The League of Nations and the Development of International Law

I0890930

This volume examines the contributions to International Law of individual members of the Advisory Committee of Jurists in the League of Nations, and the broader national and discursive legal traditions of which they were representative. It adopts a biographical approach that complements existing legal narratives.

Pre-1914 visions of a liberal international order influenced the post-1919 world based on the rule of law in civilized nations. This volume focuses on leading legal personalities of this era. It discusses the scholarly work of the ACJ wise men, their biographical notes, and narrates their contribution as legal scholars and founding fathers of the sources of international law that culminated in their drafting of the statute of the Permanent Court of International Justice, the forerunner of the International Court of Justice. The book examines visions of world law in a liberal international order through social theory and constructivism, historical examination of key developments that influenced their career and their scholarly writings, and international law as a science.

The book will be a valuable reference for those working in the areas of International Law, Legal History, Political History and International Relations.

P. Sean Morris is Research Scholar at the Faculty of Law University of Helsinki and Affiliated Research Fellow at the Erik Castren Institute of International Law and Human Rights, University of Helsinki.

Routledge Research in Legal History

The Royal Prerogative and Constitutional Law
A Search for the Quintessence of Executive Power
Noel Cox

Socialism and Legal History
The Histories and Historians of Law in Socialist East Central Europe
Edited by Ville Erkkilä and Hans-Peter Haferkamp

A History of Divorce Law
Reform in England from the Victorian to Interwar Years
Henry Kha

The League of Nations and the Development of International Law
A New Intellectual History of the Advisory Committee of Jurists
Edited by P. Sean Morris

For more information about this series, please visit: www.routledge.com/Routledge-Research-in-Legal-History/book-series/RRLEGHIST

The League of Nations and the Development of International Law

A New Intellectual History of the Advisory Committee of Jurists

Edited by P. Sean Morris

Routledge
Taylor & Francis Group
LONDON AND NEW YORK

First published 2022
by Routledge
2 Park Square, Milton Park, Abingdon, Oxon OX14 4RN

and by Routledge
605 Third Avenue, New York, NY 10158

Routledge is an imprint of the Taylor & Francis Group, an informa business

British Library Cataloguing-in-Publication Data
A catalogue record for this book is available from the British Library

Library of Congress Cataloging-in-Publication Data
Names: Morris, P. Sean, editor.
Title: The League of Nations and the development of international law : a new intellectual history of the Advisory Committee of Jurists / edited by P. Sean Morris.
Description: Milton Park, Abingdon, Oxon ; New York, NY : Routledge, 2021. | Series: Routledge research in legal history | Includes bibliographical references and index.
Identifiers: LCCN 2021011654 (print) | LCCN 2021011655 (ebook) | ISBN 9780367897536 (hardback) | ISBN 9781032065007 (paperback) | ISBN 9781003020882 (ebook)
Subjects: LCSH: League of Nations—History. | Permanent Court of International Justice—History. | International law—History.
Classification: LCC KZ4871 .L45 2021 (print) | LCC KZ4871 (ebook) | DDC 341.22/1—dc23
LC record available at https://lccn.loc.gov/2021011654
LC ebook record available at https://lccn.loc.gov/2021011655

ISBN: 978-0-367-89753-6 (hbk)
ISBN: 978-1-032-06500-7 (pbk)
ISBN: 978-1-003-02088-2 (ebk)

DOI: 10.4324/9781003020882

Typeset in Galliard
by Apex CoVantage, LLC

Contents

List of contributors vii
Acknowledgements ix

Introduction: the 'wise men' of the Advisory Committee of Jurists (ACJ) and contemporary legal biography 1
P. SEAN MORRIS

1 **The legal conscience of a universal man: Rafael Altamira y Crevea (1866–1951)** 8
YOLANDA GAMARRA

2 **National political ideologies and international legal practices: Raul Fernandes (1877–1968)** 39
ARTHUR ROBERTO CAPELLA GIANNATTASIO

3 **A civilizational pluralist and inegalitarian: Mineichiro Adachi (1869–1934)** 74
TETSUYA TOYODA

4 **George Francis Hagerup (1853–1921): a Norwegian legal internationalist** 91
DAG MICHALSEN

5 **Elihu Root (1845–1937): architect and advocate of the Permanent Court of International Justice** 112
WILLIAM G. ROSS

6 **Forgetting Albert Geouffre de Lapradelle (1871–1955) and ignorance as remembering** 135
TONI SELKÄLÄ

7 **Edouard Descamps (1847–1933): from 'negative neutrality' to 'positive pacigerate'** 156
FREDERIK DHONDT

8 **The judicial-churchman for peace: Walter George Frank Phillimore (1845–1929)** 180
P. SEAN MORRIS

9 **'Where is your tribunal?' Bernard Loder (1849–1935) and the quest for international justice** 195
FREYA BAETENS AND VERONICA LAVISTA

10 **The Italian jurist and diplomat at the Advisory Committee of Jurists: Arturo Ricci Busatti (1868–1923)** 218
ELISABETTA FIOCCHI MALASPINA

Index 241

Contributors

Freya Baetens (Cand. Jur./ Lic.Jur. (Ghent); LL.M. (Columbia); Ph.D. (Cambridge)) is Professor of Public International Law at the PluriCourts Centre (Faculty of Law, Oslo University) and affiliated with the Europa Institute (Faculty of Law, Leiden University). As a Member of the Brussels Bar, she regularly acts as counsel or expert in international and European disputes. She specialized in the law of treaties, responsibility of states and international organizations, law of the sea, WTO and investment law, energy law and sustainable development.

Frederik Dhondt is Associate Professor of Political and Legal History at the Vrije Universiteit Brussel (VUB) and Director of the Research Group Contextual Research in Law (CORE), as well as voluntary researcher at the Gustave Rolin-Jaequemyns Institute of International Law (GRILI) and the Ghent Legal History Institute. He publishes on international legal history and constitutional history (www.vub.be/CORE/members/dhondt).

Yolanda Gamarra is Full Professor of Public International Law and International Relations at the University of Zaragoza (Spain). Gamarra is the Spanish member at the Management Board of the European Union Agency for Fundamental Rights (FRA). She has written on international legal history works such as 'Rafael Altamira y Crevea, (1866–1951). The international judge as "Gentle Civilizer"', *The Journal of the History of International Law*, 2012, vol. 14, pp. 1–49, or 'Public Uses of the history of international law', *Ius Gentium Journal of International Legal History*, 2021, vol. 6/1, pp. 7–27.

Arthur Roberto Capella Giannattasio is Professor at the International Relations Institute of the University of São Paulo (IRI/USP) and was a visiting professor or researcher in Brazilian and in non-Brazilian institutions (France, Germany, Italy, Turkey). He is Fellow of the Ryoichi Sasakawa Young Leaders Fellowship Fund (Tokyo Foundation).

Veronica Lavista is Legal Counsel on one of the Case Management Teams at ICSID. Dr. Lavista joined ICSID in September 2019. Prior to joining ICSID, Dr. Lavista worked as counsel at GST LLP in Miami (2016–2018),

Guglielmino & Asociados in Buenos Aires, Argentina (2015–2016) and for the Argentine government (2006–2013).

Elisabetta Fiocchi Malaspina is Assistant Professor of Legal History at the Law Faculty of the University of Zurich (Switzerland). Her works include: *L'eterno ritorno del Droit des gens di Emer de Vattel (secc. XVIII–XIX): L'impatto sulla cultura giuridica in prospettiva globale* (Frankfurt am Main 2017).

Dag Michalsen has been Professor in Legal History at the Faculty of Law, University of Oslo since 1997, Professor II in Legal Science at the Faculty of Law, University of Tromsø since 1998, and was Dean at the Faculty of Law in Oslo 2016–2019. Recent major publications include Dag Michalsen/Ola Mestad (eds), *Historical Commentaries to the Norwegian Constitution 1814–2020* (published May 2021) and Dag Michalsen, *Legal Historical Critique* (Oslo, 2017).

P. Sean Morris is Research Scholar at the Faculty of Law University of Helsinki and Affiliated Research Fellow at the Erik Castren Institute of International Law and Human Rights, University of Helsinki. Sean's main field of research and teaching is in public international law and private law in global governance, and he has interests in legal relations of early twentieth-century history and legal aspects of economic history since 1860–1914. Sean is the editor of *Russian Discourses on International Law: Sociological and Philosophical Phenomenon* (Routledge 2018).

William G. Ross is the Albert P. Brewer Professor of Law and Ethics at the Cumberland School of Law, Samford University, where he has taught since 1988. A graduate of Stanford and Harvard Law School, Professor Ross has published extensively on American constitutional history during the early twentieth century, the judicial appointments process, and the ethics of legal fees.

Toni Selkälä is Researcher at the Faculty of Law, University of Turku. His research focuses on questions of international legal theory and the impact of technology on international law.

Tetsuya Toyoda, DEA en droit international at the Université of Paris-II, BA in law at the University of Tokyo, Ministry of Foreign Affairs (1994–2000), has taught at Akita International University since 2007 and was Fellow at the Woodrow Wilson International Center for Scholars (2013–14). He is also the author of *Theory and Politics of the Law of Nations: Political Bias in International Law Discourse of Seven German Court Councillors in the Seventeenth and Eighteenth Centuries* (Martinus Nijhoff, 2011).

Acknowledgements

The editor would like to express his gratitude to all the contributors and other supporters of the project. While the project was intended to be a single-authored monograph by the editor, it would not have been an easy task to cover all ten members of the ACJ in an accurate and developed manner by a single author. Moreover, there was the issue of language: how to manoeuvre the various languages, such as Portuguese, Dutch, Flemish, Spanish, French, and Italian, when in typical fashion, the editor is only accustomed to research in English. Hence, the editor reached out to the respective contributors who responded enthusiastically and through their research, time and intellectual endeavour contributed to the success of the book. Two initial contributors eventually pulled out, or, due to new deadlines, never made it but were enthusiastic: Vincent Genin and Lianne Boer. Genin explained that due to the result of his successful application for a research grant, he was unable to participate as his new project required deeper attention, and Boer had an unfortunate incident during December 2020. Furthermore, Giorgio Gaja, a former judge at the International Court of Justice (ICJ), was willing to write a foreword, but he had an unfortunate accident and was only recovering when all the chapters were ready and could not proceed as planned. Nonetheless, the editor wishes to thank everyone for their support, and also the respective commissioning editors at Routledge for their time and patience, especially Alison Kirk. And, although the pandemic of 2020 contributed to substantial delays to the project, the publishers were accommodating to the editor's request for delays. Ultimately, this is a book dedicated to all the victims of Covid-19.

Introduction

The 'wise men' of the Advisory Committee of Jurists (ACJ) and contemporary legal biography

P. Sean Morris

In 1920, the Advisory Committee of Jurists (ACJ) was set up by the Council of the League of Nations to draft the statute of the Permanent Court of International Justice (PCIJ). Article 38 of the PCIJ Statute and, as retained in its successor, the International Court of Justice (ICJ) state that the sources of international law include, inter alia, *the teachings of the most highly qualified publicists.*

This acknowledgement of the importance of legal scholars to the progress and development of international law has, in fact, transformed the field of international law over the last century. In this regard, a number of questions relating to the *science* and *structure* of legal writings from the 'founding wise men' of the ACJ have remained underexplored. Some of those questions include, but are not limited to, the historical and legal context of the background and teachings of the men who sat on the ACJ. Although not all the members of the ACJ were legal scholars as such, their impact and legacy are still with us today through Article 38.

Composed of ten jurists (and political diplomats), the ACJ devised the Statute of the PCIJ partly based on the legal and political thinking of a vision of an *international liberal order* that began in earnest in the 1890s and culminated in the founding of the League of Nations. The ten-member ACJ was comprised of Edouard Descamps (1847–1933); Francis Hagerup (1853–1921); Rafael Altamira (1866–1951); Bernard Loder (1849–1935); Arturo Ricci Busatti (1868–1923); Albert Lapradelle (1871–1955); Raul Ferandes (1877–1968); Mineichiro Adachi (1869–1934); Elihu Root (1845–1937); and Walter Phillimore (1845–1929).

This volume therefore looks at the various functions, professional activities and scholarly endeavours these men engaged in leading up to their appointment to the ACJ and also, in some cases, their subsequent international activities. For example, on the one hand, an important concern is how much their early writings or views helped to shape the content of Article 38 of the Statute of the PCIJ to include 'the teachings of the mostly highly qualified publicists' or the general principles of law. At the same time, the debates during the ACJ can allow us to see how areas of international law progressively developed and were interpreted in cases at the PCIJ where some of the ACJ men later served.

Thus, prior to the founding of the League of Nations, the ACJ wise men taught and published on different aspects of 'law and the international order', or, on some occasions, served in various government functions. Hence, their contributions to

DOI: 10.4324/9781003020882-1

the annals of the history of international law prior to the founding of the League of Nations can serve as an insight into the historical origins of the sources of international law.

Given that pre-1914 visions of a liberal international order influenced the post-1919 international liberal order based on *the rule of law in civilized nations*, this volume will also concentrate on the scholarly work of the ACJ wise men, their biographical notes, professional activities and narrates their contribution as founding fathers of the sources of international law that culminated in their drafting of the Statute of the PCIJ.

A permanent feature of modern international law is the ability to resort to the International Court of Justice (ICJ) for the settlement of disputes concerning states or, as it is set out in the ICJ Statute, 'the Court shall be open to the states parties to the present Statute'.[1] Yet, this remarkable development, which has its origins in the predecessor the Permanent Court of International Justice (PCIJ), was in part the crafting of ten 'wise men' of the ACJ who were given the task of drafting the Statute of the PCIJ in the summer of 1920.[2] While some of these men were accomplished in their own right having risen to the ranks of diplomats, foreign ministers, prime ministers or university professors, others did not reach the pinnacle of state power or academic grandiosity. Yet, little is known of some of these men, and nor have their lives been shown in such a way as to reflect who they were and how they drew up the PCIJ Statute.[3] From a literature point of view, only few authoritative sources exist that give us insights into the wise men of 1920: the *Procès-Verbaux*[4] and relatively few scholarly works such as the now classic monograph by Spiermann[5] and recent anthologies on the PCIJ 'legacy'.[6]

In as much as the First World War was a turning point for the international legal order with the Paris Peace Conference and the Treaty of Versailles leading

1 Statute of the International Court of Justice, 33 UNTS 993, Article 35(1).

2 Covenant of the League of Nations, Article 14: 'The Council shall formulate and submit to the Members of the League for adoption plans for the establishment of a Permanent Court of International Justice. The Court shall be competent to hear and determine any dispute of an international character which the parties thereto submit to it. The Court may also give an advisory opinion upon any dispute or question referred to it by the Council or by the Assembly.' The Advisory Committee of Jurists (ACJ) met during the summer of 1920, at The Hague from 16 June to 24 July, to craft the PCIJ Statute. Their work has been captured in the Procès-verbaux, Advisory Committee of Jurists, *Procès-Verbaux of the Proceedings of the Committee, 16 June–24 July 1920, with Annexes* (Van Langenhuysen, The Hague 1920). For overview of the PCIJ, see Shabtai Rosenne, 'Permanent Court of International Justice (PCIJ)' (2006) Max Planck Encyclopaedia of International Law.

3 Statute of the Permanent Court of International Justice, 13 December 1920, 6 LNTS 380.

4 Procès-Verbaux (n 2).

5 Ole Spiermann, *International Legal Argument in the Permanent Court of International Justice* (CUP 2005); but see JHW Verzijl, *The Jurisprudence of the World Court, Vol. 1: The Permanent Court of International Justice (1922–1940). Vol. II: The International Court of Justice (1947–1965)* (Sijthoff 1965).

6 Christian Tams, Malgosia Fitzmaurice and Panos Merkouris (eds), *Legacies of the Permanent Court of International Justice* (Martinus Nijhoff Publishers 2013).

the changes, so too were the lives of the men who, perhaps, during their time on the ACJ crafting the PCIJ Statute did not realize the indelible mark on history they were about to make. Thus, if in the beginning, heaven and earth were created, then in 1920, the World Court, as it were, was created to keep the injustices of humankind at bay. If more comparisons are to be made, then the ACJ in 1920 had other biblical greatness. This includes the Twelve Disciples who 'advised' Christ or spread throughout the world his message of peace and redemption.

The ACJ, although officially comprised of ten men of extraordinary accomplishment in state relation and or the science of international law, was *de facto* 12 when the behind-the-scenes interventions of Leon Bourgeois (1851–1925) and Dionisio Anzilotti (1867–1950) are factored in. But if legal analogies as opposed to biblical ones are more appropriate, one could invoke the Twelve Tables of the *Institutes of Justinian* for guidance.[7] These analogies points to the legacy of the men who sat on the Advisory Committee of Jurists in 1920 and the resulting Statute of the PCIJ (and later incorporation into its successor the ICJ).

The aftermath of the First World War was a pivotal moment that allowed the victors and idealists to frame the post-war world order in a new vision. It was a vision of rules, laws, world courts, international institutions, and the ideological underpinnings that navigated the troubled waters of idealism and realism. It was also a period in which the battle for the civilizational discourse among states would further upend international society as battle lines were drawn distinguishing those states that were 'civilised' from the rest. With the Martens Clauses of the 1899 Hague Convention still fresh in memory, the ACJ capitalized on this and formulated more explicitly the concept of civilized states for a more powerful court as Article 38(4) of the PCIJ recognized the existence of 'civilised states'.[8] For nations that were still under imperial rule or have not yet made the civilizational threshold of European states, those peripheral states' contribution to the international legal developments in the aftermath of the First World War was non-existent. Their future, as it were, would hinge on the successes of the emerging Soviet State and its narrative for self-determination for colonial peoples. Thus, the international legal order of the 1920s was, in essence, a European civilizational affair with interventions from the United States or men of European pedigree entrenched in peripheral states such as Brazil. Japan for its part would, however, challenge or carve out its own form of 'civilizational pluralism' to fit into the international society.[9]

Although the League of Nations represented humankind as it were, its more powerful members and benefactors were the civilized states of Europe, the UK (the US was not a member, but contributed indirectly), and a few peripheral

7 See Ernest Metzger (ed), *A Companion to Justinian's Institutes* (Duckworth/Cornell University Press 1998); Michael Maas, *The Cambridge Companion to the Age of Justinian* (CUP 2005).

8 PCIJ Statute, Article 38(4). See also, Dhondt, at p. 173, in this volume.

9 See Toyoda, in this volume; see also, Hersch Lauterpacht, 'Japan and the Covenant' (1932) 3 Political Quarterly 174.

states who were founding members.[10] With a distinct message to promote peace and 'international security', the League of Nations was a special creature of the Versailles Treaty.[11] The notion of international security at the formation of the League of Nations was to some degree a crossover of international law with the backing of military might in order for the idealism of international security to be realized in a pragmatic way. This was perhaps the sense one gets when, through the negotiations for the League, the Americans were somewhat hesitant about treaties pertaining to the international system during the conflict.[12] However, by the time of the Peace Conference in Paris, the Leagues' Covenant had set in stone a liberal international legal order based on the rule of law, equality of states,[13] and the peaceful settlement of disputes.[14] And, through Article 14 of the Covenant, it was enshrined that a PCIJ should be established.

The Advisory Committee of Jurists met from 16 June to 24 July 1920 in The Hague and produced a draft Statute of the PCIJ.[15] It was now up to the Council of the League of Nations to adopt the draft. However, this required a number of steps including a thorough examination of the draft Statute by the Council of the League. Thus, in the first examination immediately after the ACJ produced it, the Council of the League of Nations met and, among other things, scrutinized the draft.[16] The process was to repeat itself during the Tenth Session of the Council of the League of Nations in October 1920.[17] From the Council, the draft Statute of the PCIJ moved to the Committee stage of the League Assembly, where the Third Committee of the First League Assembly fully studied the draft, followed by two plenary meetings which completed the first stage.[18]

Prior to this, the men on the Advisory Committee of Jurists had to debate and ultimately come up with the text. Furthermore, their lives prior to July 1920 were crucial to how they behaved during the ACJ meetings and what they said. It is specifically those moments that this volume captures: bringing back to life the influential men of the ACJ in 1920 and how they rose to the occasion to draft the 'new testament' of international dispute settlement. However, in contrast to 'old testament' works such as the statute of the Permanent Court of Arbitration

10 Haiti, Brazil, India, Japan, Thailand, Uruguay and Venezuela, and South Africa, for example, were founding members of the League of Nations.

11 Covenant of the League of Nations, Preamble: 'In order to promote international cooperation and to achieve international peace and security'.

12 This ambivalence was expressed by Elihu Root who would go on to sit on the ACJ, see Root to George Gibbons, 8 December 1916, box 136, Elihu Root Papers, Library of Congress, Manuscript Division, Washington DC; see also Ross, in this volume.

13 Covenant of the League of Nations, Article 4, recognizing that members have one vote.

14 Articles 12–15.

15 Procès-Verbaux (n 2) 693.

16 Eight Session of the Council of the League of Nations, San Sebastian, 30 July to 5 August 1920; Proces Verbal of 8th Session of Council of League, League Doc. 20/29/14.

17 Tenth Session of the Council of the Language of Nations, Brussels, 20–28 October 1920; Proces Verbal of 10th Session of Council of League, League Doc. 20/20/16.

18 Records of the First Assembly: Meetings of the 3rd Committee (1920) 273–318, 331–408, 436–501.

(PCA)[19] or the Prize Court of 1907,[20] the PCIJ was different: it was the product of a post-war international order.[21] That is why it is important to open up the lives and activities of the ACJ men to shed light on their upbringing, political activities, academic pursuits and the morals they displayed between idealism, realism, liberalism and conservatism, while at the same time acting according to how they were 'politically' instructed by their respective capitals in 1920.

The ACJ men navigated the political and legal minefields they were trapped in, in that, they had to ensure that the interests of their states were served during the drafting stage of the PCIJ Statute. Yet, at the same time, the men had to eliminate the political overtones of the legal language of the text, and balance how their own idealism and realism came to full fruition in Article 38 of the final text.[22] From the pre-war international legal order, to during and after the conflict, a certain idealism of international law existed. That idealism had to do with the conception of international law as a form that is practiced among civilized nations, and, as it were, only the rules of such civilized nations formed general principles of law. Another part of the idealism had to with the extent the scientific output of the men who practised international law through legal scholarship and learned societies constituted a source of international law: 'publicists' as it were.[23] This was a highly contentious issue.

19 Permanent Court of Arbitration, 1899.

20 Convention (XII) relative to the Creation of an International Prize Court, The Hague, 18 October 1907, adopted, never entered into force; see Charles Noble Gregory, 'The Proposed International Prize Court and Some of its Difficulties' (1908) 2 AJIL 458.

21 But see, Martti Koskenniemi, 'The Ideology of International Adjudication and the 1907 Hague Conference' in Yves Daudet (ed), *Topicality of the 1907 Hague Conference, the Second Peace Conference* (Martinus Nijhoff Publishers 2008).

22 Article 31 of the draft PCIJ Statute (and eventually article 38), was based on a proposal by Descamps, and stated: 'The following rules are to be applied by the judge in the solution of international disputes; they will be considered by him in the order given below: (i) Conventional international law whether general or special, being rules expressly adopted by the states; (ii) International custom, being a practice between nations accepted by them as law; (iii) The rules of international law as recognize by the legal conscience of civilized nations; (iv) International jurisdiction as a means for the application and development of law.' As reproduced in Mark Weston Janis: 'Sources in the Meta-History of International Law: A Little Meta-Theory – Paradigms, Article 38, and the Sources of International Law' in Samantha Besson and Jean d'Aspremont (eds), *The Oxford Handbook of the Sources of International Law* (OUP 2017). For discussions on the sources of international law see e.g., Lauri Malksoo, 'Sources of International Law in the Nineteenth-Century European Tradition: Insights from Practice and Theory' in Samantha Besson and Jean d'Aspremont (eds), *The Oxford Handbook of the Sources of International Law* (OUP 2017); Abkar Rasulov, 'The Doctrine of Sources in the Discourse of the Permanent Court of International Justice' in Christian Tams, Malgosia Fitzmaurice, and Panos Merkouris (eds), *Legacies of the Permanent Court of International Justice* (Martinus Nijhoff Publishers 2013); Hugh Thirlway, *The Sources of International Law* (OUP 2014).

23 Article 38(1)(d) of the ICJ Statute notes that the teaching of highly qualified publicists constitutes a source of international law. The provision is based on the original version of the PCIJ Statute.

At the ACJ, this contentious issue played out during the drafting of the PCIJ Statute where two camps essentially advocated different premises for inclusion in the draft statute. The first premise was that 'qualified publicists' were people of eminent legal training such as jurists and other secondary forms for determining the rule of law. That premise was fiercely defended by Edouard Descamps.[24] At the other end was the camp led by Walter Phillimore who espoused Anglo-American views that it was 'dangerous to "give abstract justice" to judges'[25] and who had been sceptical of the idea of 'publicists' and their scholarly writings. One recent commentator summed up the contentions regarding the drafting of Article 38 as having to do 'more about international law and international legal argument process'[26] and that the 'Advisory Committee came to the question of sources only after having considered a provision on compulsory jurisdiction.'[27] But as in 1920 to the present day, the sources of international law as formulated in the draft Statute of the PCIJ remains a point of debate similarly to how they reflected the legal and cultural background of the men on the Advisory Committee of Jurists. The sources as drafted in Article 38 reflected a cultural approach based on how law was practiced in civilized states and to the extent the domestic legal practitioner interpreted international legal instruments in a domestic context. At the same time, those sources reflected the high practice of international law by men who were able to produce scientific output which reflected their ideological views that oscillated between idealism and realism of the interwar international legal order.

The chapters in this volume capture some of those narratives but also give biographical portraits of the men of the Advisory Committee of Jurists in 1920. Traditionally, the PCIJ and the League of Nations have been subjected to a legal post mortem where the narratives invariably referred to disagreements or the shape of interwar international law. The lives, beliefs, and practice in the form of the legal biography of the men who drafted the Statute of the PCIJ have been missing from those narratives. This volume corrects that gap by providing new and archival research on the ten 'wise' men of the Advisory Committee of Jurists. By turning to the real-life situation of those men, their engagement with the practice of international law through diplomacy and academia, we can get an insight into how the PCIJ Statute came about. We can also find answers to whether idealism gave way to realism, whether the men were 'liberal conservatives', how they viewed the international law and civilizational discourse that the post-war order tamed; and finally, what factors hastened the closure of natural law thinking and paved the way for legal positivism. The volume may not answer all

24 Procès-Verbaux (n 2) 322 *et seq*.

25 Walter Phillimore, 'Scheme for the Permanent Court of International Justice' (1920) 6 Transactions of the Grotius Society 89, 94.

26 Ole Spiermann, 'The History of Article 38 of the Statute of the International Court of Justice: A Purely Platonic Discussion?' in Samantha Besson and Jean d'Aspremont (eds), *The Oxford Handbook of the Sources of International Law* (OUP 2017) 167.

27 Ibid.

the questions about the 'sources' of international law but will give an insight into among other things, 'the teachings of the most highly qualified publicists of the various nations' and the general principles of law 'recognised by civilised nations.' It is a volume about the modern era of international law and the men who drafted the Statute of the PCIJ in 1920. The contributions in this volume therefore provide a detailed history and biographical sketch of the lives and the legal and diplomatic role of the ACJ appointed members and traces how those who were law professors used their legal scholarly writings to help shape provisions of the PCIJ Statute. The chapters capture these moments and in the process underscore the value of each narrative on the ACJ members among the multitude of legal and historical forms of biographies that have emerged in recent years to shed new light on the men that were behind the formation of the statue of the PCIJ.

1 The legal conscience of a universal man

Rafael Altamira y Crevea (1866–1951)

Yolanda Gamarra

1. Introduction

The purpose of this chapter is to present and examine the history of the Permanent Court of International Justice (PCIJ) Statute through the approach of a Spanish 'wise man' at the Advisory Committee of Jurists (ACJ): Rafael Altamira y Crevea (1866–1951).[1] Altamira's background left its mark on the conceptual issues included in the PCIJ Statute[2] and on the international architecture of the interwar period. The idea here is based on the analysis of the inclusion and interpretation of 'judicial justice', the eligibility of judges and the incorporation of a list of sources (Article 38 of the PCIJ Statute), in particular the custom, the general principles of law, and the 'writings of publicists'.

Altamira was a Spanish legal historian who represented the general spirit of a liberal generation who worked for the rule of law to be applied at national and international level.[3] Altamira aimed to become the 'modern intellectual

1 For the elaboration of this work I have taken into account Y Gamarra, 'Rafael Altamira y Crevea (1866–1951). The International Judge as "Gentle Civilizer"' (2012) 14 The Journal of the History of International Law 1–49.

2 Statute of the Permanent Court of International Justice, Geneva, 13 December 1920, League of Nations Treaty Series, vol 6, 380–413.

3 He was an author of multiple axes, of theoretical inspiration, methodological claims and international projection. This is accredited by a scientific work that not only covers the History of Law, Pedagogy or Literature, but also by his introduction in the specialized path of international law. See on the biographical and historiographical reconstruction JMª Martínez Cachero, L Sela Sampil and R Prieto Bances, *Homenaje a Rafael Altamira en su Centenario (1866–1966)* (Secretariado de Publicaciones de la Universidad 1967); J Malagón Barceló, *Rafael Altamira y Crevea: el historiador y el hombre* (Universidad Nacional Autónoma de México 1971); V Ramos, *Rafael Altamira* (Alfaguara 1968); and more recently A Alberola (ed), *Estudios sobre Rafael Altamira* (Diputación Provincial de Alicante 1987); R Asín Vergara, 'Prólogo' to *Historia de la civilización Española*, by Rafael Altamira (Alianza Editorial 1990); F Moreno Sáez, *Rafael Altamira Crevea (1866–1951)* (Comunidad Valenciana 1997); E Rubio Cremades and EMª Valero Juan (eds), *Rafael Altamira: historia, literatura y derecho. Actas del Congreso Internacional celebrado en la Universidad de Alicante, del 10 al 13 de diciembre de 2002* (Universidad de Alicante 2004), and *Rafael Altamira, 1866–1951* (Instituto de Estudis 'Juan Gil Albert'/Diputación Provincial de Alicante 1987).

DOI: 10.4324/9781003020882-2

archetype',[4] a kind of 'spiritual guide'[5] to direct the rest of society from a moral standpoint after the disasters of the wars of 1898 (the Spanish-American War) and of 1914 (the First World War). Altamira became the 'intellectual' pillar of Spanish regenerationism and attempted to demonstrate the civilized character of Spanish people and Spain's civilizing role. He was the man who introduced the Spanish legal culture into the PCIJ Statute.

The PCIJ Statute adopted in 1920 constituted the expression of a new theoretical concept of international law in recognizing as sources not only treaties and customs, but also the general principles of law acknowledged by 'civilized nations', jurisprudence, and 'the teachings of the most highly qualified publicists as subsidiary means for the determination of rules of law' (Article 38 of the PCIJ Statute).[6] The PCIJ legacy has influenced the International Court of Justice (ICJ) and has continued to extend its international authority to the present day. International Human Rights Courts and International Criminals Tribunals have followed the same schemes of the PCIJ's elections of judges, the contradictory procedure, the sources to be applied, or their having a permanent secretariat.[7] The history of international criminal procedure, for example, has substantially been one of cobbling together building blocks from different traditions in order to create a new *sui generis* system based on extrapolations from Article 38(1) of the PCIJ Statute (and the ICJ Statute) and the history of Nuremberg, Tokyo and the other post-war military tribunals.[8]

The study is divided in three parts. First, I describe the Altamira's liberal education, post-university training, and access to the chair of History of Law, examining the influence of the various trends such as positivism, rationalism, or naturalism on Altamira's thought. Altamira was imbued with the traditions of nineteenth-century Spain. However, he stood out by virtue of going beyond the prevailing

4 See JL Abellán, 'Rafael Altamira como arquetipo de intelectual moderno' in P Altamira (coord), *La huella de Rafael Altamira* (Universidad Complutense de Madrid 2013) 4 *et seq.*

5 The 'spiritual guides' had existed throughout history. The features of this figure were different according to the type of society in which its presence occurred with its subsequent evolution. In the West, this evolution had a marked secularization character. Thus, in the Renaissance, the figure of the humanist (Picco della Mirandola) emerged, who later became the figure of the teacher, and later that of the scholar until reaching the figure of the 'intellectual'. Francisco de Vitoria (1483–1546) was the compiler of the ideas that prevailed on private law and *jus gentium* in the sixteenth century, and Hugo Grotius (1583–1645) was the compiler of the ideas prevailing in the seventeenth century. See Abellán (n 4) 4.

6 See S Besson and J d'Aspremont (eds), *The Oxford Handbook of the Sources of International Law* (OUP 2017); A Boyle and Ch Chinkin, *The Making of International Law* (OUP 2007) 338 *et seq.*; M Koskenniemi (ed), *The Sources of International Law* (Routledge 2000), or H Thirlway, *The Sources of International Law* (OUP 2014).

7 See on the origins of the League of Nations secretariat the work of E Drumont, 'The Secretariat of the League of Nations' (1931) 9 Public Administration 228–35.

8 M Bolhander, 'Paradise Postponed? For a Judge-Led Generic Model of International Criminal Procedure and an End to "Draft-as-You-Go"' (2014) Netherlands Yearbook of International Law 331 *et seq.*

trend of 'natural law' and for applying positivism to historical science, a method that, over time, he attempted to incorporate into international legal science.

Second, I present Altamira's work in the ACJ,[9] especially the writings that helped shape the content of the PCIJ Statute, that is, the purpose of the PCIJ, its compulsory or optional competence,[10] the eligibility of international judges, or the regulation of its dual function as a court of litigation and as a consultative body. I focus there on the judicial nature of the PCIJ and the nomination process of international judges.[11] Through the analysis of these elements, the moral character of the idea of justice in Altamira's thinking is observed.

Third, I explore the discussions on the rules of law to be applied by the PCIJ by examining the role played by Altamira and other members of the ACJ as the first jurists who established a 'closed' and 'universal' list of sources that privileges pragmatism, determinacy, and scientific technique.[12] I analyse Altamira's thought on the general principles of law and the 'writings of publicists' such as sources of international law. I refer to formalization of sources included in Article 38 of the PCIJ Statute.[13]

The chapter concludes with some reflections on the imprint of the Spanish legal culture in the PCIJ Statute. The Spanish authors turn to Francisco de Vitoria (1483–1546) as the founding father of international law.[14] The principles of the Spanish classics of the sixteenth century were projected into the League of Nations Pact and the PCIJ Statute.[15] The concepts of sovereignty, justice, universalism, or solidarity are part of the language of international law. The recovery and reconstruction of the legal discourse of Spanish internationalists before the Spanish Civil War is essential to fully participate in contemporary international language.[16]

9 Advisory Committee of Jurists, *Procès-Verbaux of the Proceedings of the Committee, 16 June–24 July 1920, with Annexes* (Van Langenhuysen, The Hague 1920).

10 He was in favour of permanent justice as opposed to the arbitrational form that had been in force until then.

11 As a 'pragmatic pioneer', see Ch Tams, M Fitmaurice, and P Merkouris (eds), *Legacies of the Permanent Court of International Justice* (Martinus Nijhoff Publishers 2013) 7.

12 See Th Skouteris, 'The Force of a Doctrine: Art. 38 of the PCIJ Statute and the Sources of International Law' in F Johns, R Joyce and S Pahuja (eds), *Events, The Force of International Law* (Routledge 2011) 69–80.

13 See the interesting chapter of MW Janis, 'Sources in the Meta-History of International Law: A Little Meta-Theory. Paradigms, Article 38, and the Sources of International Law' in Besson and D'Aspremont (n 6) 270 *et seq*.

14 See Y Gamarra, 'On the Spanish Founding Father of Modern International Law: Camilo Barcia Trelles (1888–1977)' in JMª Beneyto and J Corti Varela (eds), *At the Origins of Modernity. Francisco de Vitoria and the Discovery of International Law*. Studies in the History of Law and Justice, Series SHLJ (Springer 2017) 95–115.

15 MªA Egido León, 'Madariaga reivindicador de la figura de Vitoria como fundador del Derecho internacional' in *Salvador de Madariaga, 1886–1986. Libro-Homenaje con motivo de su centenario* (Ayuntamiento de La Coruña 1986) 106 *et seq*.

16 According to the ideas included in A Roberts, *Is International Law International?* (OUP 2017).

2. A liberal law historian

2.1 Legal education, travelling and teachings

In 1886, Altamira graduated in Law from the University of Valencia.[17] One year later, Altamira moved to Madrid and obtained a PhD degree from the Central University with a thesis titled *Historia de la propiedad comunal* (1890)[18] under the direction of Gumersindo de Azcárate (1840–1917).[19] From this moment, he combined his academic career with various public functions, travelling and social activities.

One constant in Altamira's life was his support for education. This commitment to education came from his membership of the *Free Institution of Education* (ILE).[20] The ILE was a crucible for the diverse liberal ideologies that encouraged the enlightened bourgeoisie to pursue the regeneration of Spain. At the ILE, Altamira met Francisco Giner de los Ríos (1839–1915), Nicolás Salmerón (1838–1908), and Joaquín Costa (1846–1911),[21] with whom he had a close intellectual and political relationship throughout his life.

Also, Altamira's interest in the theoretical and practical aspects of education was also fuelled by his year of study at the *Museo Pedagógico Nacional* (National Museum of Education). This institution aimed to encourage new teaching methods and scientific systems. Altamira devoted himself in large measure to science and its teaching under the direction of Manuel B. Cossío (1857–1935), a Krausits pedagogue. In Altamira's thought education should be the core element of

17 He was interested in Geography, History, Natural Sciences, Geology, Botany and Zoology and Chemistry through reading – without any guide whatsoever. He read Jules Verne, Stevenson, J. F. Cooper, Cervantes – *Don Quixote* – Guizot, Müller, Guigier, and Oncken's Universal History. At 15, he finished reading Darwin's *On the Origin of Species*, see R Altamira, 'Historia de mis libros' (October 1935) *La Nación*, Manuscript notes compiled in *Rafael Altamira, 1866–1951* (n 3) 7.

18 R Altamira, *Historia de la propiedad comunal* (Madrid 1890). As Altamira wrote: 'the history of communal property should include, not only the legislative provisions related to them and everything that . . . is called positive law, but everything that may have influenced it or contributed to its evolution, from education and feelings popular to discussions of practitioners and philosophers . . .', R Altamira, *Historia de la propiedad comunal*, compiled in *Rafael Altamira, 1866–1951* (n 3) 39.

19 Azcárate was a jurist, a historian, a politician and one of the leading lights of the Spanish regenerationism. He was Altamira's mentor in international law. He was his supporter to integrate into the social and cultural circles of Madrid. See E Storm, *La perspectiva del progreso. Pensamiento político en la España del cambio de siglo (1840–1914)* (Biblioteca Nueva 2001).

20 See A Jiménez Landi, *La Institución Libre de Enseñanza y su ambiente* (Ed. Complutense D.L. 1996) 4 Vols.

21 The most remarkable influence during these years came from Joaquín Costa who introduced him to the study of customary law. His doctoral thesis, *Historia de la Propiedad comunal*, written in 1887 and published in 1890, is a historical-legal piece of research with an extensive bibliography. The subject area was fashionable in certain university political circles headed by Costa and Azcárate. JG Cheyne, 'La relación intelectual y política entre Costa y Altamira' in Alberola (ed), (n 3) 127 *et seq.*

reform following the ideas of Johann Heinrich Pestalozzi (1746–1827) and Friedrich Fröbel (1782–1852).

Altamira was a prominent member of regenerationism.[22] This movement was an ideological stream, a form of group social psychology that was rooted in the political powerlessness and crisis of identity afflicting the Spanish *petite bourgeoisie*. After the crisis of 1898, the role of Spanish liberalism as the conscience of the nation was limited to the ILE elite – *institutionists* who would be followed by large numbers of people moved by the revolution of the bourgeoisie. In the eyes of the *institutionists*, there was a need for a structure other than the State that would put an end to the figure of the political strongman and replace moral corruption with honesty and respect for the law.[23]

It is essential to place Altamira in relation to and in terms of (Spanish) Krausism and of its most mature expression, which was that of positivism.[24] The great intellectual effort that was Spanish Krausis[25] aimed at the rationalization, education, secularization, and modernization of the Spanish system that was opening up to America and Europe. This reformist movement co-existed with positivism, giving rise to what has been called Krauso-positivism,[26] which essentially advocated national change through education and culture. This movement gradually became

22 This was a *petite et moyenne bourgeoisie* phenomenon that, at the end of the nineteenth and beginning of the twentieth century, represented the most wide-ranging expression of the rupture of the existing conservative hegemony. This tendency brought with it criticism of the ills of the previous regime, of the oligarchic practices of the *grande bourgeoisie* illustrated by an ideology that was also rooted in the previous regime. However, in his criticism, Altamira was careful not to veer too dangerously towards confusing the false parliamentarism of the oligarchic *cacique* system with true democratic parliamentarism. One of the latest reviews of the phenomenon in V Salavert Faviani and M Suárez Cortina (eds), *El regeneracionismo en España. Política, educación, ciencia y sociedad* (Universitat de Valencia 2007).

23 The leading representative of this intellectual movement was Joaquín Costa, who had a close intellectual and political relationship with Altamira. In particular, Costa introduced Altamira to the study of customary law. See further (n 21).

24 Krausism can be viewed as a spiritual, ethical and intellectual approach to living, a system of education within a life system in which its founder and his first Spanish disciples stressed the prevalence of harmony – what they described as harmonic rationalism – over the idea of contradiction which had Hegelian roots. See E Díaz, *La filosofía social del krausismo español* (Ed. Cuadernos para el Diálogo 1973) 51; JJ Gil Cremades, *El reformismo español. Krausismo, escuela histórica, neotomismo* (ed. Ariel 1969), and J López Morillas, *El krausismo español* (FCE 1980).

25 Spanish Krausism was more than a school of philosophy; it was a complex intellectual, religious, and political movement that brought together the liberal *bourgeoisie* of the Left and advocated the rationalization of Spanish culture. It was a moral movement, and as Azorín stated: 'they are the last Spanish erasmists'.

26 This was the philosophical movement that tried to harmonically synthesize idealism, with its speculative and abstract method, and positivism, with its method of experimental observation in order to overcome rationalist dualism. Among the fundamental notes that made up the Kraus-positivist Spanish movement one should, first, highlight its synthesis of rational idealism of the Krausist pattern and empirical observation rooted in positivism; second, the inductive metaphysics with which one aims to overcome the limitation of deductive idealism; and third, the acceptance of a scientific monism that propounds a unitary conception of the world. See more in JL Abellán, 'Filosofía de la Institución Libre de Enseñanza: el

the launching pad for the ideological erosion of the Restoration system – that is, conservatism.[27]

Be that as it may, the Krauso-positivist symbiosis, that is, the common ground between conceptual idealism and factual empiricism latent in Altamira's regenerationist texts, tends to have a somewhat sterilizing effect when its general idealist propositions are contrasted with a forced positivist circumspection that relies more on erudite academic contextualization than on expanding upon the propositions put forward. Altamira's methodological approaches and formulations were oriented by an underlying 'sociological idealism'.[28] This cultural approach – with its limitations – would be mirrored in the various areas in which Altamira left his mark, in particular in his studies and his writings on international law.

Altamira took every opportunity to travel abroad. He began to broaden his horizons in Europe, seeking methods, knowledge, and scientific systems that he could apply in his efforts to contribute to the cultural renewal of Spain. A tour of European cities that Altamira undertook in 1890 gave him the opportunity to reflect on the intellectual isolation of his own country, and to get to know the works of leading French,[29] English,[30] and German academics.[31]

In 1897, Altamira was appointed a chair in History of Law at the University of Oviedo, where he founded, along with other professors from the Faculty of Law,[32] the *University Extension Programme*, characterized by the optimistic and innovative work,[33] and developed his project to establish closer links with America. At the same time, he was a promoter of a 'civilized' Spain, and a defender of a tolerant policy on the treatment of nationalities especially in relation to minorities: a key question in Spain at the interwar period. Behind it lies

---

krausopositivismo' in JA Ferrer Benimeli (coord), *Masonería, Política y Sociedad*, vol I (Centro de Estudios Históricos de la Masonería Española 1989) 405 *et seq.*

27 See J Álvarez Junco, 'Identidad heredada y construcción nacional: algunas propuestas sobre el caso español, del Antiguo Régimen a la Revolución liberal' (1999) 2 Historia y Política 123.

28 Acoording to the Émile Durkheim's sociological theory in his work *Les règles de la méthode sociologique* (Paris 1919).

29 French influence was particularly represented by Charles Seignobos, Charles-Victor Langlois, Jacques Monod, and Ernest Renan. Leading French positivists whose methodology lay in selecting and gathering data and facts. See JJ Carreras Ares, 'Ventura del Positivismo' in *Razón de Historia. Estudios de historiografía* (Selection and foreword by C Forcadell, Marcial Pons & Prensas Universitarias de Zaragoza 2000) 142 *et seq.*

30 Henry Thomas Buckle (1821–1862), English positivist who was little acknowledged in his own land, author of *History of Civilization in England*, understood (following Comte) that the basic factor in historical development was intellectual progress, and he rejected the existence of moral progress.

31 Such as Ernst Bernheim. German positivist renowned for applying the rules of sociological method. His best-known work is *Lehrbuch der historischen Methode* (1889).

32 In particular, with Aniceto Sela Sampil (1863–1935), a professor of private and public international law. See more information in Gamarra (n 1) 16–20.

33 As a defined area of the university with the purpose of spreading the knowledge generated in this institution through conferences, courses, and other activities to those social classes that could not access them, following the example of several English universities that had already spread to other European states like Germany and Belgium.

a regenerationist project that endorses the Spanish nationalism, which consisted in holding that the key to opposing the Black Legend were several studies of American institutions.[34]

In March 1910, Altamira returned to Spain after a triumphal journey that he had begun in July 1909 in Buenos Aires.[35] There occurred a curious phenomenon of masses encouraged by the University of Oviedo and the Spanish Americanist Lobby, a phenomenon that was amplified by the Republican press and given political validity by their Liberal counterparts. He was received with honours in Oviedo, Madrid, Valencia, Alicante, and other places in Spain.[36]

Altamira's ideas were about to construct a renewed discourse that was built on the common elements of Spanish and America legal culture. The year 1910 was the anniversary of the crisis in imperial order.[37] That complex year saw most of the Hispanic American Republics simultaneously mark their independence and the rise of the cultural legacy of Spain. That year seemed to be destined to be a portal to an era of fruitful exchanges between the intellectual worlds of Spain and Hispanic America.[38] That ambitious project seemed feasible at the time, but it was not due only to the favourable 'Climate of the Centenary', much less to an instinctive fear of Anglo-Saxon imperialism that was spreading through the 'New World'. Rather, it was due to the surprising progress made in the space of just a few months by the Spanish Americanist movement.

The first parts of this journey did not succeed in attracting much attention from Spanish public opinion – which had been shaken by events in Morocco, the revolt in Barcelona, and the change in government – but Altamira's time in Mexico and Cuba was followed with growing interest in Spain.[39] In Cuba, Altamira maintained a controversy with Fernando Ortiz (1881–1969), an essayist, who was critical with a sector of Spanish regenerationism that claimed 'the trace of Spain in America', that is, 'the spiritual Re-Conquest of America'.[40] He

34 See R Altamira, *Medios de difusión del libro español en América* (1920); *La política de España en América* (1921); *La huella de España en América* (1924); *Colección de Textos para el estudio de la Historia de las Instituciones de América* (1926); *Últimos escritos americanistas* (1929); *La enseñanza de las Instituciones de América* (1933), and *Diccionario castellano de palabras jurídicas y técnicas tomadas de la legislación indiana* (1951), among others.

35 See R Altamira, *Mi viaje a América* (Madrid 1911). Reedited by the University of Oviedo in 2007.

36 See the articles written in press such as 'Dos Españas' *Heraldo de Madrid* (3 April 1910), *La Ilustración Artística* (18 April 1910), and other materials compiled in *Rafael Altamira, 1866–1951* (n 3) 121–30.

37 See G Prado, *Rafael Altamira en América, 1909–1910: Historia e Historiografía del proyecto americanista de la Universidad de Oviedo* (CSIC 2008).

38 See P Vélez, *La historiografía americanista en España, 1755–1936* (Iberoamericana Editorial Vervuert 2007).

39 See also those mentioned in (n 35).

40 See F Ortiz, *La reconquista de América. Reflexiones sobre el hispanismo* (Sociedad de Ediciones Literarias y Artísticas, Lib. Paul Ollendorff 1910).

thought that this sector defended Panhispanism from the claim of Spanish influence, intellectual and economic, as a means to its own Spanish regeneration.[41]

Spain, however, was a defeated and a lagging state that, at the beginning of the century, with all its social and political problems, could not be considered precisely as a model to follow. Even so, a good part of the Spanish authors elaborated a panhispanista discourse that, taking advantage of the fear of the growing hegemony of the United States of America, tried to realize its objectives by investing the old Motherland as tutor and saviour of the young Spanish-American republics. At the end, Ortiz states that 'what is underneath' the Spanish discourse is 'the expansive feeling of a people that wants to impose on others their way of being and living, all the sense of your civilization'.[42]

Altamira pursued a methodology of rapprochement and overcoming of misunderstandings and new thoughts by presenting a renewed history of Spain.[43] The Americanist programme of Altamira, on the one hand, contributed to a progressive normalization of the relations between Spain and the Americas relations. On the other hand, the journey was a starting point for new initiatives and exchanges of all types, especially of the cultural and economic variety.[44]

In 1914, he was appointed, following open competition, to a chair in *History of Political and Civil Institutions in America*, which was created as an exclusively doctoral subject in the Faculty of Law and the Faculty of Philosophy and Arts,

41 E Valero, *Rafael Altamira y la 'reconquista espiritual' de América*, n° 8 (Cuadernos de América sin nombre 2003) 99 *et seq.*

42 Criticism made by Fernando Ortiz of Cuba. See F Ortiz (n 39) 55 *et seq.*, 110, 111.

43 Altamira submitted to Alfonso XIII a proposal to set up (with contributions from the various States concerned) a Centre for Studies in Seville that would bring together teaching and research institutions 'in order to offer a common field of work and of intellectual contact between Hispano-Americans and Spaniards'. The project was very detailed, and re-submitted part of what had been presented to the governments of Latin America. Altamira's project intended that the government should contribute the refurbished building of the Archive of the Indies, the Columbus Library, land to build the new premises, and credit for general expenditure. This Centre would contain an Institute for the History of Hispano-America; a chair for Jewish, historical, and economic studies; a chair for short courses in Spanish language and in literary history; permanent research seminars; an American museum; auxiliary chairs for preparatory studies in palæography, archival science, and the history of art, as well as a period of residence for Latin-American teachers and students. In spite of the interest shown by the Spanish monarch, and given the fact that the proposal was not expressly rejected, its feasibility was sufficiently weakened for the project to die away and be replaced by other, competing initiatives that offered a model that was less costly to the state. In spite of repeated difficulties, Altamira never gave up hope of inspiring an American dimension to Spanish diplomacy and cultural policy. Naturally, his strategy was typical of an 'intellectual', not of a politician.

44 Altamira and Adolfo González Posada (1860–1944), a jurist and a politician, tried to establish a link with the former Spanish colonies and to work in a Spanish-American cultural unit by means of the legal unification of the Spanish-American 'peoples', see LM Lloredo Alix, 'Rafael Altamira y Adolfo Posada: Dos aportaciones a la socialización del derecho y su proyección en Latinoamérica' (2012) Rechtsgeschichte Legal History 209–33.

with a special focus on Americanist issues at the Central University of Madrid.[45] In that same year, Altamira joined the teaching staff at the Diplomatic and Consular Institute (the precursor to what is now the Diplomatic School of Spain).[46]

Altamira's complex personality, long life, and multiple spheres of activity, as well as his substantial body of work, suggest that it would be wrong to define him simply as a regenerationist (of 1898). Nevertheless, there was a fundamental regenerationist phase in Altamira's background that determined his initial thought, that is, the methodology of questions and answers as used by Krauso-positivists and regenerationists at the time. Altamira's historiographic work shows an obsession with defining the internal building of a 'community of culture' that can serve as the basis of an idealized 'Spanish nation'. *A fortiori*, it would be right to define the general thrust of this work as representing one of the first and most fruitful historiographical responses to the anguished concern for national destiny that was part of the regenerationism of 1898.

In general terms, Altamira shared the liberal political platform.[47] In 1916, Altamira was appointed Senator with the Liberal party by the University of Valencia. Like many of the men around him, his political ideology was defined by a series of features such as an impulse for modernization, a tendency towards compromise, and a developmental life path leading to a modern, neutral State. He reserved for the Law a role as an organizer of reforms. He also worked towards the depersonalization of power, the secular state, the differentiation of functions and powers, and rationalization of the administration.

Altamira worked within a liberal paradigm, above all upholding the universal principles of the rights of the individual[48] – religious freedom, civil freedom, the right to use one's own language, or the rights of minorities. He participated in the re-configuration of a 'post-classical' international legal system based not only on a new definition of sources, but also on a new concept of the nation state, which was more receptive to the idea of certain restrictions on its sovereign rights, and more sensitive to the rights of the individuals – dependent and non-dependent – and his legal protection.[49] In the PCIJ,[50] Altamira filled the post of

45 Altamira served in that role until his retirement in 1936 and endowed it with a good library nourished largely by his own bibliographic donations.

46 JE Togores and JC Jiménez, La Escuela Diplomática: Setenta y Cinco Años de Servicio al Estado. Los últimos veinticinco años (1992–2017) (Minsiterio de Asuntos Exteriores y de Cooperación 2018) 13 *et seq.*

47 Several doctrinal trends of the late nineteenth century influenced his thought. Of the three doctrinal trends described by Florentino Perez-Embid in the prologue to Vicente Cacho Viu, that is, the traditional attitude, bourgeois heterodoxy and the Marxist labour movement, Altamira should be placed in the second: bourgeois heterodoxy. See F Pérez-Embid 'Prólogo' a Cacho Viu, V., *La Institución Libre de Enseñanza*, vol I (Madrid 1962) 6–7.

48 R Altamira, manuscript notes (1 August 1924) compiled in *Rafael Altamira, 1866–1951* (n 3) 179.

49 See R Altamira, 'Una nueva declaración de los derechos del hombre' in *Almanaque de El Socialista* (Madrid 1929) 155–56.

50 On 16 September 1921, Altamira was appointed as a judge of PCIJ, a post he held until the court was dissolved.

judge in the Chamber for Social Affairs,[51] and his participation in oral debates shows his concern for the individual rights. In his dissenting opinions, Altamira defended the rights of individuals as being above international law itself. In the *Lotus* case, for example, he gave priority to the application of national laws as being above any other law, even international law.[52] Like many other European international lawyers, he considered that an international system within which the individual finds a place was the great challenge for international law.

To sum up, Altamira's ideology oscillated between a liberal conservative orientation and a democratic reformism – a form of bourgeois elitism. He did not want to make a clear political choice, but was ready to change opinions when he felt it necessary to do so. This apparent self-contradiction is one of the reasons that explain, to a large extent, his later disillusionment.

2.2 *A pacifist in the face of the war*

After the Spanish-American War in 1898, the calls to regenerate Spain were constant and, along with the influence of the pacifist movement, were decisive in the defense of Spain's neutral position during the First World War.[53] Altamira encountered war throughout his long life.

In 1915, Altamira published his book *La guerra actual y la opinión pública Española* (*The Current War and the Spanish Public Opinion*),[54] in which he set out his vision regarding the causes of the First World War and the response of international law. Altamira supported pacifist ideas and the neutral position of Spain, despite the differences that arose in friendships among the members of the Spanish historiographical community and French historical experts.[55] He

51 A Chamber provided for in article 26 of the PCIJ Statute. Its function is set out in Title I, Section C, articles 14 to 16 of the Rules of Operation.

52 Dissenting opinion, R Altamira, *Affaire du 'Lotus'* (PCIJ, Series A, no. 10, Leyden 1927) 106.

53 A Niño, 'Política de alianzas y compromisos coloniales para la "regeneración" internacional de España, 1898–1914' in J Tusell et al. (eds), *Política exterior de España en el siglo XX* (Biblioteca Nueva/UNED 2000) 31 *et seq.*; JL Neila Hernández, 'El proyecto internacional de la República: democracia, paz y neutralidad' in JC Pereira (coord), *La política exterior de España (1800–2003)* (Ariel 2003) 353 *et seq.*, and J Ponce Marrero, 'La política exterior española de 1907 a 1920: entre el regeneracionismo de intenciones y la neutralidad condicionada' (2007) 37 Historia Contemporánea 93–115.

54 See R Altamira, *La guerra actual y la opinión pública Española* (Editorial Analecta/Centro de Estudios Políticos y Constitucionales 2014).

55 In 1914, the outbreak of the First World War put to the test the friendships and adhesions to the French cause of fellow Spanish historians. From the first months of the conflict, the positions of the peninsular historians were cause for concern for the Hispanists who, like the rest of the French scholars, interrupted their pacifist reveries by perceiving the war as a historical obligation of the defense of the homeland. Read from the Spanish side, the French polls and reservations became part of the complex system of representations of the culture of war, born from the new conditions imposed by the conflict. And in this sense, Rafael Altamira's words in favour of pacifism suffered the special censorship of the editors of the Hispanic Bulletin. The entire group of Hispanics, and in particular Alfred Morel-Fatio, felt distrust of the

declared that he was a 'pacifist', while also ultimately recognizing the need for the war.[56] Altamira reconciled this contradiction by using the concept of 'active neutrality'.[57]

When the events of July and August 1914 occurred, Spain, which was more worried about its own internal conflicts, was ignored and once again considered as a 'subordinate' power to the Allied Powers. The Allies had no need to drag Spain into the war and could control the country without it being an official ally, and whose participation, with an army lacking resources, would have been of little help in a war that was assumed was going to be relatively short.[58]

The consensus about the Spanish 'official' neutrality did not match the consensus in the scope of the sympathies towards the warring countries. Public opinion, or rather the opinion in the circles of power, was divided into Allied and German supporters, with debates about everything in the press.[59] It should be remembered, however, that foreign policy was not the priority for the majority of Spanish society, which was more interested and concerned with domestic policy.[60] The neutrality declared during the First World War left Spain implicitly excluded from any direct influence in international affairs. This did not mean an abandonment of the defense of the interests of the Spanish abroad. It meant quite the opposite, with Allied and German supporters agreeing on the defense of Spanish interests in the Mediterranean and Latin America, not without self-interest on their part.[61]

A large volume of the sympathizers were close to the leftist movements – ranging from liberals to socialists and from intellectuals to middle-class professionals – were Allied supporters, since countries like France and Great Britain represented

---

'absurd' neutrality and ambivalence of someone who passed for being a loyal 'Francophile and Frenchified' with a long history. See, I Peiró, 'La Gran Guerra de los historiadores: la encuesta francesa de Alfred Morel-Fatio sobre la neutralidad, la beligerancia y el pacifismo de los intelectuales españoles' in Y Gamarra and C Fernández Liesa (coords), *Los orígenes del Derecho internacional contemporáneo. Estudios conmemorativos del centenario de la Primera Guerra Mundial* (Institución 'Fernando el Católico' 2015) 71 *et seq.*

56 See Altamira (n 52) 33, and R Altamira, 'Preparación para la paz', published in 1937 and included in *El derecho al servicio de la paz. Cuestiones internacionales* (Imprenta Universidad de México 1954) 449.

57 See on the scope and content of 'active neutrality', Y Gamarra, 'The Neutrals and Spanish Neutrality: A Legal Approach to International Peace in Constitutional Texts' in M Abbenhuis, A Higgins and Ch Barber (eds), *War, Peace and International Order? The Legacies of The Hague Conferences of 1899 and 1907* (Routledge 2017) 207–23.

58 Ch Clark, *Sonámbulos. Cómo Europa fue a la guerra en 1914* (Galaxia Gutenberg 2014).

59 S Juliá, *Nosotros, los abajo firmantes. Una historia de España a través de manifiestos y protestas* (Galaxia Gutenberg 2014); A Navarra Ordoño, *Aliadófilos y germanófilos en la cultura española* (Cátedra 2014), and M Fuentes Codera, *España en la Primera Guerra Mundial. Una movilización cultural* (Akal 2014).

60 See L Martin, 'Le pacifisme en Espagne, 1885–1925' in M Petricioli, D Gherubini, and A Anteghini (eds), *Les Etats-Unis d'Europe. The United States of Europe. Un projet Pacifiste–A Pacifist Project* (Peter Lang) 369–89.

61 J Becker González, *Causas de la esterilidad de la accion exterior de España*. Discourse (Academia de Jurisprudencia y Legislación 1925).

the ideals of democracy and freedom.[62] By opposition, the most conservative sectors of society – army leaders, the Church, the upper bourgeoisie, and the Carlists – favoured the Central Empires because in Germany and Austria-Hungary they saw the representation of military order and authority. They were more Francophobes than German supporters.[63]

The key to Spanish neutrality in the First World War was its powerlessness, and its full meaning becomes clear when we analyse over four years of challenges – all wars are challenges for neutrals – that Spanish diplomacy faced.[64] Among the many limitations that determined Spanish powerlessness, the lack of resources made it impossible to implement significant reforms, necessary if Spain wanted to have the effective armed forces that the war required. This shortage of financial resources deepened the technological and other backwardness that the Spanish army suffered.

Also, the realization that Spanish military forces could not contribute to its presence abroad – beyond a poor Africanism – and were not at the level required by the increasingly demanding military circumstances, helped to focus attention on the actions of the army in the resolution of national problems. These were internal problems that were aggravated precisely as a consequence of the economic impact of the First World War on the state coffers.[65] This helped increase political instability, as the State was even more incapable of dealing with military deficiencies and economic imbalances, with the subsequent social conflict caused by the war.

The First World War showed the limits of international law, and several years later, European public opinion even considered it to be responsible for the tragedy of the war because it lacked effectiveness and was not faithful to the expression of justice (in legal terms). One of the Spanish authors who came out in defense of international law was Joaquín Fernández Prida (1863–1942), a professor in public and private international law at the Central University (Madrid), who analysed the crisis in international law using a realist approach.[66] He stated that the loss of prestige of international law was the result of a mistaken understanding of reality that had led to placing the problem in the law instead of the 'imperfections in international organization, in enforcement proceedings or in how legal rules are understood and established'.[67] For Fernández Prida, the political use made of the rules, and not themselves, were to blame.

In 1919, Manuel Lasala Llanas (1875–1944), a professor of public and private international law at the University of Zaragoza wrote 'Pacifismo

62 A Navarra Ordoño, *1914. Aliadófilos y germanófilos en la cultura española* (Cátedra 2014).

63 FJ Romero Salvado, *España 1914–1918, entre la guerra y la revolución* (Marcial Pons 1999).

64 See Ponce Marrero (n 52) 93–115.

65 See JC Pereira, 'España y la Primera Guerra Mundial: una neutralidad impotente' in Gamarra and Fernández Liesa (n 54) 275 *et seq.*

66 In the discourse at the Royal Academy of Moral and Political Sciences, on 23 March 1915, see J Fernández Prida, *La crisis del Derecho internacional* (Imprenta clásica española 1915).

67 ibid 37.

reformista y pacifismo científico' (*Reform Pacifism and Scientific Pacifism*)[68] in which he defended the role of international law from an idealistic approach. He expressed his perspective of the need to promote peace through education, disarmament, arbitration, or international cooperation.[69] In particular, Lasala defended 'the proscription of war . . . as the cornerstone of all new international law'.[70] This author considered that the prohibition of war is the result of legal developments.

Altamira also came out in defense of international law in 'Observaciones sobre la realidad internacional presente' (*Observations on the Present International Reality*), published in September 1925.[71] He gave an idealistic reading of international law by emphasizing the advances made since the signing of the Treaty of Versailles (1919). The creation of the League of Nations and the PCIJ, claimed Altamira, were the two great innovations that international society had achieved in the 1920s. These advances were the result of the 'desires that for centuries and centuries had formed the dream of all the idealists in the world and the attempt, which had always failed, of social forces not available in other times'.[72] Those desires would eventually be turned into 'effective rules and powerful organizations'.[73] Altamira maintains the 'idealistic' illusion that international law plays a role in the organization of social life among states.

There was still a certain contradiction in the redefinition of Spanish neutrality, given that there was, on one hand, the commitment to collective security included in the League of Nations Pact and, on the other hand, there was the aspiration to consider peace as the backbone of Spain's domestic and foreign policy – renouncing war as an instrument of national policy as established in the Kellogg-Briand Pact. In this context were born notions such as 'positive neutrality' or 'active neutrality' – understood as 'a permanent effort for the upholding and organization of peace in the world' arose. Despite this, the Republicans, such as Altamira, among others, could not clarify the final objectives in this regard, as the contradiction between neutrality and pact was inherent to the system itself.[74]

2.3 *A cosmopolitan scholar as a 'wise man'*

Altamira's appointment in 1919 as an arbitrator at the Court of Mining Litigation in Paris – where he had the task of ruling on the dispute between France and

68 M Lasala Llanas, *Pacifismo reformista y pacifismo científico* (Real Academia de Jurisprudencia y Legislación 1919).
69 ibid 15 *et seq.*
70 ibid 39.
71 This article is included in R Altamira y Crevea, *Cuestiones internacionales y de pacifismo* (C. Bermejo 1932).
72 ibid 34.
73 ibid.
74 See Gamarra (n 56) 212–15.

Spain over mines in Morocco[75] – made him a prime candidate for a membership at the ACJ. During the mining arbitration he met Léon Bourgeois (1851–1925), Albert G. De Lapradelle (1871–1955), and Gregers W. W. Gram (1846–1929), among others, with whom he established a professional relationship that led to mutual intellectual admiration.[76] These good relationships with French, Italian, Belgian, Norwegian, English, and American experts in international law influenced his international career and influenced his appointment to the ACJ.

The culmination of Altamira's international career in the immediate post-war period came when the Organizing Committee of the Council of the League of Nations designated a Committee of Jurists with the task of drawing up plans for the PCIJ. Eric Drummond (1876–1951), as the Secretary-General of the League of Nations, invited Altamira to participate in the ACJ along with 11 other jurists.[77] For several reasons, the ACJ was finally composed of ten members. The membership of the ACJ, as was the case with the final composition of the PCIJ, was based on personal and scientific ability rather than national representation.

Nevertheless, Altamira benefited from Spain's status as a neutral country during the war when his name was put forward to be a member of the ACJ.[78] Spanish neutrality in the First World War was rewarded with a position at the ACJ and a non-permanent position on the Council of the League of Nations.[79] After many negotiations, thanks to the pressure of neutral countries and the insistence of Woodrow Wilson, Spain was invited to become a member of the League of Nations as a non-permanent member of the Council – Article 4 par. 1 of the

75 With regard to the damage caused by French troops to the *Compañía Española de Minas del Rif*, it was decided to resolve the controversial situation by turning to arbitration. That led to a decision to set up the Court of Mining Litigation, with its seat in Paris. Concerning the interests of Spain in Morocco and the difficult relations with France for the control of North Africa, see R Carr, *España 1808–1939* (Ariel 1969) 499 *et seq.*; JA Carrillo Salcedo, 'Las relaciones exteriores de España (del desastre de 1898 al desastre de 1921)' in *Historia Social de España del siglo XX* (Madrid 1967) 355–72. In a wider context, S Sueiro Seoane, *España en el Mediterráneo. Primo de Rivera y la 'Cuestión marroquí', 1923–1930* (UNED 1992). See also, R Ruze, 'Litiges Liniers du Maroc. L'affaire Mannesmann' (1920) 47 Revue générale de droit international et de législation comparée 159–68, and L Rollin, 'La Commission arbitrale des litiges Miniers au Maroc. Clôture des travaux' (1922) 32 Bulletin du Comité de l'Afrique française 302–4.

76 See R Altamira, *La Sociedad de las Naciones y el Tribunal Permanente de justicia internacional* (2ª edn, Bermejo 1931) 49.

77 The initial invitation to participate was also sent to Akidzuki, Clovis Bevilaqua, Descamps, Dagro, Fadda Fromageot, Gram, Loder, Phillimore, Root, and Milenk R. Vesnitch. List obtained from R Altamira . . . (n 75) 71.

78 With the support of neutral States it attained a position as a non-permanent member of the Council of the League of Nations and Spanish representatives eagerly took part in the debates about disarmament, minorities, and the aggression in Manchuria. See Y Gamarra, 'La ilusión española de la Sociedad de Naciones' in Gamarra and Fernández Liesa (n 54) 289–312.

79 In fact, it was a neutrality imposed by the Allied Powers, see M Espadas Burgos, 'España y la Primera Guerra Mundial' in J Tussel et al. (eds), *Política exterior de España en el siglo XX* (Editorial Biblioteca Nueva 2000) 95–116.

League of Nations Pact – along with Belgium, Brazil, and Greece. To a large extent this act defined Spain's foreign policy within the context of the League of Nations.[80]

The ten-member commission included a member from the Netherlands, one from Norway, one from Spain, and representatives of American countries – the USA, and Brazil – a member from Japan, and figures from the countries on the winning side in the war: Belgium, England, France, and Italy. No German, Austrian, or Russian 'personality' was invited to contribute to the design of the PCIJ. The ten illustrious figures of the ACJ were Mineichiro Adachi (1869–1934), from Japan, a diplomat; Édouard Descamps (1847–1933), from Belgium, Minister of State; Clovis Bevilaqua (1859–1944), from Brazil later replaced by Raul Fernandes (1877–1968), a legal adviser to the Ministry of Foreign Affairs;[81] George Francis Hagerup (1853–1921), from Norway, diplomat; Albert de Lapradelle (1871–1955), from France, Professor of the Paris Faculty of Law; Bernard Loder (1849–1935), from the Netherlands, member of the Netherlands Court of Appeal; Walter Phillimore (1845–1929), English member of the Privy Council; Arturo Ricci Busatti (1868–1923), Italian professor and counsellor of the Ministry of Foreign Affairs; Elihu Root (1845–1937), from USA, former Secretary of State, and Altamira, our protagonist. Of the ten jurists, Altamira, Loder, and Adachi were the only members of the ACJ who had been judges of the PCIJ; of the three, Altamira was the only one to be present throughout the process of designing and setting up the PCIJ and then putting it into operation.

In the ACJ, whose sessions took place between 16 June and 24 July 1920,[82] Altamira became a defender of Spanish and Latin American legal culture. The reports and the draft Statute of the PCIJ were presented to the Council of the League of Nations between 30 July and 5 August 1920.[83] The draft Statute, with the amendments inserted by the Council of the League of Nations, was presented to the Assembly, where it was unanimously approved on 13 December 1920, with a separate instrument being considered for later acceptance of competence. In September 1921, the number of countries that had ratified the Statute was sufficient for the Statute to enter into force.

Altamira considered that the PCIJ was, in his own words, the 'higher pacifist body – law is always peace, since it is at one and the same time a guarantee of the

80 See G Solé, 'La incorporación de España a la Sociedad de Naciones' (1976) 36(132) Hispania. Revsita española de Historia 131–74.

81 Halfway through the sessions of the Advisory Committee of Jurists, Clóvis Beviláqua stopped attending and was replaced by Raúl Fernandes, a Brazilian jurist. See chapter____in this volume.

82 The sessions were held on the following dates: 16 June; 17 June, 18 June; 19 June; 21 June; 22 June; 24 June; 25 June; 26 June; 29 June; 30 June; 3 July; 5 July; 6 July; 7 July; 8 July; 9 July; 10 July, 12 July; 13 July; 14 July; 19 July; 19 July; 20 July; 22 July, and 24 July.

83 The text of the preliminary draft for the institution of the Permanent Court of International Justice, mentioned in article 14 of the Covenant of the League of Nations presented to the Council by the Committee of Jurists, is contained in Altamira (n 75) 161–73.

weak and of the strong – before which would be dispelled many of the reasons that, but for the PCIJ, would lead to war'.[84] In his manuscript notes he wrote that:

> I could well see that the condition of Humanity at that moment called out for the greatest efforts to be made in that direction – the creation of a permanent tribunal.[85]

Nevertheless, Altamira's entrance onto the international stage was not an easy one. Altamira himself had to overcome his lack of confidence and fear of the international arena. He made sharp and pertinent observations on his position:

> I confess to having been a little apprehensive, not only because diplomats would be amongst the members of the Committee, but also because of my belief that in meetings of an international nature, the old practices of diplomacy were common, and that I would have to deal with concealment, with veiled thought, with a degree of reserve expressed in words with double meaning.[86]

Lack of experience in international legal practice explains his scant reflections on sovereignty, human rights, international criminal law, immunities or sources of international law, among others. Altamira himself wrote no articles or books that examined the principles and practice of international law in depth. Only in a few surviving manuscript notes can we find random ideas on what he understood by international justice and international law.

3. Moralism in the idea of justice

3.1 'Judicial justice' and 'legal questions'

The creation of the PCIJ was not free of tensions and obstacles.[87] The influence of the Great Powers forced the suppression of the compulsory competence that was necessary for controversies of a legal nature. Debates were also held on the legal form to be given to the PCIJ Statute: either to have recourse to a resolution of the Assembly of the League of Nations, or to use the option of including the Statute in an international treaty. Throughout the process, Altamira was in favour of the compulsory jurisdiction of the PCIJ.

84 Altamira (n 75) 44.

85 R Altamira, manuscript notes (August 1928) compiled in *Rafael Altamira, 1866–1951* (n 3) 180.

86 R Altamira, *El proceso ideológico del proyecto de Tribunal de Justicia Internacional* (Madrid 1921) 16.

87 See O Spiermann, *International Legal Argument in the Permanent Court of International Justice. The Rise of the International Judiciary* (CUP 2005) 129 *et seq.*

Altamira distinguished the principles contained within the PCIJ, the old sense of arbitration against the new legal principle regarding a permanent and independent judicial body, in his own words, the judicial 'justice' (objective justice). Altamira's concern focused on what should be understood by 'justice' and 'legal questions'. For him, both were the core values of the Covenant of the League of Nations and the purpose of the ACJ's mission. The aim was to distinguish between arbitration and 'judicial' justice (PCIJ) and to eliminate international disagreements 'of a political nature'.

Political disagreements were left outside of the scope of international justice in The Hague Conferences (1899 and 1907). Altamira mentioned the declaration by Bourgeois in 1907, which benefited from the distinction between legal and political matters to produce agreements. Basically, the members of the ACJ agreed with limiting all 'pretexts for violence or for abuses of others' rights, by adventurers, by bullies, by the powerful or by those who believe they are so strong that they can treat others with disrespect'.[88] In this regard there was agreement among the members of the ACJ to accept the broad system finally included in the Statute of the PCIJ.

Regarding the distinction between arbitration and judicial justice, the debate among the different approaches of the members of the ACJ remained open until the last moment. In Altamira's opinion, this was due to the resistance to transferring international differences to a field other than the field of arbitration 'which gives a free hand to opportunists'.[89] Altamira defended that the judicial justice entailed obligation, while arbitration entailed freedom, given that it was based on the consent of the parties to decide to submit a dispute to a court of arbitration.

In Altamira's thought, the governments of states that chose to settle their differences through arbitration could always use the Permanent Court of Arbitration (in The Hague). However, even if a party exposed to a controversy refused the legal examination of the question, it would have to submit to the PCIJ if the other party so requested. For Altamira:

> If this rule is approved by the Council and the Assembly of the League of Nations, an enormous step will have been taken in terms of peaceful and legal settlement of many conflicts that are, mainly, due to the resistance of one of the parties to discuss the question or have it legally examined.[90]

In the context of this discussion, Altamira wondered whether the competence of the PCIJ would be recognized and used by the states and whether the Covenant of the League of Nations would be complied with in this field. For him, this depended on the willingness of the states, in particular the most powerful states.[91] Ideally, for Altamira, the correct channel to respect the jurisdiction of the

88 Altamira (n 75) 50.
89 ibid 50–51.
90 ibid 51.
91 ibid 60.

PCIJ was the loyalty to the idea of the League of Nations and of international justice. He wondered if the world had achieved sufficient maturity to renounce war. Altamira recognized that there was a tendency to renege war – more than ever in the process of history – and inclined to use international justice. For him, the future of the world depended upon a psychological experience that fell under 'the intellectual and moral possibility of humankind'.[92]

In 1928, Altamira reflected on the idea of justice linked to his technical thought on education in the following terms:

> Laws are not enough to prevent all injustice, to liberate us from it, or even to punish it. There is another, more powerful resource that we do not consider very much or that, at least, due to its power, we do not try hard enough, believing that everything depends on external guarantees. This resource is the legal purity of our intention, of our moral sense and of the law, the only thing that will make us fair in all our actions . . . and that will truly guarantee, in practice, justice for others.
>
> Therefore . . . we have to think about educating our own sense of the law, about making ourselves, individually, increasingly fairer with others at all times in our lives: because laws cannot be effective in a social environment that is used to unfairness and tolerates it . . .
>
> Because of all the above, those of us who dream of a better humanity than the present one and use the resources that are available to us to make this truly happen, are strongly determined to support educational resources.[93]

Altamira followed, at least in part, the ideas of Georges Scelle (1878–1961), who was inspired by Léon Duguit (1859–1928), to define his idea of international social solidarity.[94] For Duguit (using his theory of solidarity) and Scelle (using his biological theory), the law was based on the action of solidarity that entails natural, biological coercion that individuals are obliged to accept because of the threat to social cohesion. The law, therefore, emerges as a social imperative that translates into a need arising from human solidarity, to which considerations of justice and moral character is added.[95] Altamira's thinking reflects the transformations of law based on a double process of socialization and internationalization.[96]

92 ibid 60–61.

93 R Altamira, 'Justicia y Escuela' in *Idella* (Elda 1928). Text collected in *Rafael Altamira, 1866–1951* (n 3) 187.

94 G Scelle, *Précis de droit des gens. Principes et systématique I-II* (Sirey 1932, 1936). See also M Koskenniemi, *The Gentle Civilizer of Nations. The Rise and Fall of International Law 1870–1960* (CUP 2001) 297 *et seq.*

95 See L García Arias, *Las concepciones iusnaturalistas sobre la fundamentación del derecho internacional* (Zaragoza 1960) 123.

96 R Asín, 'El proyecto social de Rafael Altamira. Un modelo para la cultura y la comprensión internacional' in J Ferrándiz Lozano et al. (coord), *Rafael Altamira: Idea y acción hispanoamericana* (Diputación de Alicante 2011) 13–54.

3.2 International judge

The different approaches of the members of the ACJ could be seen in problems such as the choice of language, the different legal systems and 'civilization groups', and the appointment of judges. Altamira did not participate a great deal in the discussions of the ACJ, his contributions being mainly confined to the requirements to be met by members of the PCIJ, and considerations on the principles of international law such as sovereignty, good faith, or non-interference, and the procedure and requirements that judges had to comply with.

One important element that Altamira had supported was set out in Article 9 of the Statute. This article stated:

> the whole body . . . should represent the main forms of civilization and the principal legal systems of the world.

The sought-after universality of the League of Nations and of the PCIJ itself made it easier for the representation of principal cultures, including that of Spain and Latin America. Altamira emphasized the originality of 'Spanishness', even within the domain generically described as Latin or Romance:

> (W)e Spaniards, *lato sensu*, i.e. people who speak Spanish and who are branches of the tree of Spanish civilization, are a world apart. We have an original degree of orientation and a Western mode of civilization that has important characteristics, even within the so-called Latin group.[97]

Altamira attempted to promote Spanish legal culture in the Statute of the PCIJ over Anglo-Saxon culture. It was Root who, advised by James Brown Scott (1866–1943), came out in defense of Altamira's position on the very identity of Spanish civilization.[98]

With regard to the procedure for electing PCIJ judges, Altamira defended the principle of selection from a single list of candidates drawn up in view of their merits and capacity and not based on nationality grounds.[99] He defended this idea with energy, stating that

> judges shall be elected on the basis of a list of candidates designated by the States. Each State shall be entitled to present a maximum of . . . candidates who are nationals of that State. In addition, with the purpose of showing clearly that each judge is at the sole service of justice, each State shall be entitled to propose a number of candidates of other nationalities, that

97 Altamira (n 85) 20.

98 Altamira (n 75) 81–82.

99 Article 4 of the Statute stipulated that PCIJ members were to be elected 'from a list of persons proposed by national groups in the Court of Arbitration'. Article 5 limited the nomination of candidates to 'members of the Court of Arbitration who are nationals of the States listed in the Annex to the Convention, or of the States that are members of the League of Nations'.

> number being greater than the number of candidates of the State's own nationality.[100]

Not all the members of the ACJ thought the same way.

Moreover, after the ACJ's first meeting in 1920, Manley Ottmer Hudson (1866–1960), a US lawyer who specialized in the process of PCIJ, defended the system of selecting candidates from national groups because:

> (i) the system is intended to secure the independent judgment of competent men who are not necessarily government officials or political leaders; (ii) it leaves the representatives of members of the League of Nations freer in their voting in the election by the Assembly and the Council; and (iii) it provides a useful link between the Permanent Court of Arbitration and the Permanent Court of International Justice.[101]

A new system to select candidates was discussed in the ACJ. It was based on the principle of sovereign equality – with there being no more than one judge per country – by appointing temporary judges on an ad hoc basis for each case, so that each litigant would have a defender in the PCIJ.[102] Altamira had serious doubts over this approach, since it presumed that the confidence placed in the elected judges was not absolute. For him, there was a continuing fear that the rights of each state would not be defended if that state did not have its own representative at the PCIJ who knew the case well. Altamira went even further, saying:

> What did this mean, and what effect would it have on the PCIJ, with a fixed number of components, to have these special judges who stopped being special judges once the case was brought before the PCIJ? Would this not lead to the denaturing of the PCIJ, making it closer to an arbitration body?

Basically, this debate raised a problem typical of international law: the equal sovereignty of states. On repeated occasions, Altamira insisted that the law was the guarantee of the small and the weak and called for equality for all. Such arguments were not without criticism. For William Rappard (1883–1958), a Swiss academic and diplomat, weak states agreed to consider the League of Nations 'primarily as an instrument for promoting peace through justice',[103] thereby allowing themselves to be considered the most loyal champions of the League of

100 Altamira (n 75) 34.

101 MO Hudson, 'The Election of Members of the Permanent Court of International Justice' (1930) 24 American Journal of International Law 721.

102 Altamira referred to the method adopted by the Conference of Associations for the League of Nations, held at Brussels, December 1–3, 1919. See more information in *Mémorandum sur les différentes questions concernant l'établissement de la Cour Permanent de Justice Internationale présenté à la Commission de juristes chargé de préparer le projet relatif à l'établissement de cette Cour*, p. 41.

103 WE Rappard, 'Small States in the League of Nations' in *Problems of Peace* (London 1935) 49–51.

Nations. This was due, according to Rappard, less to their superior virtue than to their inferior power since 'by serving the League of Nations, they were not only defending justice, they were also promoting their national interests more effectively'.[104]

Altamira returned to his constant concern, that is, the conditions that an international judge must meet. He said:

> Was it certain that there would be a sufficient number of persons who met the conditions, so that any special judges who might be subsequently appointed could fulfill those conditions with the same or similar rigor as PCIJ judges?[105]

Our protagonist strongly defended the selection of judges paying more attention to moral criteria than to technical competence. This may have been due to his reformist project based on education through humane and moral postulates. Article 2 of the PCIJ Statute set out the conditions required for a person to carry out the work of a judge.

The drafting of this article gave rise to a curious debate between Root and Phillimore on the one hand, and Altamira on the other. The former defended 'the need to leave open the possibility for certain countries to choose their international judges in their senior magistracy'. To which Altamira replied that certain 'national judges rarely have the opportunity to deal with international questions'.[106] Lord Phillimore accused Altamira of 'quixotism'. Altamira's response was clear and forceful in the following words:

> I do not feel myself to be a compatriot of Don Quixote. Rather, I feel myself to be a citizen of the world who knows what is wanted and sought not by minorities governing people, but by the masses, the university youth of all peoples, people of whom much will be needed in the future, those who will increasingly want to know exactly what they are involved in and committing themselves to.[107]

Perhaps Altamira was right to speak out against the scant experience of national judges in international matters, but it was no less true that Altamira's own experience of international language and structures was also far from solid. James Brown Scott wrote:

> Mr Altamira repeatedly expresses the view in the proceedings of the Committee, that the success of the court would depend upon the quality of its judges, and that moral qualities had more importance than scientific ability.[108]

104 ibid 50.
105 Altamira (n 75) 55.
106 Advisory Committee of Jurists (n 9) 612.
107 Altamira (n 75) 24.
108 J Brown Scott, *The Project of a Permanent Court of International Justice and Resolutions of the Advisory Committee of Jurist* (Washington, DC 1920) 51.

Those moral qualities in the eyes of Altamira were reason, education, justice, conscience, purity, effort, tolerance, austerity, and good manners. It is revealing that a man of Altamira's solid intellectual background and moral authority concentrated more on defending the moral quality of aspirant judges than on their technical abilities. In his defense of the moral and scientific quality of judges, Altamira promoted the role of writers and intellectuals, that is, his role as a spiritual guide of Spanish legal culture.[109]

4. Pragmatism and scientific technique

4.1 The general principles of law

Once the nature of the competence of the PCIJ had been dealt with, the debate moved on to the sources to be included in an article of the PCIJ Statute. The attention to Article 38 of the PCIJ Statute is an exercise in reflection on the scope and meaning of the sources of international law.[110] This exercise allows us to understand the process that produces binding norms. Before 1920, the doctrine of sources was unable to establish an instrument to define what was law and what was not.[111] The members of the ACJ managed to agree, after several discussions, on a list of sources of international law that favoured scientific expertise and pragmatism.

The inclusion of this list of sources of international law in Article 38 of the PCIJ Statute was the result of the theory and practice accumulated during the nineteenth century.[112] The members of the ACJ found justification in Article 15 and Article 37 of the 1899 Convention and 1907 Convention for the Pacific Settlement of International Disputes, respectively, and Article 7 of the 12th Convention of the Hague Conference of 18 September 1907. This latter instrument established the International Prize Court (IPC) in order to interpret and apply the law on prizes in a consistent manner. Article 7 of the IPC referred to the sources of international law as follows:

> If a question of law to be decided is covered by a treaty in force between the belligerent captor and a Power which is itself or whose subject or citizen is a party to the proceedings, the Court is governed by the provisions, the Court shall apply the rules of international law. If no generally recognized

109 More or less, a man with project. See on this idea A Lang and S Marks, 'People with Projects: Writing the Lives of International Lawyers' (2013) Temple Int'L &COMP. L.J, (27)2, 437–454.

110 M Fitzmaurice, 'The History of Article 38 of the Statute of the International Court of Justice. The Journey from the Past to the Present' in S Besson and J d'Aspremont (eds), *The Oxford Handbook of the Sources of International Law* (OUP 2017) 179 et seq.

111 Skouteris (n 12) 69 *et seq.*

112 See A Pellet and D Müller, 'Article 38' in A Zimmermann and Ch J Tams (eds), *The Statute of the International Court of Justice* (3ª edn, OUP 2019) 822 *et seq.*, and MW Janis, 'Sources in the Meta-History of International Law. A little Meta-History. Paradigms, Article 38, and the Sources of International Law' in S Besson and J d'Aspremont (eds), *The Oxford Handbook of the Sources of International Law* (OUP 2017) 270–71.

> rule exists, the Court shall give judgments in accordance with the general principles of justice and equity

The expression 'the Court shall apply the rules of international law' was rejected by the British government. It was presented again at the London Naval Conference in 1908. This was the origin of the London Declaration of 1909, *non nata* as a consequence of the lack of ratification by United Kingdom. The 1907 Hague Convention, along with the other cited instruments, were used as a foundation by the members of the ACJ for the drafting of Article 38 of the PCIJ Statute, by referring to the sources that at a certain time were known or were taken into practical consideration as applicable rules. The article referred to treaties, justice, and even fairness. In a certain way, Article 38 of the PCIJ Statute bears certain similarities to Article 7 of the IPC Statute.

The members of the ACJ entered into a difficult discussion on the rules to be applied by the PCIJ.[113] Three positions are identifiable in the ACJ discussions: first, members who considered the definition unnecessary, as was the case with Lapradelle; second, members who accepted the definition proposed by Descamps (except paragraphs 3 and 4), for example Root, who thought that the PCIJ should only apply to international treaties and customary law; and, third, members who supported Descamps' proposal – the majority of the ACJ members.[114]

In fact, the discussions in the ACJ included reflections on the scope of international law not just limited to positive rules – treaties and customs – but also considered a wider range of sources.[115] The sources of treaties and customs did not generate any debate among the jurists of the ACJ. The differences between the members of the ACJ were focused on questions such as what would happen if no treaty or custom existed. The members of the ACJ debated 'what question of international law' to apply. It was not a closed discourse connected to the establishment of a *non liquet*. Many members, including Altamira, were reluctant to consider this *non liquet*, and, therefore, debates were held on other sources to be included in Article 38.[116]

If neither a treaty nor custom could be identified or if the customary rule were inadequate, the President Descamps asked whether a judge could invoke the *non liquet*.[117] The President of the ACJ was convinced that an international judge could not refuse to issue a ruling on a case that was his responsibility to hear, even if there were no clear applicable rules.[118] In this scenario, Descamps asserted that

113 This led, among other reasons, to James Brown Scott or John Bassett Moore to recognize that the ACJ's opinion on Article 38 of the PCIJ Statute was not unanimous. This is reflected in the work of Janis (n 112) 273.

114 The three positions were established by A. Pellet and D. Müller on the rules of law to be applied by the PCJI, see Pellet and Müller (n 112) 828.

115 Spiermann (n 86) 61.

116 O Spiermann, 'The History of Article 38 of the Statute of the International Court of Justice. "A Rurely Platonic Discussion"?' in S Besson and J d'Aspremont (eds), *The Oxford Handbook on the Sources of International Law* (OUP 2017) 165 *et seq.*

117 Advisory Committee of Jurists (n 9) 318.

118 ibid.

the general principles of law should be applied.[119] However, in order not to let a judge act on his own opinion, the decisions to be taken had to be in accordance with the legal conscience of civilized peoples and 'for this same purpose make use of the doctrine of publicists carrying authority'.[120]

The proposal was not without opposition from other members of the ACJ, such as Root and Phillimore.[121] Root repeated that the states would only accept compulsory jurisdiction (of the PCIJ) if the sources to be applied were clearly defined.[122] Root objected to the third point, that is, the rules of international law as recognized by the legal conscience of civilized nations. The American representative did not understand the significance of this argument. Root considered that

> nations will submit to positive law, but will not submit to such principles as have not been developed into positive rules supported by an accord between all states.[123]

Descamps and Lapradelle considered that this did not affect the PCIJ jurisdiction,[124] although Lapradelle approached the problem when he proposed that

> it was only in connection with paragraph b: 'any point of international law' that Root felt he must oppose the application of the principles mentioned in numbers 3 and 4 of the President's draft, dealing with the rules to be applied.[125]

For Phillimore, the general *principles* recognized by civilized nations were those recognized in the national law of the various states such as certain principles of procedure, the principle of good faith and the principle of *res judicata*, among others.[126] Ultimately, for Phillimore the general principles of law meant the 'maxims of law'.[127]

Loder and Hagerup felt that they could agree with Phillimore on the basic principles. Root made a proposal that included the rule 'the general principles of law recognized by civilized peoples'.[128] Finally, Root's proposal on the basis for Descamps' project was approved by consensus.

119 ibid.
120 ibid 319.
121 See Spiermann (n 86) 170.
122 Advisory Committee of Jurists (n 9) 286, 287, 308, 310.
123 ibid 287.
124 ibid.
125 ibid 313.
126 ibid 335. See also GA Finch, 'Les sources modernes du droit international' (1935) 53 Recueil de Cours de l'Académie de Droit International 629.
127 ibid Italics are from the author to emphasize the importance of the word.
128 ibid 344.

As representative of the Spanish legal tradition, Altamira defended the inclusion of the general principles of law recognized by civilized nations as a source of international law in the terms used by the President Descamps in his PCIJ draft,[129] as well as the positive custom. The Statute of the PCIJ embodied the recognition of the universal principles proclaimed by the Spanish legal culture of the sixteenth century, that is by Vitoria and his successors, concerning the universality of international law, justice, and solidarity.[130] Altamira was a strong supporter of including the various sources in the draft of the PCJI Statute in order to define differences through the practice of arbitration.

Finally, a new discussion problem dealt with the inclusion of 'successive order'. The Belgian Descamps, in opposition to Ricci Busatti, defended that the different sources should be applied in successive order. Ricci Busatti was in favour of the suppression of the words 'succesive order' because these words might also suggest the idea that

> the judge was not authorised to draw upon a certain source, for instance point 3 (general principles of law), before having applied conventions and customs mentioned respectively in points 1 and 2.[131]

Ricci Busatti's argument was that '(i)t is a fundamental principle of law that a special rule goes before general law'.[132] For Ricci Busatti, many phrases were superfluous. Other members such as Hagerup or Lapradelle joined the Italian's argument. Altamira characterized the phrase as a 'pleonasm' and pointed out that 'keeping this expression . . ., they would only be following an age-old tradition'.[133] In the end, the ACJ members agreed with the argument that the successive order of the sources was due to the principle *lex specialis derogat legi generali*.

Eventually, the jurists of the ACJ adopted a normative approach to international law whose relevant criterion was provided by source theory. This approach to international law underlines the regulations of the law, their ability to oppose the policy of the state as a key element of its obligation.[134]

129 On this point see J Basdevant, 'Sur quelques opinions du Judge Altamira' in *Estudios de Derecho internacional. Homenaje al profesor Camilo Barcia Trelles* (Universidad de Santiago de Compostela 1958) 257 *et seq*. Also referred to in several other articles: R Altamira, 'Le Droit Coutumier espagnol moderne' *Recueil d'Études sur les sources du Droit en l'Honneur de François Gény. Les sources générales des systèmes juridiques actuels*, vol I (Paris 1934) 269 *et seq*., and 'La costumbre jurídica en la colonización española' (1946–1948) n° 31–40 Revista de la Escuela Nacional de Jurisprudencia.

130 See M Koskenniemi, 'Empire and International Law: The Real Spanish Contribution' (2011) 61 University of Toronto Law Journal 3 *et seq*.

131 Advisory Committee of Jurists (n 9) 337.

132 ibid.

133 ibid 338.

134 See M Koskenniemi, *The Politics of International Law* (Hart Publishing 2011) 40 *et seq*.

4.2 The 'writings of publicists' as elements of interpretation

The debates about the sources continued when both the character and nature of the doctrine were addressed. The 'writings of publicists' as a source of international law are and were controversial.[135] Their inclusion could be explained by the need to define and identify the sources listed in the paragraphs preceding Article 38 of the PCIJ Statute, in particular the custom and the general principles of law.

In 1908, Lassa Oppenheim (1858–1919) provided an insight on the relevance of introducing the 'writings of publicists' into the PCIJ Statute in the following terms:

> The writers on international law, and in especial the authors of treaties, have in a sense to take the place of the judges and have to pronounce whether there is an established custom or not, whether there is a usage only in contradistinction to a custom, whether a recognized usage has now ripened into a custom . . ., the writers have again to take the place of the judges and have to ascertain the precise meaning of those rules with the help of interpretation. It is for this reason that text-books of international law have so much more importance for the application of law than text-books of other branches of the law.[136]

The use of textbooks was a common practice among judges in international arbitration proceedings, among other pre-existing international courts. The doctrine was universally recognized as a source of international law. The Spanish author Rafael Conde y Luque (1835–1922), a professor in international law at the Central University in Madrid, who was a positivist realist, considered that scientific doctrine had an important role to play in international law because legal science was what specified and defined popular feelings and beliefs regarding the law.[137] Science sowed the idea, or accommodated it, and formulated and submitted it to the conscience of the legislator to be accepted.[138] Conde y Luque stated that in public international law the field of science was extensive and its efficacy undisputable.[139]

The ACJ members agreed that the function of the PCIJ was defined by its legal basis and that it did not allow any sources for the settlement of disputes except those in compliance with the law. The final version of Article 38 of the

135 See M Vec, 'Sources of International Law in the Nineteenth-Century European Tradition-The Myth of Positivism' in Besson and d'Aspremont (n 6) 121 *et seq.*
136 L Oppenheim, 'The Science of International Law: Its Task and Method' (1908) 2(2) AJIL 315.
137 See R Conde y Luque, *Derecho internacional público* (Athenaica 2015) 72 *et seq.*
138 ibid 72.
139 ibid.

PCIJ Statute differs to the text proposed by the ACJ in its draft as Article 35.[140] The modifications were made by the Council and the Assembly, adding the final paragraph: '(t)his provision shall not prejudice the power of the Court to decide a case *ex aequo et bono*, if the parties agree thereto'. For Altamira, the inclusion of this final paragraph distorted the character of the PCIJ and confused its function with that of the Court of the Arbitration.[141]

Article 38 (4) states that 'Subject to the provisions of Article 59, judicial decisions and the teachings of the most highly qualified publicists of the various nations, as subsidiary means for the determination of rules of law'. The final version was the result of the conflict between two legal systems: the Anglo-Saxon and Romano-Germanic systems. The adapted version was an attempt to limit the effects of the *stare decisis* rule in common law in the application of the doctrine established by Article 38.[142] It also attempted to define the functions of international courts through a cross-reference to the identification and application of the rule to be applied.

The debates on the inclusion or not of the 'writings of publicists' as a source were led by Ricci Busatti and Phillimore. The Italian jurist Ricci Busatti opposed the argument that the 'writings of publicists' could be considered as a source of law.[143] He even said he was 'astonished that Root had agreed to a formula containing this idea'.[144] Nevertheless, Phillimore thought that the doctrine could be considered as a source for international law.[145] In response to this assertion, Ricci Busatti asked Phillimore

> whether England would accept a sentence based not on a rule of law accepted as such, but upon the doctrine of legal writers.[146]

Phillimore himself thought that 'this was possible'. Ricci Busatti doubted

> whether states would really accept rules which would be the result of the doctrine rather than of their own will, or of their usages.[147]

140 The text of Article 35 of the ACJ Draft submitted to the League of Nations states as followed: 'The Court shall, within the limits of its jurisdiction as defined in Article 34, apply in the order following: 1. international conventions, whether general or particular, establishing rules expressly recognized by the contesting States; 2. international custom, as evidence of a general practice, which is accepted as law; 3. the general principles of law recognized by civilized nations; 4. judicial decisions and the teachings of the most highly qualified publicists of the various nations, as subsidiary means for the determination of rules of law'.

141 Altamira (n 75) 251.

142 On the institution of *stare decisis* see G Guillaume, 'The Use of Precedent by International Judges and Arbitrators' (2011) Journal of International Dispute Settlement 5–23.

143 Advisory Committee of Jurists (n 9) 332.

144 ibid 333.

145 ibid.

146 ibid.

147 ibid 333–34.

Phillimore thought that

> the sources mentioned in point 3 might be included in point 4, because it was through custom that general principles came to be recognized, and on the other hand, custom is formed by the usage followed in various public and formal documents, and from the works of writers who agree upon a certain point.[148]

Ricci Busatti observed that the ideas of Phillimore coincided with his own ideas.[149] At the end of the discussion, the 'writings of publicists' were recognized as an 'auxiliary source', that is, an element of interpretation of international law.[150]

To analyse Altamira's thoughts about the importance of the 'writings of publicists', it is essential to turn to the old and polemic debate between jurist and historian. He made a statement to the effect that the historian has a notable advantage over the jurist, fully conscious of all the risks that such a statement implies. Thus, he declared the historian to be

> a spirit who has 'a historical sense' of human rights, and who always views them and judges them on that basis.[151]

Going even further than this, Altamira felt that the jurist was characterized by stagnation and the historian by a capacity for action. In his own words:

> The jurist tends to see a problem from the perspective of legal texts . . .; the historian views the same problem through a genetic sense of the facts that are to be perceived in each one, and above all, . . . that could be described as fluid, taken from a moment in the process of historical movement that attends to the past whilst moving towards a future that may be quite different.[152]

Altamira was fully aware that his role as an international jurist meant that he would not only have to decipher texts and documents, but that in order to provide a generalized explanation, he would also have to set them in the context of their time, that is, in their historical context. For this reason, Altamira had no confidence in the vision or reading of the pedestrian jurist who, he would have said ironically, 'is no more than a jurist'; that is, a person who neither sees nor goes beyond the written word, without paying the slightest heed to its genesis, to the series of elements that brought it into being. Altamira rejected the model of jurist as a person for whom 'the text alone suffices, of whom it is only necessary

148 ibid 334.
149 ibid.
150 ibid.
151 Altamira (n 75) 310.
152 ibid 311.

to ask, based on purely legal criteria, what the text says', a person to whom something different would appear as being 'prohibited' and 'dangerous'.[153]

With this approach that was at once methodological and ideological, Altamira gave a coherent setting to the criteria and the standards that would mark his work at the PCIJ. He wrote:

> (T)he historian is naturally drawn to historical research, because for the historian, a legal text is no more than the result of a process of preparation that carries within it the end logic and explanation of the result itself.[154]

Through this rigorous sentiment, Altamira unequivocally claimed the definitive characteristic of the historian. He said:

> to make use of voices that already have a classical significance, the study and contemplation of history leads on naturally to being 'liberal' or 'progressive' rather than 'conservative' or 'retrograde'. It is no surprise that one of the most liberal of modern philosophies should have been substantially historicist.[155]

Altamira finds in the classics, in particular in Hugo Grotius (1583–1645), the foundations of the 'law of nations'.[156] In 1926, Altamira published an article entitled 'Hugo Grotius and Spain' (*Hugo Grocio y España*) in which he referred to the Dutch international law expert as a 'chosen spirit',[157] a man with an 'elevated spirit and self-confidence'.[158] This was a way of supporting the figure of Grotius as a reference for international law. For Altamira, when examining the history of international law it could be seen how public conscience and the disasters caused by the war had inspired Grotius in his celebrated work *De jure belli ac pacis* (1625). In Altamira's thought, Grotius was not a legislator in the true sense of the word, but he recognized that the states were eager to take the rules of international law from his book. In his article, Altamira connected Grotius to Spanish legal culture and asserted that his work had been of great use for the history of international legal historiography.[159]

Additionally, Altamira was a defender of resolutions adopted by international conferences and congresses. He had participated in numerous international conferences related to the history of the law and education and in the preparatory congresses for the creation of the League of Nations. In fact, in 1919, he was

153 ibid 312.
154 ibid 314.
155 ibid 311–12.
156 Altamira read and cited the work of J Kosters, *Les fondements du droit des gens. Contribution à la théorie generale du droit des gens* (Brill 1925).
157 R Altamira, 'Hugo Grocio y España' (1926) 36 Revista de Ciencias Jurídicas y Sociales 290.
158 ibid 292.
159 ibid 297.

a member of a Spanish delegation to the Brussels Congress organized by 27 associations from various countries that laid the foundations for the League of Nations.[160] For Altamira, modern science created doctrine through international legal congresses that brought together men of science from all states to discuss preliminary or agreed-upon theories, with a practical emphasis, the results of which were offered to governments to put them into practice.[161]

5. Conclusions

Through his pragmatism, Altamira contributed to the scientific technique of international law as a member of the ACJ by supporting a list of sources for international law, recognizing the (compulsory) competence of the PCIJ and the procedure for selecting judges, among other matters. In this way, Altamira contributed to the formalization of international law. His legacy continues to guide the discipline of international law, especially the settlement of disputes through legal channels. The concepts of universality, justice, solidarity, and active neutrality, among others, are part of contemporary international legal language.

Altamira's idea of justice was based on a sum of virtues and values, welcomed in the social, political and legal world, and linked to security, liberty, tolerance, equality and solidarity.[162] Obviously, the theoretical and practical aspects of education implemented by Altamira in his years of teaching at the ILE and at the National Museum of Education were reflections of his idea of justice. His approach to the concept of justice cannot be understood without considering its relevance to Spanish regenerationist circles. In these circles, education was the keystone to solving society's problems. When working as a jurist on the ACJ, Altamira combined the concept of justice with education.

Article 38 of the PCIJ Statute includes, for the first time, a list of sources to be applied by the PCIJ Statute. Altamira was a supporter of the formalization of law and of history and this drove him in his decision to support the inclusion of Article 38 of the PCJI Statute. Altamira kept a low profile in the ACJ. Altamira did not participate a great deal in the discussions of the ACJ as his contributions were mainly confined to the requirements to be met by judges of the PCIJ, and considerations on the principles of international law such as sovereignty, good faith, and non-interference. Nevertheless, through his discourse, Altamira helped

160 The Congress of Brussels was a Congress of Associations to study problems relating to the creation of the League of Nations, and for spreading this idea. The meeting was between 27 associations representing all the warlike states of Europe except Germany and Austria, some from Asia, such as China and Japan, and all the neutral states of Europe. On the other side, the American Republics were not represented. Altamira (n 74)10. For a useful study of the international and national organizations working for the creation of an international organization see R Altamira, *Problèmes modernes d'enseignement en vue de la conciliation entre les peuples et de la paix morale* (Presses Universitaires de France 1932).

161 Altamira was elected associate of the *Institute de Droit International* (IDI) in 1927, and member in 1934.

162 See Gamarra (n 1) 40.

to expand the sources of international law to be applied by international courts (Article 38 of the PCIJ Statute), including the 'writings of publicists', which was without doubt a useful tool for the interpretation of the rules of applicable international law.[163]

Like most European liberals, Altamira was, in the end, an amateur who conceived the discipline of international law at an abstract level. He was ready to change his opinion, influenced by politics, whenever he felt it necessary to do so. In the final analysis, Altamira's amateurism was one of the reasons for his disillusion and bitterness. History has recognized Altamira and other international jurists as 'the legal conscience of the civilized world'. His work paved the way towards a professional awareness of the significance of the international judge and the practical uses of this profession for the benefit of the rights of individuals and of nations.

163 In the terms used by RY Jennings, 'What is International Law and How Do We Tell It When We See It?' in M Koskenniemi (ed), *The Sources of International Law* (Routledge 2000) 29.

2 National political ideologies and international legal practices

Raul Fernandes (1877–1968)

Arthur Roberto Capella Giannattasio

1. Introduction

Barão do Rio Branco (1845–1912) and Rui Barbosa (1849–1923) are not the only main Brazilian international legal scholars of the first half of the twentieth century.[1] Raul Fernandes was a Brazilian legal scholar who has also contributed positively to the development of international law and to the public defense of its main institutions.[2]

The Council of the League of Nations (LoN) originally invited the Brazilian jurist Clovis Bevilaqua (1859–1944) to take part in the Advisory Committee of Jurists (ACJ)[3] – an organ created to prepare a draft statute of the Permanent Court of International Justice (PCIJ). The ACJ's meetings were held between 16 June and 24 July in 1920 at the Peace Palace at The Hague (Netherlands) and, due to personal reasons, Clovis Bevilaqua was unable to attend the meetings and

1 It would be impossible to indicate in a single footnote all the Brazilian literature which highlights the different contributions from both. Just to mention a few examples, see Carlos Cardim, 'A Luta pelo Princípio da Igualdade entre as Nações' in Fundação Alexandre da Gusmão (FUNAG), *II Conferência de Paz, Haia 1907: A Correspondência Telegráfica entre o Barão do Rio Branco e Rui Barbosa* (FUNAG 2014), Paulo Casella, *Fundações do Direito Internacional Pós-Moderno* (Quartier Latin 2008), Luís Corrêa, 'Introdução da Primeira Edição' in Luís Corrêa (ed), *O Brasil nas Nações Unidas (1946–2011)* (3rd edn, FUNAG 2012), Celso Lafer, *A Identidade Internacional do Brasil e a Política Externa Brasileira* (Perspectiva 2001) and Rubens Ricupero, *A Diplomacia na Construção do Brasil (1750–2016)* (Versal 2017). For a critical appraisal of their contributions, see Arnulf Lorca, *Mestizo International Law* (CUP 2015) and Alexandre Moreli, 'Estranha Ordem: O Brasil e o Liberalismo Político Internacional do Pós-1919' in Silvia Correia and Alexandre Moreli (eds), *Tempos e Espaços de Violência*, (UFRJ/Autografia 2019).

2 For instance, Hans Kelsen's proposal in 1944 on the construction of international peace through legal institutions – i.e., via an international court with compulsory jurisdiction – is directly associated to the efforts of Raul Fernandes at the ACJ – see Hans Kelsen, *Paz pelo Direito* (Martins Fonte 2010). This will be mentioned below.

3 See the respective chapters in this volume; see also, PCIJ, Advisory Committee of Jurists, *Procès-Verbaux of the Proceedings of the Committee, 16 June–24 July 1920, with Annexes* (Van Langenhuysen, The Hague 1920), III–IV and 1) (hereinafter « Procès-Verbaux » or « PCIJ »).

DOI: 10.4324/9781003020882-3

was subsequently replaced.[4] After the ninth session, Raul Fernandes was included in those meetings as the substitute of Clovis Bevilaqua.[5] Although Fernandes was mentioned as absent from the ninth meeting, he only started during the tenth session towards the very end of that meeting. While performing his activities, Raul Fernandes' duties at the ACJ were originally restricted to present and defend the project proposed by Clovis Bevilaqua and to discuss the proposals presented by the other members. During the twenty-fifth session of the ACJ[6] – when the reading of the first consolidated version of the entire draft proposal had begun – Raul Fernandes was granted voting rights to decide, on an equal footing with the other members of the Committee, on the final version of the document.[7]

The practical and theoretical results of the debates developed within the ACJ and the corresponding draft are widely known: the establishment of one of the pillars of contemporary international legal order, that is, an international judicial mechanism with compulsory jurisdiction to solve conflicts between states.[8] After the Second World War, the successor of the PCIJ, the International Court of Justice (ICJ), would continue to form the World Court.

The debates on the institutional design of this new international public authority[9] focused on several aspects: its legal mandate,[10] its procedural and normative legitimacy,[11] and the corresponding enforcement mechanisms.[12] The ACJ also worked on the establishment of the normative criteria upon which this judicial institution would be authorized to exercise its technical authority – that is, the rules to be applied by the Court.[13]

4 Procès-Verbaux (n 3) 1. During ACJ's debates, Raul Fernandes has tried to present Clovis Bevilaqua's project for a Permanent International Court of Justice, but his initiative did not succeed – see below item 4.1. For a brief analysis of Bevilaqua's proposal, see Paulo Macedo, 'Clóvis Beviláqua e a Justiça Internacional: Entre o Sim e o Não a Rui Barbosa' [2016] Revista de Direito Internacional 423, 433–21.

5 Procès-Verbaux (n 3) 203.

6 19 July 1920.

7 Procès-Verbaux (n 3) 551.

8 Paulo Casella, *Tratado de Versalhes na História do Direito Internacional* (Quartier Latin 2007), Kelsen (n 2), Antonio Trindade, *Os Tribunais Internacionais Contemporâneos* (FUNAG 2013).

9 For the distinction of those three aspects (legality, legitimacy, and enforcement) as constitutive elements of international public authorities, see Armin von Bogdandy, Matthias Goldmann, and IngoVenzke, 'From Public International Law to International Public Law: Translating World Public Opinion into International Public Authority' [2017] EJIL 115 and Arthur Giannattasio et al., 'International Constitutional Court: Rise and Fall of an International Debate' [2019] Revista de Direito Internacional 130.

10 PCIJ (n 3) 11, 45, 104, 107–9 and 224–32.

11 ibid 307–20, 552–57, 574–98, 613–24 and 620–50.

12 ibid 125–26 and 128.

13 ibid 331–51. It should be noted that these are set out in the famous art. 38 of the Statute of the ICJ as the traditional place of the so-called sources of international law. For a criticism of this idea, see, for instance, Arthur Giannattasio, 'Contra um Fetichismo nos Estudos Empíricos em Direito Internacional: Moldura Intencional e o Esvaziamento Significativo da

This text examines the contribution of Raul Fernandes in the institutional design of the PCIJ. The idea is to indicate that, on the pretext of shaping the legal framework of this new international judicial body, the contributions presented by Raul Fernandes at the ACJ's sessions express a certain Brazilian approach to international law at that time – an approach directly bound to domestic material and immaterial conditions. Such discussion was not until now explored by academics in international law – and it should not be underestimated.

In fact, Raul Fernandes is recognized as one of the champions of the PCIJ. Indeed, he not only admonished international powers after the negotiation for not accepting the jurisdiction of the Court,[14] but was also responsible during the negotiations for presenting the main compromise proposals for two sensitive issues which threatened the success of the ACJ:[15]

(i) the adoption of the so-called 'Fernandes Formula', according to which if no state was legally obliged to accept the jurisdiction of the PCIJ, once it declared its voluntary acceptance, the state would be legally bound by its declaration – the optional clause on the compulsory jurisdiction of the PCIJ[16] and
(ii) the rejection of special procedures for the nomination of judges: one procedure for permanent judges (appointed by international powers) and other procedure for non-permanent judges (appointed in a rotative basis by the other countries) – following Rui Barbosa's efforts on the legal equality of states since the Second International Peace Conference held at The Hague in 1907.[17]

Empiria' [2018] Revista de Estudos Empíricos em Direito 9 and Onuma Yasuaki, Direito Internacional em Perspectiva Transcivilizacional (Arraes 2016).

14 Raul Fernandes, *The United States and the Permanent Court of International Justice* (American Foundation 1928).

15 Antônio Carvalho, *Raul Fernandes – Um Servidor do Brasil* (Agir 1956), Ramiro Guerreiro, 'Homenagem da Comissão Jurídica Interamericana ao Doutor Raul Fernandes' in Organización de los Estados Americanos (OEA), *XIV Curso de Derecho Internacional* (Subsecretaría de Asuntos Jurídicos de la Secretaría General de la OEA 1988) xi–xxii, Juan Quintana, 'The Latin American Contribution to International Adjudication: The Case of the International Court of Justice' [1992] Netherlands International Law Review 127, Vicente Ráo, 'Saudação do Prof. Vicente Ráo ao Embaixador Raul Fernandes' [1952] Revista da Faculdade de Direito da Universidade de São Paulo 454, Antonio Trindade, 'Compulsory Jurisdiction of the Inter-American Court of Human Rights under the American Convention on Human Rights' in Antonio Trindade (ed), *The Construction of a Humanized International Law* (Brill Nijhoof 2015) 521–42.

16 Albert Guani, 'La Solidarité Internationale dans l'Amérique Latine' [1925] Recueil des Cours de l'Académie de Droit International de La Haye, 204, 329; Quintana (n 15) 136–38, Ráo (n 15) and Trindade (n 15) 525.

17 One of the many reasons why Rui Barbosa was elected in 1921 to be one of the first 15 judges of the PCIJ from 1.1.1922. Rui Barbosa died in 1.3.1923 and another Brazilian jurist was elected to take office in his place from 10.9.1923 – Epitácio Pessoa, former Brazilian President (1919–1922) and former Chief of the Brazilian Delegation for the Treaty of Versailles (1919). He occupied this role in the PCIJ until 31.12.1930 – PCIJ, *Rapport Annuel*

Both proposals from Raul Fernandes are today still regarded as core institutional requirements for the success of any international judicial mechanism – like the ICJ,[18] the Inter-American Human Rights Court,[19] and, although with some differences, the International Criminal Court (ICC).[20] But the presence of Raul Fernandes at the ACJ debates reveals something else: one should not only focus on his individual achievements and proposals to understand the range of his contributions to international law. It is important also to understand the structural roots of his agency.

Since the Second International Peace Conference at The Hague (1907) there was a shared perception that Latin American countries had an important role in the development of international law.[21] And, among the 27 signatory states of the Treaty of Versailles, 11 were Latin American countries: Bolivia, Brazil, Cuba, Ecuador, Guatemala, Haiti, Honduras, Nicaragua, Panama, Peru, and Uruguay.

However, despite the common perception that Latin American countries could provide relevant contributions to international law and in spite of the fact that almost half the signatory states of the Treaty of Versailles were Latin American countries, only jurists from Brazil – first, Clovis Bevilaqua, then, Raul Fernandes – took part at ACJ debates.[22] This raises several questions. What could explain only the participation of Brazilian jurists from all the Latin American countries at the ACJ? Was there a shared *mentalité internationale*[23] among Latin Americans? Or what could have motivated such 'preference for Brazilian jurists'?

Raul Fernandes' role at the ACJ highlights other reasons that might justify the preference for Brazilian jurists. Instead of simply repeating the traditional narrative which emphasizes his individual achievements, this text will develop a structural approach of Raul Fernandes' agency. After all, if one takes seriously the argument that individuals cannot be understood as entities with exceptional *ex nihilo* creative capabilities,[24] it is important to identify some structural

---

de la CPJI (1er Janvier 1922–15 Juin 1925) (AW Sijthoff 1925) 9–10. See also Cardim (n 1), Lorca (n 1) 158–68 and Ráo (n 15).

18 Quintana (n 15) and International Court of Justice, *Selected Documents Relating to the Drafting of the Statute* (US Government Printing Office 1946) *apud* Hans Kelsen, *Law of the United Nations* (Frederik Praeger 1964) 523.

19 Trindade (n 15).

20 Kai Ambos, *Treatise on International Criminal Law*, vol I (OUP 2013) 26–29.

21 Cardim (n 1), Juliette Dumont, 'A América Latina na Sociedade das Nações: Reflexões a partir do Caso Argentino, Brasileiro e Chileno' [2016] Revista Escrita da História 139, Guani (n 16) 328–30 and Lorca (n 1) and Quintana (n 15) 128.

22 The Argentine jurist Luis Drago (1859–1921) was also invited, but due to personal reasons could not attend the meetings, See Quintana (n 15) 136. This does not necessarily affect the present argument, but the research of material and immaterial conditions of Argentina at that time lies outside the aims of this text. I, however, reserve those discussions for another time and place, especially if the savvy reader should reach out to me for collaborative research project.

23 Raul Fernandes, 'L'Amérique du Sud et la Société des Nations' in Peter Munch (ed), *Les Origines et l'Œuvre de la Société des Nations* (2nd supp, Gyldendalske 1924) 137 *apud* Quintana (n 15) 126.

24 Pierre Bourdieu, 'Campo Intelectual e Projeto Criador' in Jean Pouillon (ed), *Problemas do Estruturalismo* (Jorge Zahar 1968) 105 and Karl Marx, 'O Dezoito de Brumário de Luís Bonaparte' in Karl Marx, *Textos Escolhidos* (first published 1852, Abril Cultural 1978) 323.

incentives both at the international and national levels to which Raul Fernandes corresponded.[25] By doing so, this text suggests reasons that might clarify such preference for Brazilian jurists.

In this sense, the idea is to connect the arguments presented by Raul Fernandes at the ACJ debates – highlighting his contributions on the subject of the writing of publicists as applicable rules by the Court (art. 35.4, of the draft proposal; nowadays, art. 38.4 of the current Statute) – with other documents authored by him. The idea is to unveil (i) a domestic structure in his responsiveness to international law issues, and (ii) the relation of his agency to the international preference for a certain Brazilian approach to international law.

This chapter is divided into four parts. The first part (2.) discloses and justifies (i) the materials used to develop the qualitative research based on primary and secondary sources (2.1), and (ii) the critical framework used to examine the information gathered (2.2). The second part (3.) presents a general biography of Raul Fernandes according to Brazilian political and economic structure during his lifetime. The third part (4.) examines the contributions of Raul Fernandes at ACJ debates (4.1) and identifies a common ideational structure among his texts (4.2). The fourth part (5.) discusses Raul Fernandes' agency at the ACJ and explains the preference for Brazilian jurists at that time.

2. Materials and methods

2.1 Qualitative research based on primary and secondary sources

The information gathered for this text was extracted according to a qualitative approach of primary sources (document analysis) and secondary sources (literature review). The majority of the primary sources and some of the secondary sources were examined thanks to the access granted to the physical archive of the Peace Palace Library in The Hague (Netherlands), and to the online archives of the *Centro de Pesquisa e Documentação de História Contemporânea do Brasil da Fundação Getulio Vargas (CPDOC-FGV)* in Rio de Janeiro (Brazil) and the ICJ for documents produced by the PCIJ – specially the following series: (i) Series D: Acts and Documents concerning the Organization of the Court, (ii) Series E: Annual Reports, and (iii) the 'Other Documents' session.

Some of the documents analysed were authored solely by Raul Fernandes, namely:

(i) his contributions registered in the proceedings of the ACJ debates (1919) as the substitute of Clovis Bevilaqua;[26]
(ii) three speeches on the LoN and on the PCIJ as a former member of the ACJ, namely: (i) one delivered in French at the *Real Academia de Jurisprudencia*

25 Arthur Giannattasio, 'Fundamentos de uma Análise Sociológica Crítica das Instituições Jurídicas Internacionais: Negatividade e Política na Metodologia dos Estudos em Direito Internacional no Brasil' [2018] Revista Brasileira de Estudos Políticos 113.

26 Procès-Verbaux (n 3) III.

y Legislación (Madrid, Spain) on 21 May 1921,[27] (ii) one delivered in Portuguese at the *Sociedade Brasileira de Direito Internacional* (Rio de Janeiro, Brazil) on 28 July 1925,[28] and (iii) one delivered in French at the *Université de Bruxelles* (Brussels, Belgium), on 11 November 1927, which was later translated to English and published by the American Foundation;[29]

(iii) three speeches on other international legal issues, in which his discourse reveals elements characterizing his structure of thought on international responses to national material and immaterial conditions, namely: (i) one given at the Third Regular Session of the General Assembly of the United Nations (Paris, France) on 28 September 1948, as the Brazilian Ministry of Foreign Affairs – later translated to Portuguese by Fundação Alexandre de Gusmão (FUNAG),[30] (ii) one given in Portuguese at the *Faculdade de Direito da Universidade de São Paulo – Largo São Francisco (FD/USP)* (São Paulo, Brazil) in 1952, when Raul Fernandes received from this University the doctor *honoris causa* degree,[31] and (iii) the one given in Portuguese when he took the office of Brazilian Minister of Foreign Affairs for the second time in 1954;[32] and

(iv) two academic texts in Portuguese on the international responsibility of the state, in which his proposals follow the same pattern of argumentation mentioned above: one originally published in 1929[33] and the other originally published in 1952.[34]

All those texts were not analysed to understand Raul Fernandes' personal academic contributions on their respective subjects. Rather, the idea was to extract from them a certain pattern of institutional responses to international legal issues in Raul Fernandes' arguments. Thus, these academic texts are considered documents (primary sources) that register and represent a permanent structure of thought – and not the register of academic outcomes (secondary sources).

27 Raul Fernandes, *El Principio de la Igualdad Jurídica de los Estados en la Práctica Internacional después de la Guerra* (Reus 1921).

28 Raul Fernandes, *A Sociedade das Nações: Sua Gênese, Seus Fins, Sua Estructura, Meios de Acção e Resultados* (Imprensa Nacional 1925).

29 Fernandes (n 14).

30 Raul Fernandes, 'III Sessão Ordinária da Assembleia Geral da ONU – 1948' in Luis Corrêa (ed), *O Brasil nas Nações Unidas (1946–2011)* (3rd edn, FUNAG 2012) 73–75.

31 Raul Fernandes, 'A Velha Academia' [1952] Revista da Faculdade de Direito da Universidade de São Paulo 444.

32 Raul Fernandes, 'Discurso de Posse de Raul Fernandes, Ministro das Relações Exteriores' (27 August 1954) <www.funag.gov.br/chdd/index.php/ministros-de-estado-das-relacoes-exteriores?id=442> accessed 26 August 2020.

33 Raul Fernandes, 'Responsabilidade do Estado por Dano Irrogado aos Estrangeiros – Um Aspecto da Questão' in Luiz Baptista and Valerio Mazzuoli (eds), *Doutrinas Essenciais – Direito Internacional* (first published 1929, Revista dos Tribunais 2012) 807.

34 Raul Fernandes, 'A Responsabilidade dos Estados em Direito Internacional' [1995] Boletim da Sociedade Brasileira de Direito Internacional 9 (first published 1952).

The literature review consisted basically of texts authored by other scholars on (i) Raul Fernandes' biography and personal achievement concerning international law, (ii) Raul Fernandes' contributions to the development of international law, and (iii) the traditional legalist identity of the Brazilian approach to international issues.

Some of the biographies analysed were published during his lifetime[35] while others were written after his death.[36] Although the non-biographical texts do not address specifically Raul Fernandes' role or life, while discussing the development of the LoN or of international judicial mechanisms – such as the PCIJ and the ICJ – those texts do mention his contribution to international legal order. Those non-biographical texts will be properly mentioned below.

As for the texts concerning the legalist identity of Brazil in international issues, the focus was on texts written by (i) Brazilian scholars in international law and international relations, who, from an interdisciplinary perspective, tried to identify and to qualify the idea of such Brazilian identity, and (ii) non-Brazilian scholars in international law, who, from a contemporary critical perspective, tried to identify and to qualify a pattern of response of former European colonies to international legal issues. The idea was to compare them and to understand if Raul Fernandes' responsiveness could be associated to some of those theoretical frameworks. Those texts will also be properly mentioned later.

2.2 *A critical approach to Raul Fernandes' agency: unveiling structural political tensions*

It is important to clarify the idea of (i) identifying a structure in the contributions of Raul Fernandes to ACJ debates and to the development of international law, and (ii) qualifying this as a certain pattern in the Brazilian approach to international law at that time. Of course, it does not intend to affirm that Raul Fernandes is a kind of 'representative' of an alleged 'Brazilian School' of international law.

Such statement would be problematic for several reasons. After all, it is still unclear whether or not it is possible to affirm the existence of a coherent academic Brazilian perspective on international law over time – even though some authors try to develop this idea.[37]

That aside, some authors insist that Brazil is a good apprentice in international legal tradition[38] – if only for strategical reasons.[39] Some authors argue that

35 Carvalho (n 15) and Ráo (n 15).

36 Luís Corrêa, '1948' in Luís Corrêa (ed), *O Brasil nas Nações Unidas (1946–2011)* (3rd edn, FUNAG 2012), Guerreiro (n 16) and Robert Pechman, 'Fernandes, Raul – Verbete Biográfico' in Christiane Paula and Fernando Weltman (eds), *Dicionário Histórico-Biográfico Brasileiro* (CPDOC-FGV 2010) <www.fgv.br/cpdoc/acervo/dicionarios/verbete-biografico/fernandes-raul> accessed 9 April 2020.

37 Casella (n 1).

38 Lafer (n 1) and Ricupero (n 1).

39 Gregory Shaffer, Michelle Sanchez and Barbara Rosenberg, 'The Trials of Winning at the WTO: What Lies behind Brazil's Success' [2008] Cornell International Law Journal 383.

Brazilian legalism is just further evidence of the uncritical submission of Latin American countries to Euro-American legal standards on international law[40] or a sign of Brazil's uneasy position in international relations in terms of identity.[41] However, there are several epistemic difficulties in affirming or denying 'national schools' of international law – which shall be discussed later.[42]

Moreover, such a statement would sound a comfortable – and superficial – theoretical determinism of the role of Raul Fernandes in the ACJ and in the international environment. But that is not the case: the idea of conducting a structural approach to his contributions consists precisely in identifying how he proposed institutional innovations at the international level while taking into account the legal-political disputes within his own country.[43]

In other words, such analysis will (i) focus on different contributions from Raul Fernandes over time to the development of international law institutions, in order to (ii) extract from them a pattern of domestic material and immaterial political disputes to which he himself continuously responded at the international level. This will then enable us to (iii) connect his own institutional responsiveness to a certain Brazilian approach to international law at that time, and, finally, (iv) suggest reasons that might help in understanding the preference for Brazilian jurists at the international debates – such as the one developed at the ACJ.

This critical analytical framework is based on the idea that the contribution of scholars cannot be understood as the isolated outcome of an individual biography characterized by exceptional capabilities. Indeed, it is usual to have narratives which try to magnify those personal trajectories as a progressive affirmation of a pioneering and excellent individual agency. Their exceptional character in comparison to others would then justify their capacity to innovate in their own intellectual fields. However, by falling for such biographical illusion, those narratives do miss something.[44]

'Field' is an expression which designates a metaphorical description of a system composed by agents who are bound by interdependent relations. The idea is that every field is governed by a similar structural dynamic:[45] a continuous dispute between those agents and a constant reestablishment of the balance of forces between them within the field.[46]

40 Emmanuelle Jouannet, *Le Droit International* (PUF 2016), Lorca (n 1) and Liliana Obregón, 'Completing Civilization: Creole Consciousness and International Law in Nineteenth-century Latin America' in Anne Orford (ed), *International Law and its Others* (CUP 2006).

41 Feliciano Guimarães, 'The Uneasy "Well-Placed" State: Brazil within Latin America and the West' [2020] Cambridge Review of International Affairs 1.

42 See item 5., *infra*.

43 Giannattasio (n 25).

44 Pierre Bourdieu, 'A Ilusão Biográfica' in Marieta Ferreira and Janaína Amado (eds), *Usos & Abusos da História Oral* (Fundação Getulio Vargas 1996).

45 Pierre Bourdieu, 'Quelques Propriétés des Champs. in Pierre Bourdieu, *Questions de Sociologie* (Minuit 1984) 113 and, from the same author, 'A Gênese dos Conceitos de *Habitus* e de Campo' in Pierre Bourdieu (ed), *O Poder Simbólico* (DIFEL/Bertrand Brasil 1989) 67–68.

46 Bourdieu (n 45), 'Quelques . . .' 113.

Such disputes develop between (i) those who seek entering the field and achieving a prominent position in it (heterodox); and (ii) those who already have such a position in the field (orthodox).[47] The former seek those positions via the accumulation of different signs of prestige and recognition – that is, they learn the rules and the symbols which characterize the field and follow the recognized paths. The latter are concerned with maintaining their position within the field, in order to dictate the rules of access to the field and of participation in it, and to define the legitimacy criteria (paths and symbols) of declaring something as appropriate or inappropriate to the field.[48]

In spite of those disputes, the relationship between heterodox and orthodox is characterized by interdependence: both agents are concerned with keeping the social recognition of the field as an important place for the reproduction of society itself. After all, the field is regarded as an important place in which its participants are socially legitimized to exercise a symbolic power – a power to define the direction and the sense of using 'a particular category of signs and, thus, [a power] over the view of the natural and social domains'.[49]

Thus, heterodox and orthodox seek not only acquiring for themselves such power, but also keeping the social recognition that the field is continuously authorized to exercise this power. For this reason, both behave in a complicitous way to not end the disputes and to preserve the social recognition of the field as responsible for producing something which is dear for the reproduction of society itself[50] namely: the capability of defining different symbols for 'making people see and believe [. . . experiences of the natural and social domains which were hitherto], more or less confused, fluid, unformulated'.[51]

In other words, heterodox and orthodox jointly defend the social recognition of the fields as authorized instances for selecting and consecrating legitimate 'sorcerers', who are capable of bringing 'into existence' something that did not exist before or that was not perceived as such until then.[52] That is why although the conflictual dynamic happens in every field, it does not happen necessarily in a conscious way or always in accordance with an instrumental calculation.[53]

Although all fields are similar, they are not identical[54] – and, for this, they usually operate in an autonomous relationship in relation to other fields.[55] However, the specific field of scholars – the intellectual field – has a definitive characteristic: it is

47 . . . ibid 115.

48 Pierre Bourdieu, 'O Campo Intelectual: Um Mundo à Parte' in Pierre Bourdieu (ed), *Coisas Ditas* (Brasiliense 2004) 170 and 172–74.

49 ibid 172–74.

50 Bourdieu (n 45) 'Quelques . . .' 114–16.

51 Bourdieu (n 48) 176.

52 ibid.

53 Bourdieu (n 45) 'Quelques . . .' 119–20 and Bourdieu (n 45) 'A Gênese . . .' 59–73.

54 Bourdieu (n 48) 170.

55 Bourdieu (n 24) 105–6.

related to different social instances who are responsible for cultural production – such as literature, religion, and art, among others.[56]

In this sense, the consecration of someone within the intellectual field occurs basically in two ways: by the concurrence of elements from the intellectual field itself and by the concurrence of elements from the other cultural fields. In other words, the intellectual field has relative autonomy[57] as the outcomes of its disputes are influenced by the recognition or non-recognition by elements and criteria developed within other cultural fields.[58]

The intellectual field operates, indeed, according to its own criteria of recognition.[59] Although not exclusive to international legal field,[60] the consecration of international legal scholars is usually associated with:

(i) following an educational background which is usually regarded as being the one followed by elites – that is, attending courses and pursuing degrees in prestigious national, foreign, and international academic institutions;[61]
(ii) publishing academic works (e.g., major university publishers, prestigious journals, leading commercial presses) whose recognition derives from an alleged worldwide reputation of academic excellence;[62] and,
(iii) being effectively close to and active with famous academic organizations and societies in international law and to other less formal – though equally prestigious – epistemic communities or research groups.[63]

However, meeting such requirements does not seem to suffice. The consecration of someone within the intellectual field is also related to the accumulation of signs of social prestige located in non-academic fields.[64] Once again, although not exclusive to the international legal field,[65] the consecration of international legal scholars can also be associated with the following signs of distinction:

56 Bourdieu (n 45) 'A Gênese . . .' 71.
57 . . . ibid 65–66 and Bourdieu (n 48) 174–75.
58 Bourdieu (n 48) 169–71 and 176.
59 Bourdieu (n 24) 107–9.
60 London School of Economics (LSE), *Maximizing the Impacts of Your Research: A Handbook for Social Scientist* (LSE 2011).
61 Michelle Badin, Fabio Morosini, and Inaê Oliveira, 'Direito Internacional Econômico no Brasil: Quem Somos e o que Fazemos? Evidências Empíricas de 1994 a 2014' [2016] Revista de Direito Internacional 5 and Anthea Roberts, *Is International Law International?* (OUP 2017).
62 Onuma (n 13) and Roberts (n 61).
63 Douglas Castro, 'Direito Internacional no Brasil: As Injustificáveis Raízes de Ausência do Debate Crítico' in Associação Brasileira de Pesquisadores em Sociologia do Direito (ABRASD), *Anais do IX Congresso da ABraSD: Trabalhos Completos* (ABRASD 2018), Onuma Yasuaki, 'Remarks' [1981] Proceedings of the Annual Meeting (American Society of International Law) 163 and Onuma (n 13).
64 Bourdieu (n 24) 107–9 and Bourdieu (n 48) 177–79.
65 London School of Economics (n 60).

(i) performing in self body patterns of established social stereotypes of someone 'that socially matters' for the public sphere.[66] This usually include someone who holds material and immaterial conditions in terms of gender, race, and economic independence[67] which are socially overestimated: being a white,[68] sophisticated – a euphemism for 'civilized' or not being a 'backwarded race'[69] – cisgendered[70] male person.[71]

(ii) occupying prominent positions in other fields – especially the political one – at national, international, or both levels. This means that international legal scholars accumulate signs of social recognition when they manage to progressively perform a certain 'quadruple role' in their career by means of combining two well-known concepts of *dédoublement fonctionnel*. Thus, the double role of international legal scholars both in national and international levels[72] and the double role of international legal scholars in academic and non-academic professions.[73]

In this sense, the consecration of an agent as pertaining to a specific intellectual field does not derive from an alleged individual exceptionality.[74] Rather, it derives from a combination of internal and external factors to the field which lead the agent to the acquisition of symbolic power.[75] For international legal scholars, this enables them to exercise such power as academics in national and international levels and as non-academics on national and international levels.

For this reason, the task of understanding the role of legal scholars regarded as responsible for the development of international law is something which must be carried out with a certain degree of mistrust. Indeed, it is important to ask several

66 Judith Butler, *Gender Trouble* (Routledge 1990) and, from the same author, *Bodies that Matter* (Routledge 1993) and Adilson Moreira, *O que é Discriminação?* (Letramento/Casa do Direito/Justificando 2017).

67 Nancy Fraser, 'Da Redistribuição ao Reconhecimento? Dilemas da Justiça numa Era "Pós-Socialista"' [2006] Cadernos de Campo 231, Arthur Giannattasio, 'Direitos e Democracias: Reflexos da Democracia Deliberativa' in Felipe Asensi and Daniel Paula (ed), *Direito Constitucional* (Elsevier 2013) and, from the same author, 'International Human Rights: A Dystopian Utopia' [2014] ARSP – Archiv für Rechts- und Sozialphilosophie 514.

68 Adilson Moreira, 'Pensando como um Negro: Ensaio de Hermenêutica Jurídica' [2017] Revista de Direito Brasileira 393 and Onuma (n 13).

69 Luís Eslava, 'The Moving Location of Empire: Indirect Rule, International Law, and the *Bantu Educational Kinema Experiment*' [2018] Leiden Journal of International Law 539.

70 Diane Otto (ed), *Queering International Law* (Routledge 2018).

71 Hilary Charlersworth, Christine Chinkin, and Shelley Wright, 'Feminist approaches to International Law' [1991] American Journal of International Law 613, Adilson Moreira, *Cidadania Sexual* (Arraes 2017) and Onuma (n 13).

72 Georges Scelles, 'Règles Générales du Droit de la Paix' [1933] Recueil des Cours de la Académie de Droit International de la Haye 327, 358–59.

73 Oscar Schachter, 'The Invisible College of International Lawyers' [1977] Northwestern University Law Review 217.

74 Bourdieu (n 48) 177–79.

75 Bourdieu (n 45) 'A Gênese . . .' 72–73.

questions: Who were those people regarded as examples?, Which paths did they follow to be considered like this?, What signs of distinction did they accumulate within their trajectories?, Why are they still regarded today as examples?, Why others were not recognized at that time and why are they still not recognized?

To put it simply, it is necessary to ask about the structural rationality (i) that locates some scholars closer to the centre of the international law field to the detriment of other scholars, (ii) that reaffirms the prominent position of some scholars by means of control and surveillance of the consecration dynamics within the fields, and (iii) to which agents constantly respond, seeking to enlarge or to reduce access to current signs of social prestige.

Thus, the contributions of Raul Fernandes – like the contribution of any Brazilian legal scholar on international law – cannot be regarded as singular outcomes of an individual with alleged exceptional capabilities. Rather, I argue that (i) his role at the ACJ is directly related to the process in which he accumulated social signs of prestige, (ii) his contributions to the development of international law are precisely related to his responses, at the international level, to national political tensions regarding access to those social signs, (iii) those contributions correspond to a certain Brazilian response, via international law, to domestic political disputes at that time concerning material and immaterial conditions, and (iv) such an approach can explain the above-mentioned preference for Brazilian jurists at international debates.

3. Not another 'historical background': Raul Fernandes' biography and its structural drivers

Raul Fernandes was born in Valença (São Sebastião do Rio de Janeiro Province) in 1877 and died in 1968 in Rio de Janeiro (Rio de Janeiro State).[76] This first information of his biography indicates something relevant:[77] Raul Fernandes lived during several legal and political changes in Brazilian contemporary history and developed his quadruple role in decisive moments for Brazilian public order.

Since its independence in 1822 – formally recognized in 1825 by the Treaty of Rio de Janeiro, signed with Portugal after the mediation conducted by the United Kingdom – Brazil established a total of seven Constitutions: (i) Constitution of 1824, (ii) Constitution of 1891, (iii) Constitution of 1934, (iv) Constitution of 1937, (v) Constitution of 1946, (vi) Constitution of 1967 and

76 Pechman (n 36).

77 "São Sebastião do Rio de Janeiro Province" and "Rio de Janeiro State" are terms which designate, with some geographical differences, approximately the same territory – the current Rio de Janeiro State. There are of course differences beyond their names, which are related to geographical issues (e.g., including or not the municipality of Rio de Janeiro) and to their political and legal status (Province *versus* State). Those differences will not be addressed in the text, as they simply indicate that Raul Fernandes' lifetime followed crucial changes in Brazilian political organization.

(vii) Constitution of 1988. Thus, Raul Fernandes has lived under the rule of six different Brazilian Constitutions and has passed through five – out of a total of six – constitutional changes of Brazilian public order. In other words, he spent his life basically in moments in which Brazil underwent severe legal and political disputes in its history.

In terms of institutional changes, Raul Fernandes lived through fundamental legal and political transitions in Brazilian history in at least three different dimensions:[78]

(i) forms of government: the change in 1891 from Brazilian Empire (Monarchy) to Brazilian Republic (Republic) – the former was regulated by the Constitution of 1824, while the latter is being regulated by all the other following Brazilian Constitutions since 1891;
(ii) political organization of the territory: the definitive replacement in 1891 of political centralization (Unitary System) by political decentralization (Federal System);[79] and
(iii) military coups d'états preceding constitutional changes: military interventions have put an end to the monarchical regime (1889), but during the Republican regime the military have also put an end to Brazilian democracy for three times (1930, 1937, 1964) – although they were also responsible for restoring it once (1945).[80]

The legal and political changes during Raul Fernandes' lifetime were not restricted to the institutional organization of powers in Brazil. They have also touched issues concerning the political participation of society, as those disputes were also related to the legal definition of those who were entitled to make and take political decisions. This issue is directly related to the material conditions

78 Miriam Dohlnikoff, *História do Brasil Império* (Contexto 2017), Carlos Fico, *História do Brasil Contemporâneo* (Contexto 2016) and Marcos Napolitano, *História do Brasil República* (Contexto 2017).

79 The constitutional balance between the powers given to the center (Union) and to peripheries (not anymore Provinces, but States) was modified within each Constitution. This process can be associated with the variations of the democratic legitimacy of Brazilian Republic during the twentieth century – which will be mentioned below. See Maria Souza, 'Federalismo no Brasil: Aspectos Político-Institucionais' [2006] Revista Brasileira de Ciências Sociais 7.

80 Current democratic regime established in the Brazilian Constitution of 1988 – 20 years after Raul Fernandes' death – was also organized and led by the military forces. No coup d'état occurred to put an end to Brazilian civic-military dictatorship in 1988 – see Fico (n 78). Actually, the current regime derives from a negotiation process in which old and new oligarchies achieved a conservative compromise – in this sense, see Sérgio Abranches, 'Presidencialismo de Coalizão: O Dilema Institucional Brasileiro' [1988] Dados 5 and José Afonso da Silva, 'Direito Constitucional Comparado e Processo de Reforma do Estado' in José María Serna de la Garza (ed), *Metodologia del Derecho Comparado* (UNAM 2005) 280–82.

of Brazilian public order – which is characterized throughout its history by the prominent role of economic oligarchies in political dynamics.[81]

Raul Fernandes lived during different political disputes between successive Brazilian economic oligarchies within time:

(i) Brazilian Empire's aristocracy (1822–1889), based on colonial legacy of exporting commodities – mainly coffee, sugar, cotton, tobacco and rubber – grown in monocultures with the use of slave-labor force;[82]
(ii) Brazilian Democratic Republic's aristocracy (1889–1930), also based on the export of commodities – mainly coffee, rubber, cocoa, sugar, yerba mate, and tobacco – grown largely in monocultures with the use of a wage labour-force;[83] and
(iii) the industrial aristocracy which arose between the end of Monarchy (1889) and the first military coup d'état during the Republic (1930)[84] and was financed, first by domestic private investors[85] then (and largely) by foreign investors,[86] and later via state intervention.[87] After this first breach of Brazilian democracy (1930), this aristocracy acquired progressively a more stable economic and political position – especially after the other non-democratic coups d'état (1937 and 1964) led by the military.[88]

This political dispute between oligarchies is peculiar, as none was replaced by the other. Each new oligarchy simply introduced itself in different instances in the Brazilian decision-making process, both in domestic and foreign policies.[89] Even

81 Abranches (n 80), Fabio Comparato, *A Oligarquia Brasileira* (Contracorrente 2017) 18–23, Emília Costa, 'Introdução ao Estudo da Emancipação Política' in Carlos Mota (ed), *Brasil em Perspectiva* (10th edn, DIFEL 1978), Miriam Dohlnikoff, 'A Regionalização do Jogo Político: Elites e Poder Legislativo no Brasil do Século XIX' [2004] Novos Estudos CEBRAP 33, Napolitano (n 78) 91; Caio Prado Jr., *História Econômica do Brasil* (Círculo do Livro 1986) 180.

82 Costa (n 81) and Fernando Novais, Passagens para o Novo Mundo [1984] Novos Estudos CEBRAP 2.

83 Celso Lafer, 'Uma Interpretação do Sistema das Relações Internacionais do Brasil' in Felix Penã and Celso Lafer (eds), *Argentina e Brasil no Sistema das Relações Internacionais* (Duas Cidades 1973), Prado Jr. (n 82) and Maria Souza, 'O Processo Político-Partidário na Primeira República' in Carlos Mota (ed), *Brasil em Perspectiva* (10th edn, DIFEL 1978).

84 Celso Furtado, *Análise do "Modelo" Brasileiro* (3rd edn, Civilização Brasileira 1972) 15–20.

85 Gabrel Cohn, 'Problemas da Industrialização no Século XX' in Carlos Mota (ed), *Brasil em Perspectiva* (10th edn, DIFEL 1978) 288–304 and Prado Jr. (n 82) 283–90.

86 Cohn (n 85) 313–16, Boris Fausto and Fernando Devoto, *Brasil e Argentina: Um Ensaio de História Comparada (1850–2002)* (2nd edn, Editora 34 2005) 156–57, Furtado (n 84) 19–20; Prado Jr. (n 81) 299–303.

87 Cohn (n 85) 308–13 and Furtado (n 84) 24–27 and Celso Furtado, *Formação Econômica do Brasil* (18th edn, Nacional 1982) 228–32.

88 Boris Fausto, 'A Revolução de 1930' in Carlos Mota (ed), *Brasil em Perspectiva* (10th edn, DIFEL 1978) 227–34; Furtado (n 84) 33–37, Lafer (n 83) and Napolitano (n 78) 91.

89 Abranches (n 80), Afonso da Silva (n 80) 280–82, Fernando Cardoso and Enzo Faletto, *Dependência e Desenvolvimento na América Latina* (3rd edn, Zahar 1970) 14–15, Amado

the abolition of slavery and the adoption of a wage-based labour force in 1888[90] did not imply the exclusion of old oligarchies by the new ones.[91]

In other words, if Brazilian political regime changed from Monarchy to Republic (1891) and from Republican democracies to Republican dictatorships (1937 and 1967), a political consensus on the maintenance of the capitalist foundations of its oligarchical economy was kept throughout the years.[92] This condition is particularly important to understand the international position assumed by the country and its consequences to the definition of domestic political participation during Raul Fernandes' lifetime.

Although not being a postcolonial position exclusive to Brazil[93] during the above-mentioned period, the country followed its colonial legacy.[94] To put it simply, the Brazilian economy consciously kept its ties as a complementary player to an international capitalist structure led by Euro-American players – as a commodity supplier and as the destination of foreign capital.[95]

This external condition also paved the domestic geographical distribution of economic power between Brazilian regions and its related oligarchies.[96] As a secondary player in international economic environment, the Brazilian economy was also articulated within a capitalist centre-periphery dynamic: subsistence activities from the Brazilian periphery would provide economic support – through

---

Cervo and Clodoaldo Bueno, *A Política Externa Brasileira (1822–1985)* (Ática 1986) 41–43, Cohn (n 85), Fausto (n 88), Lafer (n 83) 92–93, Francisco Oliveira, *Elegia para uma Re(li)gião* (3rd edn, Paz e Terra 1981) 88 and 94–96 and Prado Jr. (n 81).

90 Prado Jr. (n 81) 185–206.

91 One should never forget that the abolition process (first of the slave trade, later of the slave labor power) was promoted worldwide by the United Kingdom during the nineteenth century. These actions were taken at that time via diplomatic negotiations and also through unilateral actions which violated international law – see Amado Cervo, *O Parlamento Brasileiro e as Relações Exteriores (1826–1889)* (UnB 1981) 133–71. Those actions sought to establish new international legal foundations for the necessary labour exploitation required to sustain the structural survival of an international economy based on capitalist premises – see Eric Williams, *Capitalism & Slavery* (UNC 1994). This also demanded the extinction of the slavery-based economy of concurrent Empires – like the Brazilian and the Portuguese Empires – see Novais (n 83). But it did not require either the extinction of the European capitalist economic system itself, or the transformation of the not-so-uneasy secondary role of Brazil within it – see Luiz Alencastro, 'La Traite Négrière et l'Unité Nationale Brésilienne' [1979] Revue Française d'Histoire d'Outre-Mer 395 and Novais (n 82).

92 Prado Jr. (n 81).

93 Cardoso and Faletto (n 89) 24–28, Eslava (n 69), Fausto and Devoto (n 85) 154–55, Arnulf Lorca, 'Direito Internacional na América Latina ou Direito Internacional Latino-Americano? Ascensão, Queda e Recuperação de uma Tradição de Pensamento Jurídico e Imaginação Política' in Michelle Badin, Adriane Brito, and Deisy Ventura (eds), *Direito Global e suas Alternativas Metodológicas* (FGV DIREITO SP 2016) 145–46 and Prado Jr. (n 81) 371.

94 Furtado (n 87) 94–95 and Fernando Novais, 'O Brasil nos Quadros do Antigo Sistema Colonial' in Carlos Mota (ed), *Brasil em Perspectiva* (10th edn, DIFEL 1978) and Novais (n 83).

95 Cardoso and Faletto (n 89) 32–34, Cohn (n 85), Furtado (n 84) 7–9, Furtado (n 87) 240, Lafer (n 83) 93 and 114–5, and Prado Jr. (n 81) 295 and 303.

96 Dohlnikoff (n 81) and Souza (n 83).

the flow of food, labour, and income – to the exporting activities developed in Brazilian centres.[97] This process occurred with important consequences for the national political structure concerning the definition of Brazilian domestic and foreign policies.

During the nineteenth century the Brazilian economic centre shifted progressively from the Northern and Northeastern parts of the country to its Southeastern and Southern parts.[98] In the beginning of the twentieth century, alongside its peers from Bahia and Pernambuco (Northeastern Brazil), oligarchies from São Paulo, Minas Gerais, Rio de Janeiro (Southeastern Brazil), and Rio Grande do Sul (Southern Brazil) arose. Those new oligarchies sought and achieved – even via non-international armed conflicts – a better position in the Brazilian economy and in its political structure.[99]

One oligarchy has not completely replaced the other: each one was able to influence, to a certain extent, the making and the taking of political decisions at the federal level.[100] In other words, in spite of punctual changes, economic and political structures remained the same in Brazil: decisions concerning domestic and foreign policies kept its oligarchic logic. And it is relevant to perceive that Raul Fernandes' agency was developed within this movement in which old and new regional oligarchies consecutively arranged their structural positions within Brazilian economic and political dynamics.

Aiming to preserve their respective prominent positions in domestic affairs, Brazilian oligarchies conducted the country to a permanent subaltern position in international affairs.[101] They established among them formal and informal agreements to: (i) accept the uneven international structure based on (a) capitalist economic premises (international division of labour), and (b) the Euro-American political centrality (Western civilized/non-civilized distinction), (ii) give Brazil a subordinate position within this international order, and (iii) preserve the country in such subaltern conditions. This strategy enabled them to (iv) preserve (a) the unequal political and economic structure of Brazil, (b) their dominant role as oligarchies within political and economic dynamics in the country, and, consequently, (c) their self-interests as drivers of Brazilian national and foreign policies.

In terms of international law theory, the acceptance and the reinforcement of an uneven international legal framework[102] were necessary. Such self-placement of Brazil in a subordinate position was crucial to (i) receive international legal

97 Furtado (n 87) 236–40 and Oliveira (n 89) 81–96.

98 Fausto and Devoto (n 86) 153–56; Furtado (n 84) 20–22, Furtado (n 87) 238–42, Oliveira (n 89) 73–78 and Prado Jr. (n 81) 180 and 218–21.

99 Fausto (n 88) 232–34; Fausto and Devoto (n 86) 190 and 198, Furtado (n 84) 20–22 and Furtado (n 87) 171–73, Napolitano (n 78) 19–31 and 57 and Prado Jr. (n 81) 237–38.

100 Cardoso and Faletto (n 89) 14–15 and 29–30, Oliveira (n 89) 88 and 94–96, Souza (n 79) and Souza (n 83).

101 Cardoso and Faletto (n 89) 35–36 and 39–46, Fausto (n 88) 230, Prado Jr. (n 81) 376–83 and Souza (n 83) 167–69.

102 Arthur Giannattasio, 'Verità Effetuale e Paz no Direito da Integração Europeia' [2018] Direito & Práxis 610, 621–22 and Lorca (n 94) 149–51.

recognition by Euro-American countries as a sovereign and civilized state[103] and (ii) as a 'domesticated' independent state, evade foreign direct interventions in domestic affairs.[104] This would enable Brazilian oligarchies (iii) international untouchability, as a stable international legal order would refrain foreign threats, and as a consequence,[105] (iv) national domination, as those international material and immaterial conditions provided them a stable prominent role in domestic economic and political structures.[106]

Living permanently in a subaltern country in (economic, political and legal) international relations was thus crucial for the continuity of national (economic, political and legal) relations of Brazilian oligarchies. Understanding the social and political aspects of those oligarchies will give finally additional elements to understand the agency of Raul Fernandes in performing his quadruple role. After all, during Raul Fernandes' entire lifetime (1877–1968), political participation in Brazil was restricted in different ways by its polity framework.

To put things in context, during the Brazilian Monarchy, there was a representative body – the Parliament; however, its members were selected via an indirect election procedure, which was restricted to white, male, Catholic Brazilian citizens with high annual net incomes (Constitution of 1824: arts. 5, 6, 9 to 12, 40 to 45 and 90 to 95) – in practical terms, the richest landowners and slave traders.[107]

Political representativeness also faced several restrictions during the Brazilian Republic – even though the religious requirement of 'being Catholic to be eligible' disappeared.[108] Indeed, democracy was suspended three times by military coups d'état (1930, 1937, 1964) and, although there was a Parliament both in democratic and dictatorial regimes – except for the dictatorships between 1930–1933 and 1937–1946 – a number of legal restrictions were present.

The Constitution of 1891 was enacted two years after a military coup d'état and established direct elections to the Parliament (arts. 26, 28 and 30). Its members could be selected only among eligible nationals – that is, male citizens who were not beggars or illiterates (arts. 69 to 71). While still explicitly excluding women from political participation, racial and economic exclusions from Monarchical times were also preserved – now indirectly. Indeed, although slavery was abolished one year before the end of the Monarchy (1888), there was absolutely no public policy organized by the Brazilian government to promote any kind of social and economic inclusion of ex-slaves and their descendants until

103 Lorca (n 93) 143–44.

104 Cervo (n 91) 20–29 and 145–64 and Lafer (n 83) 85–88.

105 João Pimenta, *Tempos e Espaços das Independências* (Intermeios/USP 2017) and José Ribeiro Jr., 'O Brasil Monárquico em Face das Repúblicas Americanas' in Carlos Mota (ed), *Brasil em Perspectiva* (10th edn, DIFEL 1978) 152–55.

106 Lafer (n 83) 88, 110–13 and 126.

107 Comparato (n 81) 87–94, 98–107 and 108–12 and Prado Jr. (n 81) 158–65.

108 Still, it is noteworthy that every Brazilian secular republican Constitution – besides the ones of 1891 and 1937 – repeated in their preambles the confessional tradition dating from the monarchical Constitution of invoking the protection of God.

more or less the 1970s.[109] Instead, there was a clear policy towards its exclusion and its progressive reduction via the official promotion of European – and later, Japanese – migration to replace African labour and to 'improve' Brazilian civilization by whitening its population[110] – a reason also to reject Chinese migration at that time.[111] Thus, even though the Brazilian Republic was mostly formed by ex-slaves, descendants of slaves, indigenous people, and free poor white men, considering that they could not meet the two legal requirements (not being beggars, not being illiterate), racial and economic exclusions still went on: in spite of the seemingly inclusive legal provisions, only 2 per cent or 5 per cent of the Brazilian population could exercise their political rights.[112]

Similar restrictions to political representativeness continued in the other political regimes during Raul Fernandes' lifetime. The Constitution of 1934 was enacted four years after a military coup d'état which closed the Parliament in 1930[113] and adopted a mixed election procedure similar to European conservative regimes in Portugal and Spain.[114] Male and female citizens were eligible, if not beggars or illiterates (arts. 108, 109 and 112), but such gender equality was not effective until 1965,[115] as it depended on female inclusion within economic and social fields.[116] Immigration was also affected, in order to reduce the entrance of 'dangerous foreign communist and anarchist ideas'.[117] Finally, racial and economic exclusions were preserved via indirect means, as social conditions did not allow many to fulfil the social and literacy criteria.[118] The Constitution of 1937 was enacted after a military coup d'état and established an authoritarian regime allegedly created to protect the country from a 'communist threat' (second preamble). This document provided formal requirements for indirect elections for a Parliament (arts. 38, 46 and 50), but this was never created until the end of this regime.[119] The Constitution of 1946 reestablished democracy after another military coup d'état. The Brazilian Parliament (arts. 37, 38 and 134) was restored and its members would be elected directly among Brazilian

109 Giannattasio (n 67) 'Direitos . . .' 169–70 and Lilia Schwarcz and Heloísa Starling, *Brasil: Uma Biografia* (Cia. Das Letras 2015) 342–4.

110 Maria Bassanezi et al., *Atlas da Imigração Internacional em São Paulo (1850–1950)* (UNESP/FAPESP 2008) 13–14, Fausto and Devoto (n 86) 178–79 and Schwarcz and Starling (n 109) 323.

111 Cervo (n 91) 178–87.

112 Fausto and Devoto (n 86) 201, Napolitano (n 79) 25 and Schwarcz and Starling (n 109) 342–46 and 351).

113 Schwarcz and Starling (n 109) 351–66.

114 Fausto and Devoto (n 86) 265–66 and Schwarcz and Starling (n 109) 374.

115 Fernando Limongi, Juliana Oliveira, and Stefanie Schmitt, 'Sufrágio Universal, mas . . . só para homens. O Voto Feminino no Brasil' [2019] Revista de Sociologia e Política 1, 3–4.

116 Giannattasio (n 67) 'Direitos . . .' 169.

117 Arthur Giannattasio and Pedro Scudeller, 'Cidadania na Comparação Internacional' in Thomas Richter and Rainer Schmidt (ed), *Integração e Cidadania Europeia* (Saraiva 2011) 179–81.

118 Fausto and Devoto (n 86) 264 and Schwarcz and Starling (n 109) 367.

119 Fausto and Devoto (n 86) 267–68 and Schwarcz and Starling (n 109) 374–77 and 391.

citizens – male and female persons who were not illiterates and who could speak Portuguese properly (arts. 129, 132, 133 and 138). Not only racial and economic exclusions were preserved via social conditions,[120] but also migrants and their descendants were marginalized in any political participation.[121] The Constitution of 1967 was enacted three years after another military coup d'état and was responsible for establishing the last official Brazilian dictatorship – once again, politically and economically motivated by an alleged 'communist threat'.[122] This new constitutional order also established a Parliament (arts. 29 and 30), whose members would be directly elected among Brazilian citizens – with the same requirements of previous Constitutions (arts. 142, 143 and 145).[123]

This is not simply a 'small outline of Brazilian history' or a mere 'background'. Bearing in mind all those legal, political, economic, and social aspects of Brazilian public order, it is crucial to understand the development of Raul Fernandes' agency in his quadruple role. After all, in spite of all those ruptures and continuities in Brazilian contemporary history, Raul Fernandes' academic and non-academic career both at national and international levels was never directly compromised. To put it simply, his agency can be identified in its actions towards the preservation of Brazilian structures – that is, to decisions and movements which preserved continuities and blocked ruptures.

Raul Fernandes was a white cisgendered man born during the Brazilian Monarchy in 1877. His birthplace was a farm located in Valença, a city of São Sebastião do Rio de Janeiro Province. He was the grandson of Mr. Peregrino José de Américo Pinheiro, a landowner of Rio de Janeiro who was granted with noble titles (baron and viscount of Ipiabas) during the Brazilian Monarchy. Raul Fernandes' father was Mr. Antonio José Fernandes, a doctor and landowner who also acted as a legislator at Rio de Janeiro's legislative body during the Brazilian Republic (Constitution of 1891).[124]

The discussion enables us to perceive that simply by birth, Raul Fernandes held several layers of social prestige in Brazilian public order. Not only because he was born a white cisgendered man, but mainly because he was born in one of the new economic centres in Brazil (Southeast region, alongside with Minas Gerais and São Paulo) and as an heir of one of the Brazilian economic and political oligarchies. Indeed, his family originated from landowners from the Brazilian Monarchy which constantly met the restrictive legal requirements for political

120 Fausto and Devoto (n 86) 284 and Schwarcz and Starling (n 109) 396–97.

121 The language requirement was thus a way to hinder such possibility – as Brazilian census of 1940 a slow linguistic assimilation. See Bassanezi et al. (n 110) 81–82. This restriction was removed later, in the Constitution of 1988.

122 Comparato (n 81) 191–92 and Fausto and Devoto (n 86) 380–83 and 392.

123 Other restrictions arose in this regime: all individual and collective civil and political freedoms could be suspended by the administrative, judicial, and political acts (arts. 151 to 156), several regulations temporarily suspended the Parliament, among others. See Schwarcz and Starling (n 109) 455–59.

124 Pechman (n 36).

participation as already described – both in the Brazilian Monarchy and in Brazilian First Republic. But there is more.

His agency developed at national and international levels in academic and non-academic fields only reinforced his conditions acquired by birth. In this sense it is possible to identify actions taken towards not only the accumulation of additional signs of social prestige, but also the conservation of the structural conditions which foster and value those signs.[125] And this, not only at the national level, but also at the international level.

At the national level, Raul Fernandes' academic path was associated with the most prestigious educational background at his time. First, he followed a law degree course – which was always associated in Brazil as a branch responsible for preparing those who would occupy the core bureaucratic positions in Brazilian civil public service.[126] Second, by the time of his enrollment in the undergraduate course in Law (1895), the country held at least four Law Schools: (i) two created in 1827 – one in São Paulo (Southeast) and other in Pernambuco (Northeast), and (ii) two created in 1891 in Rio de Janeiro (Southeast).[127] Yet, he graduated from the São Paulo Law School in 1898,[128] the first and – until today – the most prestigious Law School in Brazil[129] located by the time of his graduation in the economic and political centre of Brazil (São Paulo). Third, he was recognized as the best law student of his time, due to his outstanding performance in all disciplines in the course.[130] Finally, based on his academic performance and on his non-academic achievements in Brazilian public service, the same São Paulo Law School granted him the *doctor honoris causa* degree in 1951.[131]

His non-academic achievements at the national level are also associated with the outlined logic of use and accumulation of additional signs of conservative prestige.[132] Indeed, among other professional activities, not only did he (i) act as a lawyer in Rio de Janeiro – the capital of Brazil at that time, but he (ii) was also elected as a representative of Rio de Janeiro state at the Brazilian Parliament five times (four times during the First Brazilian Republic (1909–1917 and 1921–1922) and once during the short-term Constitution of 1934), (iii) was elected as Governor of Rio de Janeiro in 1922 (but could not take office, due to political opposition), (iv) supported the candidacy of Getulio Vargas in 1930 (who, although losing the elections, was responsible for the coup d'état in 1930 and, while acting as the President of Brazil between 1930–1945, was also responsible for the first official dictatorship in Brazil), (v) was nominated to the position of General Consultant of Brazilian Republic, between February and November

125 Fernandes (n 31) 445–46; Guerreiro (n 16) xi–xii; Ráo (n 15) 454–56.
126 Carvalho (n 14).
127 Rodrigo Bordignon, 'As faculdades de direito e o recrutamento de professores de ensino superior na Primeira República' [2017] Revista Sociedade e Estado 749.
128 Pechman (n 36).
129 Sergio Adorno, *Os Aprendizes do Poder* (Paz e Terra 1988) and Fernandes (n 31) 453.
130 Fernandes (n 31) 450–51, Pechman (n 36) and Ráo (n 15) 471–72.
131 Fernandes (n 31) and Ráo (n 15) 454–56 and 471–73.
132 Pechman (n 37) and Ráo (n 15) 455–56 and 472–73.

of 1932, (vi) was one of the jurists responsible for writing the Constitution of 1934, and (vii) was one of the founders in 1945 of the political party called União Democrática Nacional (UDN), which, in spite of its alleged 'democratic origins', (i) was an oligarchical political party[133] with a 'conservative, moralistic and antidemocratic profile'[134] and (ii) supported the military coup d'état in 1964 responsible for Brazilian last official dictatorship.[135]

For the purposes of this text, Raul Fernandes' academic achievements at the international level cannot be neglected. Although he is not known for his academic writings[136] he (i) is recognized worldwide for cleverly applying academic ideas to solve practical international law issues (as already mentioned), (ii) is regarded as one of the main heirs of Brazilian legalist tradition on international law,[137] (iii) is identified as an 'ardent and tireless'[138] disciple of Rui Barbosa's tradition on the international legal equality of states,[139] (iv) gave several speeches on international law (doctrines, practice and issues) to academic audiences in Brazil and in other countries, which were later transcribed and properly published as academic contributions to international law (192?, 1921, 1925, 1995, 2012b), and (v) received in 1947 a *doctor honoris causa* degree from the Universidad de la República Uruguay.[140]

Finally, his non-academic activities at the international level are also related to several experiences associated with the acquisition of signs of prestige.[141] After the First World War – and still during Brazilian First Republic – he was appointed (i) in 1919 as a member of Brazilian delegation to the Peace Conference, (ii) in 1920 as a substitute of Clovis Bevilaqua to the ACJ meetings, (iii) between 1919 and 1925 as the Brazilian representative at the LoN, (iv) from July 1926 to January 1927 as the Brazilian ambassador in Brussels (Belgium), and (v) in 1928 the Head of the Brazilian delegation to the VI Panamerican Conference in Havana (Cuba). Although refusing in 1934 – during Getulio Vargas' regime – the position of the Brazilian Minister of Foreign Affairs, after the Second World War – and after the end of the first Brazilian dictatorship – he was appointed (vi) in 1946 as a member of the Brazilian delegation to the Peace Conference, (vii) in 1947 as the Head of the Inter-American Conference for the Maintenance of Continental Peace and Security held in Rio de Janeiro (Brazil), (viii) in 1948–1949 as the Head of the Brazilian delegation to the III Regular Session of the General Assembly of the United Nations, (ix) from December 1946 to February 1950

133 Fausto and Devoto (n 86) 286–88.
134 Schwarcz and Starling (n 109) 392.
135 ibid 458.
136 Actually, he authored oral presentations, but no academic paper, article or book. See Guerreiro (n 16) xii.
137 Ráo (n 15) 457–58.
138 ibid 462–64.
139 Fernandes (n 26) 33–34 and Guerreiro (n 15) xv–xvi.
140 Pechman (n 36).
141 Corrêa (n 36) 72, Fernandes (n 30), Guerreiro (n 15) xvi–xvii, Pechman (n 36), Ráo (n 15) 455–56.

and from August 1954 to November 1955, as the Brazilian Minister of Foreign Affairs, and (x) between 1958 and 1968 – that is, during the second Brazilian dictatorship – as the President of the Inter-American Juridical Committee (IAJC) of the Organization of American States (OAS).

Finally, it is still important to emphasize three additional non-academic achievements of Raul Fernandes: he (xi) was responsible, alongside representatives from the US, Chile, and Peru, for writing and proposing, at the IX Panamerican Conference (1948) held in Bogotá (Colombia), a resolution against 'communist threats' in America,[142] (xii) advocated in 1946–1947 the need for closer diplomatic relations with Francisco Franco's authoritarian regime in Spain (1936–1975) to fight communism in the entire Western world,[143] and (xiii) was awarded by the Portuguese President two honorary orders: (i) on 24 December 1948, the Ordem Militar de Cristo (Military Order of Christ) and, (ii) on 6 May 1955 the Ordem Militar de Sant'Iago da Espada (Military Order of St. James of the Sword) – honorary orders which are historically associated with the promotion and preservation of Christianity dignity (Alvará 19.6.1789) were regulated into new terms during the twentieth century (Decreto n. 5.030/1918, n. 14.172/1927 n. 16.449/1929) and were granted to him during Antonio Salazar's authoritarian regime in Portugal (1926–1968).

Raul Fernandes was able to occupy different prominent positions in several intellectual and political fields until his death in 1968. Such stability derives not from exceptional individual capabilities. Rather, it derives from a certain combination of the accumulation of signs of social recognition within his own agency – both at the national and international levels – towards the outlined political disputes in Brazilian public life. His progressive identification with the conservative structure of Brazilian oligarchical economic and political dynamics in national and foreign policies helps to understand the way he contributed to the development of international law.

4. Raul Fernandes' quadruple role at the international level

The year 1919 was a turning point for the new international (legal) order as it was the year in which the Treaty of Versailles was signed and its institutional innovations such as the LoN, the PCIJ, and the International Labour Organization (ILO) were inaugurated. However, the end of the First World War was also an important period for several political disputes within Brazilian domestic history, besides the different aspects of the those indicated before. Understanding some

142 Pechman (n 36) and José Salgado, 'La Guerra Fría Llega a América Latina: La IX Conferencia Panamericana y el 9 de Abril' [2013] Análisis Político 19.

143 Adna Oliveira, 'O Itamaraty, o corpo diplomático e a ONU no início da Guerra Fria: a atuação brasileira entre 1947 a 1956' in Associação Nacional de História (ANPUH), *Anais do XXIX Simpósio Nacional de História – Contra os preconceitos: História e Democracia* (ANPUH 2017) and Pechman (n 36).

of the issues at that time is also of particular relevance to understanding Raul Fernandes' quadruple role at the international level.

In general terms, the economic crisis related to the First World War stimulated social movements towards legal reforms in Brazil. General strikes were organized across the entire country by Labour Unions in 1907 and 1917 – the last one starting in São Paulo.[144] Those movements were not simply 'inspired' by European migrants: rather, they were also arranged by them, as Italian, Spanish, and Portuguese immigrants – motivated by the success of the Soviet Revolution of 1917 and influenced by anarchist and by anarcho-syndicalist ideologies[145] – were directly engaged in such activities.[146]

Also related to the outlined dispute, the continuity of the prominent role of the Catholic Church in this period was also important. Although the Brazilian Republic was allegedly a secular political regime (Constitution of 1891), the close relationship between the Brazilian state and the Catholic Church did not disappear in this period and was little by little reestablished. This happened because the Catholic Church would, not only tame social movements against the recent Republican regime, but also help rejecting leftist demands – culminating, for instance, with the creation of Catholic workers' associations.[147]

Those issues were not exclusive to Brazil: similar oppositions towards capitalism spread worldwide after the Soviet Revolution in 1917. That is the reason why 1919 was also an international political compromise directed to minimize – also worldwide – such movements and 'leftist temptations' via international institutions established by international law – like the ILO, created by the Treaty of Versailles.[148] In the same sense, the religious solution to social issues and to socialist and communist demands at that time were mostly guided by *Rerum Novarum*, the Encyclical of Pope Leo XIII (1891) on the conditions of the workers. In this document, the Church explicitly rejected socialist and communist ideologies (on the family, on the state), demands (collective property) and activities (strikes, revolution), and, at the same time, defended capitalist premises (state, private property, bourgeois family) as natural rights derived from God and God's will.[149]

It is not surprising, thus, that Raul Fernandes – who progressively identified himself with the conservative structure of Brazilian oligarchical economics and

144 Fausto and Devoto (n 86) 187–89 and Napolitano (n 78) 38.

145 Socialist and communist ideologies assumed a prominent position in Brazilian Labor Unions only after 1930 – Paul Singer, *A Formação da Classe Operária* (3rd edn, Atual 1986) 59.

146 Comparato (n 81) 159 and Schwarcz and Starling (n 109) 334–37.

147 Comparato (n 81) 152 and Fausto and Devoto (n 86) 214–19.

148 Casella (n 8); Jürgen Habermas, 'A Idéia Kantiana de Paz Perpétua – À Distância Histórica de 200 Anos' in Jürgen Habermas, *A Inclusão do Outro* (2nd edn, Loyola 2004) 202–3, Michael Hardt and Antonio Negri, *Empire* (HUP 2000) 51 and 240–41 and Singer (n 145) 73.

149 Papa Leão XIII, 'Carta Encíclica *Rerum Novarum*' (15 May 1891) <www.vatican.va/content/leo-xiii/pt/encyclicals/documents/hf_l-xiii_enc_15051891_rerum-novarum.html> accessed 26 August 2020.

politics in national affairs – was also identified at the end of the First World War with similar conservative international legal solutions. To put it in other way: while performing his quadruple role at the international level in the legal field, his agency was also directed towards the preservation of local and global signs of social prestige.

4.1 Raul Fernandes' contributions to ACJ debates

As mentioned before, Raul Fernandes was the substitute of Clovis Bevilaqua at ACJ meetings. In this sense, he started to participate only after the ninth session (25.6.1920). One year later, at the *Real Academia de Jurisprudencia y Legislación* (Madrid, Spain), Raul Fernandes spoke about his experience at ACJ meetings. Through this opportunity, he not only expressed his gratitude for participating in those discussions, but also clearly identified himself with the jurists from the other so-called civilized nations.[150]

The reader of ACJ meetings proceedings might encounter a different perception. Although being invited to take part as the substitute of Clovis Bevilaqua at those meetings, Raul Fernandes' role at the ACJ cannot be understood as being effectively developed on an equal footing compared to the more active jurists at the time such as Edouard Descamps, Walter Phillimore,[151] Albert Lapradelle, and Elihu Root. In other words, in lieu of the usual narratives which magnify Raul Fernandes' role at the ACJ meetings, a critical perspective reveals additional layers of his non-academic role at the international level.

From the 26 sessions he attended, he did not speak at all in seven of them: Sessions 10, 11, 14, 27, 32, 33 and 34. Of course, his silence was expected in the last three as they were simply final meetings – that is, meetings in which there were no discussions at all, but only the reading of the final version of the draft, the reading of the final report of all meetings, the final approval from the representatives and the signatures. However, his silence is critical for the purposes of this text: Session 14 was one of the few sessions where the focus was precisely to discuss the normative references ('sources of international law') to ground the decisions of the Court, and Session 27 was the one in which the first version of the proposal was approved, after a brief discussion between Edouard Descamps, Walter Phillimore, and Albert de Lapradelle.

To put it simply, Raul Fernandes' contributions to the discussions concerning the role of the writing of publicists as normative references for the decisions taken by the PCIJ was minimal – not to say, none.

Indeed, Sessions 13, 14, and 15 were the ones in which the jurists were responsible for discussing (i) if it was necessary to present a list of sources of law, (ii) which items would be present at this list (treaties, custom, general principles

150 Fernandes (n 27) 14–16. See also the respective chapters in this volume.

151 Editors' note: Walter Phillimore did take a likening to Fernandes as he thought he was an intelligent man, the two would also in later years co-author a paper on Brazil and international law.

of law, equity – as one of the many general principles of law, judicial decisions and writing of publicists, (iii) which of those items were or were not redundant (general principles of law *versus* equity, judicial decisions, and writing of publicists), (iv) what would be the role of each of the sources (main or subsidiary), and (v) if the Court should apply them in a specific order or hierarchy. These discussions were taken in order to make the PCIJ project feasible by avoiding two undesired scenarios: (i) giving too large powers to the Court – that is, leaving states to a possible arbitrary *quasi*-legislative international judicial organ, and (ii) giving too narrow powers to the Court – whose role would be unnecessary to international order, as it would frequently declare *non liquet*.[152]

In Session 13 he only presented a very short opinion, which is not relevant for the purposes of the discussion here.[153] In Session 15 he was, however, rather precise with his views on the modification of the original proposal regarding the sources of international law.[154] Thus, for Fernandes, it was important that the text reflects 'the authority of judicial decisions . . . as a means for the application and development of law', the writing of publicists as sources of international law, as follows: 'the doctrines of the best qualified writers of various nations[, as . . .]'.[155]

However, Raul Fernandes' contribution at Session 15 was not related to the discussion regarding the role of the writing of publicists. He only prepared and presented a discourse on the general principles of law, in order to settle a theoretical dispute between Edouard Descamps (Belgium) and Elihu Root (US) concerning this last issue.[156] This was in fact a useless discourse: just after Raul Fernandes' presentation, Edouard Descamps (the President of the ACJ) simply stated that his remarks were 'interesting, but [the problem was] already solved [by the new Root-Descamps proposal]'.[157] After that, Raul Fernandes did not given any contribution on this issue until the end of the Session – in which the idea was finally approved.

In Session 25 the first consolidated version of the draft proposal was publicly read for adjustments. In this procedure, every article was read by the President of the ACJ and each jurist was able to propose changes and to approve or refuse each legal provision. This procedure lasted until Session 30. The second and final read of the draft occurred in Session 31, in which final minor adjustments were possible. In this sense, Raul Fernandes had at least two more opportunities to express his opinion concerning the sources of international law and to propose modifications on the issue examined in this text – the writing of publicists.

However, the legal provision on this issue (originally, art. 31.4) was discussed in Session 27 – the one in which Raul Fernandes did not present any contribution at all, as already indicated. The proposal was approved by all jurists at

152 PCIJ (n 3) 293, 307–21, 336–37.
153 ibid 293.
154 ibid 331, 344.
155 ibid 351.
156 ibid 345–46.
157 ibid 331.

Session 27 – except Albert de Lapradelle.[158] Walter Phillimore' and Edouard Descamps' proposal declaring that 'teachings of the most highly qualified publicists of the various nations', alongside 'judicial decisions', are 'subsidiary means for the definition of rules of law' was finally approved at Session 31 without any kind of discussion. The only modification was a technical one: the text was renumbered from art. 31.4 to art. 35.4.[159]

The assignment of a subaltern position to Raul Fernandes at ACJ meetings was not exclusive to the discussions concerning the sources of international law. This was not because only in Session 25 – the one in which the first conclusion round started – was he definitely granted equal legal possibility to interact (voting rights): it is possible to perceive in the proceedings a certain pattern of disregard by the other members of many of his contributions during the sessions in which he effectively participated.

Indeed, one should not ignore that some of his commentaries on other issues were (i) simply disregarded and not even discussed – Sessions 9,[160] 19,[161] 20,[162] 28,[163] and 29,[164] (ii) promptly dismissed because he not aware of usual international practices – Session 12,[165] (iii) mere confirmation of the position of other jurists – Sessions 18,[166] 22,[167] and 23.[168] It was usually in these situations in which he only agreed with the others that his commentaries were taken into account by the other representativeness and eventually approved – Sessions 28[169] and 31.[170]

In the same sense, Raul Fernandes' proposals on other issues were (i) simply disregarded directly by the President – Sessions 15,[171] 20,[172] and 21,[173] (ii) immediately opposed by other members – Session 16,[174] or (iii) promptly rejected by the other representatives – Sessions 21,[175] 22,[176] 24,[177] and 30.[178]

Apart from these situations, his commentaries were usually compact, with no effective contribution to the development of discourses during ACJ meetings, for

158 ibid 584.
159 ibid 646, 648.
160 ibid 215–16.
161 ibid 423–24.
162 ibid 447 and 460.
163 ibid 587–89.
164 ibid 612–15.
165 ibid 263, also further, at 266–69.
166 ibid 421.
167 ibid 481–83.
168 ibid 504–5.
169 ibid 591–92.
170 ibid 646.
171 ibid 340–41.
172 ibid 460.
173 ibid 473.
174 ibid 371–72.
175 ibid 469–71.
176 ibid 492.
177 ibid 526–27.
178 ibid 618–19, 628.

example, during Sessions 25[179] and 26.[180] Sometimes he even explicitly refused to present additional commentaries – Session 17[181] – or to submit a proposal for discussion, as the proposal of another representative was already approved, in spite of the fact that the other jurists were already aware of his own suggestions – Session 24.[182] In other moments, Raul Fernandes tried to present the project from Clovis Bevilaqua to the ACJ, but this document was never properly examined by the Committee.

Besides the proposition of the so-called Fernandes Formula, Raul Fernandes' agency in ACJ meetings was effectively heard at least once: in Session 16 in which he declared that he attended that meeting not only as a Brazilian representative, but possibly also as a representative of all Latin American countries.[183] In this statement, he emphasized that the Great Powers should stop unduly underestimating other countries and he publicly threatened the success of the ACJ's works. In that opportunity, after explicitly recognizing that he was aware that he had no right to vote or to reject any of the proposals made until that moment, he argued that 'if . . . the proposals [on keeping the inequality among countries to select judges to the Court] were to be accepted by the Committee, Brazil, in agreement with the majority of States interested, when the time came, would, without fail, vote against the [Court] project'.[184] As seen previously, Raul Fernandes was later granted voting rights.

For the purposes of this text, the analysis of Raul Fernandes' agency in ACJ meetings cannot be viewed as disappointing.

Of course, Raul Fernandes was not responsible for making any effective contribution to the development of the idea of establishing the teaching of publicists as sources of international law. However, his non-academic role at the international level revealed something more important: although he identified his country and himself – as a jurist – as being one of the members of the civilized nations, he felt and he knew that, in comparison to the other jurists of the ACJ – especially the ones from Europe and from the US – he and his country were located in a subaltern position in international relations.

Only after threatening to 'caus[e] the fall of the institution which the whole world wished to see powerful and lasting'[185] and affirming that Brazil would profit from such inequality when the time came[186] did he felt more comfortable to present his positions in other sessions, and his voice started to be heard and discussed by others and he finally earned voting rights. Still, even after that, his commentaries and proposals were never welcomed – that is, were never discussed,

179 ibid 553–54, 557.
180 ibid 574.
181 ibid 385.
182 ibid 530, 536.
183 ibid 365–67.
184 ibid 366.
185 ibid.
186 ibid 367.

or able to influence or even approve – to the same degree when compared to the contributions from other jurists who originated from European countries or from the US.

In this sense, I argue that Raul Fernandes was aware of the subaltern position of his country in international relations and of his personal recognition as an international jurist – as he also recognized, in his speech in 1921 at the *Real Academia*: at the ACJ, he knew that he was 'much less than the most obscure collaborator'.[187] Such a condition was not a concern for him, as the maintenance of such a subaltern position would be important to keep his country in its due condition of representing other subaltern countries and to keep its own independence by preserving its image as a disciplined and well-behaved country.

4.2 National concerns in Raul Fernandes' writings on international law

In 1948, as the Brazilian Minister of Foreign Affairs, during the Third Regular Session of the General Assembly of the United Nations, he indirectly criticized the USSR by saying that freedom and the protection of individuals were being effectively conducted only in some regions of the world.[188] Although pretending that Brazilian participation in international affairs followed a 'neutral and balanced' evaluation of international affairs, Raul Fernandes continuously affirmed that his country always stood beside those countries who protected individual freedom.[189]

With this information in mind, it is possible to properly understand the argument of Raul Fernandes. Behind the goal of preserving civilization 'under the rule of law',[190] Raul Fernandes' actions taken after the ACJ on an international level progressively indicated which was the civilization and which was the rule of international law he thought it was necessary to preserve.

At various times Raul Fernandes wasted no opportunity in openly confronting the USSR regarding possible 'communist threats' to existing institutions. In his discourse to the *Sociedade Brasileira de Direito Internacional* (Rio de Janeiro, Brazil) in 1925, Raul Fernandes argued that Soviet dislike for international law – in his argument, represented by the LoN and the PCIJ – was a logical consequence of such leftist movements, as it envisaged 'the subversion of world political and economic organization'.[191]

Similarly, in 1952, by occasion of the ceremony to receive the *doctor honoris causa* degree from São Paulo Law School, a similar statement was repeated. By simply ignoring US derogations to international law at that time,[192] Raul

187 Fernandes (n 27) 15.
188 Corrêa (n 36) 72 and Fernandes (n 30) 75.
189 Fernandes (n 30) 73–74.
190 Guerreiro (n 15) xii–xiii.
191 Fernandes (n 28) 11.
192 Jon Frappier, 'Above the Law: Violations of International Law by the U.S. Government from Truman to Reagan' [1984] Crime and Social Justice 1.

Fernandes opportunistically argued that the only reason for the absence of world peace lay exclusively in the USSR's continuing opposition to the established legal and political terms of international relations – explicitly referred to by him as the *Pax Americana*.[193]

Even when criticizing the conflicts between the US and the USSR[194] and the opposition to the same international law by these two countries[195] Raul Fernandes always explicitly presented arguments in favour of the international agenda which was already known to Brazilian foreign affairs: the liberal one, represented by the US.[196]

Indeed, according to his perspective, it was necessary to cultivate liberal premises in order to ensure national and international stability and peace.[197] This condition was necessary to enable the preservation of international political, economic, and legal liberal frameworks – which were responsible for preserving the subaltern conditions of Brazil – and of the national signs of social prestige within Brazil: an oligarchical economy, restricted political participation, and moral conservatism.

As Raul Fernandes explicitly recognized, in Rui Barbosa's time (Brazilian Monarchy and Brazilian First Republic), the centre of gravity of international law was based on the *Pax Britanica*, while in his own time, such centre of gravity was based on the *Pax Americana*. As he himself stated, the terms of this world peace were based on economic liberal premises – to which not only Brazil, but all other countries should abide.[198]

That is precisely the reason why he followed the argument of Rui Barbosa from the Second International Peace Conference at The Hague (1907) concerning the legality of the use of force to collect public debts.[199] Using that opportunity, Rui Barbosa publicly refused Luis Drago's proposal on rejecting the legality of the use of force in international relations to collect public debts.[200] In other words, the Brazilian government repeatedly sustained – even in legal terms – its international subaltern position – first to the *Pax Britanica* (Rui Barbosa), then to the *Pax Americana* (Raul Fernandes).

The preservation of this subaltern position was necessary to maintain Brazilian credibility towards past and future foreign loans – tools which were allegedly important to promote 'national development'.[201] It is due to this condition that the country should accept and follow these liberal terms of international world order. In spite of this argument, it is undisputed that those loans were used to sustain the economic and political positions of Brazilian oligarchies within the

193 Fernandes (n 31) 453.
194 Fernandes (n 30).
195 Fernandes (n 28) 17–18.
196 ibid.
197 Fernandes (n 31) 453.
198 ibid.
199 Fernandes (n 34) 24–25.
200 Lorca (n 1) 143–51.
201 Fernandes (n 34) 25.

country – especially the oligarchies from São Paulo.[202] This explains why, at his speech at the São Paulo Law School in 1952, he declared that Brazilian future generations of law graduates should be continuously trained in (international and national) liberal terms.[203]

Similarly, in 1921 at the *Real Academia de Jurisprudencia y Legislación* (Madrid, Spain) Raul Fernandes indirectly condemned actions taken by the USSR as undesired and short-term 'political arbitrariness' – actions which were characterized by him as 'sinister experiences, just like the Apocalypse'.[204] However, in a text published in the same decade, he criticized the opposition of the US to the LoN and to the PCIJ by (i) simply calling the US to refrain from denying its '(moral)' tradition of adhering to international law and international justice,[205] (ii) curiously affirming that 'the world owes a great moral debt to the US'[206] – and not that the US was in debt to the world!, and (iii) stating that, without the US, the entire system of international justice would lose its centre of gravity – in his own words, it would be just like 'the Church without Rome'.[207]

One should note that Raul Fernandes' main issue was neither simply the fight of supposed 'left threats', nor the mere opposition to the USSR. Rather, it was the preservation of international conditions which would enable the preservation of his domestic social structure and its respective signs of prestige.

Indeed, the intertwining of those issues within Raul Fernandes' academic and non-academic agencies both in national and international spheres is clear. Once again, we mention his speech at the *Real Academia*, in which he explicitly stated that legal changes derived from 'social solidarity' were severe economic 'attacks on ancient institutions'. The alleged damages were 'the limitations to [the absolute right of private] property and the principles of unionism' – which were, according to his perspective, not only 'serious derogation[s] to individual freedom of contract', but mainly the source of severe 'disruptions of world economy' and of the war.[208]

In the same speech the Christian moral weight of his discourse appeared with all his strength: the outlined situation – which he indirectly associated with the USSR – is explicitly identified with the image of the Apocalypse.[209] It is at least interesting to mention that, according to his perspective, if the USSR was the Antichrist, the US would be Rome for the (Catholic) Church.[210]

The use of Catholic religious terms as a rhetorical strategy is a pattern in his speeches – just like the concluding words of the speech at the *Real Academia*:

202 Fausto (n 88) 227–30, Furtado (n 87) 177–85, Napolitano (n 78) 32–34, Oliveira (n 89) 52–56 and 88, Prado Jr. (n 81) 228–30 and 240–44 and Souza (n 83) 168.
203 Fernandes (n 31) 453.
204 Fernandes (n 27) 8.
205 Fernandes (n 14) 3–4.
206 ibid 7.
207 ibid.
208 Fernandes (n 27) 7–8.
209 ibid 8.
210 Fernandes (n 14) 7.

'Help yourself and heaven will help you'.[211] But there is more: even fables from the Catholic religion are suggested as inspirational lessons for international relations: world peace would be similar to Christ(ian) peace.[212]

Raul Fernandes consistently presented a conservative position concerning legal frameworks and practical solutions at an international level – that mentioned at the ACJ meetings is just an example. By doing this, he would be able to protect the domestic structures to which his quadruple agency adhered – and from which he benefited: a capitalist legal framework and Catholic moral and restrictive political participation indirectly benefiting national oligarchies – all outlined previously.

For this reason, when taking the office of Brazilian Minister of Foreign Affairs for the second time (1954), it is not surprising that his speech clearly addressed the intertwining of Brazilian national affairs and the position of the country in international affairs: 'The problems that Brazil are facing are immense. As a patient, the country would have to undergo a real surgical process, which would restore its lost health. If the patient recalcitrated, fearful of the operation, a fatal outcome was expected.'[213] In this sense, Raul Fernandes understood that his responsibility as the Brazilian Minister of Foreign Affairs was crucial to fully take in the 'seriousness of the situation' and, alongside other 'national sectors', be able to lead everyone to 'not measure personal sacrifices, for the good of Brazil'.[214]

The proper handling of domestic economic and political oppositions was thus crucial to preserve the country – and this, even by sensitive measures to deal properly with the urgent challenges posed within the country. As the new Brazilian Minister of Foreign Relations, it was necessary for him only to reinforce the domestic legal framework – in order to restore the old social, political, and economic stability based on an oligarchical economy, moral conservatism and political restrictions, but also to use the international environment to promote this 'healthy, yet abrupt and necessary' backlash. As mentioned above, he was traditionally associated at that time with (i) the different successful participation of Brazil in diplomatic conferences directed to fight 'communist threats' (US, Chile and Peru), and (ii) international initiatives from Brazil to enable closer foreign relations with Catholic and authoritarian regimes (Portugal and Spain).

To put it simply, the external opposition of Raul Fernandes to alternative political, economic, legal, and moral patterns of society meant, thus, a strong domestic political concern of refraining the diffusion of modes of existence. After all, this situation could deny not only his own personal prominence within the country, but mainly the proper social structure in Brazil which recognized his collective and individual achievements as worthwhile.

211 Fernandes (n 27) 35.
212 Fernandes s.d. *apud* Ráo (n 15) 471.
213 Fernandes (n 32).
214 ibid.

5. Raul Fernandes and Brazilian approaches to international law: conservative international response to national political disputes

Brazilian traditional legal literature does not address directly the issue of the underlying political tensions which might have framed the international legal practices of Raul Fernandes.[215] Based on a triumphalist perspective, such literature regards Raul Fernandes as one of the many followers of – and contributors to – a coherent historical construction of a so-called Brazilian legalist tradition in international relations – whose origins are associated with Barão do Rio Branco and Rui Barbosa.[216]

However, this narrative is not sufficient to understand the information gathered thus far. Indeed, as those authors do not directly deal with underlying political tensions in the formation of a Brazilian approach towards international law, this literature is unable to perceive and to qualify the interplay between domestic material and immaterial conditions as drivers of Raul Fernandes' agency.

Within and outside the international legal field, there are contemporary analytical keys developed within critical and interdisciplinary perspectives which could help articulating this information. Yet, although apparently promising, they still do not enable taking steps forward.

Some authors on international relations argue that the period in which PCIJ Statute was discussed is characterized by establishing the basis of Brazilian unease at the time as 'well-placement' in foreign relations.[217] According to this position, ACJ debates were developed at a time when Brazil consolidated one of the main foundational oppositions of its diplomatic drivers: the interplay between Americanism and Portuguese-Brazilian identity.

In this sense, while constantly hesitating between Latin American and Western/European identities, Brazil was pressed to develop innovative legal and political solutions within its foreign relations. The presence of Brazilian representatives (first, Clovis Bevilacqua, then Raul Fernandes) at the ACJ – as mentioned before, the only ones with Latin American origins – could thus be simply understood as a successful outcome of a Brazilian clever balance between those two identities.

Due to the fact that this argument takes into account underlying political tensions in the design of new legal solutions, it is indeed an interesting source of alternative interpretations of Brazil's role in international relations. Yet, as it emphasizes non-domestic political tensions, it does not help understanding the role played by material and immaterial conditions in shaping the driver of the Brazilian approach to international law at that time.

Mainstream critical legal literature states broadly that international legal studies developed in non-centre countries – broadly speaking, the ones other than US and some European countries – are thoroughly pure and applied branches of the

215 Casella (n 1), Corrêa (n 36) and Lafer (n 1).

216 Ráo (n 15) and Ricupero (n 1).

217 Guimarães (n 41) 4–9.

one developed within central countries.[218] In other words, aiming to denounce, to evade, and to tackle Eurocentrism, westerncentrism or first-worldism in international legal scholarship, this literature argues that there is a shared condition of international legal studies in non-centre countries: their international legal mindset derives from either a willing mimicry[219] or an unwilling acceptance of domination.[220]

Of course, this text does not aim to deal once again with the never-ending dispute between two epistemic fields – international law *versus* international relations.[221] Rather, I simply argue here that none of the three mentioned analytical keys is able to fully explain the path followed by Brazilian legal scholarship in international law as a response to domestic material and immaterial conditions at that time.

In other words, Raul Fernandes' role at the ACJ cannot be understood as: (i) a naive adherence to a legalist depoliticized tradition, (ii) a simple legal response generated within an 'uneasy' external search for an international identity, or (iii) a mere voluntary or involuntary replication of Euro-American standards on international law. Rather, the aspects highlighted in his contributions at ACJ debates and other writings suggest something else.

As a legal scholar built into the structure just described, Raul Fernandes' quadruple role might be better understood as the agency of someone seeking to preserve his prominent position in national political disputes. Thus, his agency can be regarded as a subaltern action on the international level towards a conservative solution of national political disputes concerning material and immaterial conditions. The preference for Brazilian jurists in international discussions might then be associated with their ability to use international law to keep their respective national domination and (oligarchical) public order and to reaffirm locally and globally the required signs of social prestige.

218 Onuma (n 13) and Roberts (n 61).

219 Luís Eslava, Liliana Obregón, and René Urueña, 'Imperialismo(s) y Derecho(s) Internacional(es): Ayer y Hoy' in Antony Anghie, Martti Koskenniemi, and Anne Orford (eds), *Imperialismo y Derecho Internacional* (Siglo del Hombre/Universidad de los Andes/Pontifícia Universidad Javeriana 2016), Lorca (n 93) and Obregón (n 40).

220 Antony Anghie, 'La Evolución del Derecho Internacional: Realidades Coloniales y Poscoloniales' in Antony Anghie, Martti Koskenniemi, and Anne Orford (eds), *Imperialismo y Derecho Internacional* (Siglo del Hombre/Universidad de los Andes/Pontifícia Universidad Javeriana 2016); Jedidiah Kroncke, *The Futility of Law and Development* (OUP 2016); Makau Mutua, 'Critical Race Theory and International Law: The View of an Insider-Outsider' [2000] Villanova Law Review 841 and Onuma (n 13).

221 It would not be possible to exhaust in a single footnote the already widely known debate between the two fields. For a Brazilian approach of such subject, see for instance Michelle Badin, Lucas Tasquetto, and Nathalie Sato, 'As Trilhas de Anne-Marie Slaughter na Defesa da Interdisciplinaridade entre Direito Internacional e Relações Internacionais' [2014] FGV Direito SP Research Paper Series and Roberto Yamato and Florian Hoffman, 'Counter-disciplining the Dual Agenda: Towards a (Re-)Assessment of the Interdisciplinary Study of International Law and International Relations' [2018] Revista Brasileira de Política Internacional 1.

Thus, on the pretext of shaping the legal framework of international institutions – in this case, not only the PCIJ, but also the contributions he presented to the development of international law – Raul Fernandes expressed a certain Brazilian approach to international law at that time – that is, an approach directly concerned with using international law to handle, in a conservative way, domestic material and immaterial political disputes.

One final remark should be addressed before concluding. There is almost a hundred-year time lapse between Raul Fernandes' agency at the international level and the authorship of this text. Still, structural drivers concerning material and immaterial conditions which characterized 'that time' are similar to the ones present in Brazilian contemporary political disputes. Indeed, there is still:

(i) a non-official social prestige and preference for people who publicly meet the criteria of being a white cisgendered male person[222] in spite of several social initiatives and public policies aiming to tackle those discriminations based on gender, race, and related symbolic and economic stereotypes;[223]

(ii) a higher trust on armed forces than on the Judiciary and Legislative Powers[224] – including the rise of acceptance of a constant and regular military solution for domestic issues;[225]

(iii) a higher trust in the Catholic Church than on secular institutions of the state – reinforcing the perception of a progressive return of[226] religious paradigms – especially of Pentecostal origins – in national politics;[227] and

(iv) an official state discourse and a public opinion: (i) backing a capitalist economy – favouring (1) national, transnational and international neoliberal premises[228] and (2) once again Brazilian traditional economic oligarchies,[229] and, because of that, (ii) embodying the anachronic and conceptually inconsistent revival of the hate speech against an alleged 'communist/left threat' to those premises.[230]

222 Abranches (n 80) 21 and Moreira (n 66), Moreira (n 68), and Moreira (n 71).

223 Giannattasio (n 67) 'Direitos . . .'.

224 Escola de Direito de São Paulo da Fundação Getulio Vargas (FGV DIREITO SP), *Relatório do Índice de Confiança na Justiça Brasileira*, vol 24 (FGV DIREITO SP 2017) 13–14.

225 Anaís Passos, 'The Military Mystique: Democracies and the War on Crime in Brazil and Mexico' (Dphil, Institut d'Études Politiques de Paris – SciencesPo 2018).

226 Escola de Direito de São Paulo da Fundação Getulio Vargas (n 224) 13–14.

227 Marilena Chauí, 'O Retorno do Teológico-Político' in Sérgio Cardoso (ed), *Retorno ao Republicanismo* (UFMG 2004) and Maria Machado and Joanildo Burity, 'A Ascensão Política dos Pentecostais no Brasil na Avaliação de Líderes Religiosos' [2014] Dados 601–31.

228 José Faria, *Direito e Conjuntura* (Saraiva/FGV DIREITO SP 2008).

229 Gilberto Bercovici and Luís Massoneto, 'A Constituição Dirigente Invertida: A Blindagem da Constituição Financeira e a Agonia da Constituição Econômica' [2006] Boletim de Ciências Econômicas 3, 13–21.

230 Daniel Andrade, 'Neoliberalismo: Crise Econômica, Crise de Representatividade Democrática e Reforço de Governamentabilidade' [2019] Novos Estudos CEBRAP 109–35.

In this sense, if Brazilian structural drivers have not deeply changed since 'that time', one could argue that international legal responsiveness to domestic material and immaterial conditions would nowadays remain the same. In other words, 'that time' is somehow still 'this time'.

However, such responsiveness is clearly not determined by structural drivers: bearing in mind the social, economic, political, and legal consequences of previous institutional responses, history cannot be understood as a cycle of necessity and mimicry. Rather, history is a cycle of opportunities in which humankind's knowledge is tested and provoked in different moments to use institutions in innovative ways – either to reinforce public freedoms, or to undermine it.[231]
In this sense, without denying the relevance of the rule of international law[232] the awareness of similar institutional drivers pushes contemporary Brazilian international legal scholars to an important challenge: deciding whether their institutional responses to international issues *vis-à-vis* domestic material and immaterial conditions will follow the example of Raul Fernandes or not.

231 Nicolau Maquiavel, *Comentários sobre a Primeira Década de Tito Lívio* (first published 1531, UnB 2010).

232 Martti Koskenniemi, 'What should International Lawyers learn from Karl Marx?' [2004] Leiden Journal of International Law 229.

3 A civilizational pluralist and inegalitarian

Mineichiro Adachi (1869–1934)

Tetsuya Toyoda

1. Introduction

Among the ten members of the Advisory Committee of Jurists (ACJ), Mineichiro Adachi was special in two important ways: his non-European background and his hierarchical subordination as a career diplomat in the service of the Ministry of Foreign Affairs. These two peculiarities very much defined his position in the Committee.

The ten seats in the Committee were attributed to five great powers (Japan, France, UK, Italy, and US) and five middle powers (Spain, Brazil, Belgium, Norway, and the Netherlands). Among them, if Brazil and the US were geographically out of Europe, their representatives were ethnically European and had been educated in European languages in European traditions. In any way, the two countries had been developed earlier as European colonies. Adachi was different. He grew up in a non-European country, spoke a non-European language, and was educated in the East Asian tradition up to secondary school. As we will see below, he even claimed that his country represented the East Asian civilization.

It is no less important to point out that he was different from most of the other members for his professional status. He was a career diplomat and did not enjoy freedom of speech as much as many others did. Rafael Altamira and Albert de Lapradelle were university professors and enjoyed the largest freedom of speech. Édouard Descamps and Elihu Root were politicians of importance who enjoyed much freedom. Bernard C. J. Loder and Walter Phillimore were judges and expressed their beliefs to the best of their professional conscience. The other four were diplomats: George Francis Hagerup was Norway's Minister Plenipotentiary in Sweden; Arturo Ricci Busatti, Legal Adviser to the Italian Ministry of Foreign Affairs; Raoul Fernandes, a former member of the Brazilian delegation to the Paris Peace Conference, and Adachi, Japan's Minister Plenipotentiary in Belgium. But Hagerup was a former Prime Minister and his younger colleagues seemed to have dispensed him with specific instructions, and Ricci Busatti was in the position to advise the Foreign Minister rather than being instructed on legal issues. Adachi and Fernandes were the only members in the Committee whose arguments needed endorsement by their respective home governments.

DOI: 10.4324/9781003020882-4

We will see how his two peculiarities affected his position in the Committee, including his attitude towards the 'the teachings of the most highly qualified publicists of the various nations'. After examining Adachi's legal education at the Law School of the Ministry of Justice and the University of Tokyo and his diplomatic career in Japan, Mexico, and Belgium, we will examine how he contributed to the foundation of the Permanent Court of International Justice and how he engaged in political-academic activities at the *Institut de Droit International.*

2. Adachi's education and professional career and Japan's overcoming of the unequal treaties

2.1 Education

Adachi was born on 27 July 1869 (or 19 June of that year in the lunar calendar which was still in use in Japan) in the village of Takadate in the province of Uzen in Northern Japan, just a month after the end of the Boshin War, the Civil War which ended the long rule of the Tokugawa Shogunate. His father was an educated farmer who also taught at the local school. Having ended the class-based feudal society, the new government opened opportunities of higher education for farmers and townsmen. The Law School of the Ministry of Justice (Shihōshō Hōritsu Gakkō), established in 1871, was one of such new opportunities, of which Adachi took great advantage. Students at that school were not only exempt from tuition but also benefited from a stipend. Adachi entered that school in October 1884. Sixteen years after the end of the feudal system, the entrance exam was mostly on Chinese classics, Chinese history, and Japanese history. Japanese education was still in a period of transition from Sino-centrism to Euro-centrism.

The Law School of the Ministry of Justice taught mostly French law under the guidance of Gustave Boissonade (1825–1910), the French professor of law who drafted the first Japanese Civil Code. One day during the five years of his study there, Adachi read in a newspaper an article on the Normanton Incident in 1886, the case of a British merchant vessel sinking off the coast of Japan which drowned many Japanese passengers. The incident sparked a national uproar when the British Consul at Kobe declared innocent the British captain who had taken only European passengers in lifeboats and let perish all the 25 Japanese on board. The Consul-General at Yokohama overruled the judgment and sentenced the captain to three months' imprisonment, but refused any compensation to bereaved families. The perceived lenience of the sanction and the refusal of reparation provoked fury of the public and accelerated Japanese political moves for the abolition of the extraterritoriality, which was granted to the Western powers during the last years of the Tokugawa Shogunate.

By the time Adachi graduated from the Law School of the Ministry of Justice, that school was reorganized to become a school preparatory to the Law Faculty of the University Tokyo, to which he moved up in September 1889. By that time, he was determined to study international law. Just before entering the University of Tokyo, he wrote a letter to the Dean of the Law Faculty, Prof. Shigenobu Hozumi. Adachi emphasized the importance of international law with following words:

> If we wish for a perfection of domestic and foreign policy with dignity for our small and weak empire in the midst of great powers, we need people who devote themselves to diplomacy with a deep understanding of the law of reason among nations and an ability to apply it to complex situations of the time.[1]

The Normanton Incident may have been one of the reasons for Adachi's choice.[2] Japan in the 1880s was a second-class country, and was suffering unequal treatment by the Western powers. Young Adachi was determined to make the best use of international law to protect the interests of his own weak nation.

Adachi was a brilliant student at the University of Tokyo. His three years there mostly overlapped with Alessandro Paternostro's sojourn in Japan, who was invited there to advise the government on the unequal treaties' revision and other legal issues and give lectures on international law. The lectures were given in French through Adachi's interpretation, and were later published as a book. While giving a series of lectures on international law at the university, Prof. Paternostro delivered a public lecture in 1890 on 'La révision des traités avec le Japon au point de vue du droit international'.[3] That lecture was published a year later in *Revue générale de droit international et de législation comparée*, the most authoritative journal of international law in Europe in the late nineteenth century. Thanks to his fluency in French, Adachi, still a university student, could have been involved in such politically important academic activities of the time.

Prof. Paternostro's concept of international law was very much idealistic. We find in the Japanese translation by Adachi of Paternostro's lecture a powerful confession of belief in the science of international law:

> Without controversy, scholars agree on the existence of the most part of international law, especially public international law. States also recognize the existence of the principles of international law that have the authority superior to international treaties and regulate their relations in the same way as the civil and commercial codes regulate relations between individuals under domestic law. We can say there is a legislator among the states, which is

1 Mineichiro Adachi, 'Letter to Shigenobu Hozumi – Sep. 1889' in Masaharu Yanagihara (ed), *Peace Among All Nations – A Collection of Mineichiro Adachi's Writings* (University of Tokyo Press 2019) 5–6, 5.

2 Masaharu Yanagihara, 'Mineichirō Adachi no Shōgai [Life of Mineichiro Adachi]' in M Yanagihara and S Hatsue (eds), *Mineichirō Adachi* (University of Tokyo Press 2017) 3–32 at 5. Most of the biographical information is also from Yanagihara's article.

3 Alessandro Paternostro, 'La révision des traités avec le Japon au point de vue du droit international' (1891) 18 Revue générale de droit international et de législation comparée 5–29.

> the science. The science [of international law] does not have the means of enforcement as does the sovereign in a country, but what the science proves becomes the conviction of the humankind and gains a supreme power that binds the actions of states.[4]

Adachi was only translating the words of Paternostro and it is not certain if he was convinced by the idealistic words of Paternostro. But one thing we know for sure is that Adachi was very much familiar with the idealistic understanding of international law which gave great power to the science of international law and the writings of publicists.

2.2 *Professional experience*

Upon graduation from the University of Tokyo, Adachi joined the Ministry of Foreign Affairs in September 1892. He was posted in Rome in July 1893 (arrival in September 1893) and then moved to Paris in February 1897 where he remained until October 1903. After coming back from France, he joined the delegation to the Peace Conference at Portsmouth, New Hampshire in the US in 1905, which ended the Russo-Japanese War. He was posted to Paris again in October 1908 and then to Mexico in January 1913 as the Japanese Minister Plenipotentiary. After two years in Mexico and two years in Japan, he was appointed Minister Plenipotentiary to Belgium in May 1917, while the Great War was coming to the final stage in the Western part of Europe. He left Tokyo in September and arrived at Le Havre in November, the seat of the Belgian government in exile. Adachi stayed there for a year to wait for the withdrawal of German forces from the Belgian soil. After the war, Adachi remained in Belgium until 1927, when he was appointed Ambassador Plenipotentiary to France. He was elected judge of the PCIJ in September 1930 and resigned from the Ministry of Foreign Affairs three months later to join the PCIJ in January 1931.

If his experience in foreign service had any influence on his view on international law, one thing which cannot be omitted is his experience in Mexico. When he arrived in Mexico City in July 1913, the country was in the midst of the revolutionary war which started in 1910. In June 1914, Adachi made a visit to a Mexican port on the Pacific Ocean to greet Japanese Battleship Izumo, which was sent to Mexico for the protection of Japanese citizens in the country. Ironically, Adachi himself became a victim of the turbulent situations, as his train back to Mexico City was attacked by the revolutionary army and he and his suite went missing for ten days. Adachi contracted an acute liver failure due to polluted water he drank during the march on the mountains back to Mexico City.

In spite of the dangers and hardships he went through in Mexico, Adachi remained very sympathetic to the government and people of Mexico. In his

4 Alessandro Paternostro, *Kokusai Kōhō Kōgi [Lectures on Public International Law]* (Mineichiro Adachi tr, Kohokai Press 1897) 41. English translation mine.

numerous letters, public and private, Adachi ascribed much of the trouble in Mexico to the excessively idealistic diplomacy of US President Woodrow Wilson, who was inaugurated in March 1913. President Wilson was horrified by the murder of the democratically elected president, Francisco I. Madero, and refused to recognize the legitimacy of the government under the presidency of Victoriano Huerta. President Wilson urged European powers not to recognize the Huerta government, recalled the US ambassador who was sympathetic to Huerta, and imposed an arms embargo on Mexico in August 1913. In addition, the US government allowed arms sales to support the rebellion and let the country plunge deep into the Civil War. When a German merchant ship, Ypiranga, was discovered to be carrying arms to the Huerta government, President Wilson sent troops in an attempt to stop the ship from docking. When the US forces occupied the port of Veracruz for seven months in 1914 for a seemingly minor incident (Tampico Affair), Wilson's real objective is said to have been the overthrow of the Huerta government. Huerta resigned in July 1914 and went into exile.

In a personal letter dated 14 March 1915, Adachi wrote:

> In retrospective, Huerta was a great politician who was ruined nonetheless by the obsession of the U.S. president. Dispute between the Mexicans themselves is the primary cause for the current state of affairs, but the responsibility of the U.S. who secretly kindled it cannot be overestimated. While the European states and Japan cannot do anything there, the U.S. will soon torture Mexico to death. I only shed tears for the tragedy of a nation.[5]

Wilson was an idealist and denied the Huerta government's legitimacy. Adachi saw the danger of idealism causing a catastrophe on the ground, and people's suffering.

As mentioned above, from November 1917 to the same month the following year, Adachi was the ambassador to the Belgian government in exile at Le Havre. Belgium was liberated by the Americans and the Versailles system was established under Wilson's leadership. The last point of the Wilson Fourteen Points in January 1918 provided that 'A general association of nations must be formed under specific covenants for the purpose of affording mutual guarantees of political independence and territorial integrity to great and small states alike.' But Adachi was quite aware that such a principle would not apply to Mexico or other countries who went against Wilson's preference.

5 Tadaaki Kitagawa, 'Chū-Mekishiko-Kōshi Jidai no Adachi Meneichirō [Mineichiro Adachi as Minister Plenipotentiary in Mexico]' Reference Room for Mineichiro Adachi (Yamagata University Yamagata Chiiki Shakai Kenkyūsho [Yamagata Community Research Center, Yamagata University]) <www-hs.yamagata-u.ac.jp/laboratory/yamagata_adachi/blog/p3753/> accessed 10 August 2020.

2.3 Japan's inegalitarianism in revising the unequal treaties

At the base of Adachi's attitude toward international law lies the question of unequal treaties. The Tokugawa Shogunate concluded a series of treaties with Western powers in 1858 or a few years later,[6] which included clauses on extraterritoriality and the loss of tariff autonomy.[7] It was with the extraterritoriality clause in the 1858 Anglo-Japanese Treaty of Amity and Commerce that the captain of the merchant ship *Normanton* was exempt from Japanese jurisdiction. Exemption of British citizens from Japanese jurisdiction continued until the entry into force in 1899 of the revised Anglo-Japanese Treaty (which was followed by the revision of treaties with the other Western powers). The revision of the unequal tariff clauses took longer. The first revision of the tariff clause was made with Russia in 1907. The other Western powers agreed to restore Japan's tariff autonomy in 1911.

The Japanese government's approach to revising unequal treaties was realistic and pragmatic. It never denied the legality of unequal treaties. Claiming the equality between nations would have elicited strong reactions from the Western powers most of which were also colonial powers. Instead, the Japanese government claimed that Japan was civilized enough to be treated equally with the Western powers.

That argument was well presented by Paternostro's article in 1891, mentioned above, in which he argued that:

> La constitution politique; les codes civil, de commerce, pénal, d'instruction criminelle, et de procédure civile; l'organisation judiciaire; l'organisation scolaire en tout l'empire: jardins d'enfants, écoles primaires, moyennes, supérieures, et universitaires; l'organisation du contentieux administratif; l'organisation provinciale et communale; l'organisation de toute l'administration civile et militaire, centrale et locale, ont fait du Japon un pays qui a la culture, la vie politique, l'organisation d'État, et l'état social, en un mot, des pays d'Occident.[8]

For a country that had acquired 'the culture of the Western countries (*la culture des pays d'Occident*)', there should not be any discrimination. Paternostro continued his arguments to come to the conclusion that Japan even had the right

6 Treaties with the US, UK, France, Russia, and the Netherlands in 1858, a treaty with Prussia in 1861, and treaties with Austria-Hungary and Spain in 1868.

7 For example, Article 6 of the Japan-US Treaty of Amity and Commerce provided that 'Americans committing offenses against Japanese shall be tried in American Consular courts, and, when guilty, shall be punished according to American law' and Article 4, paragraph 3 that '[n]o higher duties shall be paid by Americans on goods imported into Japan than are fixed by this Treaty, nor shall any higher duties be paid by Americans than are levied on the same description of goods if imported in Japanese vessels, or the vessels of any other nation.'

8 Paternostro (n 3) 181.

to unilaterally denounce the unequal treaties (even if the Japanese government would not do so just for political reasons):

> La dénonciation est encore légitime, lorsque les fait qui, dans l'intention expresse ou tacite des parties, avaient été la base des dispositions d'un traité, se sont modifiés. Au Japon, les fait étaient: le silence ou la grande différence des lois, les lacunes ou la grande différence dans l'organisation judiciaire, et l'absence des garanties nécessaires pour protéger les droits d'une des parties contractantes. Ces faits sont désormais passés à l'état de simples souvenirs du temps jadis, et dès lors les conventions internationales qui n'ont eu autrefois leur raison d'être que dans ces faits, manquent de toute base solide.[9]

In other words, for Paternostro the unequal treaties with Japan should be revised because Japan was a civilized country as much as Western powers were, not because unequal treaties should be prohibited per se. The evolutionary theory of civilization was widely shared by the public in Japan, since the publication of Fukuzawa Yukichi's *Bunmeiron no Gairyaku* [An Outline of the Theory of Civilization] in 1875, which presented the three-phase developmental theory of savage, semi-civilized, and civilized nations. According to Fukuzawa, Japan was in the semi-civilized phase as of 1875. Since then it became the nation's wish to reach the status of a civilized nation or a first-class nation. This view was no doubt shared by Adachi, Paternostro's favourite disciple, as he often mentioned his wish to make Japan a first-class country.[10] As indicated in the quotation above, Paternostro believed that, at least as of 1891, Japan had already entered the stage of civilization on the same level with the European powers.

This civilizational inegalitarianism allowed Japan to impose unequal treaties on its weak or weakened neighbours. While pleading the Western powers for the revision of unequal treaties with itself, the Japanese government concluded unequal treaties with Korea in 1876 and China in 1896. A year after the unequal treaties were all revised, Adachi expressed his satisfaction with the rise of Japan in the international legal system in a public talk he gave in December 1912 before the Japanese Society of International Law,

> Gentlemen, every time I think of international law, I feel immense admiration and satisfaction with the progress made by our country. In 1888–89 when I was still at the preparatory school, Japan was clearly out of the scope of application of international law. It was clear that it was a code for the exclusive use

9 ibid 191.

10 For example, on his sea route to Europe in 1893, he wrote: 'I am saddened at every port on the route that the non-European nations are under slavery almost everywhere. It is our duty to make at least Japan a first-class nation' (Mineichiro Adachi, 'Letters to Kyoko from 31 July to 9 October 1893' 3 September 1893 in Masaharu Yanagihara (ed), *Peace Among All Nations – A Collection of Mineichiro Adachi's Writings* [University of Tokyo Press 2019] 27–45, 37).

of Western countries and not applicable to our country. Mr. Kowashi Inoue argued energetically in a newspaper, *Kokkai*, how the Japanese government should let Japan get a place within the scope of application of international law. Application of international law to Japan was an earnest wish of the Japanese nation, which must be fulfilled. The opinion of Professor Paternostro, who was then a counsel of the Ministry of Justice, was sought on this issue. He claimed good reasons for international law to be applied to Japan and published his view in the *Revue générale de droit international [et de législation comparée]*. It is beyond today's possible imagination how seriously our predecessors struggled on this question. . . . What about the situation today? Thanks to the greatest achievements of Late Emperor Meiji, Japan has risen to the honorable status in international law. . . . Gentlemen, the great question in 1889 was whether international law should be applied to Japan. The great question today, on the contrary, is whether Japan as the great power accepts to apply international law.[11]

At the Normanton Incident, Adachi was angry against the injustice of extraterritoriality. The solution he found was not to deny the system of extraterritoriality but to get a better position in the system for his country. He was angered by the injustice of extraterritoriality not because it was unjust but because the injustice was committed against his own nation. He felt no pain in Japan's imposing extraterritoriality on 'inferior' nations.[12]

3. Civilizational pluralism and inegalitarianism as a solution

Adachi participated in the Committee as an expert independent from any government, but in reality his nomination came through the Ministry of Foreign Affairs.[13]

The Japanese government did not have the slightest sympathy for the establishment of an effective international judicial system and thus refused categorically a compulsory jurisdiction, but it did want to secure a permanent seat for a Japanese judge so that Japanese interests could be secured. The

11 Mineichiro Adachi, 'Study of International Law [Lecture at the Japanese Society of International Law]' in Masaharu Yanagihara (ed), *Peace Among All Nations – A Collection of Mineichiro Adachi's Writings* (University of Tokyo Press 2019) 16–21, at 17–19.

12 In retrospective the civilizational inegalitarianism of Adachi's may be regrettable, but it perhaps suited well the international politics of the time since the Western powers were not yet ready to accept an overall equality with non-Western nations. When the Japanese government proposed in 1919 a racial equality clause as an amendment to an article of the Covenant of the League of Nations, President Wilson as the chair of the League of Nations Commission blocked its adoption.

13 Adachi was only a secondary choice after Former Ambassador in Austria Satsuo Akizuki, who declined the nomination for personal reasons.

Japanese government gave Adachi an instruction which consisted mainly of two points:[14]

1) the jurisdiction of the PCIJ must be based on the consent of both parties, and
2) the five great powers (US, UK, France, Italy, and Japan) should have the right of permanent representation among the judges in the Court.

Thus, Adachi must let the other members tolerate the Japanese reluctance towards the development of the international judicial system and also accept Japan's special right to the permanent seat in the Court. These two claims were hardly compatible. But as a diplomat, Adachi was very successful in the Committee. He obtained a solution to satisfy both. In doing so, Adachi came up with a doctrine of civilizational pluralism[15] and had it accepted by the other members.

3.1 Japan's refusal of compulsory jurisdiction

To understand Japan's categorical refusal, we should briefly review the 1905 House Tax Law case before the Permanent Court of Arbitration, which left a lasting impact on Japanese foreign policy.

In negotiating the abolition of extraterritoriality in the 1890s, the Japanese government chose to tolerate the existing leases in perpetuity within the foreign settlements and exempt them from taxation. To the Japanese understanding the exemption was limited to land, but three governments – Britain, France, and Germany – argued that the exemption should cover buildings on the land as well. The core issue was the interpretation of the concept of 'property', 'propriété', and 'Grundstück'.[16] The Court was split between the three arbitrators and the majority opinion decided in favour of Britain, France, and Germany.

Until the arbitral award was rendered, the Japanese government was optimistic and was convinced of its victory, but the result was otherwise. Harukazu Nagaoka,

14 'Telegram from Foreign Minister Uchida to Minister Adachi in Belgium, 18 May 1920' in Ministry of Foreign Affairs (ed), *Documents on Japanese Foreign Policy 1920. Vol. 3. Book 1.* <www.mofa.go.jp/mofaj/annai/honsho/shiryo/archives/t9-31.html> accessed 10 August 2020, 324–26.

15 Adachi may have developed his idea of civilizational pluralism in Mexico. In his speech for the Board of Education of Yokohama City in June 1916, he talked of 'the vocation of the Japanese nation' to establish a special civilization of its own by mixing what they have inherited from the ancestors with that of the Europeans' (Mineichiro Adachi, 'Situations in Mexico [Lecture for the Yokohama City Board of Education, 20 June 1916]' in Masaharu Yanagihara (ed), *Peace Among All Nations – A Collection of Mineichiro Adachi's Writings* [University of Tokyo Press 2019] 142–61 at 158).

16 Douglas R Howland, 'The Japan House Tax Case, 1899–1905: Leases in Perpetuity and the Myth of International Equality' (2015) 75(2) Zeitschrift für ausländisches öffentliches Recht und Völkerrecht 413–34 at 422.

later a judge of the PCIJ, regretted that the Japanese government 'thought too simply that we could expect someone from a country which does not have any conflict of interest with Japan could make fair arguments'.[17] The House Tax award caused a 'shattering disillusionment' and a 'lurking suspicion born in the mind of Japan in the manipulative aspect of international law'.[18] The Japanese government was determined not to put itself ever again under the authority of an international jurisdiction.[19]

3.2 Combination of civilizational pluralism and inegalitarianism

Adachi secured a virtually permanent seat for a Japanese judge in the PCIJ with the idea of civilizational pluralism. The provision in Article 9 of the Statute, 'the representation of the main forms of civilization' as a condition for the election of judges was a brainchild of Adachi's.[20]

But his civilizational pluralism should not be taken synonymously with civilizational egalitarianism. On the contrary, he was claiming Japan's superiority over others in East Asia:

> all different kinds of civilisation must be taken into account, among them the civilisation of the Far East, of which Japan was perhaps the principal representative.[21]
>
> . . . the Japanese system was fully entitled to be represented upon the Court, more especially as there was a distinct tendency for it to spread throughout Asia. Thus it was Japanese jurists who had prepared the new constitution of China and who had drafted the laws of that country.[22]

The combination of civilizational pluralism and inegalitarianism was the solution he found to make compatible the two seemingly incompatible objectives the government ordered him to achieve. He was successful in 1920 as an astute diplomat.

17 Harukazu Nagaoka, 'Nihon Gaikō Tsuikairoku [Mémoires on Japanese Diplomacy] (1900–1935)' (1983) in Ministry of Foreign Affairs (ed), *Documents on Japanese Foreign Policy*, vol 1, 5. <www.mofa.go.jp/mofaj/annai/honsho/shiryo/archives/st-11.html> accessed 10 August 2020.

18 Urs Matthias Zachmann, 'The Reception and Use of International Law in Modern Japan, 1853–1945' (2014) 37 Zeitschrift für Japanisches Recht 109–38 at 118.

19 For Japan's refusal of compulsory jurisdiction, see Shōichi Sekino, *Kokusai-Shihō-Seido Keisei-Shi-Ron Josetsu [Preliminary Discussion on the Formation of an International Judicial System]* (University of Tokyo Press, Tokyo, 2000).

20 Tetsuya Toyoda, 'Japan's Early Challenge to Eurocentrism and the World Court' in F Rösch and A Watanabe (eds), *Modern Japanese Political Thought and International Relations* (Rowman & Littlefield International 2019) 43–55.

21 Procès-verbaux, Advisory Committee of Jurists, *Procès-Verbaux of the Proceedings of the Committee, 16 June–24 July 1920, with Annexes* (Van Langenhuysen, The Hague 1920) 136.

22 ibid 384.

3.3 Adachi's failure in persuading the Japanese government for compulsory jurisdiction

Taking as an opportunity his election campaign in the 1930s for a judge's post in the PCIJ, he tried to convince the Japanese government and the public of the need for accepting the compulsory jurisdiction. In a speech he gave on 8 May 1930 before the members of various business associations, he presented his ideas as follows:

> The voluntary system of jurisdiction is a system where no country is forced to accept the jurisdiction of the Court in any case which was brought before it by the other party. This was the way the PCIJ worked until now. Ten years ago, in 1920, I was the only one to claim the voluntary system, which became the present system.[23] That was because after the failure in the arbitration on the House Tax case, we were convinced that Japan would lose any case before the international court whatever the strength of our legal arguments. We have maintained until now the policy never to accept the compulsory jurisdiction. But in spring last year the Kellogg-Briand Pact entered in force[24] and Great Britain, France, Italy, and others decided to accept the compulsory jurisdiction of the PCIJ one after another.[25]

In other words, after the unfair judgment on the House Tax case (unfair at least to Japanese eyes), it was very much understandable that the Japanese government could not accept the compulsory jurisdiction of the PCIJ, but ten years later, especially after the entry into force of the Kellogg-Briand Pact, Adachi argued it was time to accept the compulsory jurisdiction, as did the European great powers.

Twelve days later, Adachi argued again before the Tokyo Bankers' Club for the importance of the compulsory jurisdiction:

> Under the conditions ten years ago, I strongly argued that the compulsory jurisdiction should be a stumbling block to a sound development of the Permanent Court of International Justice. That is the reason why the present Statute made it an optional clause. That is the result of my reservation against the other nine members [in the Advisory Committee of Jurists]. But

23 In fact, Adachi was not the only one to refuse the compulsory jurisdiction in 1920, even if they were not as vocal as Adachi in this regard.

24 Article of the Pact provided that '[t]he High Contracting Parties agree that the settlement or solution of all disputes or conflicts of whatever nature or of whatever origin they may be, which may arise among them, shall never be sought except by pacific means.'

25 Mineichiro Adachi, 'Ōshū no Kinjō narabini Sekai Tōmen no Jūyō Shomondai [Recent Situations in Europe and the Important Current Issues of the World] Lecture for Japan Business Association and Japan Industrial Club, 8 Mai 1930' in Masaharu Yanagihara (ed), *Peace Among All Nations – A Collection of Mineichiro Adachi's Writings* (University of Tokyo Press 2019) 221–40 at 235.

> the Kellogg-Briand Pact entered in force and the Labor Party came to power in the U.K. in June last year. In September last year at the League's General Assembly, Mr McDonald and Mr. Henderson, representing the British government, declared the British acceptance of the compulsory jurisdiction. Germany accepted it earlier. So did France. . . . So did Italy. Ambassadors from various countries told me: 'The compulsory jurisdiction you opposed as a jurist in 1920 is now accepted by all the members of the international society. It was ten years ago you opposed it. You said the world in those days was not ready for it, but it is ready today. Why don't you accept it now.' This made me think deeply. This is a serious question and our government should consider it carefully. So, I didn't give them an answer. But the question remains. The Japanese government is in a peculiar position regarding the Permanent Court of International Justice.[26]

But the government did not seriously consider the possibility of accepting the compulsory jurisdiction or even the possibility of the judicial settlement of international disputes as the rest of history tells us.

3.4 Adachi's view on scholarly opinions as a subsidiary source of law

Among the ten members of the committee, Elihu Root expressed the strongest opposition to including in the list of applicable rules anything other than positive international law. He was at first very critical of the proposal by Descamps on 1 July,[27] which included not only treaties and international custom, but also 'the rules of international law as recognised by the legal conscience of civilised nations' and 'international jurisprudence as a means for the application and development of law' in the list. According to Root, '[the] two clauses constituted an enlargement of the jurisdiction of the Court which threatened to destroy it'[28] and 'the Committee must limit itself to rules contained in the conventions and positive international law'.[29]

However, two days later, on 3 July, Root came with a proposal which was substantially the same with Descamps' proposal. Root's proposal included 'the general principles of law recognised by civilised nations' and 'the authority of judicial decisions and opinions of writers as a means for the application and development of law' as the third and fourth sources of law.[30] The addition of 'and opinions of writers' was only to fully translate the French concept of *jurisprudence* in English,

26 Mineichiro Adachi, 'Sekai Taisengo no Gaikō to Niko no Jūyō Jiken [Diplomacy after the Great War and Two Important Issues] Lecture for the Tokyo Bankers' Club, 20 May 1930' in Masaharu Yanagihara (ed), *Peace Among All Nations – A Collection of Mineichiro Adachi's Writings* (University of Tokyo Press 2019) 275–90 at 286.

27 Procès-Verbaux (n 21) 306.

28 ibid 294.

29 Ibid.

30 Ibid 344.

which included not only case law but also the science of law. Only de Lapradelle found it useless to include 'opinions of writers', but de Lapradelle did not go far as to oppose it.[31] In addition, Ricci Busatti expressed hesitation to the inclusion of 'opinions of writers' in the list as he 'thought it was inadmissible to put them on the same level as positive rules of law'[32] and made a proposal to mention the fourth source of law only as a means of application.[33]

While the debate continued on the sources of applicable law before the PCIJ, Adachi did not express either opposition to or support for the proposals made by Descamps, Root, and Ricci Busatti.[34] He sent the resulting text to Tokyo without reporting the initial divergence of views between Descamps and Root.[35] The Ministry of Foreign Affairs was much more worried by the discussion on the compulsory jurisdiction and gave its approval to the list of sources without reservation, and perhaps without serious considerations.[36]

It is thus impossible to determine Adachi's attitude towards the legal validity of scholarly writings even as means of interpretation. But what Elihu Root said in the committee about the US position probably applies to the Japanese position, too: 'America would never give its adherence to a treaty for compulsory jurisdiction outside the limits of recognised rules.'[37] For Adachi to convince the Japanese government to accept the compulsory jurisdiction, there was no room for expanding the scope of applicable rules with such ambiguous notions as 'writings of publicists', even if he perhaps remembered the idealistic understanding of international law which he learned from Prof. Paternostro in his younger days. We do not have any writings of Adachi on international law for the period between his university years and the ACJ meetings, but it should be noted that the Japanese government had good working relations with Elihu Root when he was the Secretary of State (1905–1909) and that Adachi was a junior member of the Japanese Delegation to the Portsmouth Peace Conference in 1905. It is probably no accident that at the ACJ meetings Adachi and Root very much shared a kind of realism with liberal ideals.

Adachi was also an active member of the *Institut de Droit International.* In the Brussels session in August 1923, he co-authored with Charles De Visscher a report on the interpretation of articles 10 and 18 of the Covenant of the League of Nations. The Canadian government had even proposed the deletion of Article

31 Ibid 335–36.

32 Ibid 334.

33 Ibid 351.

34 The Committee provisionally adopted the text as 'the authority of judicial decisions and the doctrines of the best qualified writers of the various nations (l'autorité des décisions judiciaires et la doctrine des publicistes les plus qualifiés des différentes nations)'(Procès-Verbaux (n 21) 337).

35 Telegram from Minister Ochiai in the Netherlands to Foreign Minister Uchida, 4 July 1920, in Documents on Japanese Foreign Policy (n 14) 343–44.

36 Telegram from Foreign Minister Uchida to Minister Ochiai in the Netherlands, 10 July 1920, in Documents on Japanese Foreign Policy (n 14) 348.

37 Procès-Verbaux (n 21) 309.

10, which provided that '[t]he Members of the League undertake to respect and preserve as against external aggression the territorial integrity and existing political independence of all Members of the League'. The Canadians feared being entangled in European wars because of the obligation 'to respect and preserve . . . the territorial integrity and existing political independence'. Gilbert Gidel's proposal at the session of the *Institut* at Grenoble was rejected altogether as going beyond the texts of the Covenant. Adachi worked with Charles De Visscher, a brilliant young scholar of international law who was 14 years younger than Adachi, to come up with a new draft interpretative resolution on that article, which provided among other things:[38]

> III. Il appartient aux Etats membres de la Société de décider dans quels cas s'ouvre l'obligation de garantie./IV. Toutefois, par application de la disposition de l'article 10 *in fine* du Pacte et en vue de réaliser entre les membres de la Société l'accord indispensable à une action collective efficace, le Conseil . . . pourra émettre un avis sur le point de savoir s'il y lieu à garantie.

That is because, according to Adachi and De Visscher, '[o]n ne saurait, en bonne logique, reconnaître ici au Conseil un pouvoir de décision qui ne lui appartient pas' and they only accepted that 'à défaut de décision, le Conseil peut émettre un avis sur le point de savoir s'il y lieu à garantie',[39] but nothing more than just an opinion (*avis*).

The *Institut* adopted the resolution as proposed by Adachi and De Visscher with some minor modifications. Virtually the same proposal was adopted by the First Committee of the League of Nations on 24 September in the same year, even though it was not adopted by the Plenary of the League because a resolution containing an interpretation of the Covenant could be adopted only with unanimity.[40] Discussion on the interpretation of Article 18 was postponed and eventually abandoned. Adachi and De Visscher were again co-rapporteurs next year at the *Institut*, on the question of interpretation of Article 7, paragraph 4, and Article 12 of the Covenant.[41] Even if Adachi was a realist and knew only agreements between states can lay the solid basis for international law, he was nonetheless aware of the importance of scholarly discussion and engaged actively

38 M Adachi and Ch De Visscher, 'Rapport [sur les article 10 et 18]' (1923) 30 Annuaire de l'Institut de droit international 22–64, at 46.

39 ibid 34.

40 'Art. 5(1). Except where otherwise expressly provided in this Covenant or by the terms of the present Treaty, decisions at any meeting of the Assembly or of the Council shall require the agreement of all the Members of the League represented at the meeting.' See also James Brown Scott, 'Interpretation of Article X of the Covenant of the League of Nations' (1924) 18(1) The American Journal of International Law 108–13.

41 M Adachi and Ch De Visscher, 'Rapport sur l'art. 7, alinéa 4: privilèges et immunités diplomatiques des agents de la S.D.N.' (1924) 31 Annuaire de l'Institut de droit international 1–19 and id, 'Rapport préliminaire sur l'article 12 du Pacte' (1924) 31 Annuaire de l'Institut de droit international 22–32.

in the activities of the *Institut de Droit International*. He was realist enough to understand that the discussion at the *Institut* and other scholarly forums could exercise influence on discussions in diplomatic forums.

Even after he became too busy to be directly involved in scholarly activities, Adachi certainly kept his interest in scholarly writings on international law. When he wrote a preface to a book of international law by his old friend Prof. Sakutaro Tachi, Adachi wrote:

> j'eus la chance de collaborer étroitement pendant quatre ans avec un juriste italien, le Professeur Paternostro, appelé au service du gouvernement de mon pays et qui donna à ces écoles [de droit crées à Tokyo dès 1889] un excellent cours de droit international public. Mon rêve le plus cher fut alors de consacrer toute ma vie à l'étude et au progrès de ce droit, dont je devinais la très haute destinée. Le destin en disposa autrement. Me voici, depuis 38 ans, absorbé par le règlement des affaires courantes de la vie internationale.[42]

Daily work, however, did not entirely absorb Adachi's time and energy and he left print in the resolutions of the *Institut de Droit International* and, as discussed above, he did what he could to promote the rule of law in the international society until his last days.

4. Conclusion – realism and idealism in the World Court

Adachi's successful opposition to the introduction of compulsory jurisdiction can mostly be explained by his subordination to the position taken by the Japanese government. Adachi's insistence on civilizational pluralism can be explained as an argument of convenience, which drew on his cultural background. On a positive note, Adachi brought realism to the PCIJ, but on the negative side, he handed the death sentence to the ephemeral hope for universal justice. Later he became more and more isolated in Japanese political and diplomatic circles because of his idealism. He was an idealistic realist, or an idealist with an acute sense of realism.

As a realist, Adachi must be quite aware how much influence the scholarly writings had on discussions in the PCIJ: after all, many of the judges were from the academic milieux and those who were from other professional circles must equip themselves with knowledge of scholarly writings.[43] Also, as a realist, Adachi was

42 Mineichiro Adachi, 'Préface pour Sakutaro Tachi, La Souveraineté et l'indépendance de l'Etat et les questions intérieures en droit international, Paris, Les éditions internationales, 1930 (1930)' in Masaharu Yanagihara (ed), *Peace Among All Nations – A Collection of Mineichiro Adachi's Writings* (University of Tokyo Press 2019) 2–3 at 2.

43 For example, when the Director-General of the Bureau of Legal Affairs of the Ministry of Foreign Affairs asked Adachi how the withdrawal of Japan from the League of Nations should affect the relationship between Japan and the PCIJ, Adachi referred to an article of André Becker that appeared in the Revue de droit international et de législation comparée, 'La Cour permanente de justice internationale en 1930–1931', in its volume 13 (3rd Series) in 1932 at 524–63 ('Renmei Dattaigo no Wagakuni to Kokusai Shihō Saibansho tono Kankei

aware of the power of idealism. In the speech before the Tokyo Bankers' Club (the one quoted above), he talked about the power of Wilsonian idealism:

> When Woodrow Wilson came to Paris as the U.S. president and created the League of Nations, the majority of people including myself had much doubt as to the soundness of his ideas. But he was a great man. The enterprise he started there developed for more than ten years and has become key to the peace and war at least in Europe and South America. People are now aware of its importance because many potential wars have been prevented by the League of Nations. Had not been the League there, there should have been three or four wars after the Great War.[44]

For Adachi, it was important to establish the authority of the PCIJ and have it accepted by the public and the government in Japan. At the first session as a judge of the PCIJ, Adachi declared:

> Gardiens de l'idée pour un laps de temps qui ne sera certes, dans la vie de l'institution, qu'un instant bref, les juges qui ont, à un moment donné, le redoutable honneur de composer la Cour, se souviendront surtout de leur devoir de transmettre un jour à leurs successeurs, au moins intact et si possible accru, le capital de confiance et d'autorité qu'il sera le mérite ineffaçable de leurs prédécesseurs d'avoir su gagner à la Cour auprès de l'opinion publique.[45]

In spite of Adachi's hope and efforts, the Court could not win confidence from public opinion in his own country.

Seven months before his death, Adachi wrote a preface to a French translation of a Japanese classical work, *Notes de chevet de Sei-Shōnagon*. He commended the work of translation and the Japanese spirit for peace:

> Il suffira simplement de parcourir cet ouvrage pour comprendre que l'âme millénaire du peuple japonais est une âme d'une sensibilité infinie, s'éprenant de tout ce qui est beau, juste et noble, et que cette âme cherche

nitsuiteno Shiken [Personal View on the Relationship between Japan and the Permanent Court of International Justice after the Withdrawal from the League], 18 May 1933' in Ministry of Foreign Affairs (ed), *Documents on Japanese Foreign Policy*, Showa Period-II, Second Collection, vol 2 <www.mofa.go.jp/mofaj/annai/honsho/shiryo/archives/pdfs/showaki222_07.pdf> accessed 10 August 2020, 311–13 at 312). Adachi referred to this article, of course, not because this purely academic article can be an authoritative means of interpretation, but simply because it explained well the legal effects of the ratification of the PCIJ Statute without joining the League of Nations (which was sought with the US).

44 Adachi (n 25) 276.

45 Mineichiro Adachi, 'Discours devant la séance d'ouverture de CPJI, 20 January 1931' in Masaharu Yanagihara (ed), *Peace Among All Nations – A Collection of Mineichiro Adachi's Writings* (University of Tokyo Press 2019) 73–73 at 74.

> toujours la paix et le rapprochement des peuples, partout où il est en son pouvoir de le faire.[46]

His term as judge of the PCIJ coincided with the turbulent events for Japanese diplomacy, the Manchurian Incident in September 1931 and the withdrawal from the League of Nations in March 1933. For more than a decade since then, the 'âme qui cherche toujours la paix et le rapprochement des peuples' did not have any space 'où il est en son pouvoir de le faire'. He died in Amsterdam in December 1934.

46 Mineichiro Adachi, 'Préface pour André Beaujard, Notes de Chevet de Séi Shōnagon (Paris: Maisonneuve 1934) (1934)' in Masaharu Yanagihara (ed), *Peace Among All Nations – A Collection of Mineichiro Adachi's Writings* (University of Tokyo Press 2019) 107–8 at 107.

4 George Francis Hagerup (1853–1921)

A Norwegian legal internationalist

Dag Michalsen

1. Francis Hagerup as a legal scientist and politician

Norwegian lawyer, politician and diplomat Francis Hagerup died in February 1921, and he died, so to speak, at his post. Already not in good health, Hagerup had in early spring 1918 been appointed leader of the Norwegian governmental committee that was responsible for ensuring the interests of the neutral states at the end of the war. Among its tasks was to prepare for the Scandinavian states' participation in The League of Nations and Hagerup became involved in the collective process of the Scandinavian states in December 1918 aiming at a common draft to this effect – formed by the idea of a world that now should be governed by law.

At the same time, Hagerup was active in the preparatory work of the Scandinavian states' opinion on the International Court that was to be set up according to Article 14 of the Covenant of the League of Nations. In spring 1920, Hagerup was invited to join the international committee of lawyers in Hague, which task was to draft a proposal for establishing the court. As the *Procès-Verbaux* of the proceedings of the committee testify,[1] Hagerup was very active during the six weeks of meetings. Then, he headed the Norwegian delegation to the first meeting of the Assembly of the League at the end of 1920 in Geneva. Even though he was then very sick, he accepted the task of chairing the sub-committee which aimed at finalizing the draft for the Permanent Court of Justice (PCIJ). With minor adjustments, the Assembly accepted this proposal. At that point, Hagerup had just come home to Oslo,[2] and some weeks later he died.

Francis Hagerup was, as academic lawyer and politician, well prepared for the legal and diplomatic work in the years between 1918 and 1921. He was born in 1856 into an old family of civil servants and politicians.[3] He himself became

1 Advisory Committee of Jurists, *Procès-Verbaux of the Proceedings of the Committee, 16 June–24 July 1920, with Annexes* (Van Langenhuysen, The Hague 1920).

2 For practical reasons I use the name Oslo – even though the capital of Norway's name was Kristiania during Hagerup's life, until 1925, when it resumed its old name Oslo.

3 Unfortunately, there is still no biography on Francis Hagerup. Given his central position as politician and lawyer at the turn of the century, 1900, this is indeed a lack. See, for a short introduction, Dag Michalsen, 'Hagerup, Francis' in Michael Stolleis (ed), *Juristen. Eine Biographisches Lexicon* (Verlag C.H. Beck, München 1995) 265–67.

DOI: 10.4324/9781003020882-5

one of the leading politicians of his generation, being twice Prime Minster of Norway. He finished legal his studies in 1876 and set out almost immediately to travel abroad, primarily to study modern capital law and private law, in Munich, Leipzig, and Paris. He became fluent in three major foreign languages that helped him immensely in his later career as a diplomat.

Hagerup became Professor in Law in 1887 and he made a name for himself as a legal scientist with theoretical depth and international outlook. From 1888 to his death 1921, he edited *Tidsskrift for retsvitenskab* [*The Journal of Legal Science*], his own brainchild, and at the time the only Nordic legal journal.[4] The journal had significant influence on Nordic legal thinking and it created a network of elite lawyers and politicians in the Nordic countries that had not existed before.[5] In the years after 1905, the journal, moreover, became an important Nordic mouthpiece for scholarly exchange on international law. At the outset, Hagerup wrote a number of books and articles on private law, contributing to a new systematic approach and an almost striking internationalization in the science of private law. Somewhat before 1890, Hagerup turned to criminal law and procedural law. He contributed significantly to both the academic study and the legislative reforms of these disciplines. His major achievement was to apply new forms of systematic methods for both criminal and civil procedure and thereby understand them as independent branches of law. By comparative means, he set the Norwegian and Nordic procedural law both in the context of continental law and common law as he had explicitly studied both European traditions. In addition, his work on civil procedure became the scientific basis for a new code on civil procedure (1915). His works on penal law and criminal procedure were influenced by the contemporary movement of criminology and had profound legislative effects. In particular, his book on general penal law (1911) is still regarded as a classic in Nordic legal literature.[6] Overall, there can be no doubt that Hagerup's deep knowledge on procedural law equipped him well for future work on the establishment of the International Court.

Hagerup wrote a number of influential works on legal methods and legal philosophy. In constant exchange with international legal science, in particular the German one, he formulated three general points of view: first, he emphasized the need for a systematic approach to the legal dogmatic work as the increase of legal sources and more complicated social facts made this necessary. Second, Hagerup upheld a radical concept of law by defining it in psychological terms as those facts that motivate people to action and what motivates judges to declare law. Thus,

4 See the important study Sten Gagnér, „Hagerups Zeitschrift“ [1999] in Sten Gagnér (ed), *Abhandlungen zur europäischen Rechtsgeschichte* (Keip, Goldbach 2004) 615–750.

5 Dag Michalsen, 'The Making of Public Legal Sphere' in Michael Stolleis and Thomas Simon (Hg), *Juristische Zeitschriften in Europa* (Vittorio Klostermann, Frankfurt a.M. 2006) 29–54.

6 See on this book in Serge Dauchy et al. (eds), *The Formation and Transmission of Western Legal Culture. 150 Books that Made the Law in the Age of Printing* (Springer, Cham 2016) 436–38. See further Jørn Jacobsen, *Hagerup og den strafferettslege ansvarslæra* (Fagbokforlaget, Bergen 2017).

Hagerup was able to understand radical breaks in constitutional and international law politically and legally better than more formalistic-tuned lawyers were. Third, Hagerup formulated a balance between a strict theory of legal adjudication and the contemporary free-law movement that he in essence regarded as unconstitutional. His contributions on this issue helped him later to conceptualize the character of the legal workings of the Permanent Court and, by extent, other international tribunals.

At the same time, Hagerup became an active politician on the conservative side, although with strong liberal leanings as, for example, advocating almost passionately women's rights to education and vote.[7] Due to the growing tensions in the Norwegian-Swedish union, which had existed since 1814 (see more below), the King asked him to enter a minority government in the early days of Parliamentarism that de facto had been introduced in 1884. In 1893, he became Minister of Justice, facing fierce opposition from the majority liberal left that, among other things, proposed to withdraw Hagerup's professorship. The government fell in 1895. On the brink of war with Sweden in 1895, Hagerup felt compelled to form a new, broad multiparty government with the intention of negotiating truce with Sweden. As the government consisted of members with conflicting political opinions, little reform of politics was conducted as long as it lasted, until 1898. War, however, was avoided. From 1900, Hagerup was member of *Stortinget* (The Parliament).[8] As leader of the conservative party, he won the general election in 1903 with a programme to negotiate a comprehensive deal with Sweden. Thus, he became Prime Minster for a second time, again heading a multiparty coalition government. As he was politically and personally unable to move to a more radical stance in the union question, which would eventually entail a Norwegian unilateral dissolution of the union, he resigned as Prime Minister early 1905. However, he continued as an important and influential Member of Parliament through the union crisis and the subsequent dissolution of the union in 1905, and then until 1906.

Hagerup was a typical professor-politician connected both to the university and to the interests of the state. As for many of his generation in Europe, the political task (both as an active politician and as a top bureaucrat) was often the most important part of the professional lives of law professors. To understand this activity as a kind of operational legal research signifies the interconnections between legal expertise and the expertise related to political institutional activities. The operational character shaped these professor-politicians in their plural public activities, being in Parliament, state administration, the close connections to executive power, often doing much judiciary work, and being expert in administrative reform processes. These professors also often had important international contacts with professors on equal levels, both in other Nordic countries, in other European states as the professor type often resembled each other in

7 Francis Hagerup, *Om Kvindesagen* (Cammermeyer, Kristiania 1884).

8 To make it easier to read I use the English name Parliament instead of the Norwegian Storting.

Europe, and followed the same political and social patterns. All this points to the work in international law and legal politics done by law professors and their ability to enter into political negotiations aiming at settling international treaties, also with an eye to the increasing role of the public opinion in the decades after 1900.

2. Francis Hagerup and international law 1890–1919

It is a common notion that international law plays an important part in the politics of the Nordic countries.[9] Nordic governments have the reputation of promoting international law and its further development. Also, even though there are frequently divergences between the Nordic countries as to how to support international law, the Nordic states are generally perceived as representing one block, in particular on the issue of promoting rule of law and human rights in international relations. This has not always been the case and this image of Norden as a peace-seeking region adherent to international law is the result of the later twentieth-century Nordic history, but first evident in the processes leading up to work on the League of Nation in 1919. In this transformation, Hagerup played an important role.

In order to understand the general attitudes among the leading legal Nordic scholars to international law one should draw attention to the fact that during nineteenth century all Nordic states were bound up in a number of interstate relationships. This triggered a large amount of legal and political debates that stimulated the study of international law. A great many law professors were heavily engaged in dealing with these external-internal legal relationships: the Finns argued for as much autonomy as possible within the Russian empire. The extremely complicated historical and legal relationships between Denmark and the Dukedoms Holstein and Schleswig were the source of blending constitutional law and international politics, eventually leading to two wars. The shadows of the old pre-1814 relationship between Denmark and Norway popped up now and then in the form of unfinished businesses (as late as the Norwegian occupation of East Greenland in 1930–1933, resulting in the Greenland case at International Court in The Hague 1933).[10] After 1860, the relationship between Sweden and Norway became increasingly challenging concerning the legal nature of the Swedish-Norwegian union established in 1814. These conflicts reached their climaxes, as already mentioned, in 1895 and 1905.

The Nordic law professors and politicians became extremely well versed in analysing and understanding the idea of international relationship by practising the complicated Nordic issues, almost as a kind of laboratory of international law. These Nordic internal conflicts shaped legal thinking at the turn of the century. Hagerup regarded the dissolution of the Swedish-Norwegian Union in 1905 as an extreme experience. Norway and Sweden were at the brink of war both in

9 See e.g., 'Nordic Histories of Human' (2018) 3 Nordic Journal of Human Rights.

10 PCIJ, 'Legal Status of Eastern Greenland (Denmark v. Norway)' (PCIJ (Ser. A/B), no. 53, 1933).

1895 and in 1905, and Hagerup was Prime Minister in both those years. Hagerup was a man who knew the risks of war. He had to tackle a difficult dilemma: Was it possible to solve this conflict peacefully, according to international law, at the same time as Norwegian and Swedish nationalism worsened the inter-state relationship to the outmost? Again, we are reminded about the challenges that confronted international law in that epoch of forceful nationalism and the idea of an unchallenged national sovereignty.

Whatever might have been the 'correct union law', in 1905, the conflict came to its conclusion when the Norwegian Parliament unanimously decided that the union was dissolved as it simply stated that the common King did not act according to the Norwegian Constitution and, as an effect, the union had ceased to exist. Hagerup disliked this unilateral dissolution without negotiations, but he accepted the new fact and as Member of the Parliament, he contributed on solving a number of questions, regarding both constitutional law and international law. This must be viewed at the backdrop of a surge in popular interest in international law in Nordic countries at the turn of the century. The movement for peace and international arbitration was particularly strong. There can be no doubt that the intense conflict with Sweden, with the possibility of war, triggered the Norwegian Parliament to radical politics on international arbitration, starting in 1890. At the same time, the Norwegian Parliament became an active member of the Inter-Parliamentarian union for peace and arbitration in international affairs.[11] As a politician, Hagerup had to debate these pertinent issues in the Parliament and elsewhere and later, as a diplomat from 1906, he was equally engaged in these themes, originating from Nordic experiences.

As a law professor, Hagerup had already debated the challenges to classical international law from these new movements, having their basis in parliaments and civil society rather than among the academic elites and ministries. In 1897, Hagerup published his first article on international arbitration by reviewing new works by Alexandre Mérignhac and Eduouard Descamps.[12] Both works drafted new proposals for regimes of international arbitration, Descamps in the capacity of being president of the Inter-Parliamentarian Peace Movement. Hagerup's scepticism to a radical form of international arbitration was based upon geopolitical considerations, namely that no great power would concede to such arrangements. Still, Hagerup accepted the draft concerning the idea of a Permanent Court of Arbitration, but questioned the procedure for electing judges. Furthermore, he saw the importance of the choice of the location of the court; he went into detail about which members of the court should vote on which cases; he wrote about how the suggestion of two instances should be organized and much more. All these themes would be repeated during the next two decades.

A new impetus for a more radical view on international law came with the testament of Alfred Nobel who bequeathed the task of administrating a Nobel

11 Cecilie Schjatvet, *Fredssak og selvbestemmelse 1890–1909* (Akademisk Publisering, Oslo 2013).

12 Francis Hagerup, «International Voldgift» in *Tidsskrift for Retsvidenskab* (1897) 351–56. In that year, Hagerup was elected to *Institut de Droit international.*

Peace Prize and a Peace Institute to the Norwegian Parliament.[13] The reason why Alfred Nobel gave this task to the Norwegian Parliament is uncertain, but its outspoken view of the need for compulsory arbitration in international law was one. Another reason was the widespread popularity of the peace movement championed by the famous Norwegian author Bjørnstjerne Bjørnson. Last, Alfred Nobel, as he wrote his will in 1895, was formed by the fact that Norway and Sweden were at the brink of war and discreetly wanted to support Norway. Whatever was the background for Nobel's decision, the Norwegian Parliament in 1897 accepted the task given by Nobel and began formulating guidelines for the work. Immediately Hagerup (who then was Prime Minster) started to contribute to this cause. As expertise in international law would be vital for any committee electing prize winners, Hagerup was influential in the shaping the infrastructure of the Nobel Peace Prize. Descamps was asked to contribute with ideas on the character of a possible Nobel Peace Institute and Hagerup and his colleagues had high hopes and ambitious plans for a new academy in international law located in Oslo. Even though these plans were realized only in more modest forms, there can be no doubt that the presence of the Nobel Institute in Oslo enhanced the prestige of international law in Norway and in particular that kind of international law that was connected with preserving peace. To ensure that the expertise in international law was secured, the Parliament elected Hagerup as member of the Nobel Peace Prize Committee in 1906 and he stayed on until his death in 1921. Thereby he exercised important influence on the elections of Peace Prize winners.

The concept of neutrality continued to be politically and legally important and Hagerup wrote a lengthy article on the so-called permanent neutrality, in connection with Descamps' book on the subject.[14] He disagreed with Descamps on several points – and Hagerup's general observation was that the importance of distinguishing between positive international law and politics of international law was not sufficiently kept. He complained that the current politicization of international law would have counterproductive effects, as the blurring of law and politics would lead to a more uncertain international law enabling states (read Great Powers) to disregard international law. To discuss permanent neutrality legally would be to understand its character as law. On that note, Hagerup discussed a number of issues (as relation of neutrality to sovereignty, the legal character of unilateral statement of neutrality, the duration of permanent neutrality, guarantee of neutrality, etc.). What came out of his article was certainly a more distinct legal conceptualization of permanent neutrality – as he saw it important to stress this point of view addressing the ongoing political debates, also in

13 For this paragraph, I rely on Bjørn Arne Steine, *Fred, forskning og formidling* (PhD, Oslo University 2016) ch 2–6.

14 For the following paragraph see Francis Hagerup, 'Permanent Neutralitet [Permanent Neutrality]' in *Tidsskrift for retsvitenskab* (1902) 277–311 cfr. E Descamp, *La neutralité de la Belgique* (Larcier, Bruxelles 1902). Hagerup discussed this further in 'La neutralité permanente' in *Revue générale De Droit International Public* (1905) 577–602.

Scandinavian countries. He regarded, for example, unilateral declared permanent neutrality not as a legal act, but rather a mere political statement without legal consequences.

The danger of war and the eventual dissolution of the Swedish-Norwegian union in 1905 initiated a policy of peace, international arbitration, quest for disarmament, and the use of neutrality as a legal instrument, both from Norway and Sweden.[15] The termination of this inter-state relationship in 1905 was the first peaceful dissolution of a union between two Western nation states by then, a largely forgotten fact. In the negotiations that took place after Norway's unilateral decision both countries strived for peace and both countries had important political segments that had adhered to the radical peace movement. The Karlstad treaties of 1905, that ended the union according to international law, instituted a de-militarized zone between Norway and Sweden and it initiated two important arbitration clauses.[16] Initially Norway wanted a general arbitration clause that could solve all disputed issues rising from the treaties, whereas Sweden was skeptical to such a broad clause and insisted on legal instruments that were more precise.

From 1906 until his death, Hagerup was among the highest-ranking diplomats in the Norwegian Foreign Service, first as ambassador to Copenhagen, then to Stockholm, and on several occasions to Hague. He led the Norwegian delegation to The Hague Conference of 1907. The results of the conference were rather meagre, but Hagerup – now part of an international network of international lawyers – deliberated the difficult issues that would remain difficult ahead of the establishment of League of Nation.[17] In The Hague, Hagerup maintained a strict small-state view on the issue of international organization and he was very reluctant to deviate from the principle of sovereign equality of states. Still, he contributed significantly to the work on a Prize Court Convention (and he chaired the commission that prepared the treaty text) that, however, was not ratified.[18] Equally, he worked in favour of an obligatory arbitration court. On this issue, the differences between the greater and smaller states proved impossible to bridge, and the resistance from the great powers to obligatory arbitration, first of all Germany, but Great Britain also, was well known.[19] In these debates Norway had to tread carefully not to offend the great powers as Norway's position after 1905, before the closing of the Treaty of Integrity of 1907 (that was nicknamed 'the British guaranty'), was precarious.[20]

15 See Cecilie Schjatvet, *Fredssak og selvbestemmelse 1890–1911* (Akademisk Publisering, Oslo 2013) ch III on the Norwegian Parliament's arbitration policy in years around 1905.

16 Karlstad Treaties 1905. See *Karlstadkonferensen 1905: protokoll och aktstycken* I–II (Almqvist och Wiksell, Uppsala 1953).

17 For European historical panorama of this epoch centered on the international lawyers, see Bo Stråth, *Europe's Utopias of Peace* (Bloomsbury, London 2016), in particular 190–201.

18 See for a contemporary assessment James Brown Scott, 'The International Court of Prize' in *The American Journal of International Law* (1911) 302–24.

19 Marcus M Payk, *Frieden durch Recht* (De Gruyter, Oldenbourg 2018) 577–83.

20 Generally Patrick Salmon, *Scandinavia and the Great Powers 1890–1940* (Cambridge University Press, Cambridge 1997) 53–82. See for historical sources Cecilie Schjatvet (ed),

In retrospect, Hagerup still could not quite agree that the Second Hague Conference had been a failure. Just the fact that the conference was the first real worldwide conference was noteworthy, and he was happy that the word 'European international law' could be deleted from the vocabulary of international law. In addition, Hagerup acknowledged the possibility that international conferences of this kind could and should become a permanent part of the life of international community.[21]

Between 1910 and 1914, diplomatic negotiations and conferences were held in Oslo on the legal status of Svalbard, first a smaller conference between Norway, Sweden and Russia, then the international conference that aimed at finalizing a treaty.[22] Hagerup chaired both conferences.[23] Underneath the negotiations, there were different rivalries, between both Norway and Sweden, but far worse, between the great powers involved, Germany, Russia, Great Britain, and the United States, all as a foretaste to what would soon come. The instruments of international law, as neutrality and arbitration, and the typical *streit* on the difficulty of agreeing on the location of the administration of the treaty, were all played out at the conference. At the last meeting in Oslo in June 1914, the news of the assassination in Sarajevo sent shockwaves in the international community and ended the conference and the subsequent story of the Svalbard treaty belongs to history of the Paris Conference of 1919.[24]

3. Hagerup's vision of international law and the First World War, 1915

As the First World War broke out, the three Scandinavian countries declared themselves neutral and they stayed out of the war.[25] However, this was a testing

---

Dossier – Norges folkerettsbaserte utenrikspolitikk 1890–1909 (Institute for Public Law, Oslo 2002). See details from the Hague 1907-conference on the Norwegian delegation, Øyvind Tønnesson, 'With Christian L. Lange as a Prism: A Study of Transnational Peace Politics, 1899–1919' (PhD, University of Oslo 2013) 45–59. Particular on Germany's position in 1907, see generally Maxi Ines Carl, *Zwischen staatlicher Souveränität und Völkerrechtsgemeinschaft* (Nomos, Baden-Baden 2012) 83–124.

21 Francis Hagerup, 'Folkerettens problem [The Problem of International Law]' in *Tidsskrift for retsvitenskab* (1915) 139–77 (here 154).

22 Trygve Mathisen, *Svalbard in international politics 1871–1925* (Brøgger, Oslo 1954) in particular 75–100 (on Hagerup see in particular 96) and Roald Berg, *Norge på egen hand 1905–1920* (Universitetsforlaget, Oslo 1995) 265–93. See also Geir Ulfstein, *The Svalbard Treaty. From Terra Nullius to Norwegian Sovereignty* (Scandinavian University Press, Oslo 1995) 33–71.

23 In between *The Institut de Droit International* had its 1912 meeting in Oslo. Hagerup was at the time president of the *Institut*. See *Annuaire – Institut de droit international*, vol 25 (A. Pedone, Paris 1912) in particular 543–55.

24 Hagerup was reluctant to claim Svalbard for Norwegian sovereignty alone, as he thought this would look too antagonistic, but his reservation was kept within the Norwegian diplomatic services, see Mathisen (n 22) 115.

25 Salmon (n 20) 118–68.

position and it was challenging for the politics of neutrality. During the whole war, the Scandinavian states had to balance between the belligerent states (especially between Germany and Great Britain) to avoid becoming part of the war. Norway and Sweden, especially, had different interests, both due to traditions and to economics, as Sweden was inclined to favour Germany whereas Norway favoured Great Britain. As Hagerup was ambassador to Stockholm from 1916, he was in the middle of these tensions. As the war progressed, Norway came ever closer to Great Britain, and after the war, it stood in a rather favourable position having made the merchant fleet available for warfare to the Allied states.[26] This would be beneficial for Norway as the treaty of Svalbard came to the table as an indirect part of the Versailles settlement.[27]

In 1915, in the middle of the war, Hagerup summed up his vision of international law. One can understand his initial question: 'Does a true international law exist? If so – on what legitimate ground can it be built?'[28] As was well known to his audience, a number of authors had denied outright the legal character of international law in the sense that it did not possess the qualities of positive law beyond that of being acknowledged by the nation states. A variation of this point of view was to regard international law as positive law of another kind due to its lack of enforcement. Both these views, Hagerup stated, were part of an intended politics to minimalize the independent role of international law in politics of the world. He formed his argument by geopolitical realism of an experienced politician and diplomat. He explicitly addressed, critically, the ideas about a possible 'World State' or similar futile hopes of global federative utopias – even though they are referred to with much respect.[29] For him, as a lawyer, there could be no other way to proceed academically than to give a realistic analytical description of the structures and content of international law, as it existed as an entity separate from each state's law, at that time.

To Hagerup the question was to what extent international law was similar to state law, in the sense that international law 'motivated human actions' as only then 'those normative statements could be rules that evoke notion of duties that are to be obeyed'. As I noted earlier, Hagerup had developed a psychological theory of law: law exists primarily as a psychological phenomenon that attained identity by motivating human actions. To differentiate legal from non-legal normative facts, Hagerup narrowed the psychological motive: these intentions had to lead to notions of a duty to submit to the normative order and accept the

26 See the important book Ola Riste, *The Neutral Ally: Norway's Relations with Belligerent Powers in the First World War* (Universitetsforlaget, Oslo1965).

27 Ulfstein (n 22) 44–52.

28 Hagerup (n 21) 139–77. All translations by me. On the European debate on international law in this respect, see fundamental Martti Koskenniemi, *The Gentler Civilizer of Nations. The Rise and Fall of International Law 1870–1960* (Cambridge University Press, Cambridge 2001), in particular ch 3 and 4.

29 See generally on this 'utopian' thinking that Hagerup viewed critically, Mark Mazower, *Governing the World. The History of an Idea* (Allen Lane, London 2012) 94–115.

activities of collective organs, as courts. When these normative orders motived judges to their judicial actions, law came about.

What Hagerup called 'the modern states' had in the course of a long time reached an advanced level of legal institutionalization of judicial organs, what international law had not. In addition, Hagerup maintained 'that within the international society the solidarity of interests has been less developed and the feeling of cohesion was weaker than what bound the citizens to the state'. The modern basis for international law was the result of the development of nineteenth century and its massive increase in international conventions of many kinds and levels. There, Hagerup stated, one should rather be surprised by the growth of international law and not the other way round, and one should not look too pessimistically ahead. Hagerup retained that there were trends that ultimately would make the legal system of international law increasingly similar to that of the nation state. As he analysed the modern arbitration system, the interconnected systems of conventions, the many international economical multilateral treaties, and much more, Hagerup acknowledged a new legal massiveness that indeed 'evokes the motivating force of the normative directive'.

Hagerup had taken an important step in his own legal thinking and he was more than he perhaps admitted approaching a progressive view on international law, insisting it to be an autonomous entity – that international law actually existed, as Léon Bourgeois commented at the time.[30] Hagerup saw this confirmed by the recent history, by the institutional frameworks that already were in place, and by the proposals that eventually would reinforce it.

4. 'The ideal judge would be one that dropped from the skies': Francis Hagerup in Advisory Committee of Jurists

The Scandinavian countries wanted to contribute to the formation of the League of Nations.[31] Even though having been outside the warfare, the Scandinavian countries had still been very much affected by the war, in various ways. In addition, the collapse of the Tsar regime resulting in the new Bolshevik state and an independent Finland and the new state structure in the Baltic area had direct effects on the Nordic region. However, to transform neutrality into a League membership proved difficult in all three countries, both externally and internally. Norway was quite divided over the issue of membership, but its close ties to Great Britain meant that membership eventually became imperative.[32] Already in

30 See also similar Léon Bourgeois, *Le Pacte de 1919 et la Société des nations* (Charpentier, Paris 1919 [1916]) 2–22. See also Bourgeois, 'Speech delivered in 1920' in *Procès-Verbaux of the Proceedings of the Committee, 16 June–24 July 1920, with Annexes* (Van Langenhuysen, The Hague 1920) 5–11 and Bourgeois, *Nobel Peace Prize*, written acceptance, 1921 <www.nobelprize.org/prizes/peace/1920/bourgeois/biographical/>. See also Koskenniemi (n 28) 284–97.

31 Most recent treatment Marta Stachurska-Kounta, 'Norway and the League of Nations 1919–1939. A Small State's Quest for International Peace' (PhD, University of Oslo 2017) 42–74.

32 Shepard Jones, *The Scandinavian States and the League of Nations* (Princeton University Press, Princeton 1939) and summary by Salmon (n 20) 180–83.

October 1918, the Scandinavian governments asked the French to be consulted about the formation of the League, but nothing came out of that request. As several neutral countries were eventually asked to respond to the draft on the League in March 1919, they all stressed the significance of international law and the political role of the smaller states in the future organization.

The Norwegian government asked Francis Hagerup at an early stage to contribute to this legal and political process, which he did. The first important outcome of these preparations was undoubtedly the common Scandinavian work on the League of Nations and this draft was delivered in Paris in December 1918, the so-called *Draft for an International Juridical Organisation*, having a distinct legal character.[33] Hagerup's role here was very evident.[34] Another important outcome was the Scandinavian draft for an international court, a draft that was later integrated with that of the five neutral powers (the three Scandinavian countries plus Switzerland and Netherlands). The Committee of Jurists referred frequently to both of these drafts in their proceedings.[35] As Hagerup then came to Hague, he was indeed well prepared for the discussions as almost all the issues that were to come up during the meetings had already been debated successively in the preparatory works of the Scandinavian countries and then among the five neutral powers.

In May 1920, the Council asked Hagerup to become a member of the Advisory Committee of Jurists (ACJ), at the same time representing smaller nations and being a recognized international expert in international law.[36] In addition, Hagerup personally knew Lapradelle, Root (awarded Nobel Peace Prize 1912), Loder, and Descamps.[37] Overall, Hagerup played an active part in the proceedings of the Advisory Committee of Jurists in June and July 1920.[38] In what follows, I analyze Hagerup's major contributions in the discussions within the ACJ.

33 *Betenkning angående spørsmålet om Norges tiltredelse til Folkenes forbund. Den Norske komité til utredning av visse spørsmål vedkommende Folkenes forbund* [Govermental I on Norway's acceding to the League] (O. Fredr. Arnesens bok. & akcidenstrykkeri, Kristiania 1919) 11–13 on International court.

34 Stachurska-Kounta (n 31) 50–53.

35 See James Brown Scott, *The Project of Permanent Court of International Justice and Resolutions of the Advisory Committee of Jurists* (The Endowment, Washington 1920) 203–12 and 215–18.

36 See for details Karl Erik Haug, *Folkeforbundet og krigens bekjempelse. Norsk utenrikspolitikk mellom realisme og idealisme* (PhD, NTNU 2012) 265–69 and Scott (n 35) 2–4.

37 See for these men in their respective chapters in this book.

38 For the following analysis, see *Permanent Court of International Justice. Advisory Committee of Jurists. Procès-Verbaux of the Proceedings of the Committee* (1920). I cite from the English translation and insert the page number in the text. For a first account of Hagerup's role in meetings in 1920, see Christian Lange, «Hagerup som internasjonalist» in *Tidsskrift for Retsvidenskab* (1921) 89–93 and for a critique of Lange's biased view on Hagerup, see Cecilie Schjatvet, «Folkerett og småstatspolitikk: Francis Hagerup om opprettelsen av faste folkerettsdomstoler» in Sverre Blandhol and Dag Michalsen (eds), *Rettsforsker, politiker, internasjonalist: Perspektiver på Francis Hagerup* (Akademisk Publisering, Oslo 2007) 161–92. In recent years, there are two new contributions that touch upon Hagerup's role in ACJ: See foremost Haug (n 36) 265–77 (277–90 focuses on the discussions at the first meeting in Genève), and secondly and more general, Stachurska-Kounta (n 31) 111–31.

On a general level, Hagerup based his approach to the negotiations on two fundamentals: first, he maintained, almost dogmatically, the difference between law and politics and that his task was that of law, not politics. This is evident on numerous occasions and his belief was that to blur this difference was to undo international law as an autonomous body of law. In this sense, Hagerup was a rather conservative internationalist. In addition, this attitude formed Hagerup's view of the court as a court of law, not as a court of arbitration that would by its own logic become more political than legal. Second, Hagerup held an almost inflexible view on the principle of the legal equality of all states. He had been active in 1907 Hague Conference where he had fought for the position of the smaller states against the great powers' demand for dominance. He could not quite see (as a lawyer) that factual differences should lead to legal differences. Nevertheless, now in 1920, Hagerup expressively accepted geopolitical realities and, to a certain extent, conceded. Still, coming from a small neutral nation in a time where great powers ruled as they did (and perhaps had to do), was to him intrinsically contrary to what international law should be.

The question of legal equality came to the surface very early in the negotiations. The issue was how generally to deal with different views within ACJ: Should there be majority votes when there were different opinions on a topic? Lord Phillimore 'made it clear that, as a representative of Great Britain, he was unable to agree to any decisions being taken by a simple majority vote' and he maintained that matters of real importance would have to be decided unanimously.[39] This was an argument that Hagerup rejected as a typical great power attitude, and furthermore, as a misunderstanding of what ACJ was about. Therefore, Hagerup replied that 'the members of the Committee were not representatives of individual countries; they were independent jurists; their countries had complete liberty of decision on the proposal which would be the outcome of the work of the Committee. The Committee was not a diplomatic conference'.[40] Without doubt, Hagerup had a point here, and even though on many occasions one can read the voice of the country in the voice of the man, often that is not a dominant feature.

How to select judges was the difficult question that had to be solved and this looming issue was interwoven with the conflict between smaller and greater states. In the meetings, this was a large topic and the inventive result of the ACJ's deliberations, based on Root's proposal, was certainly what saved the new court. At the start of the debate on this issue, there was an interesting confrontation between Lord Phillimore and Francis Hagerup, relating to the tensions between smaller and greater states. Phillimore asked rhetorically: 'Is it possible to conceive the peoples of the Great Powers consenting to have their country submit to the judgement of a Court on which they are not represented.'[41] This was stated after Hagerup had maintained that the 'principle of the equality of States is the

39 Procès-Verbaux (n 1) 22.
40 ibid.
41 ibid 105.

Magna Charta of the smaller States and it is an outstanding juridical argument. Political considerations should not come into account for the solution of juridical problems' . . . 'if one tried to introduce an element of inequality into the scheme for the Court of Justice, this scheme would fall to the ground as did the scheme of 1907'.[42]

Lord Phillimore's argument that a court without members from the great powers would lack backbone[43] was met by Hagerup with the fact that 'the League of Nation was at present the backbone of the Court. Therein lay a new fact'.[44] This was also part of another argument for Hagerup which he stressed several times, also in connection to the composition of the court and the role of the Great powers, namely that 'it was of primary importance to find a solution which made the judges as far as possible independent of their governments'.[45] In addition, Phillimore underlined repeatedly the role of the public opinion at home,[46] namely that 'the great Powers would be prevented by public opinion from taking action in support of a judgment of the Court, unless they were represented on it'.[47]

Based on Root's proposal Hagerup acknowledged 'different points of view, which seem to be irreconcilable if supported inflexibly'.[48] Approaching Root's idea, Hagerup thought anchoring the election of judges in a much more complex election process, involving the organs of the League, would avoid to 'give to the great Powers a clear and formal preponderance',[49] namely by making the Council in which the great Powers are in the majority, a part in the election.[50] To Hagerup this also strengthened the idea to bind this new international court to the League as thoroughly as possible as it now became a question of using its institutions to the greatest possible advantage. However, to what extent was there consistency between Hagerup's accept of the model of Root, involving political organs like the Assembly and Council, and Hagerup's dogma of an unpolitical court, asked president Descamps. Hagerup answered 'that he did not see any greater incompatibility between these two tasks than between the normal functions of any national government. The ideal judge would be one that dropped from the skies; what they had to do was to find a practical solution.'[51] Overall Hagerup was swift to acknowledge the importance of Root's idea.[52]

In close connection to his view of the court as liberated from the control of the nation state, Hagerup was skeptical to suggestion that national legal systems

42 ibid 103.
43 ibid 121.
44 ibid.
45 ibid.
46 ibid 123.
47 ibid 126.
48 ibid 136.
49 ibid 137.
50 ibid 138.
51 ibid 157.
52 See also Scott (n 35) 35 who attributes to Hagerup's acceptance of Root's idea to be the turning point in the deliberations on this issue.

should be part of the workings of the court. This theme surfaced on several occasions, but chiefly during the debate that would lead to Article 9 stating that the whole body of the court should represent 'the main forms of civilization and the principle legal systems of the world'.[53] Hagerup formulated this in a terse way by stating that 'The Court was not to administer justice in accordance with national laws, but in accordance with international law which, in principle, was common to all States.'[54] This point of view would have consequences for the election of judges. As the court was to 'deliver judgement according to international law . . . there was no need to have national systems of law represented'[55] on the court. He was also skeptical of the civilization-clause as even though a civilization might be 'national in origin', history had shown there over time had evolved a civilization that was general in character, and 'more or less common to all countries.'[56] Not surprisingly, not all agreed, in particular Adatci.[57] Some meetings later, the topic and the arguments were repeated. Hagerup (and Loder) still held the opinion, 'but he would not press it in face of the opposition of several members . . . who attached much importance to this phrase'.[58] It is no surprise that Hagerup would be skeptical to denominate entities of legal systems, whether national and cultural in content. To him that would be to connect international law to national legal systems and thus lessen the detached character he envisaged for the new court. In addition, as Loder, coming from a small European country (and not pleading Nordic laws as a specific legal family) Hagerup saw this argument in the light of the great power debate. Still, he was less sensitive to the fact that references to legal systems and civilizations in general might reduce the power of European and Anglo-American international law in a new international world, an argument he had himself used on an earlier occasion (see earlier). Nevertheless, accepting so quickly the proposed formulation of what would become Article 9 is perhaps an indication of this sentiment.

The interest of the court's autonomy in the sense of being as unpolitical as possible guided Hagerup on many occasions. A good example was the long and complex debate on the process of electing judges. The Committee agreed quite early on that the members of the Permanent Court of Arbitration should nominate the candidates, but the Committee could not agree upon the role of the member states in nominating candidates. Hagerup argued that upon

> the main question, the question whether the nomination should be carried out by the governments or by the members of the Court of Arbitration . . . the intervention of the Governments before the nominations must be avoided in order to make the elections as authoritative as possible.[59]

53 Procès-Verbaux (n 1) 674.
54 ibid 156.
55 ibid 365.
56 ibid.
57 ibid.
58 ibid 437.
59 ibid 415.

To break the connection between the national governments and the court was of paramount importance. He stressed this opinion more forcefully than others did. Moreover, in view of the election mechanisms, states now 'would have every opportunity of expressing their views in the Council and the Assembly'.[60] To mention the Council here was to point to the great powers that were worried about this matter. Hagerup stressed this point by connecting his two main arguments – that of the interest of small states and that of an unpolitical view of the court: 'The essential point was to give the right of nomination to persons who were independent of their governments and above political considerations.'[61]

Following the same interest Hagerup argued in favour of exclusive legal qualifications of the judges and a relative long duration of the tenures. As to the legal qualification, he stated unequivocally that he wanted 'the word "jurisconsults" . . . retained',[62] in what would become Article 2. Then he underlined the opinion that non-juridical qualities were not sufficient. He deplored that governments 'had, on several occasions, appointed persons to the Court of Arbitration, who were not jurisconsults. This must not happen in the case of the Court of Justice',[63] and he pursued the point by asserting that 'the holding of an administrative post would not be considered as a qualification for the position of international judge. In his opinion, this point was most important because legal qualifications were not always required for administrative appointments.'[64] This issue was connected to the debate on the duration of the appointment as judge. Hagerup said that 'a life term had not been advocated by any member', but he was 'in favor of a fairly long term. It is wished to make the judges irremovable in order to ensure their independence. This is a principle universally recognized in national law; there is no objection to its application in international life.'[65]

It is reasonable to say that Hagerup was the one among the members that most persistently argued in favour of establishing a sub-division of the International Court as eventually resulted in Article 26.[66] He had advocated a similar idea in Hague in 1907.[67] The debate on this proposal was partly connected to the number of judges and partly more generally to the competence of the court during the ACJ discussions.[68] Hagerup drew attention to the fact

> that the archives of the various Foreign Offices contained many questions left unsolved, because there had been hesitation to set going the cumbersome

60 ibid.
61 ibid.
62 ibid 447.
63 ibid.
64 ibid 450.
65 ibid 195. See further Hagerup's formal proposal on the difficult issue of salary for the judges to which Hagerup paid much attention, 487.
66 ibid 719.
67 Article 26: «With a view to the speedy dispatch of business the Court shall form, annually, a chamber composed of three judges who, at the request of the contesting parties, may hear and determine cases by summary procedure." This article was close to *Draft Convention of 1907 for the Court of Arbitral Justice* [Haag] Article 16.
68 Procès-Verbaux (n 1) 167–82.

> machinery of arbitration to solve them. He wished to see a chamber composed of a limited number of judges formed to consider these cases.[69]

Again, Phillimore and Hagerup were somewhat at odds with each other, even though they seemed to come to an agreement.[70] Hagerup maintained that to establish such a sub-division would make possible 'a rapid and inexpensive procedure for dealing with many questions' and he 'thought this method would also meet the argument [made by Phillimore] . . . to keep the judges busy'.[71]

Another long-winding debate concerned what states may appear before the court.[72] Early in the discussions, Hagerup drew a distinction between four types of parties that one had to regulate differently:

> 1. A dispute between two State Members of the League of Nation 2. A dispute between a Member State and a non-member of the League of Nation. 3. A dispute between two States, neither of which is Member of the League of Nations, but which have been invited by the Council of the League to come before the Court

He then added as a fourth, 'Two States' that were not members but invited to join the League of Nations'.[73] By this typology, it was easier to narrow the issue at hand. One example here was the question whether 'a party [state] may arraign another before the Court unilaterally'.[74] Here there were two possibilities that had to be taken into account, 'either the Members have concluded an individual or a general convention, or such a convention does not exist. If a convention exists, one party no doubt can summon the other to appear'.[75] Hagerup further inquired: 'Ought a general convention to be proposed defining the cases of compulsory jurisdiction?'[76] Hagerup's experience with the difficulties, which arose at the Conference of 1907 'when it attempted to define cases in which arbitration should be compulsory had a great weight with him'.[77] On the proposal of a model of compulsory arbitration, Hagerup was rather pessimistic, given the stance of the great powers, and 'even if the Committee should succeed in agreeing on a list of cases for obligatory jurisdiction, all the States represented in the Assembly would never be brought to accept this list'.[78]

A sub-question here was whether there were limits as to what the Court could judge upon. Hagerup had understood Root to have the opinion that 'if in a given

69 ibid 173.
70 ibid 176.
71 ibid.
72 ibid 219.
73 ibid 221.
74 ibid 227.
75 ibid.
76 ibid.
77 ibid.
78 ibid 228.

case there were no actual rules, the Court might declare: *non liquet* – we cannot decide'.[79] However, Hagerup thought that this attitude might involve important consequences as it would limit significantly the Court's competence and, as Hagerup said, place 'the Court in an entirely different position from that of an ordinary Court, which may not declare *non liquet*'.[80] This issue was important as it involved the fundamental question what was international law.[81] Thus,

> Hagerup insisted on the two following points: 1. it must not be possible for the Court to abstain from giving a decision, alleging that no positive applicable rule exists; 2. if there is a rule of international law, the Court must apply it. The Court should only have recourse to equity if authorized to do so by the parties.[82]

He summarized his attitude that the committee must avoid 'the laying down of a formula which would limit the activity of the Court'.[83]

The debate became intensive. Hagerup later connected his opinion on the court's competence by stating that one of the 'tasks of the new Court would be to develop jurisprudence', and he addressed Root, having stated 'that if there were no positive rules of law, the Court would not be competent; otherwise certain States would not accept the convention establishing the Court'.[84] However, given this limited opinion of the Court, Hagerup said: 'the Court would be unable to contribute to the development of law'.[85] Later in the debate Hagerup eventually modified his rather broad concept of international law combined with his view of the court's law-making interpretive methods. He accepted that the proposal from the neutral countries 'goes too far in giving to the Court the right to act in the absence of a generally admitted rule, according to the rule which it thinks should be the law'.[86] However, he would accept as a limit that the court would not be allowed to declare specific law where there were no legal sources, as, for example, not being allowed to 'fix any limit whatever for territorial waters'.[87] Otherwise, Hagerup was more anxious for having to narrow competence as the opposite. This opinion was based upon the conception of the court as an independent legal entity entailing a law-making function.

Hagerup then wrote a memorandum about the non-appearance of the defendant before the Court.[88] He took as a starting point how different legal systems

79 ibid 307.
80 ibid.
81 ibid 296.
82 ibid.
83 ibid 297.
84 ibid 307–8.
85 ibid 308.
86 ibid 319.
87 ibid.
88 For what follows see Hagerup, Annex No. 2 concerning the question raised in article 43 of the Scheme of the Five Neutral Powers ibid 607.

might give ideas to the organization of the Court on this issue. How should one regulate the plaintiff's claim to have delivered goods to the other party? According to continental law the Court must not demand proofs of the fact that the goods were delivered before it needs to do so; under English law, however, one would have 'to prove that the goods were delivered'.[89] Hagerup himself had earlier recommended the first model being the most practical. To international law, however, comes other considerations than just legal practical concerns. Would it be

> in conformity with the dignity of sovereign States that a State should unilaterally be able to summon another State and should, in the absence of the other party, be in a position to demand that the Court should admit without proof any allegation made against that other party?[90]

Hagerup weighed these interests and found the solution in a wide competence of the Court. It would be on the one hand unnecessary for 'the Court in every case to demand proofs of the facts brought forward by the plaintiff';[91] on the other hand, the interest of any State must be considered. Thus, Hagerup favoured the wording that gave the Court 'free powers to appraise the circumstances'.[92] In the final wording of Article 52, this balance of interest found its solution in the first and second part of that article. These questions were related to the larger debate on the question of compulsory jurisdiction; here Hagerup seconded and amended a proposal by Lord Phillimore by defining a wide competence of the court.[93]

My final theme from Hagerup's participation in the Committee is his reaction to the proposal from Descamps to establish a High Court of International Justice for the purpose of trying crimes against what was called 'the universal laws of nations'.[94] The background for this proposal, made by the distinguished Belgian lawyer and politician, was obvious. The brutal German attack on the neutral Belgium in 1914 led to an unparalleled international outcry. The War in the west was mainly conducted on French and Belgian territory, as the Versailles Treaty negotiated the issue of German war guilt and the personal responsibility of the German Emperor (Article 227) became a complex and delicate issue.[95] It

89 ibid 607.
90 ibid.
91 ibid.
92 ibid.
93 Procès-Verbaux (n 1) 243.
94 See Descamps' proposal (The President), first at 498–99 and Annex 2 on 521 and then eventually as The Second Resolution of the Committee, 748–49.
95 See William Schabas, *The Trial of the Kaiser* (2018) 157–73 on debates during the negotiations in Paris about a possible international criminal court. De Lapradelle, French member of ACJ, wrote one of the initial proposals for such a court in 1918, see op. cit. p. 157 with note 3. See also in the book by Schabas on the Commission of Responsibility where these debates were mainly conducted.

is difficult to say how close one was to establishing such a court then. However, it was well known that the Americans were very much against an international court of justice, partly because of the tricky legal difficulties arising out of the so-called immunity of Head of States.

What Descamps proposed was first of all that the Committee should acknowledge that the proposal of a High Court of International Justice 'was not unconnected with the object which the Committee had in view, but a necessary complement to it in the organization of international justice'.[96] Beyond that, Descamps wanted to formulate four questions that had to guide any further work on the matter, and by inviting the Committee to debate these questions, he would anchor this issue at large in another international body than those of the Versailles Treaty. The four questions were:[97] Did crimes against the law of nations exists? Should one establish such a tribunal ad hoc or permanently? How should such a permanent tribunal look like? What guarantees should be imposed to ensure the just and timely operation of such a tribunal? A complicating matter for a general discussion was undoubtedly that neither did Descamps present any plan for a possible legal basis for the operation of the court nor how this court ought to be composed. To avoid an obvious objection de Lapradelle 'thought that the proposed institution was only intended to deal for future events'[98] so that there would be no debate concerning the problems connected to the Versailles Treaty Article 227.

Hagerup was the first of the members to make a principled stance on the matter[99] – and he did so in a rather undiplomatic form. What was at stake to Hagerup was that the committee's work was that of law, not of politics. The good thing about Hagerup's intervention was that the debate became transparent, but as a former politician from a neutral country not being devastated by war, Hagerup might have chosen other words. He had a formal argument. The League had invited the members to debate and organize 'only an international tribunal to which parties should have a free access'.[100] What Descamps had proposed 'was indisputably of a political nature' and if he were forced to have opinion on the matter, 'he would even retire from the Committee'.[101] Then he invoked his 'neutrality' and maintained that his presence during a debate on this matter might 'be binding upon his country'[102] – the last sentence was not too consistent with his earlier view that the members were not representing their national countries.

Not surprisingly, de Lapradelle reacted with emotions on Hagerup's statement[103] as he, as mentioned, had been working with a tribunal of this kind at the

96 Procès-Verbaux (n 1) 498.
97 ibid 498–99.
98 ibid 499.
99 ibid 499–500.
100 ibid 499.
101 ibid 500.
102 ibid.
103 ibid 500–1.

start of the Paris negotiations. De Lapradelle could not understand that this was politics, as it was not a question of particular crimes and the aim was to establish an institution for the future. 'The League of Nations was born of the sufferings of the nations, and its object was to prevent a repetition of the calamities which gave rise to its creation.'[104] Hagerup had to retreat somewhat, in order to absorb the emotions of the meeting, but after some reverences, he maintained that – apart from the formal argument – one had to look at it practically and theoretically. Thus he 'could not see how an international penal code could be drawn up, or how the enforcement of penalties was to be organized'.[105] By that, he touched upon the problem of sovereignty that would be a difficult argument in the future international criminal law. As it turned out, Hagerup was not alone, although other members were more subtle in their formulations.[106]

At one point Hagerup intervened with a proposal that would be the starting point for a common ground: 'During the deliberations of the Committee, reference was made to the advantages of the establishment of a tribunal with an international criminal jurisdiction. The Commission recommends that the various problems connected with this question be considered by a future international Conference.'[107] The outcome was somewhat different but all members accepted the issue to be worthy of a resolution. Compared to the debate, the end text was now narrowed down just to an acknowledgement of the proposal made by President Descamps and that the committee recommended the League of Nation to examine it.[108]

5. Aftermath

The last meeting in the Advisory Committee was 24 July 1920, but did not end Hagerup's involvement with the International Court. In November and December 1920, he headed the Norwegian delegation to the First Assembly at the League of Nations.[109] There he became member of Third Commission which task was to finalize the proposal of the Advisory Committee. Another four members from that Committee belonged to the Commission. Hagerup was elected chair of the sub-commission whose work was to evaluate the many proposed amendments on the report from the Advisory Committee. Later Hagerup, on behalf of the Third Commission, gave the report to the Assembly on the proposed alterations.[110] Overall, the Assembly accepted the proposal from the

104 ibid 500.

105 ibid 501.

106 ibid 503–13.

107 ibid 513; the debate 513–16.

108 ibid 748–49.

109 See the official document St. med. Nr 9. 1921 [*On the First Meeting of Delegates at the League of Nation in Geneva*]. The most prominent Norwegian delegate however was undoubtedly Fridtjof Nansen.

110 League of Nations (1920), *Official Journal: Records of the First Assembly. Meetings of the Committees*, 526–48. See also Lord Phillimore, 'The Third Committee' in Oliver Brett (ed), *The First Assembly* (1921) 147–81 (on Hagerup 171).

Advisory Committee. Later, in his report to the Norwegian government, Hagerup observed that the work of the Committee had been accepted, except for the proposal of obligatory jurisdiction in the areas stipulated in the Covenant Article 13. Hagerup was not surprised by this fact, but he referred to the option of individual treaties on obligatory jurisdiction (the so-called optional clause) that would in practice remedy this lack.[111] Hagerup's work on the establishment of an international court had started in 1919 and ended in 1921. To Hagerup this had been an important personal experience and it had given him faith in the role of law in the international society. The many difficulties ahead were not for him to see and he died in February 1921.

111 St. med. Nr 9. 1921 (n 110) 27.

5 Elihu Root (1845–1937)

Architect and advocate of the Permanent Court of International Justice

William G. Ross

Elihu Root, the principal American proponent of the Permanent Court of International Justice, used his background as an attorney and his experience as an internationalist Secretary of War and Secretary of State to help frame the PCIJ's charter and to advocate American membership.

Root produced no significant publications, he wrote no autobiography, and his extensive correspondence, which is at the Library of Congress, tends to be less revealing of his personal thoughts than are the letters written by other leading persons of his day. Root devoted much care, however, to his preparation of speeches to meetings of prestigious organizations, which were published in a series of eight volumes by various leading presses between 1916 and 1925. Although such speeches, not surprisingly, are laced with platitudes, they also provide significant insights into his thinking about various subjects, particularly the law and international organizations, and espouse visions of how international courts can help to promote a more humane and peaceful world.

Root was born on 15 February 1845 in Clinton, New York, the son of Oren Root, a mathematics professor at Hamilton College, and Nancy Whitney Buttrick Root, both descendants of early English settlers in New England. After graduating from Hamilton at the age of 19, Root taught in a private secondary school for a year and considered becoming a Presbyterian minister before enrolling in New York University's law school, from which he graduated in 1867. Following a year of clerking for a Manhattan law firm, Root formed a partnership that specialized in commercial matters. From 1883 to 1885, Root served as United States District Attorney for the Southern District of New York before resuming an increasingly successful private practice of law in which he often represented large corporations. His success as a corporate lawyer provided him with financial security that enabled him to devote the latter part of his life to public service. His background in corporate law, however, was a political liability that limited his ability to have a career as an elected official.

In 1878, Root married Clara Frances Wales, the daughter of Salem H. Wales, a philanthropist who edited *The Scientific American*. The couple had three children and a happy marriage that ended with Clara's death in 1928, shortly after their fiftieth wedding anniversary.

DOI: 10.4324/9781003020882-6

During his years as a Manhattan attorney, Root gradually became active in Republican politics, speaking on behalf of candidates, and chairing the Republican Committee of New York County. Although he originally was closely associated with the authoritarian Republican machine and served as an attorney for the party's notorious boss, William M. Tweed, in Tweed's corruption trial, Root later successfully advocated various anti-corruption measures that helped to reform municipal and state governments. As chair of the judiciary committee at the New York state constitutional convention in 1894, he was instrumental in reorganizing the state's court system, a task that provided useful experience for his later work in structuring the PCIJ.

Root first achieved national prominence when he became Secretary of War on 1 August 1899. Root's only military experience was his brief service in the New York militia during the Civil War, but McKinley made clear that he wanted a lawyer in this position to assist with the legal issues arising out of the nation's acquisition of a colonial empire during the Spanish-American War of 1898 and to reorganize the War Department in ways that reflected the nation's emergence as a world power.

Root's immediate challenge as war secretary was quelling an insurrection in the Philippines, which the United States had wrested from Spain a year earlier. Under Root's direction, the War Department organized and deployed a force of 74,000 volunteers. By April 1901, American troops had captured Emilio Aguinaldo, regarded by Americans as the rebel leader and by many Filipinos as a freedom fighter. Guerilla warfare, however, continued until July 1902. Approximately 5,000 American soldiers and at least 200,000 Filipinos, mostly civilians, died in the conflict. Many Filipinos and many Americans from then until the present day have complained that the suppression of the Philippine independence movement was unduly brutal and that American forces committed numerous atrocities, including the torture of captured soldiers. The repression of the independence movement became a lightning rod for anti-imperialist Americans, who opposed American retention of the Philippines, Puerto Rico, Guam, and other territories seized from Spain. Root was widely criticized for indifference, if not complicity, and for slowness in investigating the atrocities. Although Root did not deny that American soldiers committed atrocities, he claimed that they acted without authorization and that their insubordination had been appropriately investigated and punished.[1] Root publicly defended the colonial policies of the McKinley Administration during the election campaign of 1900, when William Jennings Bryan, the Democratic presidential nominee, made opposition to imperialism the primary issue of his campaign.

Root utilized his skills as a lawyer in helping commissions appointed by President McKinley to formulate a colonial government for the Philippines, designed to encourage a gradual transition to self-rule, which was not fully achieved until the Philippines became independent in 1946.

1 Philip C Jessup, *Elihu Root*, vol I (Dodd, Mead & Company 1938) 336.

Root also conceived a system of colonial government for Puerto Rico, which provided for a highly centralized system in which the President of the United States would appoint a governor and unicameral legislative assembly. Root's proposals were largely embodied in the Foraker Act of 1900, except that Congress provided for a higher degree of home rule and an elected lower assembly. Although Root, like most Republicans of his day, favoured high tariffs, he successfully persuaded Congress to sharply reduce the tariff on Puerto Rican goods because Root believed that free trade was necessary to stabilize the Puerto Rican economy.

Since the United States had pledged itself to Cuban independence when it went to war with Spain in 1898, Root worked to prepare the island for self-government during the four years of American military occupation. Root was instrumental in arranging a convention for the adoption of a constitution, which Congress approved with some alterations in 1901. The constitution embodied several of Root's proposals, including provisions allowing the United States to buy or lease naval facilities on Cuban soil, prohibiting Cuba from jeopardizing its independence through treaties or foreign colonization, and recognizing the right of American intervention to ensure independence and a stable government.

Root was instrumental in persuading the McKinley Administration that the civil liberties provisions of the Bill of Rights of the US Constitution applied to the Philippines, Cuba, Puerto Rico, and other territories won from Spain in 1898. The US Supreme Court later espoused most of Root's views in a series of decisions in 1901, the *Insular Cases*, in which the Court held that the Constitution generally follows the American flag.

In reorganizing the War Department, Root centralized military commands and restored full civilian control over an army that had splintered into a maze of bureaucratic fiefdoms that often operated without full accountability to the Secretary of War. Root also established an Army War College for the study of military strategy, a counterpart to a naval college that had existed since 1884. He also reorganized the state militia system to integrate it more closely with federal military forces.

McKinley probably would have selected Root as his running mate in 1900 to replace Garrett Hobart, who died in 1899, if Root had not insisted that he did not want the vice presidency. Root never regarded himself as a politician, and he preferred to remain in the War Department to complete the work that he had started there. If Root had become vice-president, he would have succeeded to the presidency when McKinley died in office on 14 September 1901. Root had known McKinley's successor, Theodore Roosevelt, long before Roosevelt became president. Roosevelt, who had immense respect for Root's abilities, encouraged Root to remain in the Cabinet and was disappointed when Root resigned as Secretary of War on 1 February 1904, believing that he had achieved most of his goals.

After his resignation, Root resumed his lucrative practice of law in Manhattan. He served as president of the Association of the Bar of the City of New York during 1904–1905 and he was temporary chair of the Republican National

Convention in 1904 after working to help to ensure Roosevelt's presidential nomination. Root resisted pleas from party leaders to seek the governorship of New York in 1904.

When Secretary of State John Hay died on 1 July 1905, Roosevelt persuaded Root to return to the Cabinet as Hay's successor.

Unlike most Americans at the time, Roosevelt and Root believed that the United States had a stake in the preservation of world peace.[2] The reason for part of Root's successful tenure as Secretary of State was his recognition of the importance of maintaining amicable relations with the Senate, which must consent to treaties.

Root also devoted particular care toward the cultivation of better relationships with Latin American countries. American relations with these nations had tended to be difficult even in the best of times and recently had become even more frayed as the result of the way in which the United States acquired territory in 1903 from Columbia and Panama for the construction of the Panama Canal. Root spent three years resolving financial and boundary issues involving the acquisition of the Canal Zone, which were embodied in treaties involving the United States, Columbia, and Panama.

Root became the first sitting Secretary of State to leave the United States, sailing to Rio de Janeiro in July 1906 to attend and address the Third Inter-American Conference. After leaving Brazil, Root travelled on to Uruguay, Argentina, Chile, Peru, Columbia, and Panama, a journey that generated good will among Latin nations.

As Secretary of State, Root also proposed and helped form a Central American Court of Justice, a precursor of the PCIJ, in 1907 in the wake of armed conflicts among the Central American nations. The Court's members were Guatemala, Honduras, El Salvador, Nicaragua, and Costa Rica. Although it was dissolved in 1918 after the United States ceased to guarantee its independence, the court was successful in averting wars among the Central American nations and adjudicating several civil rights disputes. As one historian has explained, it was 'the first supranational body to which states would suspend their sovereignty and submit all complaints', and it provided 'evidence that international organizations could facilitate state cooperation and create peace'.[3]

Root's belief that the law could resolve political tensions between nations likewise was reflected in his strong support for American participation in the Second Hague Conference, which met in 1907. The First Hague Conference, called by Czar Nicholas II in 1899 to formulate plans for disarmament to promote world peace, had established a Permanent Court of Arbitration (PCA). Despite its name, the PCA lacked judges or jurisdiction to adjudicate disputes. Rather, it consisted only of approximately 100 persons who were available to serve as

2 Richard W Leopold, *Elihu Root and the Conservative Tradition* (Little, Brown and Company 1954) 53.

3 Charles Ripley, 'The Central American Court of Justice (1907–1918): Rethinking the World's First Court' (2018) 19(1) Dialogos Revista Electronica de Historia.

arbitrators of conflicts among nations. Root recalled two decades later that the PCA was formed only to help 'save the Tsar's face' after some participants in the Conference, including Germany, refused even to discuss disarmament. '[B]ut the Conference was called and they had to do something, and so they considered that they would give the children something to play with, and they got up this arbitration proposal.'[4]

Root recognized that nations were reluctant to submit disputes to the arbitrators of the PCA because many were diplomats rather than jurists and tended to resolved disputes in a political manner that was not impartial or based upon rules of law. Root instructed American delegates to the Second Hague Conference to advocate the establishment of an actual court with full-time judges. Although delegates from other nations also tended to favour the creation of an actual court, the plan floundered on the issue of how to select the judges. The court presumably would be effective only if it had a small number of judges, and the delegates failed to develop a formula for apportioning or rotating seats in a manner that satisfied the less populous of the 44 nations that sent delegates to the conference. Efforts to achieve some sort of compromise were hampered by Root's ill health during the conference and his distance from The Hague.[5] The kind of court that Root envisioned was not established until 1920, when the League of Nations created the PCIJ.

Root took advantage of the limited abilities of the PCA in arbitration treaties that he negotiated with two dozen nations during his final year in office. These treaties required the PCA to arbitrate disputes about various legal issues, including the interpretation of treaties, if diplomats failed to resolve the problems. Hay had negotiated similar treaties but was unable to secure the consent of the Senate, which insisted upon reserving the right to agree to proceed with each arbitration and to alter the terms of the settlement. The more pragmatic Root persuaded Roosevelt to acquiesce to similar reservations, which the President strongly opposed when Hay was Secretary of State.

Another of Root's priorities at the State Department was improving relations with Japan, which had emerged as a world power through its victories in the Russo-Japanese War of 1904–1905. Root had the delicate task of facilitating the limitation of Japanese immigration to the United States without insulting Japan, which he accomplished through a series of notes between the two nations known as the 'Gentleman's Agreement'. Opposition to Japanese immigration was politically formidable on the West Coast and had provoked discrimination and violence which seriously jeopardized relations between the two countries. Root later opposed the elimination of Asian immigration in the Immigration Act of 1924. As Secretary of State, Root also promoted amity with Japan by exchanging a series of notes with Takahira Kogoro, the Japanese ambassador to the United

4 Elihu Root, 'Address Before the Association of the Bar of the City of New York, October 21, 1920' in Robert Bacon and James Brown Scott (eds), *Men and Policies: Addresses by Elihu Root* (Harvard University Press 1925) 403.

5 Jessup (n 1) vol II, 75–79.

States, in which the nations pledged to promote trade and peace in Asia. Japan also was the only Asian nation with which the United States made an arbitration treaty.

In an important example of American willingness to exercise global leadership, Root helped to arrange an international conference, proposed by Roosevelt, to resolve conflicts between France and Germany involving France's growing domination of Morocco. Root supervised the work of American delegates to the conference, which resolved conflicts during its sessions in Morocco during the first months of 1906. Although Roosevelt had boldly intervened in foreign affairs by personally mediating the end of the Russo-Japanese War in a conference he hosted in Portsmouth, New Hampshire in 1905, American participation in an international conference held abroad represented an even greater departure from the tradition of American isolationism.

With Roosevelt having refused to become a candidate for a second full presidential term, Root was prominently mentioned as a presidential candidate in 1908. While Roosevelt believed that Root was the best qualified man to succeed him and that Root would faithfully carry on his policies, Roosevelt feared that Root could not be elected, or perhaps even nominated, because of his background as a corporate lawyer and his lack of skill and experience as a political campaigner. Roosevelt also felt that Root, aged 63, was too old. While Root would have liked to have been President, he shared Roosevelt's reservations and discouraged efforts to promote his candidacy.[6]

Roosevelt's profound respect for Root also was reflected in his offer to appoint Root as an Associate Justice of the Supreme Court in 1906, which Root declined on the ground of advanced age since he was 61 years old. Root was mentioned as a possible successor to Chief Justice Melville Fuller after Fuller died in 1910.[7]

Although President-elect Taft in 1908 urged Root to remain as Secretary of State, Root preferred to become a candidate for the Senate to protect Mrs. Root's health, which suffered from heavy social obligations and the Washington weather. As the wife of a senator, she would not need to entertain so much and could spend more time at the Roots' permanent home in upstate New York, at Clinton near the Hamilton College campus.[8]

Root was elected to the Senate by the Republican-dominated New York legislature in January 1909. Root's six years as a senator were a rather frustrating time for a man who had become accustomed to major leadership roles. Moreover, Root, who had advocated visionary policies as a Cabinet member, now found himself opposing reform measures as the Progressive movement reached its crest.

Root strongly opposed the Seventeenth Amendment, mandating the direct popular election of United States senators, which the Senate approved in 1911 and which became part of the Constitution in 1913. Root believed that the taking the power out of the state legislatures would seriously erode the sovereignty

6 ibid 123–26.
7 ibid 126.
8 ibid 138.

of the states and that the people were not as well qualified as state legislators to select senators.[9]

Root also opposed women's suffrage, believing that it would undermine women's roles as wives and mothers.[10]

Root voted in opposition to the Federal Reserve Act, fearing that it would generate inflation.[11] He opposed the creation of the Federal Trade Commission, which he believed that government bureaucrats would use to harass businesses. He also voted against the Seaman's Act of 1915, which sought to ameliorate widespread abuses of sailors on commercial vessels and voted in opposition to the Clayton Antitrust Act of 1914, although he does not have appear to have had strong feelings about this legislation.[12]

One bright spot during Root's Senate years was his receipt of the Nobel Peace Prize in 1912, which he received 'for bringing about better understanding between the countries of North and South America and initiating important arbitration agreements between the United States and other countries'. Root used his acceptance address as an opportunity to call again for the establishment of a tribunal for the adjudication of international disputes.[13] In 1911, Root's contributions to peace also were recognized when the industrialist and philanthropist Andrew Carnegie selected Root to become the first president of the Carnegie Endowment for International Peace, a position in which he served until 1925.

Root's years in the Senate were blighted by the anguish of his permanent estrangement from Roosevelt, a dear personal friend, when Roosevelt tried to wrest the Republican presidential nomination from Taft, another close personal friend, in 1912. Root recognized that Roosevelt's candidacy would ensure a Democratic victory by splitting the Republican party, and he was increasingly uncomfortable with Roosevelt's leftward movement, particularly his proposals for curtailment of judicial review. As chair of the Republican National Convention in 1912, Root made critical decisions about the seating of contested delegates that ensured Taft's nomination and caused Roosevelt to bolt the party and run for President as a Progressive.

Unhappy in the Senate, Root chose not to seek re-election, a decision he apparently would have made even if the Seventeenth Amendment had not required him to seek popular election. Shortly after retiring from the Senate, Root chaired a convention to adopt a new constitution for New York to replace the 1894 constitution. Although Root succeeded in his goal of girding the proposed constitution

9 Elihu Root, 'The Direct Election of United States Senators: Address in the Senate of the United States, February 10, 1911' in Robert Bacon and James Brown Scott (eds), *Addresses on Government and Citizenship* (Harvard University Press 1916) 268–71, 277.

10 Leopold (n 2) 76–77.

11 Elihu Root, 'The Banking and Currency Bill: Address in the Senate of the United States, December 13, 1913' in Robert Bacon and James Brown Scott (eds), *Addresses on Government and Citizenship* (Harvard University Press 1916) 336–40, 343–59.

12 Leopold (n 2) 193, 195.

13 Elihu Root, 'Nobel Peace Prize Address' in Robert Bacon and James Brown Scott (eds), *Addresses on International Subjects by Elihu Root* (Harvard University Press 1916) 161.

with conservative principles, the voters rejected it because it was not sufficiently progressive.

In 1916, Root half-heartedly allowed conservative Republicans to promote him for the Republican presidential nomination. Root ranked third on the first ballot and placed a distant second to Charles Evans Hughes on the second ballot before losing to Hughes on the third ballot.

When war broke out in Europe in August 1914, Root immediately favoured the British, as did most members of the Anglo-American elite, but he did not publicly advocate American intervention in the conflict until much later. After the United States declared war on Germany, Root became bellicose even by the standards of the times, criticizing Wilson for not using sufficient military force, arguably an anomalous stance for a recent recipient of the Nobel Peace Prize and the current president of the Carnegie Endowment for International Peace. Root's intemperate screeds against German culture and the German people likewise were a departure from the normally saturnine nature that made him an ideal and effective advocate of judicial settlement of international disputes. In a speech at Carnegie Hall in March 1918, Root warned that a German victory meant 'the renewed ascendancy of the cruel and brutal and conscienceless power of a dark and horrid past, a wicked and heathen past, taking the place of that Christianity which we fondly hoped we were, little by little, approaching in these years'.[14] Root advocated stern measures to repress German American ethnicity, including prohibiting the teaching of German, which the US Supreme Court ultimately found to be unconstitutional.[15]

Root's principal public service during the war was leading an American fact-finding and goodwill mission to Russia in 1917 during the interval between the abdication of Czar Nicholas II and the Bolshevik overthrow of the provisional government. President Woodrow Wilson appointed Root despite long-standing distrust and conflict between the two men because Root's reputation as a foreign policy expert was so formidable. Root's quixotic ten-week journey through Russia, however, did not burnish his credentials. Root failed to prevent the provisional government from making a separate peace with Germany or to bolster its efforts to stem the growth of the Bolsheviks, whose threat Root greatly underestimated. Root also may have been a poor choice for the mission insofar as his social, economic, and political opinions may have been too conservative to influence a nation in the throes of an epic revolution.

After the war, Root probably was the most logical choice to lead the American delegation that helped negotiate the peace treaty in Paris. Wilson, however, chose to travel to France to personally participate in the formulation of the peace treaty. Wilson did not even include Root in the delegation, selecting Henry White, a career diplomat, as the token Republican in a small group that

14 Elihu Root, 'Speech at a Meeting in Honor of the Archbishop of York, New York City, March 7, 1918' in Robert Bacon and James Brown Scott (eds), *Men and Policies: Addresses by Elihu Root* (Harvard University Press 1925) 176.

15 *Meyer v. Nebraska* 262 U.S. 390 (1923).

also included Secretary of State Robert Lansing, General Tasker H. Bliss, and Edward M. House, Wilson's long-term personal adviser. Ironically, Root may have been over-qualified for the position since Wilson may not have wanted to work with someone whose opinions might carry more weight than his own. Wilson's failure to select Root also probably reflected the animosity between the two men.[16] Moreover, Wilson may have excluded constitutional experts because he regarded the League as a political rather than legal institution.[17] Root's inclusion might have made the Senate more amenable to the treaty after Wilson repeatedly offended influential Republican senators by appearing indifferent or even contemptuous when they attempted to discharge their constitutional duty of advising the President about the treaty. British Prime Minister David Lloyd George believed that the Senate would have approved the League if Wilson had included in the delegation 'constitutional lawyers of the highest standing' such as Taft and Root.[18]

Even though Root had no official role involving the treaty, he naturally took a keen interest in its formulation, particularly its provisions for a League of Nations, and he exercised considerable influence in Republican circles during the ratification process. Since Root had been such a prominent advocate of international courts, it is not surprising that he favoured American membership in a post-war multinational association of nations. Root never shared the view of critics of the League, including many of his fellow Republicans, that American membership in the League was unconstitutional because it impaired the nation's sovereignty. Root, however, adamantly opposed any organization that compelled its member nations to use military force. This is why he refused entreaties by former President Taft and Massachusetts Senator Henry Cabot Lodge to become an officer of the League to Enforce Peace, founded in 1915 to encourage the formation of a post-war international organization that would adjudicate international disputes, codify international law, and require member nations to use economic and military force against any member that went to war without first attempting to resolve its grievances through the organization's adjudicative and arbitral processes.

Root's objection to collective security pacts formed the basis for his principal reservation about American membership in the League of Nations. Root strongly objected to Article 10 of the League's charter, which required members to 'preserve as against external aggression the territorial integrity and existing political independence' of all members of the League. Although Wilson and other advocates of the League claimed that Article 10 would not require the United States to engage in war without the consent of Congress, Root shared the view of many critics of the League that the language of Article 10 did not respect national sovereignty and could embroil the United States in many overseas military ventures

16 Leopold (n 2) 132–33.

17 William G Ross, *World War I and the American Constitution* (CUP 2017) 326.

18 David Lloyd George, *Memoirs of the Peace Conference*, vol I (Yale University Press 1939) 184–85.

that were not in the nation's best interests. Root also advocated reservations to clarify procedures by which the United States could withdraw from the League and to confirm that the treaty did not interfere with the Monroe Doctrine.[19] Root apparently conceived the idea of having the Senate ratify the treaty with interpretive reservations rather than amending it or rejecting it. He was influential in persuading Republican leaders, including Lodge, the chair of the Senate's Foreign Relations Committee, to support the use of reservations.[20] Wilson's adamant refusal to accept any reservations ensured the treaty's defeat by the Senate in November 1919 and again in March 1920, when the treaty failed to receive the requisite two-thirds vote needed for ratification because Wilson's supporters refused to vote for it with reservations, the reservationists refused to vote for it without reservations, and the so-called 'irreconcilable' senators refused to vote for it under any circumstances.

Even though Root was sidelined in the deliberations about the League of Nations, he had a prominent role in the formation of the PCIJ, which was authorized by Article 14 of the League's Covenant, which provided that:

> The Council shall formulate and submit to the members of the League for adoption plans for the establishment of a Permanent Court of International Justice. The Court shall be competent to hear and determine any dispute of an international character which the parties thereto submit to it. The Court may also give an advisory opinion upon any dispute or question referred to it by the Council or by the Assembly.

Despite his advanced age of 75, Root did not hesitate to accept an invitation from the League's secretary-general in February 1920 to serve as one of ten members of a committee to prepare plans for a court that became the PCIJ. In June, Root travelled to The Hague to spend the summer working with the other committee members, who were jurists, legal scholars, and diplomats from Belgium, Brazil, France, Italy, Japan, the Netherlands, Norway, Spain, and the United Kingdom. At the outset of his work, Root admonished his fellow representatives that they spoke for 'not only the feelings of the people of the countries from which we come, but the feelings and the opinions of the people of all countries'.[21] In explaining the committee's work after he returned to the United States, Root emphasized that none of the members represented any government. 'We were called there as experts purely . . . as if a lot of engineers had been called together to propose a plan for a bridge' or 'as if physicians were called together to consult about a case'.[22]

19 Leopold (n 2) 138–39.

20 ibid 138.

21 Elihu Root, 'The Permanent Court of International Justice' in Robert Bacon and James Brown Scott (eds), *Men and Policies: Addresses by Elihu Root* (Harvard University Press 1925) 329 ("Extracts from Debate in Committee, June 17, 1920").

22 Root (n 4) 395; Elihu Root, 'Annual Address as President of the American Society of International Law, April 26, 1923' in Robert Bacon and James Brown Scott (eds), *Men and Policies: Addresses by Elihu Root* (Harvard University Press 1925) 418.

Root later explained to the Association of the Bar of the City of New York that 'one might suppose that it was quite a simple thing to get up a plan for a court; but there were some very serious difficulties involved'.[23] In formulating a successful structure for a court, the committee first needed to address the issue of judicial selection, which had stymied the Second Hague Conference and forced it to adjourn in failure. The problem at first seemed intractable since a viable court could have only a relatively small number of judges, which would mean that the judges could come from only a small number of the many countries that would be members of the PCIJ. The most populous countries naturally believed that the court should include judges from their own nation, while the less populated nations feared that judges from the populous countries would dominate the court. Recalling that the same kind of tension between the small and large states nearly prevented the adoption of the United States Constitution, Root proposed his own form of the American 'Great Compromise', recommending a method of judicial selection that drew on the bicameral model of the American Congress. Since the larger nations were represented in the League of Nation's Council while all League members were represented in the Assembly, Root recommended that both chambers select members from nominations made by the members of the PCA.[24] Differences between the two bodies could be resolved in a conference committee similar to those in which members of the American House of Representatives and Senate ironed out differences in legislation passed by the House and the Senate.[25] The involvement of both chambers, Root explained, would provide both large and small nations with a virtual veto of any unfairness by one against the other.[26] By availing itself of an existing organization, the League, the court would not be founded 'upon a postulate of national discord and intrigue'.[27] Pursuant to this method, 'no judge will have been selected by any nation – they will all be elected by the votes of the members of these two existing bodies, and there will be no objection to the Court doing what I believe it should do: establish itself in the confidence of mankind'.[28]

Root emphasized that the committee should provide only general rules for the Council and the Assembly to select the judges and should trust the League to formulate details for judicial selection 'in accordance with its convenience and its judgment as to the best way' of operating.[29] Root warned that '[e]very minute direction that we give is likely to be the cause of objection. Little things often cause stronger objections than great ones . . . and every unnecessary provision we put in is an added danger to the plan.'[30]

23 Root (n 4) 395.
24 Root (n 21) July 18, 1920, 332–34.
25 ibid 335; Root (n 4) 397.
26 Root (n 21) July 6, 1920, 373.
27 ibid.
28 ibid 374.
29 ibid.
30 ibid.

With regard to the questions of how nominations would be made for the League's consideration and approval, Root strongly opposed a proposal by the committee's reporter, M. Lapradelle of France, for nominations by governments rather than from the 130 judges of the PCA.[31] Root explained that the PCA would have a wider familiarity with the qualifications of potential judges than would governments and that this method would not bind governments to a particular candidate before the League's consideration of candidates.[32] Governments, he believed, would have sufficient power to select the judges when the nominations came before the League.[33] This, Root believed, would help ensure the selection of 'men who are known to be competent, impartial, judicial in their character and, men of character, rising above and ignoring the question of governmental politics and policy'.[34] Root also emphasized the importance of selecting judges who would come from a wide variety of judicial systems. 'Now what we want here is a court which will understand the sympathies, the thought, the opinions, the prejudices, the forms of expression, the ways of acting of all the people of the world – of the civilized world.'[35] Root further believed that individual judges should have 'the judicial habit of open-mindedness'.[36] Root, however, did not oppose a proposal to permit the League to go beyond the list to select a judge if its conference committee could not agree on names selected by the PCA.[37]

Root and the British member, Lord Phillimore, also successfully proposed that there should be only one judge from any country and that the electors should 'seek so far as practicable to have represented in the Court the different forms of civilization and judicial systems which exist among Members of the Society of Nations'.[38]

After considerable discussion, Root and his fellow committee members determined that nations who were litigants should be allowed to have an ad hoc judge from their own nation participate in the adjudication of their cases unless a permanent judge from such country already served on the court. Although the committee recognized that such an appointment contravened traditional notions of the need for judicial impartiality, Root later told the Association of the Bar of the City of New York that this would help facilitate justice for the small countries who rarely would have judges on the court, especially since these special judges could enlighten the permanent judges about the peculiarities of the law of their countries that might be relevant to the adjudication of the case.[39] As Root explained: 'there ought to be some one man at least in the Court who understood the habits, customs, and the reactions of the nation that is a party to

31 ibid July 7, 1920, 379–82.
32 ibid 381.
33 ibid 380.
34 ibid.
35 ibid July 8, 1920, 385.
36 ibid July 9, 1920, 385.
37 ibid July 8, 1920, 382–83.
38 Root (n 21) 362 (July 1, 1920, "*Annex*: The Root-Phillimore Plan").
39 Root (n 4) 399.

any proceeding'.[40] Root believed that '[t]he greatest obstacle to doing justice as between nations is a failure of nations to understand each other' and that such special judges might promote understanding.[41]

Recalling a case involving the interpretation of a contract between French and American companies he once argued before the US Supreme Court, Root explained that what would have seemed just to a Frenchman would seem unjust to an American and vice versa because of their different ways of thinking and doing business.[42] Root found that the same problem arose on the committee, where

> [w]e passed hours and hours and days . . . discussing subjects where the only difference was not in our discussion or in what we were saying, but in a different set of ideas in the backs of our heads; and it requires experience to understand that there is such a difference of ideas.

Root and Phillimore found themselves 'up against a granite wall very often' because their common law traditions were so different from the civil law backgrounds of the members from the Continent, and Root supposed that continental members were similarly befuddled by Root and Phillimore: 'It required long and patient effort to find out what we were talking about.'[43]

Root strongly supported the committee's agreement that the court should have the power to adjudicate cases rather than merely to arbitrate disputes. Root believed that adjudication would enable the court to make the legally correct decision rather than merely to reach the kind of compromise that characterizes arbitration. As he later explained,

> arbitrators too often are apt to treat the cases brought before them as a matter for settlement, for adjustment. They have come to consider . . . that their function is to do with the case what seems to them to be the wisest and most expedient thing for all parties and all interests concerned. They tend to act under a sense of diplomatic obligation rather than under a sense of judicial obligation.

Root observed that nations had been reluctant to agree to arbitration not because they were unwilling to submit to arbitration itself, but rather because 'they had not much confidence in getting impartial judgment', having 'found that the arbitrators, when they got together, went into negotiations as diplomats, and no one could tell what would come out of it', particularly because arbitrators generally are 'selected by one side or the other in a particular controversy' and 'tend to represent that side of the controversy with the result that there is

40 ibid 400.
41 ibid 399.
42 ibid 399–400.
43 ibid 400.

negotiation and compromise rather than judicial decision'.[44] A nation that was absolutely right as a matter of law 'might find itself defeated because it seemed to the arbitrators on the whole that it perhaps would be better that it should not have its legal rights, but that the case should be settled as conveniently as possible'. In contrast, the PCIJ 'was designed to be a court in which judges would sit and decide according to the law, and let the consequences take care of themselves'.[45]

In considering the scope of the court's jurisdiction, Root believed that the court generally should adjudicate only cases between nations rather cases involving individuals, except when individuals had acted outside the law of any nation. Root believed that many or most nations would oppose prosecution of cases in which individuals were accused of violating the law of nations even though they had acted in accordance with the law of their own nation.[46] Root explained that

> [i]t would be impossible for the nation, for certain states, to admit that their own citizens might be punished upon the initiative of the Assembly or the Council of the Society of Nations for what the Assembly thought, or . . . for what . . . the Council or any court might judge, to be crimes against international public order, because that general authority would mean indeed creating a super-government.

This, Root pointed out, would create

> a central authority which would have control over all theretofore independent sovereign states, and would be able to seize upon the individual and punish him irrespective of the views of his own country; the exercise of such a power must be most carefully limited.[47]

Root also advocated that the court's decisions be binding on its members even though this, by definition, would require the members to sacrifice at least some of their sovereignty.[48] Root emphasized, however, that such obligatory jurisdiction would need to be very narrow and definite if the court were to have any real power.[49] He favoured limiting it to cases involving the interpretation of treaties; questions of international law; and breach of contractual obligations among nations.[50] Recognizing that many nations would be loath to surrender any sovereignty, he warned that the committee should permit the court broad discretion

44 Root (n 22) 407.
45 Root (n 4) 394.
46 Root (n 21) July 13, 1920, 387.
47 ibid.
48 See ibid July 1, 1920, 363–64.
49 ibid 365.
50 ibid 372.

in determining how to make its decisions binding.[51] 'Let us first get the civilized world to agree to accept the judgments of the Court upon questions of law, and then let us go further,' he admonished his fellow committee members. 'You cannot get them now to agree to anything beyond that.'[52] He explained that the committee ought to 'place before the world a proposition which will help the friends of judicial settlement, the friends of arbitration, to win consent from their countries and not make it a proposition so broad as to lead to their certain defeat.'[53] Root favoured allowing the court to apply general 'principles of justice' only in cases in which the court's jurisdiction was not compulsory.[54] Although Root believed that members of the League of Nations were willing to accept obligatory interpretation of contracts and interpretation of long-established principles of international law, he did not think that the nations were ready to accept obligatory jurisdiction over 'principles of justice, which have not been agreed so as to become part of the law of nations' because there are 'widely different conceptions' among 'different countries and different races, and under different conditions, as to what those principles of justice require'.[55]

In urging limitation of obligatory jurisdiction to a narrow class of cases, Root recalled that the Senate had failed to ratify treaties that Taft had negotiated between the United States and Britain and the United States and France for submission of all 'justiciable' questions to arbitration because the Senate regarded the term justiciable questions as too vague, and permitted the court to decide whatever the court thought fit, without being limited by rules of law and would enable the court to make decisions that were significantly at odds with American conceptions of justice.[56]

Although the committee accepted Root's proposal for obligatory jurisdiction at least in a broad form, the League ultimately rejected it because the most powerful nations, particularly Britain, opposed it. The League substituted a provision permitting nations to accept obligatory jurisdiction on terms of reciprocity. Professor Jessup explained that 'Root, while regretting the failure to accept the proposal for obligatory jurisdiction, appreciated the reasons for its rejection and considered the final plan satisfactory.'[57]

Root's service on the committee also enabled him to promote the codification of international law to enable judges of international disputes to be guided by more objective and predictable rules, a cause which he long had favoured.[58] As Root explained in his Nobel Peace Prize address:

51 ibid 365.
52 ibid 367.
53 ibid 372.
54 ibid 371.
55 ibid 367–68.
56 ibid July 1, 1920, 367–68; Root (n 4) 393.
57 Jessup (n 1) vol II, 422.
58 *E.g.*, 'The Function of Private Codification in International Law: Presidential Address at the Fifth Annual Meeting of the American Society of International Law, Washington, April 27, 1911' in Robert Bacon and James Brown Scott (eds), *Addresses on International Subjects by*

> There are multitudes of events liable to occur frequently in the intercourse of nations, regarding which there has never been any agreement as to what is just, equitable, or convenient . . . so that in a large part of that field with which an arbitral tribunal or international court should deal there is really no law to be applied. Where there is no law, a submission to arbitration is an appeal, not to the rule of law but to unknown opinions or predilections of the men who happen to be selected to decide. The development of the peaceable settlement of international disputes by the decisions of impartial tribunals waits therefore upon the further development of international law by a more complete establishment of known and accepted rules for the government of international conduct.[59]

The First World War had intensified Root's passion for codification and convinced him that international laws must have sanctions behind them. As Root explained in 1915, the war had

> outstripped the growth of international law . . . The pressing forward of the codification of international law is made necessary by the swift moving of events among nations. We cannot wait for custom to lag behind the action to which the law should be applied.[60]

Article 38 of the PCIJ's charter, which Root helped to draft, took a long step forward in promoting codification of international law by listing the sources of international law. Article 38, which was incorporated into the International Court of Justice statute in 1945, provided that the Court would apply:

> 1 International conventions, whether general or particular, establishing rules expressly recognized by the contesting States;
> 2 International custom, as evidence of a general practice accepted as law;
> 3 The general principles of law recognized by civilized nations;
> 4 Subject to the provisions of Article 59 [providing that decisions were binding only on parties to a lawsuit], judicial decisions and the teachings of the most highly qualified publicists of the various nations, as subsidiary means for the determination of rules of law.
>
> Article 38 also provided that this enumeration of sources of law 'shall not prejudice the power of the Court to decide a case *ex aequo et bono*, if the parties agree thereto'.

Elihu Root (Harvard University Press 1916) 57–72; '"Should International Law Be Codified?" Address at the Joint Meeting of the Subsection on International Law at the Second Pan-American Scientific Congress, Washington, D.C., April 27, 1916' in Robert Bacon and James Brown Scott (eds), *Addresses on International Subjects by Elihu Root* (Harvard University Press 1916).

59 Root (n 13) 162.

60 Jessup (n 1) vol II, 374.

As one scholar recently has observed, Article 38 still 'serves as the basic building block for international law and international lawyers everywhere'.[61]

The committee made only general recommendations for procedure because, as Root explained, '[w]here you have a great many countries, all with different procedures, it is necessary to be quite general in your rules'.[62]

The committee recommended the continuation of the PCA 'for the purpose of dealing with questions which involve subjects not altogether justiciable but appropriate for arbitration'.[63]

The League quickly ratified the charter and the PCIJ met for the first time in 1922. By 1923, 46 of the League's 52 nations were members of the Court. Root declined several offers of nominations to serve on the court because he felt that he and Clara Root were too old to transplant themselves to the Netherlands.[64] Root, however, worked, unsuccessfully, for the next 15 years to encourage the United States to become a member of the court. In advocating American membership, Root tried to disentangle the court from opposition to American membership in the League of Nations since many of the most ardent opponents of the League suspected that American membership in the court would encourage membership in the League.[65] It was not until February 1923 that President Warren G. Harding sent the PCIJ treaty to the Senate, in language drafted by Secretary of State Hughes. Harding recommended ratification subject to four reservations proposed by Hughes which would provide the United States with the same rights as League members. Lodge, whose reservations about the League were instrumental in preventing American membership, raised various objections to the Court, particularly the ability of the British Empire to have six judges since Canada, India, South Africa, Australia, and New Zealand were allowed seats separate from the United Kingdom itself.[66] Lodge and other opponents of the League had raised the same objection to undue British influence in their opposition to the League.

In advocating American membership in the PCIJ, Root emphasized that the question of joining the two organizations was 'quite distinct' because they 'approach the great problem of preserving peace from different angles and by different methods. They differ radically in their nature and effects.'[67] As he explained in his presidential address to the American Society of International Law in 1923, the Court was strictly a judicial body rather than a political or diplomatic body, and the judges did not follow the orders or policies of their governments, but instead sat to 'hear and decide upon the evidence and the law in accordance with

61 Mark Weston Janis, 'Sources in the Meta-History of International Law: A Little Meta-Theory – Paradigms, Article 38, and the Sources of International Law' in *Oxford Handbook of the Sources of International Law* (OUP 2018) 11.

62 Root (n 4) 404.

63 ibid 401.

64 Jessup (n 1) vol II, 424.

65 ibid 428.

66 ibid 429.

67 Root (n 22) 408.

[their] own personal judgment'.[68] He also explained that the court 'did not originate in the League of Nations'. Rather, it was conceived in the American proposal to the First Hague Conference of 1899, and most of the details other than judicial selection were formulated in The Hague Conference of 1907.[69] Root pointed out that the court was 'a world court and not a League court' because all nations, including the United States, could institute litigation in the court; all members of the PCA, including the United States, were eligible to make nominations for judgeships; and citizens of all nations, including the United States, were eligible to serve as judges.[70] Indeed, three Americans served as judges – John Bassett Moore (1922–1928), Charles Evans Hughes (1928–1930), and Manley Ottmer Hudson (1931–1945).

Root emphasized that the only obligation that the United States would acquire by joining the court would be the payment of money to help support the court, but that this expenditure would be 'negligible' and within the sole discretion of Congress.[71] He believed that American membership in the court would 'give nobody authority or power to do anything to us. The question is merely whether we shall give our moral approval to the establishment of the same kind of court which our government has been advocating for a generation.'[72] Root opposed a proposal by former Attorney General George W. Wickersham to convene a World Conference in Washington to encourage support for the League. He wisely feared it would backfire because senators would resent any attempt to influence their deliberations, and that senators from beyond the Northeast would be particularly offended since most of the participants would be eminent lawyers, scholars, and diplomats from the Eastern seaboard.[73]

Root strongly hoped that American membership in the PCIJ would help to promote world peace. He believed that the court represented 'the highest point yet reached by agreement of the nations in affording the same substitute for war by judicial decision of international cases that has been so effective in doing away with private war among individuals'.[74] Root looked forward 'to the time when the rules so formulated and accepted as universal law, will declare all wars of aggression to be criminal violations of the law of nations'.[75]

After Harding's death on 2 August 1923, President Calvin Coolidge supported ratification with Hughes' reservations, but the Senate did not begin debate until 17 December 1925. After defeating a filibuster by opponents of the League, the Senate on 27 January 1926 consented to ratification of the treaty, subject to reservations, by a vote of 76 to 17. One of the reservations, however, was

68 ibid 410.
69 ibid 416–17.
70 ibid 419–20.
71 ibid 421, 425–26.
72 ibid 426.
73 Jessup (n 1) vol II, 430.
74 Root (n 22) 424–25.
75 ibid 425.

unacceptable to members of the PCIJ and proved fatal to American membership. That reservation would have barred the court from issuing advisory opinions to the League's Council and Assembly, as its charter allowed, without American consent when an opinion affected what the United States regarded as an American interest. Advocates of the reservation feared that such opinions might adversely affect American interests by addressing such issues as immigration and the Monroe Doctrine, and they pointed out that the United States could not oppose requests for such opinions insofar as it was not a member of the League.[76] Jessup has explained that this was a 'tempest in a teapot' because the reservations would not be binding, and that the United States would have indeed been in a better position to oppose advisory opinions if it were a member of the court.[77] Opponents of advisory opinions feared, however, that they could embarrass the United States.[78] Coolidge, after consulting Root, had supported a reservation that would allow the United States to ignore advisory opinions, but the Senate added the stronger reservation to permit the United States to prohibit proceedings altogether, which Root did not oppose.[79] Members of the League and the PCIJ naturally resented such modification of part of the court's charter and feared the cumbersome American political processes would unduly delay determinations of American consent.[80] A special conference in Geneva rejected it in September 1926. In November 1926, Coolidge refused to support any modification of the reservations.

The prospects for American membership in the court were revived in November 1928 when Herbert Hoover, an ardent and longtime advocate, was elected president. A month later, prospects improved when the League announced the formation of a committee to revise the court's 1920 charter. Root accepted the League's invitation to serve as delegate to the committee, which convened in Geneva in March 1929. Before leaving for Europe, Root travelled to Washington to meet with Secretary of State Frank B. Kellogg and influential senators, including William E. Borah of Idaho, who seemed likely to continue to oppose American membership.[81] During the conference, Root helped to formulate a compromise on advisory opinions, proposing that the United States be permitted to register its objection to an opinion that affected American interests. If a majority of the members of the court proceeded with the opinion, the United States could resign from the Court.[82] Although the League quickly accepted the compromise, the Senate delayed final action for nearly six years before once again voting to reject American membership in the League on 29 January 1935. The 52 to 36 vote in favour of membership fell seven short of the requisite two-thirds majority.

76 Leopold (n 2) 163.
77 Jessup (n 1) vol II, 432.
78 Leopold (n 2) 163.
79 ibid 163–64.
80 Jessup (n 1) vol II, 433.
81 ibid 435.
82 Leopold (n 2) 166.

Despite his advanced age, Root laboured in support of American membership throughout the six years between the 1929 Conference and the final vote, which was delayed for so long because the Senate and Presidents Hoover and Franklin D. Roosevelt were preoccupied with more urgent foreign policy issues, as well as the Depression. During this time, Root corresponded with senators, and he was the sole witness at hearings before the Senate Foreign Relations Committee in February 1931. During the night before the final Senate vote, as opposition by the Hearst press and various isolationists reached a crescendo, Root – only two weeks shy of his 90th birthday – was roused from his bed to advise Roosevelt on tactics that might turn the tide.

After the final vote, Root issued a statement to the press averring that the majority of the senators represented 'with the President the sober judgment and the sincere conviction of the American people who hate war and wish their country to do its share toward promoting peace with justice in the world', and he expressed a firm conviction that the United States eventually would become a member of the court.[83]

One study has concluded that Root contributed to the defeat to the extent that he underestimated American opposition during the Geneva Conference since he 'regarded American fears over advisory opinions as baseless' and therefore did not work to achieve a compromise that responded more fully to the Senate's objections.[84] This scholar has concluded, however, that Root's optimism was not unreasonable since '[t]he legendary reputation of Root, the prestige of the new Hoover administration, the enthusiasm generated by the Kellogg Pact [to outlaw war], and the tranquil nature of the world situation encouraged a belief that the compromise would be accepted'.[85]

In addition to his protracted efforts to promote American membership in the PCIJ, Root in many other ways maintained a high public profile during the 1920s.

After Republicans regained the presidency following the election of Harding in 1920, Taft and other prominent Republicans urged Harding to have Root return as Secretary of State. Root's appointment encountered opposition among 'irreconcilable' Republicans who had opposed American membership in the League of Nations, and there also was concern that Root, now 76, was too old.

In 1921, Root became one of four American delegates to the Conference on the Limitations of Armament, which was held in Washington from November 1921 to February 1922. The Conference established ratios of tonnage for ships maintained by the United States, the United Kingdom, Japan, Italy, and France; barred expansion of American, British, and Japanese naval bases in the Pacific; and included an agreement among the United States, Japan, and seven European nations to respect China's territorial integrity.

83 Jessup (n 1) vol II, 444.
84 Leopold (n 2) 166.
85 ibid.

Root also was instrumental in the creation of the American Law Institute (ALI), an organization of prominent judges, legal scholars, and lawyers who since 1923 have tried to systematize and improve the common law by formulating a series of model laws known as 'Restatements', which often have influenced judges and legislators. Root chaired the committee of the Association of American Law Schools that formed the ALI, and he helped to persuade the Carnegie Corporation to finance it. He turned down the presidency on account of age but served until the end of his life as honorary president and member of the executive committee.[86] Root's role in encouraging greater systemization of American law complemented his long-term efforts to promote codification of international law.

Root died of pneumonia at his home near Clinton on 7 February 1937, one week before his 92nd birthday.

Few such prominent Americans of the early twentieth century are so little remembered today, perhaps because so many of Root's contributions to public policy and international cooperation were made in the shadows of presidents and other more visible public figures. He remains, however, a key figure in the transformation of the United States into a major force in world affairs and in the creation of international political and judicial institutions.

First and foremost a lawyer, Root viewed most public issues from a lawyer's perspective. Although erudite, he was never an intellectual, and his practical and non-ideological approach to the formation of international courts may have reflected his origins as a lawyer even though Root's legal practice rarely touched on issues of international law and nothing in his many years at the bar could have foretold his equally long career in international affairs. Throughout his public career, however, Root made careful use of the technical skills he acquired during his 33-year career as an attorney. The extensive negotiating experience he received as a lawyer was particularly valuable during his public career, whether in brokering agreements for the government of the nation's new colonies; arranging treaties with foreign nations; trying to convince the Senate to consent to treaties; or mediating among the competing interests of highly diverse and far-flung nations in helping to forge rules for the PCA and the PCIJ.

Root's lawyer-like career as a statesman may be one of the reasons he is not better remembered, for the craftsmanship of the law does not tend to engage the public imagination. Root's place in history also might suffer from the ill-repute of the colonialism he fostered, particularly the brutal repression of the revolt in the Philippines, even though he improved social and economic conditions in American colonies and helped to prepare Cuba and the Philippines for self-government. Root also may be little remembered because the PCIJ no longer exists, the work of its successor is not well known outside international legal circles, and he failed in his long quest to secure American membership in the PCIJ.

In promoting international cooperation, Root consistently urged incrementalism and pragmatism. One of his favourite aphorisms was 'leg over leg, the dog went to Dover'. Root observed that '[a]ll the processes of civilization are slow.

86 Jessup (n 1) vol II, 470–72.

All advances shock somebody, and an attempt to go too far, too fast, almost always ends in failure.'[87] As Root remarked to the organizational meeting of the ALI, '[i]nstitutions which try to do everything do nothing'.[88] In explaining why he supported the formation of PCIJ even though its charter failed to provide for the compulsory jurisdiction he had advocated, Root declared that '[i]f you insist upon all or nothing at the outset, you fail'.[89] Root keenly appreciated the fragility of international accords and organizations, conscious of their dependence upon the political will of the nations that created them. As he observed, '[o]ne should always remember that the only international agreement that is worth anything is a real agreement; that opinion and feeling cannot be changed by force; that such change is an internal process that naturally requires time.'[90] Root also was a successful diplomat because he recognized the personal and emotional factors in diplomacy, once observing that '[m]ore fights come from insult than from injury'.[91]

Although Root was somewhat of a visionary in foreign affairs, his political views were fundamentally conservative, as his record as a senator demonstrates. Even though Root was an avowed Hamiltonian who favoured federal measures to promote economic growth and prosperity, he cleaved to a moderate version of laissez-faire government, generally opposing state and federal economic regulatory legislation, intrusions on personal liberty, and social reforms that significantly altered the status quo. Although he believed that government should be accountable to the people and sensitive to public opinion, he generally favoured keeping governance in the hands of upper-class men such as himself. As Richard W. Leopold observed in a 1954 biography, Root

> emphasized efficient administration, balanced power with responsibility, venerated the judicial process, and sought stability in all aspects of human relations. Order was his passion, whether he was concerned with . . . the management of colonies, military command relationships, or the codification of international law.[92]

Another biographer has aptly observed that 'Root's passion for international law was motivated by an innate sense of fairness'.[93]

87 Root (n 4) 402.

88 Elihu Root, 'The Restatement of the Substantive Law: Opening Address as Chairman of the Bench and Bar Meeting to Organize the American Law Institute at Washington, February 23, 1923' in Robert Bacon and James Brown Scott (eds), *Men and Policies: Addresses by Elihu Root* (Harvard University Press 1925) 165.

89 Root (n 22) 423.

90 ibid.

91 Elihu Root, 'The Education of Democracy in Foreign Affairs: Speech in the Committee on Foreign Relations and National Defense of the National Civic Federation, Washington, January 17, 1923' in Robert Bacon and James Brown Scott (eds), *Men and Policies: Addresses by Elihu Root* (Harvard University Press 1925) 496.

92 Leopold (n 2) 9.

93 Warren Zimmerman, *First Great Triumph: How Five Americans Made Their Country a World Power* (Farrar, Straus and Giroux 2002) 488.

Root often emphasized that his passion for adjudication of international disputes arose from his abhorrence of war. Although Root understood that the PCIJ and other international tribunals and assemblies would not eliminate war, he frequently expressed hope that such organizations would help lay the foundations for international cooperation that might prevent at least some wars in his own day and eradicate most or all wars at some future time. Root, however, forfeited the best opportunity of his life to help prevent war when he supported American entry into the First World War. It is difficult to explain why a man who otherwise worked so diligently for peace failed to try to preclude American military involvement in a war that many other prominent Americans, along with masses of ordinary citizens, regarded as wholly unnecessary and ardently and publicly opposed. Although Root probably could not have persuaded Congress and Wilson to keep the United States out of the war, his voice could have been particularly influential because of his towering experience and prestige in matters of foreign policy, and because he would have been the only major figure in the Eastern Establishment to oppose the war.

Root's confidence in the ability of courts to promote justice and help to resolve underlying political conflicts reflected his dedication to the rule of law and his veneration for the American judicial system and his strong belief in judicial review. Root was an outspoken critic of various proposals to curtail the US Supreme Court's power of judicial review that progressives and trade unions advocated in the wake of state and federal court decisions nullifying social and economic regulatory legislation, and he staunchly opposed efforts to politicize the courts. It is ironic that he died two days after Franklin D. Roosevelt announced his so-called Court packing plan.

6 Forgetting Albert Geouffre de Lapradelle (1871–1955) and ignorance as remembering

Toni Selkälä

1. Introduction

'A die is cast!', extols Albert Geouffre de Lapradelle as he outlines the atrocity of German submarine warfare against neutral commercial vessels in an opinion piece in the *New York Times*.[1] During the international career of Lapradelle, the Rubicon of international law would be crossed countless times more, as the edifice of classical international order he had been educated on eroded and disappeared. For the first decades of the twentieth century, Lapradelle was writing, teaching, and organizing the new international order that would succumb to the flames of yet another war. For an internationalist whose contemporaries saw him as one of the leading voices of international law, it would be easy at present not to know the work and influence of Albert Geouffre de Lapradelle;[2] his voluminous writings are seldom quoted, his influence rarely mentioned.[3] As such, his is a perfect figure to reflect not only the fate of the interwar internationalists, but the way the profession creates its past in equal measures through amnesia as it does it through reverence.

There are obvious caveats in approaching Lapradelle as an ignored or forgotten figure. There is no subaltern voice to be unearthed from hearing and reading Lapradelle. He is a liberal internationalist through-and-through with all its inherent inconsistencies: a stern supporter of small European states to stand as

1 Albert Geouffre de Lapradelle, 'Germany's Psychological Blockade' *New York Times* (New York, 10 February 1915).

2 Charles Rousseau, 'Albert de Geouffre de la Pradelle' (1955) 68 Bulletin de la société de legislation comparée 383.

3 By far the most recurrent reference in contemporary scholarship to Lapradelle is his introduction to Vattel's *Le droit des gens*. See, 'Introduction' in Emer de Vattel, *Le droit des gens* (Carnagie Institute 1916). Otherwise, he appears as a 'canonical' reference to some of the ideas he is considered to be among the first to have presented, such as, idea of a common heritage for resources (see, 'Le droit de l'état sur la mer territoriale' (1898) 5 Revue générale de droit international public 264; see this contribution being referred, among others, Antônio Augusto Cançado Trindade, *International Law for Humankind* (Brill 2013) ch XIII and Virgiliu Pop, *Who Owns the Moon?* (Springer 2009)), his contribution to drafting of the crime of aggression (see infra), and, as a name in committee responsible from formulation of PCIJ in general or a doctrine of sources in particular.

DOI: 10.4324/9781003020882-7

equal members among the family of nations,[4] while supporting colonialism and expecting Latin American countries 'to take a modest attitude' rather than expect equality;[5] an international lawyer calling for a respect of historical legal developments and one reading international law from a spate of decisions by a handful of European courts.[6] Thus, recentring our attention to Lapradelle is unlikely to change much in the larger frame. His is the gently civilizing international law, one wedded to a bourgeois liberalism with all its antinomies. And yet, reading through his oeuvre provides ample evidence from the lost possibilities, from the *longue durée* of arguments seen as novel or rapturous at present – a perfect illustration from contingency of international law.[7]

The chapter is divided into three parts. In the first part, I provide a short summary of Lapradelle's life and work in a fashion that would appear immediately recognizable from numerous other stories of international lawyers of yore. It is not a story of Albert Geouffre de Lapradelle as a human and a person, it is a story of him as it appears in his scholarly and public writings. Thus, there are no attempts to suggest that I would trace mentalities, ideologies, or anything of the like of Lapradelle. How he might have felt writing his texts, how he might have seen the world outside his scholarly position would provide important insights from his comfort or discomfort towards the masks of law he chose to endorse, yet those questions will not be addressed in the following. The second part, however provides a summary of Lapradelle's enounters at the League of Nations. Yet, that discussion is only to frame Lapradelle in the context of this volume in a way that legacy within the formation of international law is seen in some intellectual way. In the third part, I look at his work through the lens of more recent scholarship that has made claims on ruptures, changes, and discontinuities in areas of law Lapradelle contributed to. I look especially at areas where such ruptures turn into more modest changes when seen through the interwar developments Lapradelle recorded in such detail. In conclusion, I will bring these three parts together to reflect briefly how international law's selective and structural ignorance of its past affects its present.

2. Albert Geouffre de Lapradelle, a lawyer

Albert Geouffre de Lapradelle (1871–1955) was a French international lawyer. Born in a commune of Tulle in central France, he conducted his legal studies in

4 Louis Clerc, 'A Feeling for Justice: French Reactions to the "Finnish Cause" between 1890 and 1917' (2007) 38 Journal of Baltic Studies 235.

5 Albert Geouffre de Lapradelle and Ellery C Stowell, 'Latin America at the Hague Conference' (1907–1908) 17 Yale Law Journal 270, 277.

6 See e.g., Albert Geouffre de Lapradelle, *Nationalité d'origine* (A. Giard & E. Brière 1893) for employment of a 'historical' method, for Lapradelle's Eurocentrism, see Martti Koskenniemi, *Histories of International Law: Dealing with Eurocentrism* (Universiteit Utrecht 2011) 11.

7 Recent years has seen a revival of research on contingency of international law. See e.g., Susan Marks, 'False Contingency' (2009) 62 Current Legal Problems 1; Ingo Venzke and Kevin Jon Heller (eds), *Contingency in International Law: On the Possibility of Different Legal Histories* (OUP 2021).

Paris. During his studies, he frequented lectures of Louis Renault – the chair of international law in Paris – whose mentorship and guidance influenced his future career.[8] Together with other disciplines of Renault's positive international law, Lapradelle was a central figure in French international legal scholarship during the interwar years.[9] Lapradelle defended his thesis on laws of nationality in 1893. It contains many elements of Lapradelle's later work, while being markedly a product of an era with its steadfast belief in Comtean positivism and emergent sociology at large. In the published version of his dissertation, he tells the reader that he has given up on strict chronological exposition of laws, and instead,

> *nous avons fait effort pour suivre les principes dans leur histoire, comme on suit, dans le leur, soit un people, soit un homme. Les différentes legislations, les discussions et les difficultés qu'elles provoquent, dans leur application, tant en doctrine qu'en jurisprudence, se déroulent indirectement dans le tracé des principes.*[10]

A self-proclaimed reason for Lapradelle's choice of method lies in its seductive scientificity. For Lapradelle, law was an evolving network of norms, principles, and treaties that paved a way for progress – a belief he held till the end of his career.

But there is more in Lapradelle's method than meets the eye. If others of the 'sociological' French school were anti-formalist in their leanings, Lapradelle threads his argument through a meticulous analysis of law.[11] If his illustrious contemporaries and fellow protégées of Renault, Nicolas Politis and Alejandro Alvarez, were anti-formalists in search of a sociological explanation to transgress the chains of legal form, Lapradelle was reading international law's historical tapestry with a much more conservative intent: there is progress in international law, but it is not *dehors* international law.[12] Rather, progress is weaved in the very fabric of law through innumerable threads of more or less ancient origin. Thus, for

8 For a contemporary account of his importance, see James Brown Scott, 'In Memoriam: Louis Renault' (1918) 12/13 Proceedings of the American Society of International Law at the Meeting of Its Executive Council 35.

9 Martti Koskenniemi, *The Gentle Civilizer of Nations: The Rise and Fall of International Law 1870–1960* (CUP 2002) 266–412.

10 [I have made every effort to follow these principles as I would have followed people or men in their respective history. The acts of legislation, discussions, and difficulties caused by their application, in doctrine as in case law, can be indirectly found in the outline of these principles.] Lapradelle (n 6) vii.

11 There are markedly few definitions of this school of thought. It is being referred to as one in Koskenniemi (n 9) but more as a mentality than a practice. As a more precise style in conducting international legal scholarship, see Thomas Skouteris, *The Notion of Progress in International Law Discourse* (T.M.C. Asser Press 2010) 103–4 (footnote 280 and the accompanying text). For an ideological mapping of its emergence, see Robert Kolb, 'Politis and Sociological Jurisprudence of Inter-War International Law' (2012) 23 European Journal of International Law 233.

12 An intriguing argument for Nicolas Politis anti-formalism is provided in Umut Özsu, 'Politis and the Limits of Legal Form' (2012) 23 European Journal of International Law 243; for a like argument on Alvarez, see Arnulf Becker Lorca, 'Alejandro Álvarez Situated: Subaltern

transformation of nationality law from primacy of familial ties to primacy of territorial ties, and back again. The story tells of exiled English royalty barred from their status in fourteenth century as much as it looks at biopolitical aspirations of states in the eighteenth century to accept everyone even with remote connection to citizenship.[13] For Lapradelle, the progress of international law is subtle and slow; motivated by changes in society and reflective for power; but always encoded in the language of law. This does not prevent Lapradelle from perceiving universal international law as an emanation of precisely French spirit or presence of a natural law, but his chosen method from early on mandates a legal framework for this uniquely French spirit to work its ways.[14]

In 1897, soon after having defended his dissertation, Lapradelle passed *concours d'agrégation*, a formal competition to become Professor in Law at a university in France. Lapradelle became a faculty member at the university of Grenoble where he eventually started as a professor in 1902, teaching public and private international law. While acting as a professor in Grenoble, Lapradelle also taught in Paris from 1907 onwards and became in 1912 a professor in administrative law, and after Louis Renault died in 1918, a professor in international law. From his *agrégation* to the end of the First World War, Lapradelle wrote extensively on international law and acted as a jurisconsult and a legal adviser for Quai d'Orsay, the French Foreign Ministry. During this period there is also a notable drift in Lapradelle's view of international legal project: from celebratory to sombre. In a celebratory key, he writes after the second Hague Peace Conference in 1908 how, more than a legal connection is created between the nations:

> *c'est un esprit nouveau, de justice et d'humanité, qui se forme; c'est la société des Ètats qui s'organise sous la loi, de plus en plus consciente, de la solidarité des hommes et des peuples.*[15]

The more sombre tone is notable in his analysis of the criminal responsibility of the German Kaiser, Wilhelm II.[16] Where before the war Lapradelle saw spirit

---

Modernities and Modernism that Subvers' (2007) 19 Leiden Journal of International Law 879.

13 Lapradelle (n 6) passim.

14 Reference to Lapradelle's French allegiance is, for example, made by Rafael Altamira, see Advisory Committee of Jurists, *Procès-Verbaux of the Proceedings of the Committee, 16 June–24 July 1920, with Annexes* (Van Langenhuysen 1920) 145. That Lapradelle was widely seen as a representative of France rather than being present in his personal capacity as an international lawyer in the work of the Committee, see Ole Spiermann, '"Who Attempts Too Much Does Nothing Well": The 1920 Advisory Committee of Jurists and the Statute of the Permanent Court of International Justice' (2003) 73 British Year Book of International Law 187, 219.

15 [it is a new spirit of justice and humanity that has been formed; it is a society of nations that organize under law increasingly aware from the solidarity of men and of peoples.] Albert Geouffre de Lapradelle and Nicolas Politis, 'La deuxième conference de la paix: origine – convocation – organisation' (1909) 17 Revue générale de droit international public 385, 388.

16 In general from the history of crime of aggression and Kaiser's trial as a precursor, see Kirsten Sellars, *'Crimes against Peace' and International Law* (CUP 2013) ch 1.

of humanity as the most remarkable achievement of the Second Hague Peace Conference, immediately after the war he saw law and law alone as the right way to correct the atrocities perpetrated:

> *La solution que nous adoptons a d'ailleurs le mérite d'être en harmonie avec ce principe nouveau des peuples libres et honnêtes qui veulent que tout droit s'accompagne d'un devoir. Le droit moderne ne connaît plus d'autorités irresponsables, même au sommet des hiérarchies. Il fait descendre l'État de son piédestal en le soumettant à la règle du juge. . . . Chef d'État, l'Empereur allemand avait droit à toutes les prérogatives du droit international . . . Au regard du droit international, il doit avoir aussi la charge des responsabilités internationales.*[17]

In a sense, Lapradelle oscillated between morality and power, between natural law and positive law. But more than that, his writing immediately predating his work in the Advisory Committee of Jurists (ACJ) was reflective of a legalistic internationalism: the failure of pre-War international law was not that of impotency of law as a tool, but rather a sign of its missing enforcement.

During the First World War, Lapradelle worked as a visiting professor in the Columbia University in New York.[18] He was tasked to counter the German wartime propaganda by the French Foreign Ministry and continued to do so from September 1914 till the United States joined the war in 1917. Already before the visiting professorship, Lapradelle had forged close contacts with a fellow member of the *Institute du Droit*, James Brown Scott, whose connections allowed Lapradelle to present his work widely among the American international legal circles. Also, with the support of the Carnagie Foundation and the American Society of International Law, Lapradelle together with Scott held a tour in Southern American countries in 1916, which further extended his renown among the legal internationalists of the era. While in the United States, Lapradelle also published numerous articles and opinion pieces in, for example, *Scribner Magazine* and *the New York Times.*[19] In *Scribner*, he wrote from aerial warfare, in the *New York Times* from naval warfare – it was precisely as a scholar on international law of war that Lapradelle was acting during his time in Columbia.

17 [Moreover, the solution we adopt has the merit of being in harmony with this new principle of free and honest peoples, which states that every right is accompanied by a duty. Modern law no longer recognises irresponsible authorities, even at the top of the hierarchy. It brings the state down from its pedestal by subjecting it to the rule of the judge [. . .] Kaiser as head of a state enjoyed all the prerogatives of international law [. . .] Under international law, he must also have duties emanating from his international responsibilities.] Ferdinand Larnaude and Albert Geouffre de Lapradelle, 'Examen de la responsabilité pénale de l'empereur Guillaume II d'Allemange' (1919) 46 Journal du droit international 131, 150.

18 Catherine Fillon, 'La mission américaine du professeur Geouffre de La Pradelle (1914–1917)' (*Des facultés sur le front du droit*, 5 July 2018) <http://expo-grande-guerre-biu-cujas.univ-paris1.fr/la-mission-americaine-du-professeur-geouffre-de-lapradelle-1914-1917/>

19 Albert Geouffre de Lapradelle, 'Aerial Warfare and International Law' *Scribner's Magazine* (New York, July 1915) 19; Lapradelle (n 1).

As with many interwar era internationalists, the War marked a rupture in Lapradelle's interests. He inherited the position of Louis Renault both in academia as in Quai d'Orsay, but as the League of Nations materialized as an anti-formalist and anti-legalist organization,[20] Lapradelle's focus seemed to gravitate from public international law to private international law. His attention was less on the relationship of states and the grand conferences of treaty codification and more on the intricate domestic responses to international influences and vice versa. This change in focus reflects the more general focus of the French interwar international law to composite elements of a society instead of a monolithic fiction of a State.[21] Yet, Lapradelle's analysis remains grounded to the form of law irrespective of his varying central focus. Certainly, the trope of much of Lapradelle's discussion is 'progress' or 'evolution', while the telos of progress or means to recognize it remain unarticulated throughout his career. When welcoming the members of the *Institut de Droit International* to Aix-en-Provence in 1954 as the president of the Institute, Lapradelle suggests the continued relevance of the progress narrative even after the Second World War:

> *La construction juridique suppose l'institution et la norme. Elle ne peut être avancée dans le sens du progrès que par l'imagination critique, avec la double idée de procéder parallèlement à la création de l'une et au redressement de l'autre. Une telle entreprise ne peut être opérée que par la science.*[22]

Comtean posivitism that had invigorated Lapradelle when writing his doctoral dissertation, was the measure of science and the purpose of international law for him till the end of his life.

These terse bookends of Lapradelle's life hardly do much merit for him as a scholar and even less as a human. Yet, it allows to situate his oeuvre temporarily with relative neatness to years immediately before the First World War and before the Second World War. His years in Paris as a professor of international law between 1918 and 1939 are also years when he edited major French international legal publications and established and led the *Institut des Hautes Etudes Internationales.* He was an internationalist, an interwar international lawyer disappointed with the anti-legalism of the League of Nations. While a stern believer in the natural course of progress towards universal law, Lapradelle was also pragmatist to the boot that is also reflective of the choices he made in provision of his

20 See e.g., Stephen Wertheim, 'The League of Nations: A Retreat from International Law?' (2012) 7 Journal of Global History 210; Mark Mazower, *Governing the World: The History of an Idea* (Penguin 2012) ch 5.

21 In addition to the wider sociological movement, see also, for example, Oliver Diggelmann, 'Georges Scelle (1878–1961)' in Bardo Fassbender and Anne Peters (eds), *Oxford Handbook of the History of International Law* (OUP 2012).

22 [A legal entity presupposes an institution and a norm. It cannot progress without critical imagination with the twofold idea of simultaneous creation of institutions and recovery of norms. Such an enterprise can only be carried out through science.] Institut de Droit International, *Annuaire. Tome 45 1954*, vol II (Schmidt Periodicals 2001) 39.

legal services. He wanted no restrictions to his freedom to counsel states in their legal matters, and therefore withdraw from the service of Quai d'Orsay, but as his grandson reminds, he was equally much motivated by the money and status those services brought to him – making his service as a jurisconsult for the Prince of Monaco during the Second World War all the more characteristic choice of Lapradelle the jurist.[23]

3. Albert in the wonderland: Lapradelle and the early years of the League

In the last year of the First World War, Lapradelle returned to France from his prolonged exchange in the United States. In many ways, he returned to a world sundered that had to be made anew. For Lapradelle, as for many international lawyers of the era, the only means to quell the fire was to rely on law. Law was a precise instrument, yet capable of evolution in the hands of skilled gubernators guided by an 'esprit de corps' formed between professional judges as Lapradelle formulated it in his final report for the ACJ.[24] Lapradelle and other eminent jurisconsults fell through a rabbit hole into a small pocket inside the League where legalism was triumphant and, like for Humpty Dumpty, words meant what the internationalists chose them to mean – neither more nor less. Peace, justice, and cooperation were for this brief moment crystal clear. International society, like all societies, ought to be built on justice, which can 'take account only of a rule defined and fixed by law'.[25] And, as Lapradelle had written in 1919 together with Ferdinand Larnaud, Dean of Faculty of Law in Paris, justice ought to be served to everyone, irrespective how potent they might have been.

Charting Lapradelle's work in the early years of the League as part of his greater oeuvre appears at first relatively painless. He had embraced fully the pacifist message of international law prominently supported by, for example, the Carnegie Foundation.[26] He was part of a transnational elite that was actively nourished both in France as well as elsewhere, granting him a status of an expert in all matters international while commanding connections all over the world.[27] And he had a lifelong interest on tribunals of a different kind. Many of these themes are echoed in comments and reports Lapradelle produced in the ACJ. A case in point is his summary of the debates on election of judges to the court, which seems to lead both to universalism and particularism. After all, why does a nationality

23 Dzovinar Kévonian, Philippe Rygiel, and Géraud de Geouffre de La Pradelle, 'Entretien avec Géraud de Geouffre de La Pradelle' (2015) 7 Monde(s) 155.

24 Procès-Verbaux (n 14) 695.

25 ibid 696.

26 Impact of Carnegie Foundation for the development of international law, especially in the United States, see e.g., Benjamin Coates, *Legalist Empire* (OUP 2016).

27 In France, Lapradelle was part of le Comité national d'études sociales et politiques financially supported by a French banker Albert Kahn, see Florance Prévost-Grégoire, 'Pacifisme et universalisme: le cas du Comité national d'études sociales et politiques (1916–1931)' (2018) 129–30 Matériaux pour l'histoire de notre temps 42.

of a judge matter if international law is universal?[28] The answer, according to Lapradelle's summary, rests in the differences in legal education, not of legal ideas themselves. This allowed for Lapradelle to both support the grand projects of early twentieth-century international law and his French sociological and individual-oriented understanding of international law. The progress of international law is an iterative process and having a representation of 'main forms of civilisation'[29] on the bench would allow different forms of reasoning around the universal flourish, even if the universality itself would remain uncontested. Lapradelle employed a similar narrative of progress in his collection of arbitral cases for much the same reasons: legal systems were on a march to perfection. Learning from the constitution of a successful tribunal was a natural process, much like the PCIJ would naturally evolve its jurisprudence by bringing international in contact with distinct national traits: 'The intention is to try and ensure that, no matter what points of national law may be involved in an international suit, all shall be equally comprehended.'[30]

This demand for mutual comprehension leads to the most lasting legacy of the work of the ACJ – the sources doctrine – and the most remarkable victory of the Continental lawyers, Lapradelle among them, over their Anglo-American counterparts. As illustrated in Lapradelle's report and his later oeuvre on the role of private international law in the development of public international law, Lapradelle saw unity in multiplicity. There was a shared, predefined trajectory of progress for law that aligned with the idea of international justice (and equity). The role of general principles of international law thus was to ensure the completeness of woefully inadequate positive international law. To avoid a situation where the Court would be forced to declare its incapacity to decide (*non liquet*), it had to have at its disposal a recourse to sources beyond positive and customary law, namely, the general principles of international law.[31] Opposing this idea were Elihu Root and Walter Phillimore. According to Root, international community was not ready to embrace as of yet a court that would have an expansive competence – what Root called a right to legislate granted to a Court. For Root, then, when tasked to deliberate on a principle of justice, the Court ought to either 'declare itself incompetent' or 'limit itself to making a recommendation instead of pronouncing sentence'.[32] In brief, Lapradelle promoted an idea of completeness of international law – through general principles if need be – while Root and Phillimore saw admittance of *non liquet* as the only possibility to prevent the Court from become a legislator.

The conviction of Lapradelle on the matter of general principles was adamant. He criticized Root and the United States from continentalism rather than an open embrace of 'world' and in Phillimore's formulations he saw a defence of

28 Lapradelle nominates unity and universality as guiding principles in the establishment of the PCIJ. See, Procès-Verbaux (n 14) 710.

29 League of Nations, *Statute of the Permanent Court of International Justice* (16 December 1920) art. 9.

30 Procès-Verbaux (n 14) 710.

31 ibid 312ff.

32 ibid 309–10.

Thrasymachus' idea of justice where the powerful make the law.[33] In hindsight, it is easy to see that all parties of the debate were right; the Italian ACJ member, Arturo Ricci Busatti's claim that *non liquet* would not emerge as where there is no precise stipulation of law states remain at liberty to act without restrictions (i.e., *Lotus* principle),[34] Root and Phillimore that states would be reluctant to subject themselves to jurisdiction of a Court with too wide competence, as well as Lapradelle's insistence that there is no possible way to understand custom or general principles without jurisprudence and teachings of scholars. In light of the later works of Lapradelle, the debate over the nature of general principles seems, however, decisive. It is possible to understand all subsequent work of Lapradelle as an attempt to document public international law in 'non-traditional' setting. His editorship of the decisions of the mixed arbitral tribunals of the interwar era as well as his attentive focus on the disappearing distinction between public and private international law seem all to point towards the same conclusion: here, documented, lies the progress of international law, here is the fertile soil from whence to grow general principles of international law.

4. Forgotten or simply ignored? Lapradelle's lost legacy

Irrespective of the way Albert de Geouffre de Lapradelle's merits as an international lawyer are dissected, they are impressive. A long-standing member, vice-president, and eventual president of the *Institut de Droit International*, an editor-in-chief for several leading academic publications in the field in France, a founder of a leading educational institute of international law in the interwar period, a jurisconsult for numerous states, representative before the Permanent Court of International Justice (PCIJ), member in the committee responsible from setting up said court, an author first suggesting the crime of aggression in international law, and a central chronicler of the early arbitral practice to name but some of his numerous achievements. Yet, there are remarkably few references to him in contemporary scholarship, even in literature charting the interwar era international law. While his contemporaries in France – not to mention those closer to Anglo-American international legal academia – Nicolas Politis, Alejandro Alvarez, and Georges Scelle have all been subject to rather persistent attention, Lapradelle has been quietly forgotten, or maybe more accurately, ignored.

I want in the following briefly explore whether this ignorance is a bliss or a detriment to our understanding of international law at present. Following Robert Proctor, I maintain that there are many ways to conceptualize ignorance. On most instances ignorance or obliviousness is not a natural state of affairs, but something actively construed.

> Ignorance can be the flipside of memory, what we don't know because we have forgotten, parts of which can be restored by historical inquiries

33 ibid 314 and 320.
34 S.S. Lotus (France v. Turkey), 1927 PCIJ Ser A, No. 10.

> but most of which is forever lost. (And we often cannot say which.) Ignorance can be made or unmade, and [scholarship] can be complicit in either process.[35]

The reasons for ignorance in Lapradelle's case are beyond the reach of this chapter, but I will briefly first look at ways it materializes at present before I turn my attention to a specific instance of arbitration on concession contracts during the 1950s. The way those arbitral decisions are at present construed in the literature as a marked rupture with the past, chiefly animated by a deeply felt distrust to the governing capacity of recently decolonized countries, might be in part because the work of Lapradelle and others charting the arbitration and private international law during the interwar years has been forgotten or ignored. Reading Lapradelle will not eradicate racist tropes and centre subjecting periphery to its distorted gaze, but it might highlight the mundaneness of those arbitral awards. Rather than gateways to newly emerged transnational law, those decisions would in the light of Lapradelle's oeuvre appear as *fait accompli* already decades earlier within the European context.

In the classification of ignorance provided by Proctor, the one over work of Lapradelle would fall on one that perceives ignorance as a lost realm or a selective choice. He suggests that 'ignorance, like knowledge, has a political geography . . ., has a face, a house, and a price: it is encouraged here and discouraged there'.[36] Part of such selectivity or political geography of ignorance is the fact underlined also by Proctor that our attention comes with a direction, 'the decision to focus on *this* is therefore invariably a choice to ignore *that*'.[37] Yet, as I suggest below, neither the era nor the topics explored by Lapradelle have been out of focus. There is a body of scholarship on virtually all his contemporaries and a sustained interest on many of the areas of law he contributed to.[38] Thus, the ignorance seems not solely a product of a direction of a gaze but by who is looking and on whose behest. There seems to have been more interest in figures arriving from periphery to centre than looking at the figures restive at the epicentre of power. Maybe also the politics of academic reproduction and the triumph of English as scholarly lingua franca has had a natural effect on persons focused: there is interest in French interwar internationalists that has also been receptive

35 Robert N Proctor, 'Agnotology: A Missing Term to Describe the Cultural Production of Ignorance (and Its Study)' in Robert N Proctor and Londa Schiebinger (eds), *Agnotology: The Making and Unmaking of Ignorance* (SUP 2008) 3.

36 ibid 6.

37 ibid 7.

38 Georges Scelle was a subject of a special issue in the European Journal of International Law's first volume in 1990, see (1990) 1 European Journal of International Law 193–249; Alejandro Alvarez was a subject of a special issue in Leiden Journal of International Law's Periphery Series, see (2007) 19 Leiden Journal of International Law 875ff.; and, finally, Nicolas Politis was a subject of a special issue in European Journal of International Law in 2012, see (2012) 23 European Journal of International Law 215ff.

to the impact Lapradelle has had, but it is chiefly produced in French in French publications.[39]

As such, it is easy to align with the more programmatic calls of Proctor's project on ignorance, namely

> [c]rucial also is: ignorance for whom? and against whom? Ignorance has a history and is always unevenly distributed, the geography of ignorance has mountains and valleys. Who is ignorant and why, and to what extent? How can we develop better agnometric indicators? What keeps ignorance in one place, while it evaporates in some other? And which among our myriad ignorances will be tolerated or combated?[40]

It is arguably of relatively little importance if we ignore a white, European man hailing from an affluent background – irrespective of his pedigree. Among the multiple ignorances of the field, this must certainly amount to a minor faux pas. My interest is then not with the cosmic wrong committed to Lapradelle, but on the ways the ignorance is construed as such construction of ignorance – whether benign or malign – can contribute to our efforts to trace the more wholesale ignorances of international law both as a trade and as a field of inquiry embodies.

The locus classicus for much of international legal history for the past two decades has been Martti Koskenniemi's *the Gentle Civilizer*, where he provides a substantive account on the works and lives of French internationalists before and during the interwar period.[41] On this account, Koskenniemi assesses the importance of Lapradelle's tutor, Louis Renault, as well as his fellow mentees Nicolas Politis and Alejandro Alvarez. He also accounts for the influence of figures of not particularly significant later following, such as, Louis le Fur.[42] Despite this, Lapradelle is chiefly missing. He appears as a co-author and co-founder of Politis and Alvarez, but also as an author through whose work Koskenniemi charts his own narrative.[43] Yet, this absence of Lapradelle from Koskenniemi's account is seemingly of relatively little concern for Koskenniemi himself. He refers to Lapradelle as a conservative sharing the same view of French sociological interpretation as most of his contemporaries, but beyond that Lapradelle appears only in footnotes, and even there without much context for his writing. A good example is Koskenniemi's account of Lapradelle's pamphlet against Marxism, published

39 Even among the French general publications, Lapradelle's role is modest at best, see e.g. Dominique Gaurier, *Histoire du droit international: De l'Antiquité à la création de l'ONU* (Presses universitaires de Rennes 2014), where Lapradelle's contribution covers two pages (535–6). I am indebted to Louis Sicking for this and other insights on Lapradelle's position in later French scholarship.

40 Proctor (n 35) 26.

41 Koskenniemi (n 9) 266–352.

42 ibid 317–27.

43 Koskenniemi uses throughout the chapter Lapradelle's *Maîtres et doctrines du droit des gens* (Éditions inter-nationales 1950) as a source for lives and deeds of French internationalists.

in 1942.[44] For Koskenniemi, this booklet is a testament of his ultimately conservative leanings, while Lapradelle's grandson sees the book as a screed against scholarly rivals who Lapradelle perceived bypassing his trustees.[45]

This latter version of the book's origin and purpose does appear more in line with the countless academic feuds Lapradelle had during his time. For example, reading his first editorial in the *Nouvelle revue de droit international privé* he found together with Paul Goulé clearly illustrates how vehemently and openly Lapradelle often disagreed with his perceived scholarly opponents.[46] Lapradelle certainly was a conservative, with whatever connotations such a moniker might carry, but the account provided by Koskenniemi might still be needlessly one-dimensional. But it is not only Koskenniemi and authors of the twenty-first century who have ignored Lapradelle. During his career, Lapradelle wrote extensively from several international legal topics yet reading international legal treatises on those topics immediately after the war well into the 1960s, Lapradelle, together with most interwar authors of international law, is entirely missing from the referred sources. This early renunciation of Lapradelle and other internationalists is likely related to the perceived failure of the international law during the interwar period.[47] In this sense, the immediate denouncement is eminently more understandable than later forgetting when other contemporaries of Lapradelle have been brought back to attention of international lawyers at large in recent decades as important precursors to the present state of international law.

In a sense, Lapradelle has been then twice forgotten. He was forgotten first in the wholesale denouncement of the internationalists by those forging the emergent, more realist international order after the Second World War. This forgetting was an active undoing of the past. The scholars who survived the purge were chiefly those whose audience were the Anglo-American international lawyers who came to define the new international order in 'realist' or 'pragmatist' terms. In a sense, Lapradelle would have fit the mould by his keen focus on compromise between different powers of international law. Yet, this willingness to compromise might appear antediluvian in a world quickly moving towards the Cold War. Also, many of his ideas, such as allowing individuals to appear before the World Court, were for long deemed utopian in a more realist or apologetic international law of the post-Second World War. And as the time went by, the

44 Albert Geouffre de Lapradelle, *Le Marxisme tentaculaire: la formation, la tactique et l'action de la diplomatie soviétique 1920–1940* (Issoudun 1942).

45 Koskenniemi (n 9), Kévonian et al. (n 23).

46 Albert Geouffre de Lapradelle, 'Tout un passé' (1934) 1 Nouvelle revue de droit international privé 5. For an intriguing account on Nouvelle revue de droit international privé, see Silvia Falconieri, 'Le refus d'un "nouvel ordre" géopolitique bâti sur la "race"' (2012) 149 Relations Internationales 89.

47 This renunciation of the interwar project in one of its most lasting modes appeared already before the Second World War in EH Carr, *The Twenty Years' Crisis, 1919–1939* (Macmillan 1939). For an influential international law take on the abandonment of the interwar project and its repetition in subsequent international institutions, David Kennedy, 'The Move to Institutions' (1987) 8 Cardozo Law Review 841.

body of international legal literature kept on growing, making it altogether easier to not refer to authors of the interwar period when charting new developments of international law, such as the raise of the non-aligned states and the North/South and the East/West confrontations.

The second forgetting is therefore of a more interesting nature. It is almost as if telling a story of French internationalists without referring to Lapradelle is a form of art. On special issues focusing on the works of Politis and Alvarez, Lapradelle appears only as a name annexed to their work without a figure of his own; a passive actor who contributed little to the intellectual projects of his collaborators.[48] In appraisal of other prominent figures of the same generation of internationalists, such as Georges Scelle, he appears even less.[49] And while recent years have seen an acute interest on histories of international law, and some of those histories place work of Lapradelle at the centrefold, none of them devote much attention to the person or influence of Lapradelle more in general. In his work on Kaiser's trial, William Schabas clearly attributes the origin of the idea of criminalization of crime of aggression to Lapradelle, yet he is, throughout the book, only a French professor of not particular interest.[50] Schabas spends more time telling of the stolen ashtray of Kaiser and the fate of the man who did it than on the person he identifies as the father of the idea.[51] Also, the recent revival of interwar mixed arbitral tribunals and individual claims therein has largely forgotten Lapradelle despite his centrality in the contemporary debate by French, German, and Anglo-American authors.

I will look somewhat more closely to this latter forgetting and its consequences for the present scholarship. I do not intend to suggest that Lapradelle would have been the only one making the claims at the time or that he would have single-handedly defined the field and its expertise, but his was a voice of notable authority then and linking his opinions presented at the time would illuminate some of

48 See (n 26) for some of the recent volumes dedicated to the works of Alvarez and Politis. In contrast, see e.g., an obituary of Nicolas Politis by Hans Wehberg, 'Nic. Politis als Völkerrechtsgelehrter' (1942) 42 Die Friendens-Warte 96. There Wehberg on numerous occasions refers to close relationship of Politis and Lapradelle and their mutual influence on one another as well as the centrality of Lapradelle's work in publishing the collection of arbitral awards – work deemed by Wehberg as one with '[d]ie grösste Bedeutung für die Völkerrechtwissenschaft' (p. 98) of all work of Politis.

49 See e.g., Diggelmann (n 21); 1 European Journal of International Law 193ff.

50 William Schabas, *The Trial of the Kaiser* (OUP 2018). In page 36, Schabas suggests the project was initiated by Larnaud and Lapradelle. He writes, '[t]he likelihood, then, is that the trial of Kaiser Wilhelm was really a French initiative, developed by French academics and embraced by Clemenceau, who then persuaded Curzon during their tête-à-tête following armistice.'

51 The story of an attempted kidnapping of the Kaiser by a group of Americans is in, ibid ch 7. The story about ashtray start at page 109 and runs better part of the subsequent six pages, concluding with the following: 'MacPhail never returned the stolen ashtray, which adorned the study of his Bel Air, Maryland home for many years. He had a very public career as part owner and general manager of several major league baseball teams, including the Cincinnati Reds and the Brooklyn Dodgers' (p 115).

the contingent choices made, both in state-to-state judicial processes as well as in ad hoc arbitrations of a different sort. To set the scene, I will re-tell the story of arbitration of state concession agreements and emergence of transnational law as it appears in Anthony Anghie's seminal *Imperialism, Sovereignty and the Making of International Law*.[52] There, as is familiar, Anghie suggests through a close reading of arbitral awards in a handful of cases, most notably in that of *Abu Dhabi*,[53] that these cases presented a novel way for international law to respond to the numerical majority of the new states in the international community by bypassing the established doctrine of national law of a sovereign state being the one applied in conflicts between private parties and sovereign states.

The doctrine of domestic law being decisive when applying international law on contracts concluded between a private party and a state was, as Anghie reminds, established in *Serbian Loans* decision of the Permanent Court of International Justice.[54] At the time of *Serbian Loans* decision, the problem was already an established one in international law. After all, states had long sought loans from private actors to fund their wars, construction projects, and for other purposes.[55] There was already an established doctrine in the beginning of the twentieth century of such loans being 'quasi-international' in their character with a full recognition of the inherent problems associated with state's sovereign capacity to retroactively alter the legislation and, therewith, the terms of the loan contract with private parties. Yet, in the PCIJ's decision on *Serbian Loans*, these concerns were pushed aside, and an act of some clarity was established: lacking any specific provisions contrary, the sovereign party's domestic laws were the laws applicable to any conflicts arising from their execution. This, according to Anghie, was the prevalent understanding of international law when the *Abu Dhabi* concession case was brought before an arbitrator to decide the fate of oil drilling rights in the seabed adjacent to Abu Dhabi.

In the end, the initial arbitration had failed to provide an agreement between the parties, wherefore an umpire was set to the task.[56] The umpire, Cyril Asquith,

52 Anthony Anghie, *Imperialism, Sovereignty and the Making of International Law* (CUP 2005). The role of concession arbitrations is assessed in ch 4.

53 The decision is reproduced in 'In the matter of an arbitration between Petroleum Development (Trucial Coast) Ltd. and the Sheikh of Abu Dhabi' (1952) 1 International and Comparative Law Quarterly 247.

54 *Case Concerning Various Serbian Loans Issued in France* (1929), PCIJ Ser. A., No. 20.

55 Ripples from these debates reached even Finland. See Thorvald Becker, *Les Emprunts d'État Finlandais Au Point de Vue Juridique* (University of Helsinki 1913) and its critical examination in; Rafael Erich, 'Kirjallisuutta' (1913) 11 Lakimies 185. Rafael Erich returns to the topic in his Finnish textbook of international law, where he placates this discussion on the German tradition without providing a source. The most likely source for his coinage of Finnish words modelled after 'völkerrechtsähnlich' and 'quasi-völkerrechtlich' is Franz von Liszt's German treatise on international law and Günther Siegfried Freund's book on foreign debt from 1910, *Der Schutz der Gläubiger gegenüber auswärtigen Schuldnerstaaten, insbesondere bei auswärtigen Staatsanleihen*. See, Rafael Erich, *Kansainvälinen Oikeus* (Lainopillinen ylioppilastiedekunta 1915) 30, 74–75.

56 *Abu Dhabi Award* (n 53).

son of a former British Prime Minister and a justice with a conservative track record in the Court of Appeal and in the House of Lords, ignored the precedent of *Serbian Loans*.[57] He first refers to the existing custom, noting that '[I]f any municipal system of law were applicable, it would prima facie be that of Abu Dhabi.' But he continues immediately thereafter that 'no such law can be reasonably said to exist'.[58] The basis for this latter conclusion is that in the supposedly primitive status of law in Abu Dhabi 'it would be fanciful to suggest [. . . that] any settled body of legal principles applicable to the construction of modern commercial instruments'[59] would exist. Based on this interim conclusion of his, Asquith construes a precedent-setting international law that is not found on any domestic legislation or among any norms of international law either. Where the PCIJ in its *Lotus* decision had found states to be bound only to those norms they have precisely agreed upon, Asquith precluded the possibility of *non liquet* as a solution.[60] This, according to Anghie, paved the way for the introduction of a specific body of transnational law, whose formation was largely dictated by the North Atlantic states and corporations.

The analysis that ensues in Anghie's book is consistent and illustrative of a power of even a denounced precedent in formation of a practice. There is little to add to that analysis. My point of contention is with the rupture marked by the *Abu Dhabi* decision and later concession arbitrations from the earlier arbitration and private international law traced in the oeuvre of Lapradelle. I set my contention on two points. The first point is against Anghie's argument that there would have been a notable novelty in Asquith's decision as an umpire to set aside domestic law and favour closely the law of 'civilized states' as a shorthand for adherence to the law of the land most familiar to the umpire themselves. I point to earlier instances of arbitration where similar conclusions had been drawn as well as the wider debate on acquired rights, which is seen undergirding the decisions of the early concession arbitrations.[61] The second point is targeted to the introduction of transnational law as a new mode of law through these decisions. Seen in the light of constitutional developments and cases of the mixed arbitral tribunals of the interwar era, this conclusion as well seems to put too much accent on the rupture over continuity. The European example in the interwar years, where a single state might have been subject to several legal orders of acquired rights that led to a fusion of private and public international law, seems to carry the kernel of what later became known as transnational law decades *avant la lettre*.

57 On Cyril Asquith's life and career, see Robert Stevens, 'Asquith, Cyril, Baron Asquith of Bishopstone (1890–1954)' in *Oxford Dictionary of National Biography* (OUP 2004).

58 *Abu Dhabi Award* (n 52) 250.

59 ibid 251.

60 *S.S. Lotus* (France v. Turkey), 1927 PCIJ Ser A, No. 10.

61 See e.g., Ove Bring, *Det folkrättsliga investeringsskyddet: en studie i u-ländernas inflytande pä den internationalla sedvanerätten* (Liber förlag 1979). Bring provides an account substantiated by an extensive case analysis; he also partly builds his work on insights of Alvarez and Lapradelle.

The first argument on the relative novelty of *Abu Dhabi* arbitration is associated more widely to partial ignorance over the French tradition of international law that used to have a significant role, at least still during the interwar era. Yet, in literature on international investor-state dispute settlement, the common precursors to the *Abu Dhabi* and other concession arbitrations are two decisions passed during the interwar years: *Société Rialet*[62] and *Lena Goldfields*.[63] Of these, the former has been the subject of more academic interest long after its passing, but both effectively constitute the same rule, which has been described as an important idea to further development of international arbitration, specifically, 'the application of non-national system of law to the merits of a private law dispute, namely, "the general principles of law"'.[64] But clearly closer to Lapradelle is the first decision, *Société Rialet*, a case between a Belgian alcohol producer and the state of Ethiopia. His collaborator Nicolas Politis acted as one of the five arbitrators in the case, and, without a doubt, Lapradelle and Politis shared much in terms of their assessment of how an arbitration ought to be concluded.[65] In the *Société Rialet* case, the arbitrators find that due to lack of administrative law in Ethiopia, the applicable law must be that of French administrative law, reflective of the principles of international law. Decided in 1929, *Société Rialet* predated *Lena Goldfields* by a year and Abu Dhabi arbitration by more than two decades.

The argument of the arbitrators in *Société Rialet* very much resembles the argument Lapradelle had proposed a few years earlier in an article concerning the applicable law in territories under new sovereign rule after the conclusion of the First World War.[66] In the article, Lapradelle charts three different possibilities. First, all laws of the new sovereign become directly applicable the moment territory is transferred under its command without any need to pass new legislation to that effect. Second, that this transition to laws of the new sovereign occurs only through a specific legislative act, which declares the laws of the new sovereign applicable. And third, that only a subset of laws – most notably constitution and police powers – enter into force immediately, while the civil laws only enter into force when new, precise laws to that effect are accepted. This last option, Lapradelle suggests, is the present status of constitutional law in Europe and, as

62 *Recueil des decisions des tribunaux arbitraux mixtes tome VIII* (Recueil Sirey 1929) 742.

63 The case is annexed to Arthur Nussbaum, 'Arbitration Between the Lena Goldfields Ltd. and the Soviet Government' (1950) 36 Cornell Law Review 31, 42ff. Even though it is seldom commented as such, *Lena Goldfields* also trumps another 'established doctrine' of international law, namely the effect given to refusal of a party to participate on proceedings. In the case, Soviet Russia refuses to participate, yet the arbitral award is passed, nonetheless. This can be compared to Soviet Russia's success before the Permanent Court of Justice in the case of *Eastern Karelia* to abstain from international jurisdiction by merely refusing to appear.

64 VV Veeder, 'The Lena Goldfields Arbitration: The Historical Roots of Three Ideas' (1998) 47 International and Comparative Law Quarterly 747, 748.

65 Wehberg (n 48).

66 Albert Geouffre de Lapradelle, 'De l'influence du changement de souveraineté sur la loi territoriale' (1925) 32 Revue générale de droit international public 388.

such, reflective of a more general principle of private international law as well. Lapradelle refers to numerous court cases throughout Europe to establish his understanding of the present state of law, with main analysis focusing on a Polish case where simultaneously four different civil laws are in force concerning companies with limited liability. The acquired rights of different corporations depend on the area of Poland in which they were first established and any lacunae in law being filled by general principles of law emanating from those foundational laws of the land for which no specific act of enforcement was called for. Without much distortion, it appears non-controversial to apply these European constitutional doctrines to international law, as indicated by *Société Rialet* case; when no rules exist, apply general principles.[67] If that was the rule in Alsace and in Poland, why not in Ethiopia?

The other point I will briefly raise is the march of transnational law through the 1950s concession arbitrations. Here as well, it seems that much of what Anghie argues occurring in the aftermath of those arbitral awards had already been cemented in the views of many continental international lawyers, Lapradelle's among them. A useful point of departure is Philip Jessup's Transnational Law lecture.[68] There he points to the origin of his own thought on the matter, referring to two European authors: Alf Ross and Georges Scelle. Ross in his coursebook to international law had in 1942 coined the term interlegal law to signify a similar phenomenon as the one Jessup came up with to nominate transnational law.[69] Likewise, Scelle in his *Précis de droits des gens*, when referring to his idea of individuals being the only true subject of international law is something Jessup finds illuminating, while retaining a more moderate position where states still occupy a central role as specific corporate bodies. Comparing Jessup's project with that of Lapradelle when he charts the purpose of *Nouvelle revue de droit international privé* between public and private international law in 1934, and one is struck by the notable similarities between the two projects.[70] Both recognize the notable overlap between public and private international law,[71] and call for a 'critique' of the prevailing understanding, but unlike Jessup, Lapradelle sees no purpose to change the terms, merely to readjust the understanding of the interrelationship of public and private international law.[72]

67 Cf. however J Vanderlinden, 'Civil and Common Law Influences on the Developing Law of Ethiopia' (1966) 16 Buffalo Law Review 250, suggesting that French law might have had a more profound impact and Napoleon's Code Civil even being the default law to apply in case of a missing local legislation.

68 Philip Jessup, *Transnational Law* (Yale University Press 1956).

69 Alf Ross, *Lærebog i Folkeret. Almindelig Del* (Munksgaard 1942).

70 Albert Geouffre de Lapradelle, 'De la delimitation du Droit International Public et du Droit International Privé' (1934) 1 Nouvelle revue de droit international privé 9.

71 Jessup, though, refers to conflict of laws rather than private international law.

72 ibid 20. In some ways Lauterpacht could also be invoked in the discussion when looking at Scelles, Jessup and Lapradelle, however, in all this, I think that Lauterpacht sits in a way in the middle. He is the one who diverts the attention away from the French administrative law discussion – one that certainly animated Société Rialet – to the chiefly German debate

While it is easy to dismiss the relevance of Lapradelle for the later constitution of transnational law, his entire scholarly career during the interwar years was focused on tribunals and arbitrations that most closely resemble that of the concession arbitrations immediately after the Second World War. He edited volumes on the case law of mixed arbitral tribunals that were established after the First World War to hear cases of individuals against states, he continued to edit the collection of nineteenth and early twentieth-century inter-state arbitral awards, and he participated actively in formation of new international organizations that seemed to escape easy classification of them either under traditional international law or private international law.[73] He, if anyone, was acutely aware from the difficulties encountered by the mixed arbitral tribunals to maintain neat classifications as well as from the often complex legal questions emanating from long delay, tumultuous events, and a change of legislation.[74] Thus, his refusal to admit a neat demarcation of international inquiries depending on the subject targeted by such inquiries was motivated by the very same concerns as those that moved Jessup, and to a lesser extent Asquith and other arbitrators. In light of Lapradelle's work, there was little novel in the arbitral award Asquith provided in *Abu Dhabi*. The private and public international law had already been mixed in ways that made it difficult, if not impossible, to separate the origin of different rights to either public or private realm. Moreover, there was already an established practice to rely on general principles of law found in interwar arbitration.[75]

---

with an Anglo-American flair. The reason for the disappearance of Lapradelle is then maybe achieved partly by him, but equally much by the US authors whose French source of authority is virtually always Georges Scelle who developed much the same ideas as Lapradelle, but often couple of decades later. A proper commentary on Lauterpacht's role would require more research than I can provide, although in later work of Lauterpacht, he endorses a position close to that of Jessup and Friedmann – hailing the greatness of this particular decision (see e.g., Hersch Lauterpacht, *International Law – The Collected Papers of Hersch Lauterpacht*, vol 1 (Arranged and edited by E Lauterpacht, CUP 1970) 77–78 and 131–32. See also, FA Mann, 'Law Governing State Contracts' (1944) 21 BYIL 11; G Kaeckenbeeck 'The Protection of Vested Rights in international Law' (1936) 17 BYIL 1; Alexander Fachiri, 'Expropriation and International Law' (1925) 6 BYIL 159.

73 Apart for his seemingly life-long interest to arbitration, Lapradelle was fascinated by airplanes and regulation of air. See, e.g., *Quatrième Congrès international de legislation aérienne tenu à Monaco du 19 au 22 décembre 1921 sous la présidence de M. A. de Lapradelle* (A. Pedone 1922).

74 His role in the case concerning property rights of Hungarians in Romania is a good example of such a turbulent event, leading to Lapradelle being noted as also by the British parliamentary debate as a 'most eminent lawyer', see HL Deb 17 November 1927, vol 69, col 126. Lapradelle also provided fierce commentary in support of the Hungarians in Albert Geouffre de Lapradelle, 'De Lausanne a Genève' *Le Temps* (Paris, 5 September 1927) NP. Lapradelle's opinion is followed with a repudiation of Lapradelle's stance by Nicolas Politis.

75 The internationalization of private-public agreements has also, since mid-1950s, been the practice of the World Bank, see International Bank for Reconstruction and Development Loan Regulations, vol 4 (adopted 15 June 1956) 260 UNTS 376. These loan regulations were applicable to loans made by the Bank to borrowers other than member state, in essence to private corporations performing the project funded by the Bank. The section 7.01 on enforceability (at 396) states '[t]he rights and obligations [. . .] shall be valid and enforceable

Would our understanding of international law be drastically different if the ignorance of Lapradelle's work would have been less complete? Hardly. But what Lapradelle's fate indicates, is the constant practice of active forgetting on which international legal scholarship participates. It is consoling to note that such amnesia can lead to ignorance of even the most illustrious representatives of an era, but at the same time the reasons of this ignorance remain unclear. Was Lapradelle forgotten because his works did not resonate with later scholars? This does not seem to be the case as much of his work has had a surprising value as a precursor to many more recent legal developments. Was he forgotten for the lack of networks? This does not seem a plausible explanation either for someone with such a long-standing presence in the foremost scholarly organization of the era. Was it the language on which he wrote most of his works? This doesn't seem plausible either, as most of the authors in early UN-era refer widely to French literature – just not on Lapradelle. In the end, it would be easy to suggest that it was all because of timing, but why, then, did Nicolas Politis not suffer the same fate?

As Anthony Anghie argues, the centre defines itself in interaction with the periphery.[76] Lapradelle never occupied a peripheral position during his lifetime but gazing from the present his is a peripheral figure. That we have come to ignore Lapradelle does not mean that we have ignored the system of international law Lapradelle was centrally shaping. It simply means that we lack the means to understand those multiple contingent choices that appear self-evident when perceived in the light of Lapradelle's work. His was the work others contrasted and built theirs in interwar France and in the interwar international law more generally. The contingent choices international law came to embrace and their opposition appears in a different light when the partial ignorance over Lapradelle is lifted. And still, one needs to resist the temptation to populate the centre of international law's disciplinary narrative with more figures of international law's great male figures. As Proctor reminds, our focus is always targeted somewhere: the more we cast a light on the likes of Lapradelle, the less we are likely to find those who truly are ignored. A search for such figures is unlikely to start from the list of professors of international law at Paris, no matter how unduly ignored they might appear at present.

5. Conclusion

The creation of Permanent International Court of Justice marks the beginning of an era for international law. A transition from ad hoc arbitral tribunals to a permanent court did not flourish at first, but the dream of its drafters as a venue

in accordance with their terms notwithstanding the law of any state', and further, as all controversies are to be settled in arbitration (section 7.04, 396–400) the contracts are by their very nature subject to only rules of international law.

76 Anthony Anghie, 'Finding the Peripheries: Sovereignty and Colonialism in Nineteenth-Century International Law' (1999) 40 Harvard International Law Journal 1.

for peaceful settlement of disputes lives on in countless international tribunals established since. As with the system of the League of Nations that gave birth to the Court, also the work of international lawyers and officials instrumental for its establishment and operation has been the subject of new-found interest in recent years. This interest has provided a more nuanced image of the League of Nations and international lawyers of the interwar era. Rather than sounding the death knell for the utopian aspirations of its progenitors, the international law of the interwar era paved the way for much international law to come, and, maybe more importantly, trained a generation of administrators that would lead the restructuring of world order after the Second World War.

It is in this light of revitalization of the League of Nations, and the interwar era of international law more in general, that I have sought to understand the seeming ignorance of Albert Geouffre de Lapradelle. Why and how we came to forget his work remain unanswered, but our collective amnesia on the work of Lapradelle tells a story from the particular geography of ignorance in international law. That some life projects are revered and reproduced in international law reveals, obviously, much from projects of those participating in their reproduction; it is easier to ignore a narrative than account for its complex relationship with the present. Lapradelle has an uneasy position in his own time and an even more complicated position for the present for none of the overarching narratives of the interwar era seem to capture his eclectic approach. The fact that many of the life projects of Lapradelle were considered marginal at best for international law after the Second World War and almost till the end of the twentieth century is a testament of the shifting priorities of scholars of international law, not necessarily of shifting priorities of international law as such. This is most notable in the development of mixed arbitral tribunals and concession arbitrations to the present-day investor-state dispute settlement, and a simultaneous move from bifurcated public/private international law to transnational and ultimately to global law. These fields would merit exploring the legacy of Lapradelle more closely.

At the same time, it might be that it is precisely the success of Lapradelle as an international lawyer that he is nowhere to be seen despite the fact that much of the following generation of international lawyers learned from early state arbitration through his works.[77] His commentary and interpretation were so steadily in the mainstream of international law that his figure could disappear from the scene; to embrace his interpretation appeared as a neutral act of merely following positive law rather than following the thoughts and ideas of Lapradelle. Seen in this light, the later borrowing of his ideas as 'natural' could signal the triumph of Lapradelle the jurist over Lapradelle the ego.

But as with all acts of illumination, there is also a shadow being cast. I have been reluctant to highlight the importance of our collective forgetting of the work of Lapradelle. There are many notable stories from the margins that would certainly

77 I would like to thank professor Wouter Werner for pushing me to think of Lapradelle from this angle.

be more deserving of our attention; maybe it is due to the deeply felt burden of the field's Eurocentrism that Nicolas Politis and Alejandro Alvarez have appeared more enlightened choices of focus for the French interwar period. But such token pluralism does little service to our collective inquiry. There have likely been female as well as non-European authors, authors writing in non-European languages or writing in small European languages whose impact would merit much more attention. But their ignorance is too complete, too original for them to be found from the membership list of prestigious committees and the erudite scholarly organizations. It is, I feel, this actively produced ignorance of the past we ought to look at, following the tentative footsteps set by Immi Tallgren in reflecting the absence of women from the vaunted halls of international law.[78] As the example of Albert Geouffre de Lapradelle indicates, ignorance can befall even on the most cherished experts of an era, but as their ignorance is hardly original it remains easy to reintroduce these forgotten figures. Revealing their presence will only reintroduce a new flavour to our favourite dessert. Those silenced to the abyss of ignorance originally, on the other hand, would allow us to savour a new dessert, to enjoy a new mixture of the familiar ingredients, and would, most certainly, allow us to question with ever greater vigour the contingent choices of those heroes of the past whose scholarship we have decided to reproduce.

78 Immi Tallgren, 'Absent or Invisible? "Women" Intellectuals and Professionals at the Dawn of a Discipline' in Frédéric Mégret and Immi Tallgren (eds), *The Dawn of a Discipline: International Criminal Justice and Its Early Exponents* (CUP 2020).

7 Edouard Descamps (1847–1933)

From 'negative neutrality' to 'positive pacigerate'

Frederik Dhondt[1]

1. A man of many networks

Descamps occupied a central place within several elite networks, both in Belgium and abroad. Multiple threads holding together the fabric of the Catholic majority, which governed the country from 1884 to 1914, converged in Descamps.[2] The French-speaking Walloon Descamps had studied in Namur and Leuven, where he obtained the degrees of doctor of law (1869) and doctor in political and administrative sciences (1870). Just like Ernest Nys (1851–1920), who would teach international law at the Université libre de Bruxelles, or cabinet leader and 1909 Nobel Peace Prize Winner August Beernaert (1829–1912), Edouard Descamps travelled to follow courses at German universities in 1871.[3] Only a year later, he became a professor to succeed Charles Delcour (1811–1899), who had become Minister for Home Affairs. Descamps was only 25 years old. He was a pupil and admirer of the Catholic professor of political economy Charles

1 My thanks to the participants at the *5th ESCLH Biennial Conference: Laws Across Codes and Laws Decoded* (Paris, 28–30 June 2018), as well as to Wim Decock, Raphaël Cahen, Wouter De Rycke, Laure Hendrickx and Arno Swyngedouw for comments on an earlier version of this paper.

2 Els Witte, Jan Craeybeckx and Alain Meynen, *Political History of Belgium. From 1830 Onwards* (ASP 2010).

3 Frederik Dhondt, '"Inter Ruinas Publicas Scriptum". Ernest Nys, A Legal Historian in Defence of Belgian Tax Payers During the Great War' (2015) III Comparative Legal History 131–51, <https://doi.org/10.1080/2049677X.2015.1041730>; Maxime Jottrand, 'Les bourses de voyages de l'État, un instrument de circulation des savoirs juridiques? Exploration sur les séjours d'études dans la formation des juristes belges au 19ème siècle' in Raphaël Cahen, Jérôme de Brouwer, Maxime Jottrand and Frederik Dhondt (eds), *Les professeurs allemands en Belgique. Circulation des savoirs juridiques et enseignement du droit (1817–1914)* (ASP, forthcoming). Descamps founded the *Société juridique* in Leuven in 1880, in order to provide scholarships for exchanges. Both Nys and Beernaert had travelled with a government grant, Descamps had not. Romain Yakemtchouk, 'DESCAMPS (Edouard-François-Eugène, baron)' in *Biographie Nationale de Belgique*, vol XLI (supp, t. XIII, fasc. 1, Bruylant 1979) col. 201. In 1872, Descamps was admitted to the Bar of Leuven, which he would preside three times. JM Jadot and J Lejeune, 'Descamps (Édouard-Eugène-François, baron)' in *Belgische koloniale biografie-Biographie coloniale Belge* (Belgisch koloniaal instituut-Institut colonial belge 1955) col. 219.

DOI: 10.4324/9781003020882-8

Périn (1815–1890), who equally taught the law of nations.[4] Périn refused to submit to Pope Leo XIII (1810–1903). At his resignation from the University, his pupil Descamps took over the latter course (1881).[5] Four years later, Descamps changed the title to *Droit international et législation consulaire*.[6] In 1896, he became the president of the newly founded School for Political and Social Sciences within the Law Faculty. Within the School of Commercial, Consular and Colonial Sciences, created in 1910, Descamps taught a course on colonial law. He would only abandon teaching at the age of 85, a year before his death. The universities of Paris, Edinburgh, Lille, and Oxford awarded him honorary doctorates.[7]

Charles De Visscher (1884–1973), who wrote Descamps' obituary in the *Annuaire* of the Royal Academy, emphasized the 'constant attraction' exerted by religion and philosophy in his work as a lawyer.[8] Roman Yakemtchouk (1925–2011), who dedicated a lengthy entry in the *Biographie Nationale* to Descamps, links his religious ardour with the work of Cardinal Désiré-Joseph Mercier (1851–1926), whose fervent neo-Thomism was at the basis of the foundation of the Higher Institute for Philosophy.[9] Descamps' naturalism resulted in a rejection of a purely state-centred positivist legal order. The development of the term '*pacigérat*', which Descamps links to permanent neutrality, ought to be situated in this broader moralist outlook on international affairs.[10]

Descamps hoped to prove that 'the old conception of negative neutrality, founded on ideas of compression and erasure of peaceful states', had given way

4 Yakemtchouk (n 3) col. 198–99; Laurent Waelkens and Fred Stevens, *Geschiedenis van de Leuvense Rechtsfaculteit* (Die Keure 2014) 196. Périn favoured labour organizations under the employer's authority, and resented state intervention in the economy. Emiel Lamberts, *Het gevecht met Leviathan. Een verhaal over de politieke ordening in Europa, 1815–1965* (Bert Bakker 2011) 305; see also Fred Stevens, 'Charles Périn' in Wim Decock and Janwillem Oosterhuis (eds), *Great Christian Jurists in the Low Countries* (CUP forthcoming).

5 Yakemtchouk (n 3) col. 201. Descamps was a member of the *Confrérie de St-Michel*, a corporatist association sponsoring the revival of medieval corporatist ideas.

6 Yakemtchouk (n 3) col. 202.

7 Descamps was succeeded in Leuven by former Prime Minister Prosper Poullet for colonial legislation, and for international law by Charles De Visscher, who had left the State University of Ghent after this institution had abandoned teaching in French. François Rigaux, 'An Exemplary Lawyer's Life (1884–1973)' (2000) nr. 4 EJIL XI 881, <https://doi.org/10.1093/ejil/11.4.877>.

8 Charles De Visscher, 'Edouard Descamps' (1936) CII Annuaire de l'Académie Royale de Belgique 16, cited by Yakemtchouk (n 3) col. 204. Hence the publication of works as *L'action du christianisme dans les sciences et dans les lois* (Peeters 1880) or *Le génie des religions. Les origines. Avec un essai liminaire sur la vérité, la certitude, la science et la civilisation* (F. Alcan 1930).

9 Jadot and Lejeune (n 3) col. 221. See Wim Decock, 'Neo-Thomism, Law and Society: A Prolegomenon to Further Study' in Wim Decock, Bart Raeymaekers, and Peter Heyrman (eds), *Neo-Thomism in Action: Law and Society Reshaped by Neo-Scholastic Philosophy, 1880–1960* (Leuven University Press forthcoming).

10 Edouard Descamps, *La neutralité de la Belgique au point de vue historique, diplomatique, juridique et politique* (Larcier/Pedone 1902).

to the idea of a '*pacigérat positif*'.[11] The latter term covered 'the neutral's disinterested and active role in favour of the maintenance or restoration of peace', founded on the principle of common peace and equal sovereignty.[12] Before the First World War, the fundamental opposition between classical neutrality (derived from and necessarily linked to an actually existing state of war between two states) and Descamps' absorption of neutrality by peace was very clear, to the extent that his ideas were rejected by several legal scholars, as for instance at the *Institut*'s own conference in Edinburgh in 1904.[13] At the same time, it provided inspiration for the Scandinavian peace movement.[14] Furthermore, the '*pacigérat*' came back even stronger in his later writings, as Descamps explained that his ideas, which he considered as the logical historical consequence of the development of the law of neutrality, could be found in the system of the League of Nations. The League's Council could impose sanctions against states resorting to war in violation of its Covenant (art. 16). Member states that were not involved in the conflict were under the obligation to comply with these sanctions, which was seen as an active contribution to the restoration of peace.[15]

At the time of his monograph's publication, Descamps was the secretary-general of the Institute of international law,[16] a member of the Permanent Court of Arbitration, member of the Institut de France, as well as of the Belgian Royal Academy, the Belgian Senate, and Professor at the University of Leuven.[17]

11 Interparliamentary Union, *Compte rendu de la Xe conférence tenue à Paris, Palais du Sénat, du 31 juillet au 3 août 1900* (s.l. 1900) 5. For the report: ibid 127–54.

12 Descamps (n 10) 597; John B Whitton, 'La neutralité et la Société des Nations'(1927) XVII RCADI 472.

13 Rejection by Pierantoni: 'une négation des principes admis par la science du droit international, des traités et des lois intérieures des États, par la jurisprudence des tribunaux des prises et par les arbitrages' (1904) XX Annuaire de l'Institut de Droit International 215. A commission was called for to examine Descamps' theory, but it ultimately failed to report. See also Andréa Rapisardi-Mirabelli, 'La guerre italo-turque et le droit des gens – III (les rapports de neutralité)' (1913) XV RDILC (second series) 86, citing Kleen, Pillet and Ottolenghi. See also Thomas Erskine Holland, *Lectures on International Law* (Sweet and Maxwell 1933) 408: 'a barbarous term', which has been 'disposed of'.

14 Fredrik Bajer, 'Neutralité federative. Exposé des motifs d'une formule de convention pour une alliance pacigérante' (1902) IV (2e série) RDILC 127–39; Maartje Abbenhuis, *An Age of Neutrals: Great Power Politics, 1815–1915* (CUP 2014) 158, <https://doi.org/10.1017/CBO9781139794695.007>.

15 Whitton (n 12) 472. Edouard Descamps, 'Droit international nouveau – l'ère juridique sans violence et l'avènement du pacigérat positif' (1929) X (third series) RDILC 159–261.

16 Descamps was first elected as associate member in the *Institut*'s Geneva meeting (September 1892). Edouard Rolin, 'Institut de droit international – Compte rendu sommaire de la session de Genève en 1892' (1892) XXIV RDILC 515. At that time, Descamps was Senator and Professor at the University of Leuven. As President, he spoke at the funeral of founder Gustave Rolin-Jaequemyns in January 1902. Yakemtchouk (n 3) col. 234.

17 Descamps' honorific memberships included the Academy for Fine Arts in Antwerp, the Academy of Catholic Religion, the International Law Association, the Academia dei Lincei (Rome), the Academies of Lisbon and Oslo. He was a corresponding member of the Royal Academy of Sciences of the Institute in Bologna and of the Barcelona Academy of

Edouard Descamps, a 'colonial enthusiast',[18] 'whose colonial engagement was total and unconditional'[19] was a member of the *Conseil Supérieur* created by Leopold II (1835–1909) for the Congo Free State (1885–1909),[20] together with fellow Institute-members Feodor von Martens (1845–1909), Alphonse Rivier (1835–1898), Gustave Rolin-Jaequemyns (1835–1902), and Maurice Vauthier (1860–1931).[21] This organ served as supreme court and court of appeal for the Congo Free State, as well as advisory organ to Leopold II as sovereign.[22] Descamps was a '*léopoldiste convaincu*'.[23] He published the apologetic *L'Afrique Nouvelle* (1903) to glorify the Congo Free State, just at the time when Leopold II was confronted with international criticism on the cruelty of colonial exploitation.[24] The King lauded the 'magistral and patriotic work', asking his advisor

---

Jurisprudence. Yakemtchouk (n 3) col. 235. He received distinctions in Belgium, Austria, Japan, Prussia (Germany), Russia, Portugal, Spain, Turkey, Italy, Romania, Persia and Liberia.

18 Martti Koskenniemi, *The Gentle Civilizer of Nations: The Rise and Fall of International Law, 1870–1960* (CUP 2001) 141.

19 Yakemtchouk (n 3) col. 206. According to Yakemtchouk, Descamps enthusiastically welcomed the colonization of Africa as a 'civilising crusade', whereby the 'spiritual emancipation of the natives' would be entrusted to the Catholic Church. He regretted the division of Christianity, and hoped that the encounter with 'peoples who had been awaiting the son of God for centuries', would lead to the realization that 'the division of the truth' was not tenable, and drove to a more oecumenical approach. Descamps adhered to the Belgian anti-slavery society in 1888. He participated in the Brussels 1889 anti-slavery conference, together with top diplomats Auguste Lambermont (1819–1905), Emile Banning (1836–1898), and Léon Arendt (1843–1921). Descamps equally wrote a play 'Africa' to promote the anti-slavery mission of the Catholic Church and Belgian colonialism. Pope Leo XIII awarded him the honorary title of count as a reward for donating the related Prize awarded by the *Institut de France*. Descamps contributed to the official celebration of African 'war heroes' Jacques de Dixmude and Storms. Both are nowadays portrayed as perpetrators of colonial violence in the Congo Free State. See also Jadot and Lejeune (n 3) col. 221–24.

20 This council acted as the Supreme Court and Court of Appeal of the Congo Free State, but only in civil and commercial matters. Applicants could invoke a violation of procedural requirements, of the law (in the material sense), or of the law of nations. This latter motive constituted a remarkable addition to the grounds enumerated in art. 17 of the Belgian Law of 4 August 1832, which had organized the Court of Cassation (Supreme Court). Contrary to the domestic Court of Cassation (which only effectuated a legality check on the previous judgment), the *Conseil Suprême* could judge the merits of the case, in order to save money for the parties in the lawsuit. Decree of the Sovereign-King of the Congo Free State, 21 August 1889, *Bulletin Officiel* 1889, 164; A. de C., 'État indépendant du Congo – Installation du Conseil Supérieur' (1889) XXI RDILC 494. On the influence of the Congo enterprise on Belgian elites, see Guy Vanthemsche, *Belgium and the Congo, 1885–1980* (CUP 2012).

21 Peter Macalister-Smith, 'Bio-Bibliographical Key to the Membership of the Institut de Droit International' (2003) V JHIL 77–159.

22 A. de C. (n 20) 495. The organ could be likened to the Privy Council in the United Kingdom. Descamps drafted the regulations on the suppression of the slave trade by land and on the acquisition of Congolese nationality. Jadot and Lejeune (n 3) col. 222.

23 Yakemtchouk (n 3) col. 213.

24 Edouard Descamps, *L'Afrique nouvelle. Essai sur l'Etat civilisateur dans les pays neufs et sur la frontière, l'organisation et le gouvernement de l'Etat Indépendant du Congo* (Lebègue/Hachette 1903); Pierre-Olivier De Broux and Bérengère Piret, 'La notion de civilisation dans

to send the book to the other courts and governments in Europe.[25] On 23 May 1903, Descamps was appointed as a Minister of State of the Congo Free State.[26] He argued that British complaints on internal affairs could not be exposed to oversight by the signatory parties to the Act of Berlin (1885). This echoes his and Ernest Nys' attempts to restrict the oversight of the guarantors of Belgian permanent neutrality.[27] Descamps was rewarded with the title of Baron by Leopold II on 28 May 1904.[28] The same year, Descamps was elected president of the Royal Academy. He used his inaugural address to castigate British criticism of the sovereign and independent Congo Free State.[29] In 1927, Descamps founded a chair for the history of Catholic missions, which later on became the African Institute of the University of Leuven.[30]

As a statesman, Descamps pleaded for electoral reform and the introduction of proportional representation in 1888, ten years before its adoption.[31] This major electoral reform would only be enacted in 1899. He equally published widely on Belgian constitutional law, just before its first major reform in 1893, when plural voting was introduced.[32] In 1892, he entered the Senate, which he would only leave in 1932, four decades later. Descamps' contribution to the constitutional revision was considerable, mainly for the reform of the Senate and the legal framework for the future take-over of the Congo Free State. In 1907, he was appointed Minister for the Arts and Sciences. The liberal press had castigated the minister for his 'Jesuitic and sectarian attitude'. Descamps had refused to validate exams for provincial non-confessional teacher schools in Hainault.[33] He lost the support of his party, and was left alone to defend this measure, which offended

---

la Charte Coloniale' (2019) n° 83 RIEJ 56–62. See also Edouard Descamps, 'Le différend anglo-congolais' (1904) VI (2ᵉ série) RDILC 233–39; Koskenniemi (n 18) 162–64.

25 Jadot and Lejeune (n 3) col. 225.

26 English version: *New Africa. An Essay on Government Civilization in New Countries and on the Foundation, Organization and Administration of the Congo Free State* (Sampson 1903). See also Descamps' panegyric on the sovereign as Senator: 'Le duc de Brabant au Sénat de Belgique. En souvenir du cinquantième anniversaire de l'entrée au Sénat de S. M. Léopold II (1853–1903)' (1903) Bulletin de la Classe des Lettres et des Sciences Morales et Politiques et de la Classe des Beaux-Arts 279–323.

27 Frederik Dhondt, 'Neutralité permanente, interprétations mutantes: la neutralité belge à travers trois traités de juristes' (2018) LXXXVI (nr. 1–2) *The Legal History Review* 188–214.

28 Yakemtchouck (n 3) col. 219. Congo became a Belgian colony in 1908–1909. After the Great War, Descamps became president of the Superior Council of Belgian-Congo (5 April 1919), which he closed five years later, since the Brussels Court of Cassation was made competent for the colony as well from 1924.

29 Koskenniemi (n 18) 162.

30 Jadot and Lejeune (n 3) col. 220.

31 Edouard Descamps, *La mosaïque constitutionnelle: essai sur les sources du texte de la Constitution belge* (Peeters 1891). See also Frederik Dhondt, 'Justice and Equality for All? Proportional Representation in Belgium and France (1883–1921)' (2020) XLI (nr. 86) *Seqüência* 28–62 <http://dx.doi.org/10.5007/2177-7055.2020v41n86p28>.

32 Yakemtchouk (n 3) col. 220.

33 *L'Indépendance Belge*, 29 June 1910.

the opposition so much that it had become indefensible even for a Catholic government, as opposition-controlled city councils uttered protest and created their own teacher schools.[34] He resigned on 8 August 1910. After the Great War, Descamps was elected Vice-President of the Senate (1922).[35]

Descamps' interventions in the Belgian Senate illustrate the weight of his academic authority in a political arena. In a debate on 19 April 1898, the 1913 Nobel Peace Prize winner Henri La Fontaine (a Socialist Senator, 1854–1943) argued in favour of a Belgian subsidy to the International Bureau of Peace (founded in 1891). Foreign Affairs Minister Paul de Favereau (1856–1922), who was a Catholic, as Descamps, stated that this would not be permissible for a permanently neutral state. The Bureau treated all pending questions of international affairs, and this constituted a risk from the Foreign Ministry's point of view. Belgium could be seen as a '*donneur de leçons*' by the great powers.[36] Descamps came to the rescue of La Fontaine, and corrected the minister. The interests of permanently neutral countries were linked with the 'general and permanent interest of the international community'.[37] Any permanently neutral state could actively sustain quests to make its own legal status during armed conflict more secure. If, as La Fontaine stated, 'neutrals could not wage [offensive] war', a mandatory convention on arbitration would preventively tie potential warmongers, the latter would not be able to escape their responsibility.[38]

Finally, on an international level, he participated in the Interparliamentary Union (founded in 1889), where he propagated the idea of *pacigérat.* Descamps presided over the 1895 Conference in Brussels, where he presented an essay on international arbitration to the various foreign ministries of the participating states.[39] Together with August Beernaert, who had left his office as cabinet leader in 1894, Descamps was a member of the Belgian delegation at The Hague Peace Conferences, acting as reporter for the committee which drafted the First Hague Convention of 1899 on the Pacific Settlement of Disputes.[40] Descamps was a

34 ibid 5 August 1910.

35 Yakemtchouk (n 3) col. 223.

36 Belgian Senate, 19 April 1898, 335.

37 ibid 336. See recently Herbert H. Reginbogin and Pascal Lottaz (eds), *Permanent Neutrality: A Model for Peace, Security, and Justice* (Rowman & Littlefield 2020).

38 (n 36) 336.

39 Descamps had sponsored a proposal to compel states to recognize unilaterally proclaimed constitutional permanent neutrality. However, this was seen as excessive. A state could not force its peers unilaterally to restrict their freedom. René Waultrin, 'La neutralité scandinave' (1904) XI RGDIP 23. Descamps took part in the efforts to create an international treaty collection for customs (Bern conference, 1894) and presided the permanent bureau of the International Parliamentary Conference for Trade. Yakemtchouk (n 3) col. 235.

40 International Convention for the Pacific Settlement of International Disputes, 29 July 1899, The Hague, 187 *CTS* 140. Maartje Abbenhuis, *The Hague Conferences and International Politics* (Bloomsbury 2018); Arthur Eyffinger, *The Hague 1899 Peace Conference: The Parliament of Man, The Federation of the World* (Kluwer 1999) 31–37.

member of the Permanent Court of Arbitration from its inception.[41] He acted as legal expert to the Belgian delegation at the Paris Peace Conference.[42]

2. *La neutralité de la Belgique* (1902) and Descamps' positive concept of neutrality

> *depuis que nous existons, on se soit contenté . . . de la nue-certitude de notre neutralité et de la pratiquer tant bien que mal, un peu à l'aventure, ou tout au moins sans avoir une vue bien nette des principes qui régissent cette matière importante . . . la constitution de notre pays en Etat neutre permanent était la vraie, la réelle, la nécessaire vocation de la Belgique.*
>
> *Le Vingtième Siècle*, 10 November 1902

> *Nous n'avons pas la prétention de faire mieux, dans leur genre, que les écrivains qui ont émis des vues sur notre neutralité. Nous aspirons plutôt à faire autre chose: nous voudrions . . . composer le Commentaire juridique de notre Constitution internationale.*
>
> Descamps, *La Neutralité de la Belgique*, 1902[43]

2.1 A new national synthesis

Descamps organized his treatment of Belgian neutrality in four parts, reflecting the constitutive aspects of permanent neutrality. History, diplomacy, international law, and politics were necessary complements of a total explanation. The presence of history is not a surprise in a nineteenth-century treatise.[44] *La neutralité de la Belgique* was devised as the ultimate synthesis of the country's national mission. It also provided pragmatic ad hoc justification of potential foreign policy options.[45]

41 He acted as counsel to the United States of America in the Californian Foundations affair of 1902. Yakemtchouk (n 3) col. 227–28 and Edouard Descamps, *Le premier arbitrage de la Cour de La Haye. Les fondations californiennes et la question de la chose jugée en droit international, avec le texte du compromis et de la sentence arbitrale* (Van Langenhuysen 1902). Descamps also represented Japan and was thanked by the country's ambassador for having advanced the cause of the recognition of Japanese as an official language of the court. Vincent Genin, 'Eurocentrisme et modernité du droit international, 1860–1920. L'« Orient » et l'Amérique latine chez les juristes belges' (2018) n° 14 Monde(s) 19–20.

42 Vincent Genin, *Incarner le droit international. Du mythe juridique au déclassement international de la Belgique (1914–1940)* (Peter Lang 2018).

43 Descamps (n 10) 302.

44 Descamps had taught legal history courses himself. Yakemtchouk (n 3) col. 200.

45 The work received a favourable review by Prosper Poullet, a Catholic politician, later Prime Minister (1925–1926) at the time of the book's publication a colleague of Descamps, teaching diplomatic history (*Revue Générale*, 1902, 779–91). The Belgian press also devoted attention to it. The liberal *Indépendance Belge* disagreed with Descamps' attack on Ernest Nys, who argued that no literal mention of Belgian borders allowed to link the guarantee of the great powers with the territorial situation of 1831. The Catholic *Vingtième Siècle* (10 November 1902) expressed admiration, comparing the author to Brice and Laband. Moraynes concluded that Descamps had authoritatively demonstrated that practice and

As an example, Descamps argued that permanent neutrality did not prevent Belgium from contracting a purely defensive and non-reciprocal ('imperfect') alliance with the Netherlands. Even more, Descamps claimed that the two states could constitute an 'indivisible' entity, provoked by an aggressor. In this view, every state's individual defensive interests would compel to act.[46] Descamps' work claimed to fill a gap since the publication of his predecessor Guillaume (Wilhelm) Arendt's (1808–1865) *Essai sur la neutralité de la Belgique*.[47] Published back in 1845, this treatise had approached the novel system of permanent neutrality with the available doctrine and state practice.[48]

Half a century after Arendt's treatise had appeared, Belgium had developed its own state practice. Descamps proclaimed the 'international constitution of Belgium' apt to be submitted to the '*méthode précise et sévère de la science juridique*'.[49] The general law of neutrality, applicable to both voluntarily and permanently neutral states, had known significant developments. Descamps thought that Belgium's foreign policy accompanied these developments. His statement on the Congo Free State's neutrality after its take-over by Belgium reads as a continuation of the country's derived historical mission in the historical part of his work.[50] In the final part on 'international policy', Descamps declared that his country had become 'an institution of order and peace for the preservation of political stability'.[51]

The book was published again in 1920, after the Great War. Belgium had desired the cancellation of its 'conventional permanent neutrality',[52] at the insistence of Minister of Foreign Affairs Paul Hymans (1865–1941) and Charles De Visscher, who acted besides Descamps as legal adviser to the delegation at the Paris Peace Conference.[53]

---

custom determined 'rules, principles and theory'. *Le Petit Bleu du Matin* (25 October 1902) reasoned accordingly, highlighting the vagueness of neutralization clauses. *Le Patriote* emphasized that Descamps' work put Belgium in a position of international immunity (*inoffensif*), and attacked Ernest Nys, who had pleaded for a sustained military effort.

46 Yakemtchouk (n 3) col. 230. Descamps (n 10) 370.

47 Guillaume (Wilhelm) Arendt, *Essai sur la neutralité de la Belgique* (Muquardt 1845).

48 Arendt had tried to distinguish Belgian permanent neutrality from the case of Switzerland, which he regarded at that time as insufficiently reliable to defend itself. '*Les vices du système fédéral*', which weakened the Swiss Confederation, were absent in a centralized and unitary state as Belgium under its 1831 Constitution. Arendt incited his compatriots to conclude treaties of commerce and navigation, in order to draw benefit from the country's neutral position and maximize its access to markets. Arendt (n 47) 71, 211–12.

49 Descamps (n 10) 301.

50 ibid 431: '*il n'est guère de peuple qui, après avoir servi durant tant de siècles de champ de bataille à des rivalités étrangères, ait mieux mérité que le nôtre de posséder ce bien médiateur de tant d'autres biens: la paix dans l'inviolabilité du sol patrial.*'

51 Descamps (n 10) 597–98.

52 ibid 304.

53 Genin (n 42) 95–120. Among the other members of the delegation were Ernst Nys and Henri La Fontaine. Art. 31 of the Paris Peace Treaty stated the abrogation of the Treaty of London (19 April 1839), which had installed Belgian permanent neutrality (see also Malbone W Graham, 'Neutralization as a Movement in International Law' (1927) 21 AJIL 79,

2.2 Non-conventional permanent neutrality

The legal part of Descamps' work amounted to almost half of the monograph. Permanent neutrality was presented as Belgium's 'international constitution'. Descamps first discussed the voluntary choice for a permanent neutralization, or the '*usage éclairé de la souveraineté*' (enlightened use of sovereignty), whereby a state abandons its facultative power to 'associate . . . itself with the armed struggles between other states'. Descamps cited the examples of Venice and the principality of Liège. The United States' abandonment of involvement in 'European wars' was still apt to be classified among 'principled neutral powers'. However, the 'traditional neutrality of certain secondary states', such as the Netherlands, did not amount to such an enlightened and selfless decision.[54] A 'more or less long series of manifested occasional neutrality' could not be equalled to an 'expression beyond any doubt of a state regarding the principled adoption of neutrality'.[55] A classic example of the latter was Switzerland, which, according to Descamps, had managed to practice permanent neutrality as a constant line of behaviour, without any kind of international treaty or protection.[56]

Declarations of permanent neutrality, '*érigé*[es] *en maxime d'État*' constituted a 'licit exercise of sovereignty' in Descamps' eyes, and were as such opposable to other states. Yet, this respect did not mean that the permanently neutral state would become 'inviolable': even if the declaration of neutrality had to be respected, other states did not lose their *ultima ratio*: '*le droit de guerre*'.[57] Conversely, the right of a voluntary neutralized state to abandon this status could not be questioned either. The repeal of a declaration did not violate any rights, although a lack of reliability and trust for the future was probable.

2.3 Permanent neutrality created by treaty

The logical next step in the development was a discussion of conventional neutrality. Would the creation of permanent neutrality by a multilateral treaty ensure an immunity, which did not exist for unilaterally proclaimed permanent neutrality?

81). The other contracting parties, the Russian Empire and the Kingdom of the Netherlands, were not a party to this treaty. Consequently, from a Dutch point of view, only the Locarno Pact (16 October 1925) would have 'abolished' Belgian neutrality (Frans De Pauw, 'La Belgique et la compétence obligatoire de la Cour Internationale' (1961) XLIX RBDI 68). Furthermore, the Netherlands were not inclined to accept any territorial or maritime modifications to the 1839 settlement without bilateral negotiations. Conversely, from a Belgian point of view, the Belgian state considered to have rewon its freedom of action, and actively sought unilateral safety guarantees, which were obtained from France in the so-called secret Belgian-French military agreement (7 September 1920). See Jean Stengers, 'L'accord militaire franco-belge de 1920 et le Luxembourg' (2004) LXXXII RBPH 431–47.

54 Descamps (n 10) 307.

55 ibid 307. On Dutch voluntary neutrality, see Maartje Abbenhuis, *The Art of Staying Neutral: The Netherlands in the First World War, 1914–1918* (Amsterdam University Press 2006).

56 Descamps (n 10) 308.

57 ibid 308–9.

Descamps reasoned according to general principles of private law. The consecration of permanent neutrality in a treaty, generated '*des obligations contractuelles spéciales*'. The contracting parties of a treaty creating a status of permanent neutrality could be held liable if they infringed the agreement.[58] A synallagmatic or reciprocal contract created rights and obligations for both parties, or both sides of the agreement. Their validity and execution were mutually dependent, but at the same time flexible.

For Belgium, conventional neutrality was at the same time congenital, since the positive source was to be found in the 1839 Treaties of London. The contracting parties created Belgian neutrality '*dans un intérêt de communauté internationale*'. This higher origin forbade the neutralized state to renounce this status.[59] Conversely, the reciprocal nature of obligations, 'without which there would not be any law of nations', equally bound the guarantors.[60] If Belgium respected its obligations, the Great Powers were equally obliged to execute theirs. No one could thus argue, as French authors had done, that the German Chiefs of Staff would not even consider the country's neutral status as a '*fêtu de paille*' in their war planning.[61]

If the status of Switzerland and Belgium were to be likened, Descamps considered them both to be 'pure' permanent neutralities: both neutralized states enjoyed their sovereignty with small restrictions, immediately linked to the '*exigences propres*' of permanent neutrality. Luxemburg, by contrast, had had to accept a formal interdiction to maintain fortresses on its territory. Cracow, which had existed as a permanently neutral state from 1815 to 1846, had to forsake the right of asylum.[62]

2.4 *Against the deniers of neutrality*

The author denounced certain 'serious organs of the press', and 'prominent politicians' who had spread doubts on the basic documents of Belgian neutrality, on the guarantees, or on the margin of interpretation left to belligerents.[63] Descamps encouraged military preparedness to fend off possible aggressions: '*être neutre,*

58 ibid 310.

59 ibid 312. Descamps refuted the idea that Belgium could decide to void its status to get rid of the entailing obligations if the corresponding advantages would come to cease or diminish considerably.

60 ibid 333, citing Théophile Funck-Brentano and Albert Sorel, *Précis de droit des gens* (Paris 1877) 357.

61 Descamps (n 10) 334.

62 ibid 315.

63 ibid 323–24. For a specific example of practical '*licences*' suffered by the diplomatic pressure of the French and British guarantors during the Crimean War: Frederik Dhondt, 'Permanent Neutrality or Permanent Insecurity? Obligation and Self-interest in the Defense of Belgian Neutrality' in Inge Van Hulle and Randall Lesaffer (eds), *International Law in the Long 19th Century (1776–1914). From the Public Law of Europe to Global International Law?* (Brill/Martinus Nijhoff 2019) 159–85.

c'est prévoir; être faible, c'est prévoir encore'. Yet, the relative weakness of a state 'of the second order' could not be a justification to downplay its conventional legal protection.[64] Descamps cited Lord Russell (1792–1878) in the House of Lords, according to whom Britain's obligations towards Belgium were 'sacred' and thus contracted both collectively with the other Great Powers, and separately, with regards to a possible bilateral request by Belgium to intervene.[65] Only the agreement of the contracting parties of 1839 could erase the Treaty of London from the positive law of nations. Even if violence could tear up the treaties, its character was resolutely binding.[66]

Descamps discarded the classical *clausula rebus sic stantibus*-argument, and defended the binding nature of Belgium's permanent neutrality, irrespective of the modifications the international system had undergone after the Italian Wars of Independence and German unification, which dislocated the system of the Congress of Vienna.[67] A second argument refuted was the conclusion of confirmatory treaties between Britain (as 'mediating guarantor') and Prussia and France respectively (as 'belligerent guarantors') in August 1870. Descamps fell back on an argument developed by diplomat Léon Arendt (1843–1924). If subsequent agreements were concluded between Belgium and its guarantors, they could only concern the execution of intervention, and not the legal basis of the obligation to intervene.[68] Arendt had cited the case of the Franco-British intervention in 1831–1832, entailing a French-led siege of the Antwerp citadel, which was at that time still occupied by the army of William I.[69] Third, Descamps contested the idea that a general war in Europe would invalidate the treaty of 1839, as agreements between states were not deprived of their binding force during an armed conflict.[70] Finally, the right of necessity was forcefully rebutted, as belligerents could use this pretext to violate a friendly nation's sovereignty and to 'oppress a peaceful people'.[71]

64 An example of this: Marcel Morand, 'Les origines de la neutralité perpétuelle' (1895) RGDIP 522–37.

65 Descamps (n 10) 323.

66 This argument has been used against Belgium after World War One by the Netherlands, the latter arguing that permanent neutrality could not have been abolished in the Belgian-Dutch relationship by the Paris Peace Treaty of 1919. The Netherlands had remained (voluntarily) neutral during the war, and insisted that the Treaty of London was still binding between them and Belgium. Dutch advisers argued that this was a 'servitude' under international law, which existed irrespective of obligations between states. See AAH Struycken, *Nederland, België en de mogendheden: een historisch-juridisch betoog* (Gouda Quint 1919).

67 Descamps (n 10) 325–26.

68 ibid 300 and 326–27.

69 Els Witte, *Het Verloren Koninkrijk. Het harde verzet van de Belgische orangisten tegen de revolutie* (De Bezige Bij 2015) 312–15.

70 Descamps (n 10) 329. Descamps saw the Hague Conferences as 'the definitive transformation into general rules of the law of nations' of his ideas, and considered the adoption of 'general treaties' as the proof of the demise of 'old customs'. Descamps in *Compte rendu de la Xe Conférence* . . ., 7. Id, 'Les grandes étapes du progrès dans le droit des neutres et vocation de notre temps à la constitution du Pacigérat' (1900) RGDIP 728–29.

71 ibid 332.

As influential politician and adviser to King Leopold II, Descamps was set on proving that permanent neutrality, albeit as a congenital condition in a synallagmatic contract with the Great Powers, did not diminish or encroach on Belgian sovereignty. The Swedish diplomat and lawyer Richard Kleen (1841–1923) had argued that permanently neutral states had abandoned their discretion in self-defence: 'permanent or perpetual neutrality is incompatible with the right . . . of any independent State, to decide by itself on the means to defend its existence, its integrity and its rights against possible violations'.[72] For Kleen, deciding on matters of war and peace was an 'inseparable function' of sovereignty, even if international law only recognised war as an 'extreme means' of self-defence against 'a criminal attack against the State's integrity'.[73]

When 'so-called permanent neutrality' deprived the State of its right to self-defence, or its right to decide on its exercise, this encroached on a sovereign right, 'condition of its political emancipation, indispensable to the very objective of the State as such'.[74] Kleen added that international law could not approve of permanent neutralization which in the case of Belgium had been 'imposed as a condition of the country's independence'.[75] For Belgium, this was 'an obligation, and not a right', 'demanded in exchange and as the price for recognition of its independence'.[76] He concluded that 'unstable and powerless'[77] Belgium had been placed in a 'false situation' by the Great Powers, who had 'sacrificed' the country to their ambitions. If the country had been kept out of the Franco-Prussian war of 1870, this was not due to promises and guarantees, but to Great Power rivalry and balancing.[78]

Kleen ended his treatment of permanent neutrality with the statement that guarantees were superfluous: if all states would abide by the general rules of international law, voluntary neutrality would be sufficient to safeguard the rights of states that knowingly decide to abstain from a conflict between two others.[79] The core of the problem was the lack of respect for 'weak States' rights', who were not shielded from 'abuse by brutal force'. Only the progress of 'education and civilisation' would be meaningful paths to a better situation.[80]

Descamps, on the contrary, defined sovereignty as 'the supreme power to govern society in view of its conservation, perfection and the common happiness of

72 Richard Kleen, *Lois et usages de la neutralité d'après le droit international conventionnel et coutumier des Etats civilisés* (Chevalier-Marescq 1898), vol I, 95; Descamps (n 10) 341.

73 Kleen (n 72) vol I, 96.

74 ibid.

75 ibid.

76 ibid 101.

77 ibid 98.

78 ibid 99.

79 ibid 100.

80 ibid 102. Compare with Descamps' own words in *Le droit international et la these de la nécessité* (Hayez 1919) 17: '*Le droit* [. . .] *isolé, faible, désarmé* [. . .] *devient facilement le jouet de facteurs politiques* [. . .] *Être neutre, c'est prévoir; être faible, c'est prévoir en Belgique* [. . .] *Plus que tout autre pays, la Belgique sait ce qu'il en coûte de ne pas posséder pleinement en soi le principe de sa sécurité.*'

its members'. International order served to co-ordinate the life of states. Externally sovereign states were not free of any kind of obligation, but only free of obligations imposed by a 'will alien to their proper will'.[81] Any state was bound to respect the 'common law of civilised peoples', as well as the specific obligations following from conventions and particular customs. Conventional permanent neutrality added an obligation, which ought to be conceived – again – as a *vinculum iuris* between creditor and debtor, analogous to the general law of obligations.[82]

If permanent neutrality obliged a state to abstain and remain impartial, these were obligations 'to abstain from a facultative act', which fell within the legitimate perimeter of obligations contracted by a sovereign. Even more, permanent neutrality, for Descamps, did not restrict, but could coincide with the state's duty of self-preservation, providing security and the enhancement of the common good. Renouncing the use of force concerned not renouncing an ordinary tool of statecraft, but only 'the most gross and imperfect way of claiming justice'.[83] Descamps likened this to the deliberate choice for arbitration, which 'did not imply an abdication, but more an enlightened use of sovereignty'.[84] Finally, Kleen's position could also be reversed. If a given state, for example Luxemburg, found itself in too weak a position to organize its defence, wouldn't the choice of a collectively guaranteed permanent neutrality enhance its sovereignty? Descamps concluded that Kleen had resided on an 'abstract, uniform and inalienable' conception of sovereignty. The 'institutions of the law of nations', by contrast, existed in the 'real world of states', in order to procure 'states entirely without the means to defend themselves' with an alternative.[85]

The previous paragraph highlights that Descamps' justifications for the regime of collective security heavily influenced his defence of permanent neutrality. His reasoning slowly segregated from the classical law of nations' emphasis on the rights of states. Clearly influenced by Aristotelian and neo-Thomist thinking, Descamps transposed the internal '*bonum commune*' to the community of states. Sovereignty was not necessarily a consequence of the internal control of a territory through institutions (among which, an army), but could also be enhanced through peer protection granted by the Great Powers as organs of the international community.

This reasoning was further developed in the discussion of the 'constitutional triad' neutrality-independence-guarantee. Descamps stated that the collective guarantee of the Great Powers was a substitute (*de caractère compensateur*) for the traditional means to ensure self-preservation, such as the right to conclude

81 Descamps (n 10) 342.
82 ibid 342–43.
83 ibid 345.
84 ibid. Descamps referred to his memorandum addressed to the main powers of Europe. Edouard Descamps, *Essai sur l'organisation de l'arbitrage international. Mémoire aux puissances* (Guyot 1896).
85 Descamps (n 10) 347.

alliances, which Belgium had forfeited under the regime of permanent neutrality.[86] In the ensuing sections, Descamps conformed to the more traditional interpretation of neutrality which had been developed by Arendt in 1845, showing his sense of pragmatism and feeling for contemporary political issues. The external guarantee was no '*prime à ne rien faire*', but more of a 'strong hand ensuring that what will be done, will not have been in vain'. In other words: Belgium could not ignore its military obligations, since the country had not externalized its defence to guarantors, as Luxemburg had.[87]

2.5 *The three degrees of permanent neutrality, or permanent neutrality transformed through arbitration*

The precise operation of the rights and obligations 'tempering' the exercise of Belgium's external sovereignty could only be understood, Descamps argued, through the system of *pacigérat* and its varying degrees. First, Descamps pleaded that 'proper' permanent neutrality or the '*pacigérat simple à titre permanent*' was the term applicable to 'a nation having renounced its power to wage war as a right to meddle in the armed struggles of other states'.[88] This stage corresponded to a purely political attitude. One stage further was the *pacigérat intégral*, or the 'extended permanent neutrality',[89] which amounted to a genuine legal regime. In the latter case, a state had renounced the use of force to satisfy its own legal claims. Only the exercise of self-defence remained. Finally, a nation could be 'radically stripped' of any effective power to employ armed force in the international order, even in case of self-defence. This was called 'radical neutralisation' or '*pacigérat désarmé*.'[90]

Descamps reaffirmed that neutrality required three parties: two belligerents and a neutral power. However, 'it is not impossible that . . . we could designate in certain cases, under the label of permanent neutrality, an institution that implies the renunciation, not only to the right to meddle in armed quarrels between other states, but also the right to wage war for one's own interest and even to exercise under an effective form, self-defence in the international order'.[91] In other words, Descamps claimed to have identified a shift in the general laws of war. Neutrality could not be applied to this legal status. However, the transformation appeared clearly and unambiguously. Henceforth, Descamps argued that a new term, '*pacigérat*' would clarify the transformations permanent neutrality had undergone between 1815 and 1900.[92]

86 ibid 348–49.
87 ibid 402, 404–30.
88 ibid 350–51, 353–54.
89 ibid 354–58.
90 ibid 358–59.
91 ibid 351–52.
92 ibid 352.

'Extended neutralisation' or '*pacigérat intégral*' necessitated a subtle interpretation. Descamps wished to demonstrate that the recent evolution of international law had altered the traditional view of a state which had renounced its right to pursue claims by force or to 'wage war for its own interest'. A neutralized state had only renounced one possible way of pursuing claims, and not the 'right to obtain justice'. Moreover, all other states were bound to recognize this new status. As a consequence, not only the neutralized state, but the whole of the international community had to incorporate the legal reality that claims could not be pursued with violence against the neutralized state. Reasoning otherwise, and refusing a request for arbitration by a neutralized state, would amount to depriving that state of 'a fundamental right, which it has not abdicated'.[93] Violating the territory of an 'extended neutralised state' would amount to 'a true crime of international felony, of which the author would be held accountable towards all tenants of this institution'.[94]

Descamps saw the elaboration of a legal regime of '*pacigérat*' as the logical overcoming of the old debate on the rights of neutrals. Permanently peaceful states needed a legal regime that guaranteed their equal sovereignty, allowing for the 'effective continuity' of their peaceful relationship with states in the same legal situation, as well as with other belligerent and non-belligerent nations. This was the sense of his report on the *pacigérat*, as adopted by the Tenth Interparliamentary Union in Paris (31 July 1900).[95] The report emphasized that the 'old' regime of neutrality had had its merits, by rendering abstention possible, discarding a Manichean world view whereby belligerents would classify all other nations as friends or foes. Neutrality was incapable, according to Descamps, of organizing a legal system. Descamps thought that only a system starting from the twin principles of peace and sovereign equality could provide a coherent and just set of rules.[96] Peace was the 'superior and unitary norm', whereas armed struggle was only 'the limited sphere . . . wherein belligerents move'.[97] The peaceful relations between belligerents, non-belligerents, and neutralized states ought to classify them all as '*pacigérants*'.[98]

Finally, 'Radical neutralisation' or '*pacigérat désarmé*' had created a situation whereby the sanction for aggression had become purely external. The neutralized state did not exercise one of the 'attributes of sovereignty'.[99] It had become materially impossible to claim its own rights, or to exercise legitimate self-defence. This status was 'fatally precarious', but 'not illegitimate'. The development of arbitration created an alternative, as well as the external aid of guarantors. The 'radically neutralised state' could thus call for a double '*Deus ex Machina*'.[100]

93 ibid 355.
94 ibid 436.
95 ibid 603, note 1.
96 ibid 604.
97 ibid 605.
98 ibid 604.
99 ibid 358–59.
100 ibid 359.

3. Descamps and the Advisory Committee of Jurists in the League of Nations: a late victory for the *pacigérat*?

It is not surprising that Descamps saw the combination of the League of Nations Covenant and the Briand-Kellogg Pact[101] as the culmination of the movement he had in part directed in the 1890s and 1900s. At the opening session of the ACJ,[102] president Descamps saw the Paris Peace Conference of 1919 as the 'third peace conference', following up on the 1899 and 1907 Hague Conferences, conformably to the final recommendation of the Second Hague Conference.[103] Descamps counted on the further 'advancement of international law' by conferences, which ought to state on the 'principles of justice in rules of law', conformably to the continuing advancement and interdependence of the nations of the world.[104]

Descamps is regularly cited as the father of the introduction of the 'general principles of international law recognized by civilised nations' in Article 38 (1).[105] This – among other sources – allowed for the progressive development and adaptation of international law by the Court and its successor, the ICJ.[106] According to the thorough and archive-based study of Vincent Genin, Belgium suffered a 'declassification' during the election of the judges of the Permanent Court of International Justice. The Chilean Alejandro Alvarez (1868–1960) was preferred to Descamps.[107] Several state delegations opined that Belgium's place in the League of Nations had become disproportionate to the country's size.[108] We

101 General Treaty for the Renunciation of War as an Instrument of National Policy, Paris (27 August 1928) 94 LNTS 47.

102 Advisory Committee of Jurists, *Procès-Verbaux of the Proceedings of the Committee, 16 June–24 July 1920, with Annexes* (Van Langenhuysen, The Hague, 1920).

103 Inaugural address by Descamps, The Hague, 16 June 1920, 'Meeting of the Advisory Committee of Jurists' (July–August 1920) LNOJ 234. A conference had been planned for 1915, but World War One stalled the preparatory work. James Brown Scott, *The Project of a Permanent Court of International Justice and Resolutions of the Advisory Committee of Jurists* (Carnegie Endowment for International Peace 1920) 136.

104 Scott (n 103) 137; See also address by Léon Bourgeois on behalf of the Council of the League of Nations (who hopes to establish '*la durée du droit*'), The Hague, 16 June 1920, LNOJ July–August 1920, 231.

105 Antônio Augusto Cançado Trindade, *International Law for Humankind: Towards a New Jus Gentium* (Martinus Nijhoff/Brill 2010) 122; Gleider Hernandez, *The International Court of Justice and the Judicial Function* (OUP 2014) 31. Descamps would have initially proposed the 'juridical conscience of the civilised nations', but was opposed by Root', who brought the discussion to a compromise. Lauri Mälksoo, 'Sources of International Law in the Nineteenth-Century European Tradition. Insights from Practice and Theory' in Samantha Besson and Jean d'Aspremont (eds), *Oxford Handbook of the Sources of International Law* (OUP 2017) 155–56.

106 Malgosia Fitzmaurice, 'The History of Article 38 of the Statute of the ICJ' in Samantha Besson and Jean d'Aspremont (eds), *The Oxford Handbook of the Sources of International Law* (OUP 2017) 192–94.

107 Liliana Obregón, 'Noted to Dissent: The International Life of Alejandro Alvarez' (2006) 19 Leiden Journal of International Law 983–1016.

108 Genin (n 42) 136–46; Vincent Genin, 'Le cas des experts belges à la Cour permanente de justice internationale, 1921–1930. Quelles expertises pour quelle autorité ?' (2017) n°

will first expound on the debate on the 'general principles of international law' as a source of law for the PCIJ, and then return to Descamps' analysis of neutrality in the new framework of the League of Nations.

3.1 'General principles of international law', or 'the law of objective justice'

In the debate on the sources at the court's disposal for the settlement of disputes, Descamps showed himself a passionate advocate of naturalism.[109] His presidential speech on the matter presented the ACJ as the logical consequence of a moment which included the 1899 and 1907 Hague Conferences and the 1919 Paris Peace Conferences as logical components of a same movement. The ACJ's task was to determine 'clear' principles, rendering the court's operation 'proof against dispute'.[110] As an astute manager of the Committee, he distributed praise for the traditional paramount sources of 'a general or special treaty between the parties', which the judge has a 'first duty' to apply, on the one hand, and, 'the very natural and extremely reliable method of development' of law through custom. Yet, this appeared insufficient in the face of the existence of 'objective justice', as a 'complement'.[111] Descamps borrowed from the common law-culture by citing the American lawyer and judge James Kent (1763–1847):

> When the greater part of jurisconsults agree upon a certain rule, the presumption in favour of that rule becomes so strong, that only a person who makes a mock of justice would gainsay it.[112]

Descamps argued strongly that the 'demands of public conscience' had already been recognized as a source of the law of nations at the 1907 Hague Conferences, as complementary to the rules of positive international law.[113] Differences in interpretation concerned only matters of secondary importance, as 'the fundamental law of justice and injustice' was 'deeply engraved on the heart of every human being'.[114] The 'legal conscience of civilized nations' was the most 'authoritative expression' of this basic human sentiment. To support these high-minded

18, n° 1 Les Cahiers Sirice 61–76. The first Belgian judge at the PCIJ was elected in 1930 (Edouard Rolin-Jaequemyns). Genin furthermore notes that Descamps' praise for Grotius at the tricentennial celebrations of *De iure belli ac pacis libri tres* in 1625 can be seen as a sign of Dutch-Belgian *rapprochement*, in the aftermath of Belgium's fruitless claims against the Netherlands at the Paris Peace Conference. ibid 123–30.

109 This went so far as to propose criminal proceedings before the PCIJ at the League's Assembly's request. See Frédéric Mégret, 'International Criminal Justice as a Peace Project' (2018) 29 EJIL 835, 838.

110 Procès-Verbaux (n 14) 322.

111 ibid 323.

112 ibid 323.

113 ibid 310.

114 ibid 310, 324.

utterances, Descamps quoted the so-called Martens Clause from the preamble of the Fourth Hague Convention on the Laws and Customs of War on Land:

> Until a more complete code of the laws of war has been issued, the high contracting parties deem it expedient to declare that, in cases not included in the Regulations adopted by them, populations and belligerents remain under the protection and the rule of the principles of the law of nations, as they result from the usages established among civilised peoples, from the laws of humanity, and the dictates of the public conscience.[115]

Furthermore, Descamps used the fundamental maxim *pacta sunt servanda* (which found its meaning in medieval and early modern theology),[116] obliging parties to respect binding treaties in good faith. For Descamps, this included an obligation for the judge to 'interpret [treaties] in the light of and with all the consequences deriving from their nature according to objective justice'.[117]

Why could this source 'not law made in any meaningful sense of the word, but . . . found by comparison of municipal legal systems'[118] have been a necessary complement to existing positive law in 1920? Descamps used a short historical digression. The days of the 'inevitably unreliable system of the balance of power' were said to be over. All civilized States had 'agreed to adopt a co-ordinated system based on the principles of justice in international affairs'. As a necessary complement to this new political situation, the judge had no choice but to apply the principles of 'objective justice' that prevented states from seeking refuge in a zone of lawlessness.[119] It is hard not to see the analogy with centuries-old Christian community-thinking, whereby shared values above positive law ensured the cohesion of the community of the faithful, giving rise to judicial controls of validity.[120]

The issue of 'perplexing'[121] 'general principles of international law' concerned the compulsory jurisdiction of the PCIJ and the determination of the justiciability of disputes brought before the court by states. Elihu Root, the American delegate, showed strong reticence against the court judging on the basis of rules without a basis in either explicit or implicit state consent. The problems of the International Prize Court under the 1907 Hague Convention had to be avoided:

115 ibid 323–24.

116 Wim Decock, *Theologians and Contract Law* (Brill 2012) 122–28.

117 Procès-Verbaux (n 14) 324.

118 Robert Kolb, 'Legal History as a Source of International Law' in Samantha Besson and Jean d'Aspremont (eds), *The Oxford Handbook of the Sources of International Law* (OUP 2017) 282.

119 Procès-Verbaux (n 14) 325.

120 Harold Berman, *Law and Revolution: The Formation of the Western Legal Tradition* (Harvard University Press 1983); Maris Köpcke, *A Short History of Validity and Invalidity* (Intersentia 2019).

121 Fitzmaurice (n 106) 181.

states abhorred of judges sentencing according to justice and equity.[122] This, in turn, was refuted by the Norwegian delegate Francis Hagerup, who considered that the consequences of a *non liquet* would be too grave with regards to the PCIJ's future role, as compared to municipal judges, who could not refuse to exercise their function when justice was sought by individuals.[123] Loder agreed: why should denial of justice be possible for the PCIJ?[124] How could the committee bow to state pressure in advance, if it was assured that this would seriously impede on the Court's responsibility to contribute to the progressive development of international law?[125]

Root opposed to Hagerup's worries that the PCIJ would indeed need to be accepted as having compulsory jurisdiction, but only for 'universally recognized rules of international law'. How could extending the scope of the applicable law before the court imply those 'principles [which were] differently understood in different countries?'[126] If the interpretation of principles differed between states and legal cultures, the dispute ought to be deferred to compulsory arbitration, and not to the PCIJ. Otherwise, neither the United States (which still had to accede to the League of Nations) nor Britain would accept the Court's jurisdiction.[127] 'General principles of international law' risked endangering the confidence placed by states in the PCIJ: 'It is inconceivable that a Government would agree to allow itself to be arraigned before a Court which bases its sentences on its subjective conceptions of the principles of justice.'[128] If the ACJ would decide otherwise, it risked endangering the case of peaceful dispute settlement in domestic as well as transnational public opinion.[129]

Albert de Lapradelle tried to respond to Root's worries by pointing to the existing landscape of international courts. The PCA and a possible International Prize Court could be confronted with situations whereby the courts could be asked to settle disputes wherein no 'fixed and universally recognised rules' existed. They could continue to operate, once the PCIJ was in place.[130] Furthermore, Root's fear of American objections to a broad scope for the court, was 'the expression of American nationalism', as found in the Monroe Doctrine. Lapradelle hoped the

122 Procès-Verbaux (n 14) 309; Pierre d'Argent, 'Sources and the Legality and Validity of International Law. What Makes Law 'International?' in Samantha Besson and Jean d'Aspremont (eds), *The Oxford Handbook of the Sources of International Law* (OUP 2017) 549, note 21, noting the positivist turn taken by the ACJ with respect to the wording of the Prize Court's statute. On the International Prize Court at the Hague Conference of 1907, see Gabriela Frei, *Great Britain, International Law, & The Evolution of Maritime Strategic Thought, 1856–1914* (OUP 2020) 132–34.

123 Procès-Verbaux (n 14) 307.

124 ibid 312.

125 ibid 308.

126 ibid.

127 ibid 309.

128 ibid.

129 ibid 310.

130 ibid 313.

United States could be persuaded that 'great nations must not limit themselves to be continental' but 'must take their proper place in the world'.[131]

During the debate, it became clear that Root and Phillimore reasoned from the domestic, common law setting in their respective jurisdictions. The latter thought that his continental colleagues deduced their defence of 'general principles' from a situation whereby the judge's power is inherently limited by statute law. The use of general principles of law then allowed to expand 'freedom within these limits'. On the contrary, common law systems started from the premise that the judge was in any case obliged to 'do justice according to law'. Yet, was this a question within the mandate of the ACJ? Phillimore thought the committee had been created 'to establish the Court, not to make laws for it'.[132] Why should any reference to the applicable law be made in the statute, if an 'oath taken by the judges' could also contain 'all that might be considered necessary concerning the law to be applied'?[133]

For Phillimore, it sufficed to 'stipulate that the international judge shall have . . . the same rights as the national judge'.[134] What would the effect of such a sentence have been *in concreto*? Phillimore boasted that 'all the principles of common law are applicable to international affairs' and thus 'in fact part of international law'.[135]

Descamps' enthusiastic defence of a natural law underpinning of international law was met with another counter-argument by the Italian delegate Arturo Ricci Busatti. Why not accept *in dubio pro libertate*? If no clear international rule could be found by the court, neither international obligations or enforceable rights existed for the parties.[136] Phillimore agreed with the further development by Ricci Busatti, according to whom the division of tasks between states (legislators) and judges (administering the laws) precluded the attribution of 'legislative powers' to judges, through the recognition of their ability to decide whether a dispute presented to the court was justiciable under general principles of justice, when no specifically applicable rule could be determined.[137]

De Lapradelle firmly opposed this suggestion. He feared that in cases where the court would decline its competence, 'the strong [would] make the law'. The PCIJ would be 'limited to registering the acts of the powerful', who were suspected of having had a strong influence in the formation of positive international law.[138] Phillimore logically responded that complementary solutions existed within the League of Nations: why shouldn't the PCIJ defer a matter to the

131 ibid 314.
132 ibid 316.
133 ibid 320.
134 ibid 316.
135 ibid.
136 ibid 314–15.
137 ibid 316.
138 ibid 320.

Assembly ('to fill the gap by means of legislation') or to the Council ('for [political] decision')?[139]

Descamps perseverated in his firm conviction that the approval of 'universal public opinion' differed from the judges' 'own personal understanding'.[140] He seconded Hagerup's point of view: a *non liquet* was impossible. If conventional law and customary law were insufficient, general principles of law had to guide the PCIJ in adjudication. Logically, the 'doctrines of publicists carrying authority' could then inform the judges of their existence and content.[141] Nevertheless, in the final wording of the sources of law applicable by the PCIJ, general principles of international law as recognized by civilized nations were mentioned without an explicit reference to doctrine. For this reason, De Lapradelle and Hagerup abstained in the vote.[142]

3.2 'New international law': the victory of the pacigérat?

Descamps' study on the 'new international law', published in the *Revue générale de droit international et de législation comparée* in 1929, which he saw consecrated by the Briand-Kellogg Pact, is hard to read with the benefit of hindsight. Descamps prided himself on the installation of a '*pacigérat positif*', or the transformation of the '*pacigérat*', whose progressive development he had wished for in 1898, into positive international law.[143] He proclaimed a sweeping and self-asserting definition: 'the recognition, as universal positive law, of the final constitution of states in an inviolably peaceful society, which can resolve all international disputes internally, without any kind of violence'.[144] The legal starting point of the *pacigérat positif* was the same as in the 1890s: 'the contracted obligation by every state to respect the tranquil possession of other nations regarding their pacific state, without aggression or perturbance'.[145]

According to the relentless 'apostle of peace', the Pact had 'rejected war, to a status outside of international law'. The General Assembly of the League of Nations had completed the work by the adoption of a *General Act for Pacific Dispute Settlement*.[146] Descamps prided himself on having been the author of the first draft for the Permanent Court of Arbitration in 1895, within the Interparliamentary Union. Finally, war had been chased from the law between states.

139 ibid.
140 ibid 318.
141 ibid 319.
142 ibid 649.
143 Edouard Descamps, 'Le droit international nouveau. L'influence de la condamnation de la guerre sur l'évolution juridique internationale' (1930) 31(I) RCADI 486.
144 ibid 486–87.
145 ibid 487. On the concept of 'tranquil possession' and peace-thinking, see Frederik Dhondt, 'Renonciations et possession tranquille: l'abbé de Saint-Pierre, la paix d'Utrecht et la diplomatie de la Régence' (2020) 18 Clio@Thémis.
146 General Act for the Pacific Settlement of International Disputes, Geneva, 26 September 1928, 93 LNTS 343; Descamps (n 15) 167.

All members of the international community were now bound to recognize each other's peaceful possession, and the peaceful constitution of the international order. The despised principle of necessity had finally been excluded from international law. Quoting French Cabinet leader Aristide Briand (1862–1932), Descamps declared that war had become illegitimate, forever.[147] Arbitration had become the sole way to solve disputes.

Self-defence became an exception, restricted to two cases. First, *vim vi repellere* (as reaction to an aggression threatening the peaceful order). Second, if another state refuses an offer of arbitration, the aggrieved state could seek the approval of a competent organ. In the latter case, solely the League of Nations could elaborate a binding procedure. Descamps praised his young compatriot, the Socialist Henri Rolin (1891–1973), for having taken the lead for the elaboration of the General Assembly's General Act. Descamps recalled that the League had, at its core, the prevention of war, by reducing armaments (art. 8 of the Covenant) and by increasing the deterring effect of preventive measures.

The General Act created a three-stage procedure. First, a compulsory attempt at reconciliation, whereby a third party, alien to the conflict, or a fixed League of Nations conciliation commission of five members, would seek an agreement between the parties (art. 4).[148] The following step was arbitration by a tribunal of five members (art. 22), whereby every side could appoint a member, and three (the majority) would be designated by other states. Every case required the conclusion of a basic agreement, establishing the committee's jurisdiction. Of course, if the parties had accepted the Permanent Court of International Justice's jurisdiction prior to their dispute, this would prevail in the second stage (art. 17). If this had not been the case, a final solution consisted in the treatment of the case by the Permanent Court of International Justice, if the permanent arbitration tribunal had failed to present a solution.[149]

Consistent with the reasoning developed to counter Kleen's denigration of permanent neutrality, Descamps stated that coexistence in international society required that the 'essential attributes of power' were harmonized with the 'demands of social life'. His discourse echoed the historical research carried out for the monograph on neutrality, and, of course, his general religious inspiration. Descamps hoped for the replacement of 'bad old practices' with 'better customs',[150] and was convinced of the progressive development of 'the conscience of peoples' and the 'wisdom of governments', which would lead law to a situation of 'effective power'. The 'legal community of civilised peoples' would finally triumph.[151]

147 ibid 169. On Briand: Christophe Bellon, *Aristide Briand. Parler pour agir* (CNRS Éditions 2016).
148 Descamps (n 15) 182.
149 ibid 187.
150 Descamps (n 143) 488.
151 Descamps (n 15) 208.

Descamps repeated this message in his course at The Hague Academy of International Law in 1930.[152] He declared that the Pact of Paris had 'abolished war', and that this constituted the cornerstone of the new system of international law.[153] The 'major peoples' of the world had now entered the legal regime of '*pacigérat positif*', expressing a 'stage the civilised states have finally reached'.[154] With the same eloquence and sense of logical distinction as in his 1902 monograph, Descamps argued that he was not a utopian, since utopia and progress were distinct. The former was a pure product of 'imagination', whereas the latter consisted in the delicate 'perfecting of reality conformably to a natural tendency and true needs'.[155] The wisdom of national governments and legislatures, unconscious and conscious actors of progress, served a transnational mission.[156] The best safeguard of sovereignty was its 'wise limitation'.[157] Descamps died in January 1933, on the verge of Germany's new undoing of the international order.

4. Conclusion

Descamps' work on neutrality can only be understood fully when we combine the extra-legal context of his activism for arbitration, and the political background of his interpretation in Leopold II's Belgium. He represented the quintessence of the Belgian Catholic elite which ruled the country for three decades, and strongly identified with the national interest. Descamps staunchly defended King Leopold's personal colonial endeavours, and tried to further his country's reputation by promoting the general development of international law in several roles: as an activist in the Interparliamentary Union, as an active politician in the national aeropagus, as a member or correspondent of several academies, as an arbiter in the PCA, as a legal adviser and country delegate at The Hague Conferences, the Paris Peace Conference and, of course, as President of the ACJ. A broader assessment of his intellectual activity as a devout Catholic believer and a lawyer would require a comprehensive study of social networks and intellectual pedigree, the latter including other fields of knowledge production than international law.

Descamps intended to surpass the law of neutrality, which was premised on negative obligations. Whereas authors like Kleen explained the voluntary regime of neutrality as a natural consequence of state sovereignty and permanent neutrality as the imposition of a burden on second rate-international actors, Descamps thought neutrality could be assimilated to non-belligerence and the general pacific conduct of international relations. If peace and non-belligerence were to

152 Descamps was a member of the Academy's curatorium from its foundation in 1913 onwards. Yakemtchouk (n 3) col. 234.

153 Descamps (n 143) 486. See also Edouard Descamps, *L'influence de la condamnation de la guerre sur l'évolution juridique internationale* (Sirey 1931).

154 ibid 487.

155 ibid 488.

156 ibid.

157 ibid 493.

constitute the standard situation in international affairs, neutrality should not be seen as a restrictive status, but as a positive incitement to contribute actively to the restoration of peace. In his view, permanently neutralized states were just ahead of their time.[158] Rather than delimiting or extending the rights of belligerents and neutrals, Descamps aimed to move on to a system of collectively guaranteed security. Not state sovereignty as such, but the greater interest of the international community and its progressive evolution ought to define the role of non-belligerent states.

158 See recently Reginbogin and Lottaz (eds) (n 37).

8 The judicial-churchman for peace

Walter George Frank Phillimore (1845–1929)

P. Sean Morris

1. Introduction

In 1898 a caricature in that venerable British magazine, *Vanity Fair*, portrayed Lord Phillimore as a 'judicial-churchman'.[1] This caption perfectly captured the life and times of a man who seemed to have been lost in the pages of history. Phillimore shared a sense of obligation to the Church and the legal community to which he served equally. Phillimore was a man of many hats, and in 1885, the 'who's who' of the legal fraternity, *Men at the Bar*, wrote of the then barrister, a biographical note that summed up his many functions:

> [Sir Walter George Frank Phillimore], Bart., Q.C., D.C.L., patent of precedence, a member of the Western circuit, chancellor of the diocese of Lincoln, official of the archdeaconry of Colchester, secretary to Rt. Hon. Sir Robert Phillimore, judge of High Court of Admiralty 1867–80, student of Christ Church and sometime fellow of All Souls,' Oxon, editor of *Blunts' Book of Church Law*, a student of the Middle Temple 21 Nov., 1865, called to the bar 17 Nov., 1868, Q.C. Dec., 1883 (only son of Rt. Hon. Sir Robert Joseph Phillimore, Bart., late justice of the High Court of Justice, dec.); born 21 Nov., 1845; married 26 July, 1870, Agnes, eldest dau. of late Charles Manners Lushington, Esq., M.P., and has issue.
>
> (see Foster's *Baronetage*)[2]

Walter Phillimore (1845–1929) was born into a family of distinguished jurists ranging from his grandfather (Joseph Phillimore, 1775–1855) to his father

1 Leslie Matthew Ward, Caricature of Judge Sir Walter Phillimore entitled 'A Judicial Churchman' (*Vanity Fair*, 24 November 1898). The caricature featured Phillimore head and shoulders in judicial robes seated at the bench, facing left.

2 Joseph Foster, *Men-at-the-Bar: A Biographical Hand-List of the Members of the Various Inns of Court, including Her Majesty's Judges, Etc.* (2nd edn, Joseph Foster 1885) 363. The abbreviations in the text refers to the following: "Bart.,", Baronet; "QC", Queens Counsel; "DCL", Doctor of Canon Law; "Rt", Right; "Hon", Honourable; "Oxon", Oxford University; "dec", deceased; "dau", daughter; "Esq", Esquire; "MP", Member of Parliament. As for the title of the book mentioned in the text, it is a reference to John Henry Blunt (1823–1884).

DOI: 10.4324/9781003020882-9

(Robert Joseph Phillimore, 1810–1885), along with his own accomplishments.[3] The Phillimore clan was rather extended, however, the jurists' side (including Joseph's first son, John George Phillimore, 1808–1865) of the Phillimores were at one point either a judge, barrister, legal scholar or clergymen. They were also gifted in languages, chiefly Latin[4] and French, to which they used to their advantage in their legal writings and to some extent to navigate the canonical structure of ecclesiastical law and international diplomacy.[5] Walter Phillimore would carve out his own slice of his history in both legal and church circles, different from his father and grandfather, while he maintained the name of Phillimore as a legal institution within the confines of English law and international law. Yet, for legal historians or in the history of international law, the institution of Phillimore is missing. It is not so clear why the Phillimores, especially Walter Phillimore, have been neglected but in recent times the courts at least remind us that such canons,

3 For useful overview of the Phillimore's' see Norman Doe, 'Joseph Phillimore, 1775–1855' in Henry Collin Gray Matthew and Brian Howard Harrison (eds), *Oxford Dictionary of National Biography: Vol. 44, Phelps – Poston* (OUP 2004) 76–77; Norman Doe, 'Sir Robert Joseph Phillimore, Baronet, 1810–1885)' in Henry Collin Gray Matthew and Brian Howard Harrison (eds), *Oxford Dictionary of National Biography: Vol. 44, Phelps – Poston* (OUP 2004) 78–80; Hugh Sankey, 'Walter George Frank Phillimore, First Baron Phillimore, 1845–1929' in Henry Collin Gray Matthew and Brian Howard Harrison (eds), *Oxford Dictionary of National Biography: Vol. 44, Phelps – Poston* (OUP 2004) 80–81.

4 For example, Walter would occasionally write in French, but most of those writings are sparse and or place and publisher cannot be identified, but see Walter George Frank Phillimore, *Est-il à désirer qu'en temps de guerre la propriété privée sur mer soit inviolable?* (1900); Walter George Frank Phillimore, *Droits et devoirs fondamentaux des états* (1925). The only salvageable Latin text attributed to Walter Phillimore is however, a conference paper in 1875, Walter George Frank Phillimore, *De reconventionibus in jure Romano usitatis . . .: dissertatio pro gradu Doctoris in Jure Civili* (Typis Ecclesiastico 1875). There appears to be no citation to this text elsewhere, so its totality is of course, cannot be confirmed. A German text has also been attributed to Lord Phillimore, George Walter Frank Phillimore, *[Aussage] in der Sache des Nachlasses von Francis Clement Trafford Trufort verstorben: Francis Guillaume Clement Trafford gegen Jules Augustus Francis Henri Blanc* (Erscheinungsort nicht ermittelbar 1884).

5 The elder Robert Phillimore wrote a number of books on canon law and international law, and some of those books would later be revised by the younger Walter Phillimore, who separately wrote his own books. Some of these books would also be revised or co-authored with additional help, but some of these books include, Robert Phillimore, Walter George Frank Phillimore and Reginald James Mure, *Commentaries Upon International Law* (3rd edn, Butterworth 1879–1889); Robert Phillimore, Walter George Frank Phillimore and Charles Fuhr Jemmett, *The Ecclesiastical Law of the Church of England* (2nd edn, Sweet & Maxwell 1895); Henry Offley Wakeman and Walter George Frank Phillimore, *An Introduction to the History of the Church of England, From the Earliest Times to the Present Day* (9th edn, Rivingtons 1920); John Henry Blunt, Walter George Frank Phillimore and George Morgan Edwardes-Jones, *The Book of Church Law Being an Exposition of the Legal Rights and Duties of the Parochial Clergy and Laity of the Church of England* (10th edn, Longmans 1905); Walter George Frank Phillimore, *Ecclesiastical Courts of Final Appeal: A Paper Read at the Swansea Church Congress, 1879* (English Church Union 1879); Walter George Frank Phillimore, *Three Centuries of Treaties of Peace – And Their Classic Teaching* (John Murray 1917); Walter George Frank Phillimore, *Schemes for Maintaining General Peace* (HM Stationery 1920); Jose Carlos de Macedo Soares and Walter George Frank Phillimore, *Brazil and the League of Nations* (Pedone 1928).

as it were, have been essential to the development of law (that is just, fair, and kind).[6]

Few works exist that give an account of Walter George Frank Phillimore. Apart from a tribute that captures his life and times upon his death[7] (the other exceptions are a 1933 entry,[8] a 2020 biographical expose by Charlotte Smith,[9] and a 2004 biographical note by Norman Doe),[10] there is not much on the insights of Lord Phillimore as he later became known. Thus, in addition to those writings on Lord Phillimore this chapter charts the writings and contributions of Lord Phillimore at the *fin-de-siècle* and his role during the formation of the League of Nations and the Permanent Court of International Justice (PCIJ). This is a compact chapter and cannot give all the details of Lord Phillimore's illustrious career. Rather, the chapter looks at excerpts of Lord Phillimore's life and time, especially in relation to his involvement in early twentieth-century international law at the Advisory Committee of Jurists (ACJ). The chapter also looks briefly at Lord Phillimore's time as a judge at the House of Lords the then court of last resort in the UK and by extension the Judicial Committee of the Privy Council (JCPC) for the British Empire which handled appeals from the colonies. This would prove pivotal for how Lord Phillimore would carve out his role at the ACJ and the drafting of the PCIJ Statute in 1920.

The intellectual life of Walter Phillimore can be easily mapped through his legal writings. Such writings can be grouped into three categories: legal doctrine/case comments;[11] Church/canon law,[12] conflicts of law (especially in relation to

6 See *Viscount Tredegar v Harwood* (1929) AC 72 where Lord Phillimore attempted to make a distinction between, fair, kind and just, in a case about what type of insurance company to use for house insurance; also cited in *Ross & Anor v HRM Revenue & Customs* (2010) EWHC 13 (Ch), para. 47.

7 WAB, 'The Right Hon. Baron Phillimore of Shiplake, Barnonet, P.C., D.C.L., LL.D., J.P.' (1928) 14 Transactions of the Grotius Society: Problems of Peace and War, Papers Read Before the Society in the Year 1928 v–ix.

8 WF Geikie-Cobb, 'Lord Phillimore' in RS Forman (ed), *Great Christians* (Nicholson and Watson 1933).

9 Charlotte Smith, 'The Disruptive Power of Legal Biography: The Life of Lord Phillimore: Churchman and Judge' (2020) 41 Journal of Legal History 164.

10 Doe (n 3) 'Walter Phillimore'.

11 Walter George Frank Phillimore and DM Owen, *The Case of the Rev. Mr. Green's Imprisonment* (The Free Press 1881); Robert Phillimore and Walter George Frank Phillimore, *Judgment Delivered by the Right Honourable Sir Robert Phillimore in the Case of the Office of the Judge Promoted by Sheppard v Bennett* (Rivingtons 1870); Walter George Frank Phillimore, *Remarks on the Judgement of the Privy Council in Hebbert v. Purchas* (Swift 1871); Robert Phillimore and Walter George Frank Phillimore, *Judgment Delivered by the Right Honourable Sir Robert Phillimore in the Cases of Martin v. Mackonochie and Flamank v. Simpson* (London 1868); Walter George Frank Phillimore, *Remarks on the Judgment of the Privy Council in Hebbert c Purchas by a Barrister* (Swift and Co. 1871).

12 See also (n 5) for additional works; Walter George Frank Phillimore, The Government of the Church in Relation to the State and the Laity (The place of the publication of this title is undetermined, however, Phillimore has been credited as 'Barrister-at-Law', and 'Chancellor

marriage and divorce);[13] and to a large extent, what I will refer to as comparative international law[14] in this chapter. There are also non-legal publications by Phillimore but they are excluded from my discussion.[15] As a caveat to frame Phillimore's writings in this chapter as comparative international law it is because Walter Phillimore had to deal with both how English law was interpreted and applied in the colonies and therefore had distinct features, and at the same time, Walter Phillimore was a man of 'international law' in the traditional sense of the term. Hence, the label of comparative international law fit such amalgamation, at least for the purposes of my discussion in this chapter.

The writings of Lord Phillimore that pertained to the League of Nations including the PCIJ evolved mostly during the war, his time at the ACJ and subsequent post PCIJ life where he co-authored works such as *Brazil and League*;[16] foreign policy,[17] the Church,[18] and on the *First Assembly*.[19] Furthermore, after his death, a few more works that Phillimore authored were published (posthumously) and those works were chiefly on international law or the League of Nations (presumably were in preparation before his death) but included other topics.[20]

---

of the Diocese of Lincoln') Furthermore, the publication also stated that it is 'reprinted from the Union Review'.

13 Walter George Frank Phillimore, *Report of Committee on Divorce Jurisdiction and Procedure: Madrid Conference, 1913* (Richard Flint & Co. 1913); Walter George Frank Phillimore, *International Law of Marriage* (Review Publishing co. 1902); Walter George Frank Phillimore, *Remarriage After Divorce* (English Church Union Office 1885).

14 These writings include, Walter George Frank Phillimore, *Is It Desirable to Free Private Property at Sea from Capture in Time of War?* (Partridge and Cooper, circa 1900); Walter George Frank Phillimore, *Destruction of Merchantmen by a Belligerent* (Grotius Society 1917); Walter George Frank Phillimore, *Scheme for the Permanent Court of International Justice* (Grotius Society 1921).

15 Walter George Frank Phillimore, *The Anglican Communion in Relation to its Parts* (Society for Promoting Christian Knowledge 1908); Walter George Frank Phillimore, *How to Write the History of a Family: A Guide for the Genealogist* (E. Stock 1888); William Phillimore Watts Phillimore and Walter George Frank Phillimore, *Genealogy of the Family of Phillimore: Part I and Part II* (G. Simpson & Co. 1922).

16 See (n 5).

17 Walter George Frank Phillimore, *President Wilson's Policy* (Stationery Office 1920); Walter George Frank Phillimore, *Indemnities of War: Subsidies and Loans* (Stationery Office 1920); Walter George Frank Phillimore, *Plebiscite and Referendum* (Stationery Office 1920).

18 Walter George Frank Phillimore, *The Lawmaking Organs of the Church of England* (Church Assembly 1928).

19 Oliver Brett, Robert Gascoyne-Cecil and Walter George Frank Phillimore, *The First Assembly: A Study of the Proceedings of the First Assembly of the League of Nations* (Macmillan and Co. 1921).

20 Walter George Frank Phillimore, *Agriculture and the Preservation of the Countryside* (1932); Walter George Frank Phillimore, *The Case for Nationalist Spain, as Presented at the Great Queen's Hall Meeting, 23rd March 1938: Speeches by the Right Honourable Lord Phillimore and Others* (1938); Walter George Frank Phillimore, *Herbert Arthur Charlie Sturgess, A Collection of Books Chiefly on Foreign and International Law* collected by the Late Phillimore of Shiplake and Presented to the Library of the Honourable Society of the Middle Temple

After his death, the Hungarian Lawyer's Association in 1930 celebrated his life with a fitting tribute by the respected Hungarian jurist Emil Nagy-Böszörményi.[21] In 1908 under the presidency of Walter Phillimore, the International Law Association met in Budapest, so it was perhaps a fitting reminder in 1930 that the Hungarian Lawyers Association recognized the contribution of Walter Phillimore to Hungarian international legal relations. At that meeting in 1908, Phillimore memorably remarked that the Budapest meeting was 'a landmark in the interchange of international courtesies'.[22]

From the array of academic writings, commentaries, and revisions of texts that Lord Phillimore engaged in throughout his lifetime, they are examples of how the intellectual mind of the man was moulded in law, justice, and the moral authority of the human soul as part of a heavenly kingdom. For Lord Phillimore, the boundaries between intellectualism and legal providence would on occasions be evidence of how the right form of justice is administered. As Phillimore career progressed through the English Courts, it would not have been unusual for Lord Phillimore to find himself in other divisions of the High Court that does not include, for instance, matters of a matrimonial nature especially if such acts involved the parting of ways, which were counter to his moral convictions as a man of the cloth.

Lord Phillimore, was thus, as the *Vanity Fair* caricature of 1898 portrayed him, a 'judicial-churchman', and a man of rules, moral authority, and a (legal) scholar. As a judicial-churchman, the legal writings of Lord Phillimore, along with his ecclesiastical commentaries, and revisions of his fathers' works on international law, leave us with a picture that is largely accurate when one visualizes the context of 'judicial-churchman'. That, in some ways, is only part of the character of the man. The full and real Lord Phillimore cannot be captured in this chapter alone, so we are left to unpick two particular periods of his life in the early twentieth century, to offer further analysis of Lord Phillimore: his time at the House of Lords shortly after 1914 and his subsequent role at the ACJ.

2. Phillimore and the formation of legal authority in the House of Lords

Among the various disagreements at the ACJ meeting in 1920 two in particular stood out: disagreements over the source doctrine in international law and jurisdiction. Lord Phillimore, for his part, was also at the centre of these

(Robert Maclehose & Co. 1929). Because some the works listed here are credited to Phillimore after his death, it is not so clear to what extent Lord Phillimore are behind some of them.

21 Emil Nagy-Böszörményi, *Lord Phillimore emlékbeszéd a Magyar Jogászeglyet 1930. Január 25- iki rendkivüli közgyülésén elmondotta* (Franklin-Tarsulat 1931) (this tribute is published in Hungarian and very few references to its existence are out there).

22 Oliver E Bodington, 'Form of Will of an Alien in France' (1909) 35 Law Mag & Rev Quart Rev Juris ser 34, 42.

disagreements. Although the next part of the chapter looks at Lord Phillimore from the perspective of jurisdiction at the ACJ, the approach in this section is different. Rather, this section looks at the authority of judicial decisions from the perspective of Lord Phillimore while he was at the House of Lords shortly after 1914 and to ascertain if that period had an impact on his role at the ACJ especially in relation to jurisdiction. Although Lord Phillimore and Elihu Root hatched a plan to examine 'the authority of judicial decisions and the opinions of writers as a means for the application and development of law',[23] that part of the discussion is not taken up this chapter. That part of the narrative continues elsewhere.

The few cases that Lord Phillimore issued judgment in during his stint at the House of Lords (then the UK's final appellate court) can give us some insights into how he moulded his views from an adjudicatory perspective in relation to 'authority'.[24] From 1915 to 1917 no known judgments from the House of Lords were attributable to Lord Phillimore,[25] however, from 1918–1920 Lord Phillimore heard several cases at the House of Lords.[26] In 1914 only one judgment was attributed to Lord Phillimore, *Brooks v Inland Revenue*,[27] a case in which he dissented. The House of Lords cases were selected as they represented the final legal authority and also they established legal authority in their own right. Hence, the idea is to see how Lord Phillimore cultivated 'authority' during these cases and the impact they had on his formulation of 'authority' for the PCIJ in 1920.

In *Brooks v Inland Revenue*,[28] Lord Phillimore issued a dissent in which he said there were grounds for 'legitimate diversity of opinion'[29] and although used in a different context, it would signal the extent to which Lord Phillimore at the ACJ would also argue for the need of the PCIJ to open up to a diverse world where non-League members could have access to the PCIJ.

23 Advisory Committee of Jurists, *Procès-Verbaux of the Proceedings of the Committee, 16 June–24 July 1920, with Annexes* (Van Langenhuysen, The Hague, 1920) 344.

24 The House of Lord Cases are: *Brooks v Inland Revenue* [1914] UKHL TC_7_236; *London and North-Western Railway Co. v. Richard Hudson & Sons Ltd* [1920] UKHL 452; *Duke of Northumberland v. Commissioners of Inland Revenue* [1920] UKHL 630; *Rex v. Beard* [1920] UKHL 743; *AW Williams (Surveyor of Taxes) v WM Singer & Ors; AF Pool (Surveyor of Taxes) v Royal Exchange Assurance* [1920] UKHL TC_7_387; *Singer v. Williams* [1920] UKHL 186; *Singer v. Williams (Surveyor of Taxes)* [1920] UKHL TC_7_419; *Williams v. Singer and Others; Singer v. Williams* (1920) UKHL 386; *Pool v. Royal Exchange Assurance* [1920] UKHL 380; *London and North-Western Railway Co., v Richard Hudson & Sons Ltd* [1920] UKHL 452; *Williams v Singer* [1920] UKHL 2; *Casdagli v Casdagli* [1918] UKHL 411.

25 This is based on my search of the British and Irish Legal (BAILI) database on the cases of the House of Lords from 1913–1920 and serve as the basis of my discussion in this section. In fact, all the cases for the period were looked at year by year, and only cases attributable to Lord Phillimore, which is, where he heard those cases, were used for the discussions in this section. Those cases are listed in the previous Note, and refer to further below.

26 See (n 23).

27 ibid.

28 *Brooks v Inland Revenue* [1914] UKHL TC_7_236.

29 ibid 247.

The disputes in which Lord Phillimore served as judge at the House of Lords up to 1920 were occasionally disputes that involved many nations of the world when the British Empire is taken into account and cases on conflicts of laws involving more than one (European) state but referred to English law. In *Casdagli v Casdagli* for instance,[30] Lord Phillimore was of the opinion that 'domicile' as interpreted by the English High Court was the basis for jurisdiction over a matter concerning a suit brought against the husband by his wife.[31] It was not unusual for divorce proceedings in English Courts at the time due to the various nations of the Empire to involve different nationalities. In *Casdagli v Casdadli*, Egyptian and Greek nationalities were in contention, along with the fact that of being a British subject. These exposure to 'pluralities' would in part form part of the views of Phillimore later on at some of the discussions during the ACJ meeting. However, the case is an example in terms of the legal character of positions that Lord Phillimore held during the ACJ sessions for which he would not necessarily deviate. Another issue worth pointing out is that the *Casdagli* case involved multiple domiciles, ethnicities, and nationalities, and although Lord Phillimore looked at various cases of comparative (international) law in nature in his analysis he was of the opinion that 'foreign law' should only be 'treated as fact not law' in English jurisprudence.[32] Making this argument was crucial as it would allow Lord Phillimore to delve into the case law to support his arguments as to why the English Courts had no jurisdiction over the divorce but rather the place where 'the husband had a domicile in Egypt'.[33] Thus, through such lenses, it is easy to see how Lord Phillimore was a man of legal conscience and would only back up his statements at the ACJ with a sharp legal view to illustrate why, for instance, the jurisdiction of the PCIJ was a matter of the applicable international rules. This also includes those states that were not members of the League of Nations.

For an English jurist, legal argumentation is unashamedly shaped, in part, by how the concepts of 'contract' and 'negligence' evolve in the common law. Hence, from that premise, whether in domestic legal matters or negotiating a draft statute of an international court, the presence of an English jurist will no doubt raise questions or seek to dismiss a position of a party by employing language based on contracts or negligence. At the ACJ meeting in 1920, Lord Phillimore was no different when he agreed that the PCIJ will be established by a contract[34] and therefore contracting parties can also use to their advantage 'opening up' the PCIJ to other nations. During an exchange with Edouard Descamps, Phillimore, framed his questions in contractual terms, wanting to know 'whether the President would give compulsory jurisdiction to the Court only in case contractual agreement existed between the parties, obliging them to submit

30 *Casdagli v Casdagli* [1918] UKHL 411. Finding that English Courts had no jurisdiction to dissolve the marriage since the husband acquired Egyptian domicile.

31 ibid 427–28.

32 ibid 429.

33 ibid 430.

34 Procès-Verbaux (n 23) 222.

to the court's jurisdiction'.[35] This type of literary legal demonstration was not unusual for Lord Phillimore, and, hence, the use of 'contractual agreement' had similarities to how he also created and framed terms such as 'contractual negligence' at the House of Lords. In *North-Western Railway b Hudson & Sons*,[36] Lord Phillimore framed the dispute as 'constructive negligence'[37] and that the Lords had 'to consider the contractual relations of the parties'.[38] Apart from his ability to engage in literary manoeuvres, Lord Phillimore was also adept at setting out how authority is established, a point he made by noting that the contractual relations included a form of authorization.[39] That line of reasoning was different from how Lord Phillimore questioned the President of the ACJ at the eleventh meeting on 29th of June 1920 on the different forms of 'contractual agreements' on compulsory jurisdiction.[40] These examples only demonstrate the manner in which it was necessary for Lord Phillimore to place emphasis on the roots of his approach to authority and what legal form authority took in regards to his own approach in the ACJ.

3. Jurisdiction: Lord Phillimore and the Advisory Committee of Jurists

As a practising barrister, the question of jurisdiction by courts has been quite central to how the then Walter Phillimore strategized and argued his cases. For example, in *MacKonochie v Lord Penzance*,[41] he noted that the authority of a court can be in 'excess of jurisdiction' and therefore grounds to prohibit a court from establishing jurisdiction.[42] This was the situation in *MacKonochie v Lord Penzance* (1881) where a spiritual war of jurisdiction erupted over ornaments and the role of ecclesiastical courts.[43]

Of course, the fight over liturgy and ornaments of English churches in the late Victorian era would not be a way of viewing how the jurisdiction of the PCIJ came about in the early twentieth century. Yet, that is precisely how the issue of jurisdiction was important to the views of the now Lord Phillimore at the ACJ in 1920. In *MacKonochie v Lord Penzance* (1881), Walter Phillimore represented the appellant and argued before the House of Lords in the spiritual rift among the men of cloth in the Church of England and the jurisdiction of the ecclesiastical courts. Lord Phillimore essentially argued that the House of Lords should prohibit the High Court from deciding on the matter. To avoid doubt of my

35 ibid 224. See also, 277, Annex No. 5.
36 *London and North-Western Railway Co. V. Richard Hudson & Sons Ltd* [1920] UKHL 452.
37 ibid 459.
38 ibid.
39 ibid.
40 Procès-Verbaux (n 23) 244.
41 6 AppCas 424 (1881).
42 ibid.
43 See also Charlotte Smith, 'Martin v. Mackonochie/Mackonochie v. Penzance: A Crisis of Character and Identify in the Court of Arches' (2003) 24 Journal of Legal History 250.

interpretation, the following opening passage of Walter Phillimore's argument is worth quoting at length:

> The objection to what has been done in this case is not merely to the form of the proceeding, which might only be the subject of an appeal, but is to the very jurisdiction of the Arches Court, the lawful limits of which have been exceeded. The only proper remedy therefore is by a proceeding in prohibition. The title of the High Court of Justice is to restrain all inferior Courts where they act in excess of their jurisdiction cannot be doubted, and this is a case in which that cause for prohibition actually exists.[44]

As a skilled barrister, Walter Phillimore knew where to draw the line in the sand when it comes to courts establishing jurisdictions (whether over persons or the capacity of governments). It is through this lens which Lord Phillimore, I would argue, acted at the ACJ in relation to the jurisdiction of the PCIJ.

There are many aspects of Lord Phillimore's role and views at the ACJ one could develop in order to paint a picture of his role including the infamous Root-Phillimore plan.[45] However, this part of the chapter is concerned only with how Phillimore proposed and argued the jurisdiction of the PCIJ during the ACJ meetings in 1920. Thus, the discussion above on Walter Phillimore's legal skills before the House of Lords concerning the jurisdictions of the ecclesiastical courts is one of the obvious starting points to draw some comparisons with his proposals and arguments on the jurisdiction of the PCIJ.

From the outset the question of the court's jurisdiction has been a priority. The question was whether the jurisdiction would be compulsory or only applicable to certain subject matters. For instance, during the first meeting of the ACJ on 16 June 1920,[46] Edouard Descamps, as chair, noted in his opening remarks that the jurisdiction of the court should not be conflated with that of national jurisdiction.[47] Chairman Descamps in July 1920 was not hiding the fact that the legal contours of jurisdiction in international law were separate from the political jurisdictions of states. Rather, he was making it known that the organism of

44 AppCas 424 (1881) 426.

45 Although this plan centred on what become the 'sources' of international law, as embodied in Article 38 of the World Court, this chapter, does not discuss the Root-Phillimore Plan, or Lord Phillimore's approach in the ACJ to Article 38. But see, Procès-Verbaux (n 23), 344; Lauri Malksoo, 'Sources of International Law in the Nineteenth-Century European Tradition: Insights from Practice and Theory' in Samantha Besson and Jean d'Aspremont (eds), *The Oxford Handbook of the Sources of International Law* (OUP 2017).

46 Procès-Verbaux (n 23) 1.

47 ibid 15: 'There may possibly be a mistaken idea underlying this desire to model the organism of international jurisdiction upon the prototype of national jurisdiction. It would be well never to lose sight of what jurists mean, when, in their somewhat crude but expressive language, they assert that the 'subject-matter' is not precisely the same, as in national communities; the individuals are subordinated to the sovereign Government, while the international community is eminently one in which the States are coordinated and enjoy equal sovereignty.'

international jurisdiction was a matter of how states operated in the international community. But that was Edouard Descamps in a more diplomatic role, given that his approach to jurisdiction would be metered out more legally when he encountered the robust and sophisticated propositions of Lord Phillimore.

The jurisdiction of the PCIJ was established in Articles 34–36 under the chapter titled 'Competence of the Court'. Thus, Article 34 was compact: 'Only States or Members of the League of Nations can be parties in cases before the Court.' Articles 35 and 36 would be more explanatory but essentially contained the jurisdiction *ratione personae* and jurisdiction *ratione materiae* of the court respectively. These two confinements of jurisdiction in the PCIJ were evident from the debates between Lord Phillimore and Edouard Descamps as President of the ACJ during several of the meetings. For example at the tenth meeting of the ACJ on 26 June 1920 where the ACJ looked at the question of jurisdiction, that is, 'what States may appear before the Court?',[48] Chairman Descamps was of the opinion that the jurisdiction of the PCIJ should entail 'all Members of the League, that the court should be accessible to States non-members of the League, by means of a special procedure'.[49] This point however was not so easily digested by other members, including Lord Phillimore who backed the position of the Japanese member Adatci. The *Procès-Verbaux* captured the exchanges as such:

> M Adatci stated that the principle which had governed the establishment of the League of Nations was that, in the first place, it should be a limited organisation creating conventional obligations for its Members. This principle also, in spite of some hesitation, had been the starting point of all the work connected with the work of the Conference of Paris. The question put forward by the President, according to M. Adatci, could with advantage be dealt with in two separate articles. The first could contain general rules applicable except for contrary provisions to the Members of the League of Nations. The second article would deal with the question whether the Court should be open on equal terms to States who were not Members of the League of Nations. M. Adatci thought that these two questions were quite separate. He agreed to the solution of the latter on the lines indicated by the President. He thought that the Court might be open to all States, but naturally, under certain well established conditions.[50]

This position was in fact endorsed by a few of the ACJ members including Altamira and Lord Phillimore, although Lord Phillimore seemed to have endorse Adatci 'motives and his conclusions'.[51] Lord Phillimore argued that 'The Court in process of organisation will be established by a contract. It must therefore in the first place be open to the contracting parties, but these, if they find it to

48 Procès-Verbaux (n 23) 219.
49 ibid 220.
50 ibid 220–21.
51 ibid 222.

their advantage, may open the court to other States.'[52] Phillimore had always seen early attempts to establish an international court such as the efforts at The Hague Conferences of 1899/1907 as 'infant projects' and in any event, the times had since changed. For Lord Phillimore he never shared the same approach as some ACJ members such as those Bernard Loder had on the jurisdiction of the PCIJ. For instance, Loder believed that 'special mention should be made in the constitution of the Court of the right of non-member States to have access to the new jurisdiction by means of a special procedure'.[53] Lord Phillimore believed that 'the doors of the Court must be wide open to non-members'.[54] Apparently, sensing that the men disagreed on some aspects of the jurisdiction of the PCIJ, the astute Norwegian former Prime Minister, Francis Hagerup, attempted to shift the debate to another question relating to jurisdiction: 'to what extent may obligatory jurisdiction be admitted?'[55] It was a question that would still highlight the cordial disagreement among the men. To put it diplomatically, the cordial disagreement between Bernard Loder and Lord Phillimore over jurisdiction was 'gentle', however, Phillimore felt he had a stronger position on the matter. The verbatim quotation from the *Procès-Verbaux* speaks for itself:

> Lord Phillimore regretted that his conscience as a judge compelled him to differ with M. Loder. He did not disagree on principle; he thought that fundamentally they agreed. He thought that the international jurisdiction must be widened, and that in some way or another, parties must be induced to bring legal questions to the Court. The method suggested by M. de Lapradelle might be satisfactory. However, though he saw the object, he did not quite see the way of attaining it. At the same time it should not be forgotten that the compulsory jurisdiction of the Court is laid down for scattered cases by the main Treaties of Peace. Outside these cases, Lord Phillimore thought that the Court had the competence which the parties conferred on it by mutual agreement. He thought that it would be preferable not to specify details, but to limit themselves to saying that the Court shall be competent to deal with cases assigned to it by the treaties in force or by future conventions. From the practice point of view, Lord Phillimore pointed out the difficulty there is to define the point at issue; he quoted the case of the Atlantic Fisheries Arbitration. For this reason he thought it would be preferable to avoid the necessity for a special convention or compromise between the two parties on the competence of the Court. Finally, he again put forward the idea of defining the competence of the Court by a simple *reference* to treaties and conventions.[56]

52 ibid.
53 ibid 220.
54 ibid 222.
55 ibid 224.
56 ibid 225–26.

The above passage was classic Walter Phillimore. He cordially accepted an argument that is presented, but then meekly tore it apart and pointed to the holes and problems of such arguments. In fact, it was as if the judicial-churchman was pointing to the gates of a heavenly jurisdiction as a form of a necessity to include all nations of the world and not the privilege few that enjoyed membership in the League or who must go through complicated special procedures advanced by Bernard Loder to enjoy the fruits of universal jurisdiction. Thus, in what is an amalgamation of views shared by the Japanese ACJ member, Adatci, and also Fernandes of Brazil, Lord Phillimore would later propose what similarly ended up in Articles 36 of the PCIJ Statute.

That proposal was reprinted in the *Procès-Verbaux*:

Annex No. 2

Article on the subject of jurisdiction proposed by Lord Phillimore

In the absence of any special convention between the parties, the Permanent Court of International Justice shall be deemed to be the Court of Arbitration mentioned in Article 13 of the of the Covenant, and shall have jurisdiction in all cases of disputes between States, which involve:

a the interpretation of a Treaty;
b any question of international law;
c the existence of any fact, which, if established, would constitute a breach of any International obligation;
d the extent or nature of the reparation to be made for any such breach;
e the interpretation of its own judgements.

The Court shall also have jurisdiction in the several cases which are referred to it by the Treaties of Versailles.

In all the cases above-mentioned the parties shall be deemed to have agreed to submit the dispute to the Court so that the Court will be competent to hear and determine it according to the provisions of Article 14 of the Covenant, and either of the parties may require the Court to exercise jurisdiction without any further assent on the part of the other party.

Note by Lord Phillimore

In my view, and that, I think, of most of my Colleagues, no power is given to the Court by Article 14, unless the parties submit the dispute to it. Even if they were bound (which I doubt) to submit any dispute to the Court (except those provided in the Treaties of Versailles) unless, in fact, they submit, there would be no jurisdiction.

But the Court can only be established by a Convention, to which the Members of the Leagues must be parties, and by that Convention they can give the Court any jurisdiction which they please, though it was not given by the Original Covenant.

Perhaps we should append a note to our report, justifying our recommendation by this consideration.[57]

The Phillimore proposal was amended by Francis Hagerup[58] and in the Statute of the PCIJ adopted by the Assembly of the League of Nations in 1920, Article 36 reads:

> The jurisdiction of the Court comprises all cases which the parties refer to it and all matters specially provided for in Treaties and Conventions in force.
>
> The Members of the League of Nations and the States mentioned in the Annex to the Covenant may, either when signing or ratifying the Protocol to which the present Statute is adjoined, or at a later moment, declare that they recognize as compulsory *ipso facto* and without special agreement, in relation to any other Member or State accepting the same obligation, the jurisdiction of the Court in all or any of the classes of legal disputes concerning:
>
> (a) the interpretation of a treaty;
> (b) any question of international law;
> (c) the existence of any fact which, if established, would constitute a breach of an international obligation;
> (d) the nature or extent of the reparation to be made for the breach of an international obligation.
>
> The declaration referred to above may be made unconditionally or on condition of reciprocity on the part of several or certain Members or States, or for a certain time.
>
> In the event of a dispute as to whether the Court has jurisdiction, the matter shall be settled by the decision of the Court.[59]

The *Procès-Verbaux* has captured important elements of the debate during the ACJ meetings in relation to various Articles of the Statue of the PCIJ. And, those relating to Article 36, some of which I discussed above from the lens of Lord Phillimore, have shown that the end result took into consideration the evolution of international law. Thus, Article 36 on jurisdiction of the PCIJ Statute concerns how international law evolves to include the many nations and civilizations of the world outside of the narrow scope of League membership in 1920.

Lord Phillimore's ideas about jurisdiction were not surprising. Thus, when Bernard Loder as President of the ACJ signalled certain 'special procedures' for

57 ibid 252.
58 ibid 253.
59 PCIJ Statue, Article 36, 1920.

non-League states, it was a jab too far. First, there was the issue of 'States' within the British Empire, and second, there was Lord Phillimore's approach to the practice and interpretation of law. The latter was quite different from Edouard Loder. Lord Phillimore had intimate knowledge of how English Ecclesiastical Courts competed for jurisdiction in the long-running right to church ornaments and liturgy in the various *MacKonchie* litigations from the late 1860s through to the early 1880s. At the ACJ, Lord Phillimore was thus certain and confident that his proposal and approach to the jurisdiction of the PCIJ was the right one. And right he was, since the jurisdiction Articles of the PCIJ, Articles 34–36, still in their present form of the ICJ Statute have all the Phillimorian strokes of plurality. Article 34, for instance, is about 'State or members of the League', which satisfied the interests of the British in 1920 regarding the various 'members' of the Empire. Furthermore, Article 36 touched all the right notes as originally penned by Lord Phillimore even if those notes were later lightly diluted by the Brazilian ACJ member to break the deadlock and reach an agreement.

Although the question of the Courts' jurisdiction is an unsettled debate in modern times as it was in 1920 at the ACJ, the part played by Lord Phillimore to shape the intellectual and practical necessity on jurisdiction in the PCIJ has been as a result of how the judicial-churchman was able to combine tact, legal skills, and the need for inclusivity for a world communion of dispute settlement.

4. Conclusion: the judicial-churchman for peace

This compact discussion of the life and times and Lord Phillimore only touches the surface of the magnitude and reach of the man during his career that began as an Oxford-educated barrister, his rise to the Court of Appeal and the House of Lords, and subsequent member of the ACJ responsible for drafting the Statute of the PCIJ. Even this part of the chapter is not so much a conclusion, but rather to highlight the fact that Lord Phillimore's complete biography is not yet written. The schemes of Lord Phillimore's life as a legal writer, barrister, and canonist in the Victorian era is yet to be fully explored. At the *fin-de-siècle*, Lord Phillimore's more active participation in the movement for peace, his role in the international legal associations along with appointments at the highest judicial branches require separate monographs. Hence, this conclusion is only about reaffirming the introductory chapter of Lord Phillimore's contribution to the English and international legal space which has been lost to legal scholarship. At least, to some extent, we are further equipped with how parts of Lord Phillimore's life played out in order to appreciate the fact Lord Phillimore had been a judicial-churchman for peace.

The shaping of Lord Phillimore as a judicial-churchman for peace was perhaps evident from his single-authored work that traced the evolution of peace treaties since Westphalia to the early twentieth century.[60] In the preface, Lord

60 Phillimore (n 5) *Three Centuries*.

Phillimore wrote: 'We are looking forward to the future of peace. We are looking for it.'[61] It was a text produced during the war and like many other individuals (and nations) – all were looking forward to peace. But there was something more messianic and ecclesiastical about Lord Phillimore's observation of looking forward to the future of peace. For Lord Phillimore, a peace should be 'just' and should 'also be for higher reasons'.[62] Arguably, the higher reasons could also have been a reference to how the political masters of the belligerents sought to conclude the war or if another reading is invoked, Lord Phillimore was also making it known that peace is the desired form of humanizing the world as set out in the teachings of those beyond the heavens. Whatever interpretation we apply to Walter George Frank Phillimore's invocation for peace, his arguments were not far from those of his convictions regarding beliefs in higher humans beyond the heavens, and importantly, to apply the law in a just and fair manner. Hence, the real Lord Phillimore, when all the legal contention is stripped away, was indeed a judicial-churchman for peace.

61 ibid xi.
62 ibid 2.

9 'Where is your tribunal?'

Bernard Loder (1849–1935) and the quest for international justice

Freya Baetens and Veronica Lavista[1]

1. Introduction

This chapter provides a detailed historical and biographical sketch of the life and career of Bernard Loder, focusing on how his work as a member of the Advisory Commission of Jurists (ACJ) helped shape the statute of the Permanent Court of International Justice (PCIJ). Loder did not achieve his position as a scholar or thinker, he was not an 'eminent publicist' whose writings can be counted among the subsidiary sources of international law in the sense of Article 38 of the ICJ Statute, but he was an experienced judge with strong ideas on how to establish a functioning international court.[2] At times, the analysis in this chapter transcends the legal discipline, venturing into historical-sociological terrain. The main body of the chapter is structured into two sections, highlighting the positions held by Loder which turned out to be crucial for his contribution to the early twentieth-century development of international law: first, his background as a Dutch practicing lawyer, government representative, judge and active contributor to several international associations; second, his roles within the League of Nations system: as a member of the Advisory Committee of Jurists, as a judge at the PCIJ, and as a member of the Committee of Experts for the Progressive Codification of International Law. The chapter concludes with a commentary on Loder's legacy.

2. Loder's background

2.1 A Dutch practicing lawyer, government representative, and judge

This section focuses first on Loder's early life and university education, the historical and legal context of his background and writings in the late nineteenth

1 This work was partly supported by the Research Council of Norway through its Centres of Excellence funding scheme (project number 223274) and the FRIPRO Young Research Talents (project number 274946). The authors are grateful for the input of Jean Salmon, Jean-Marc Thouvenin and Nikiforos Panagis. The content of this chapter is the authors' alone and does not reflect the views of ICSID.

2 Loder also had a significant interest in the development of private international law as positive law beyond the issue of conflict of laws. BCJ Loder, 'La Cinquième Conférence de Droit International Privé' [1927] Grotius Annuaire International 1, 4; BCJ Loder, 'La Sixième Conférence de Droit International Privé' [1929] Grotius Annuaire International 7.

DOI: 10.4324/9781003020882-10

and early twentieth century, his contribution to legal scholarship, as well as questions relating to the science and structure of his writings. Subsequently, this section zooms in on Loder's views on the development of international law and his vision of the international legal order, providing an insight into the link between his professional background and his contributions to the ACJ's work.

2.1.1 A maritime lawyer and Supreme Court judge

Born in Amsterdam on 13 September 1849, Bernard Cornelis Johannes Loder (1849–1935) chose to pursue law studies, first at the Athenaeum Illustre of Amsterdam (the predecessor of the University of Amsterdam), then at the University of Leiden where his research was supervised by the constitutional law professor J.T. Buys. Loder's thesis (the winning submission in a competition organized by the university) was entitled *De leer der volkssouvereiniteit in hare ontwikkeling, aanbeveling en bestrijding historisch-kritisch beschouwd* ('The doctrine of sovereignty of the people in its development, recommendation and opposition: a historical-critical perspective').[3] In this thesis, he argued that the basis of the State should not be sought in the sovereignty of the people, nor in divine law. Rather, Loder adhered to the organic theory of State as developed by the German historic school, arguing that democracy is guilty of a two-pronged error: it starts from the mistaken premise that all people are equal and it denies the essence of the State.[4] Loder believed in the *in*equality of individuals, both mentally and physically, which democracy, according to him, overlooks. In regarding all individuals as equals and giving them the same rights and influence on governance, democracy disregards the very essence of the State as more than the mere sum of its citizens.[5] No individual has an *a priori* right to be part of the governing or legislative process, in the same way as not all limbs of the body have the same function: only those who are suitable to govern should be allowed to do so.[6] For this reason he dismissed the Dutch 'census suffrage' system that was in place at the time,[7] because it was insufficiently selective. His entire life, he remained faithful to this conservative outlook, leading him among others to oppose general voting rights in 1933.[8]

3 B Loder, *De Leer der Volkssouvereiniteit in hare ontwikkeling, aanbeveling en bestrijding historisch-kritisch beschouwd* (Leiden 1873).

4 ibid 222–23.

5 ibid 224.

6 ibid 226–27.

7 In accordance with Article 76 of the Dutch Constitution (version enacted in 1848), every adult Dutch person (a term interpreted by the Supreme Court as solely referring to male persons, unless the provision explicitly included women) in possession of his civil and political rights, was allowed to vote if they paid a certain sum via the direct taxation system.

8 CG Roelofsen, 'Loder, Bernard Cornelia Johannes (1849–1935)' in *Biografisch Woordenboek van Nederland* <http://resources.huygens.knaw.nl/bwn/BWN/lemmata/bwn2/loder> (12 November 2013).

After his graduation from Leiden, Loder established a legal practice in Rotterdam, where he gained a good reputation as a maritime law specialist. Apparently, he was such a persuasive advocate that other lawyers were retaining his services to plead their cases in court.[9] In 1898, he became famous for his (failed) battle against the board of the Royal Dutch Petroleum Society (currently operating as Royal Dutch Shell) that had decided to severely restrict the rights of its shareholders. After having served as elected chairman of the bar association in 1907, Loder was appointed as a judge to the *Hoge Raad* (Supreme Court of the Netherlands) in 1908, a function which he would continue to fulfil until he joined the PCIJ bench in 1921.

2.1.2 Moving to the forefront of Dutch foreign policy

From the beginning of his career, Loder was interested in international (maritime) law – an interest which did not go unnoticed in The Hague: the Dutch government selected Loder no less than four times between 1905 and 1923 to represent its interests at international maritime law conferences.[10] He also participated in the preparation of the third Hague Peace Conference which was scheduled to take place in 1915, but ultimately cancelled due to the war (although the International Congress of Women did manage to hold a peace conference in The Hague that year with over 1,100 participants from both sides of the belligerent lines).[11]

In 1918, the Dutch government (in the person of Minister H.A. van Karnebeek) appointed Loder as chair of the newly formed Board of Assistance of the Directorate of Economic Affairs within the Ministry of Foreign Affairs. This allowed him to be closely involved in the foreign policy of the Netherlands in the critical period 1918–1920. In 1919, Loder was one of the three experts advising the Dutch government to refuse (albeit not unconditionally) the extradition of Emperor Wilhelm II so he could be put on trial for his role in the First World War,[12] invoking the neutrality of their country. That same year, he accepted to serve as a member of the Dutch Advisory Commission for Questions relating to the law of nations, which was in those days mainly occupied with the drafting of Dutch policy vis-à-vis the League of Nations. Also in 1919, he acted as a Dutch delegate at the Commission for the League of Nations (Paris Peace Conference); one year later, he represented the Netherlands at the first meeting of the League. As a result, it was perhaps no surprise that the Netherlands put his name forward, first, to serve on the ACJ and, subsequently, for election to the bench of the newly founded PCIJ. Incidentally, he was not the only member of his family with

9 Van Haven tot Hoge Raad, *Advocatenblad* (1 January 2016) <www.advocatenblad.nl/2016/01/01/van-haven-tot-hoge-raad/>

10 Roelofsen (n 8).

11 F Baetens, 'International Congress of Women (1915)' in R Wolfrum (ed), *Max Planck Encyclopedia of Public International Law* (OUP 2010 – online edition).

12 W Schabas, *The Trial of the Kaiser* (OUP 2018).

international aspirations: his nephew J.A. van Hamel became the Head of the Legal Division of the League of Nations Secretariat.[13]

2.2 *Professional associations focusing on international law (1897–1935)*

Around the turn of the century, Loder started profiling himself on the international scene within a variety of professional associations, the most important of which were the International Law Association (ILA), the *Comité Maritime International* (CMI), and the *Institut de Droit International* (IDI). Before moving to an analysis of the content of his ideas, a brief word of explanation on each of these associations is due.

First, in 1873, the ILA was founded in Brussels (Belgium), making it the oldest organization in the world dedicated to 'the study, clarification and development of international law, both public and private, and the furtherance of international understanding and respect for international law'.[14] In 1910, Loder founded the Dutch branch of the ILA, which is still active today as the Royal Dutch Society of International Law (KNVIR).[15] Second, also in 1873, the IDI was established in Ghent (Belgium) as a learned society with the purpose 'to promote the progress of international law'.[16] In recognition of its efforts in endorsing arbitration as a peaceful means of settling disputes between States, the IDI received the Nobel Peace Prize in 1904. Loder became a member of the IDI in 1921, serving as its President at the IDI's 33rd meeting in The Hague in 1925, but failed to attend any subsequent meetings, except for the Cambridge session in 1931. He never served as special rapporteur for any IDI resolutions.

Third, together with Tobias Asser, Loder became involved with the CMI which had been created in Antwerp (Belgium) in 1897 by Louis Franck, Auguste Beernaert, and Charles LeJeune.[17] It was the first international organization that focused exclusively on maritime law and related commercial practices. Its purpose is to 'contribute by all appropriate means and activities to the unification of maritime law in all its aspects'.[18] In order to achieve this, the CMI promotes 'the establishment of national associations of maritime law' and cooperates with other international organizations.[19] As a specialist in maritime law, Loder became one of the earliest members of the CMI right at the outset in 1897, founding the national association of the Netherlands, namely the Dutch Committee of Maritime Law. Throughout his activities in these professional associations, two themes can be discerned that clearly captured Loder's interest: international rules

13 Roelofsen (n 8).

14 ILA constitution <www.ila-hq.org/index.php/about-us/aboutus2>.

15 <https://knvir.org>.

16 <www.idi-iil.org/en/>.

17 Arthur Eyffinger, International Maritime Law and the Comité Maritime International, *The Seas but Join the Nations They Divide*, 2 vols (T.M.C. Asser 1838–1913).

18 CMI Constitution <https://comitemaritime.org/governance/constitution/>.

19 ibid.

of responsibility for maritime accidents, and the tension between the immunity of sovereign States versus the need to establish an international court with compulsory jurisdiction.

2.2.1 International rules of responsibility for maritime accidents

In 1904, Loder co-authored the report of the Dutch Committee of Maritime Law, together with Tobias Asser and Menso Johannes Pijnappel, in the framework of the CMI draft project on the Treaty to Limit the Responsibility of Shipowners.[20] Their criticism was manifold, including on the lack of unanimity among the CMI drafters, an issue which the three authors considered a fundamental precursor to its adoption by States.[21] Moreover, they noted that the draft did not refer to the issue of jurisdiction (*compétence*) and excluded personal injury in some cases, limiting its scope to damage to property.[22] According to Loder, the objective of this project was to unify the rules on responsibility, but in allowing the parties (the shipowner, the shipwright and potential third parties) to choose the applicable law, the draft would only perpetuate and aggravate the disagreements.[23]

In relation to the responsibility for loss of human life in maritime accidents, Loder considered that the issue ought to be left to domestic legislation as it was a matter of civil and not maritime law.[24] However, in so far as it was to be regulated, the principal discussion ought to focus on the manner in which liability is assessed, not the amount of liability.[25] Regarding the codification of unified rules of maritime law, he pointed out 'that maritime law, [. . .][26] especially in these matters [the discussion was centred on the Law of Affreightment], is a living and fluctuating law, which it is necessary to adapt from time to time to new contingencies'.[27] Loder asked whether it was wise to crystallize that law at a given stage, pointing out how difficult it would be, once fixed in a particular way, to alter it by subsequent treaty. Therefore, he put forward an alternative: the best way of regulating the matter (in this case, the law of affreightment) would be to try to fix a limited number of important yet controversial matters on which State opinions are strongly divided. Though at first formulated in a context specific to maritime law, the idea that more dynamic aspects of international law should remain adaptable through State practice – instead of being codified

20 International Maritime Committee, Conference of Amsterdam, September 1904, Bulletin No. 11, p. 114.

21 ibid 115.

22 ibid 117.

23 ibid 118, 372–76.

24 International Maritime Committee, Conference of Paris, 1911, Bulletin No. 30, p. 147.

25 ibid 151.

26 He also referred to commercial law in this sense, International Maritime Committee, Conference of Anvers, July 1921, Bulletin No. 47, p. 309.

27 International Maritime Committee, Conference of Anvers, July 1921, Bulletin No. 47, p. 309.

in a treaty whose renegotiation could prove difficult – turned into a theme that is repeated throughout Loder's work, including in his dissent in the *Lotus* case at the PCIJ.

2.2.2 *Immunity of sovereign States vs. compulsory jurisdiction of an international court*

As president of a study group under the auspices of the *Organisation centrale pour une paix durable*,[28] Loder voiced his high expectations of international dispute settlement, consistently advocating the establishment of a permanent international court and a 'council for the conciliation of disputes', both to be based in The Hague. His thoughts in this regard were published in 1917 under the title '*Institutions judiciaires et de conciliation*' ('Judicial and conciliatory institutions'),[29] and repeated in a speech presented at the ILA in 1920 focusing on the distinction between the PCIJ and its predecessors.[30] He would elaborate further on these ideas in his 1923 speech (by then in his capacity as PCIJ President) entitled '*La difference entre l'arbitrage international et la justice internationale*' ('The difference between international arbitration and international justice').[31]

With regard to the immunity of State-owned vessels in particular, Loder held that, as regards maritime law, the position of States rejecting the jurisdiction of domestic courts on the basis of sovereignty was 'intolerable',[32] insisting that '[a]ll contracts must be respected, all obligations must be fulfilled, all damage must be made good and all assistance duly paid for, regardless of the position of the

28 The Central Organization for a Durable Peace has been described as being 'formed at The Hague (the Netherlands) in April 1915 by representatives from nine European nations and the United States. The deliberations of this meeting were summarized in a manifesto, and a nine point minimum-program calling for coercive sanctions, which were studied by nine international research committees and several national committees. Departing from strict pacifism, the organization expressed a willingness to accept military sanctions against countries that started hostilities without first making a good faith effort to resolve a dispute by submitting to international arbitration or making some other appeal to the existing peace machinery.' <www.swarthmore.edu/library/peace/CDGB/centralorganisation.htm>

29 BCJ Loder, 'Organisation centrale pour une paix durable' (1917) Rapport institutions judiciaires et de conciliation.

30 BCJ Loder, 'Permanent Court of International Justice' (1920) 29 International Law Association Reports of Conferences 144, 151.

31 BCJ Loder – La difference entre l'arbitrage international et la justice international: this was a recurring theme throughout Loder's interventions his different roles. He relied on this in relation to the issue of ad hoc judges on the PCIJ, see Advisory Committee of Jurists, *Procès-Verbaux of the Proceedings of the Committee, 16 June–24 July 1920, with Annexes* (Van Langenhuysen, The Hague, 1920) 531 (hereinafter 'Procès-Verbaux'); compulsory jurisdiction of the PCIJ, 251; on the issue of challenges, 170.

32 International Maritime Committee, Conference of London, October 1922, Bulletin No. 57, p. 241; see also Jasper Y Brinton, 'Suits Against Foreign States' (1931) 25(1) AJIL 50, 61.

debtor'.[33] He was quite concerned about this issue as can be seen in the following passage:

> [F]urther – and this is the most pressing grievance – national tribunals declare themselves also to be incompetent to deal with suits against foreign Governments even in cases concerning their merchant vessels, that is to say, vessels with which they enter into commercial competition with the whole world, while refusing to accept the consequences.[34]

Furthermore, Loder opined that '[i]t is right that a sovereign is not subjected to the national jurisdiction of another sovereign. It is not right that there should be no justice above all sovereigns alike.'[35] He proposed that a draft International Convention be adopted, 'dealing with the jurisdiction of national tribunals and authorizing them to administer justice against a sovereign State which, in the person of its servants, breaks the law of another sovereign State'.[36] A clause should be included calling upon the aid of the PCIJ Chamber of Summary Procedure to settle preliminary questions of jurisdiction.[37] He raised the same issue in his speech during the 33rd session of the IDI in 1925. This speech, a tribute to Grotius on the third centenary of the publication *On the Law of War and Peace*, referred to Grotius' conviction that it is an erroneous conception to consider that a consequence of sovereignty is the liberty to evade the rules of justice,[38] stressing that States must be judged by other States. Loder affirmed that it took humanity 300 years to arrive at the same conclusion, creating a supreme tribunal to apply justice to States.[39] Though he recognized the scepticism surrounding the Geneva Protocol in relation to the peaceful settlement of disputes, he stressed that the IDI had to continue to collaborate with the League of Nations, in particular regarding the codification and progressive development of international law.[40]

The importance to Loder of the existence of an international court is reflected, additionally, in the following story that he told participants at the CMI Conference of London in 1922. At the time, he was the President of the PCIJ:

> Gentlemen, this reminds me of a story which I found some time ago in an English paper. Some airmen had risen rather too high; in spite of all their

33 Maritime (n 32) 241; see also Lord Phillimore (George Grenville), 'Immunité des États au point de vue de la jurisdiction ou de l'exécution forcée' (1925) 8(III) Recueil des Cours 413, 468.
34 Maritime (n 32) 242.
35 ibid 248.
36 ibid.
37 ibid 248–49.
38 Institut de Droit International (July–August 1925) 32 Annuaire 441.
39 ibid 442.
40 The Geneva Protocol for the Pacific Settlement of Disputes was proposed to the League of Nations in 1924, but enthusiasm was lost when Great Britain affirmed that it would not ratify it.

> efforts they were carried into the sphere of attraction of the moon where they were compelled to land. They were conducted to the king of the moon who questioned them 'You come from the earth', he said. 'How is your terrestrial state carried on?' 'We have many States', they proudly replied. 'I understand', said the king. 'You have a number of communities; and where is your tribunal?' 'What do you mean by our tribunal?', said the men of the earth. 'Our communities are sovereign States.' 'But', said the king, 'if you form communities, I suppose that sometimes you have disputes, law-suits, disagreements. You must have some tribunal to administer justice among you.' 'No', replied the men of the earth peremptorily, 'that would be an infringement of sovereignty.' 'In that case', replied the king, 'how do you manage?' 'We fight', was the answer. 'We invent infernal machines; we destroy all we can; we kill each other. Ultimately one sovereign State wins, and of course that is the right one.' The king of the moon turned to his servants and said 'Imprison them all, they are a dangerous race.'[41]

The connection between the immunity of States and the need for the creation of an international court may not necessarily be obvious at first instance. However, Loder saw the interaction between both: immune States can act with impunity if there is no Court to adjudicate their conduct.

3. Loder at the League of Nations

Loder held different roles at the League of Nations, this chapter focuses on the most relevant three: he was a member of the ACJ, he later became a member (and President) of the PCIJ, and he was a member of the Committee of Experts for the Progressive Codification of International Law. From 1928 until 1935, he was a member of the Governing Body of the International Institute for the Unification of Private Law (UNIDROIT), which he combined from 1932 to 1935, with his role as a member of the International Committee on Intellectual Cooperation,[42] these last two roles were closer to private international law and are not discussed in the present chapter.[43]

41 Maritime (n 32) 247.

42 League of Nations, Intellectual Cooperation, Adjustment of the Work of the Organisation and Composition of the Committee, Doc. C.649(1).1932.XII, where he appears to have worked fundamentally on the issue of the use of broadcasting in the cause of peace (League of Nations, (1934) 15(2) Official Journal 169, Société des Nations, Avant-projet d'arrangement international concernant l'emploi de la radiodiffusion dans l'interêt de la paix, Doc. C.12.1934.XII, Annex 1, p. 2.) and Intellectual Rights (League of Nations, International Committee on Intellectual Cooperation, Report of the Committee on the Work of its Sixteenth Plenary Session, Doc. C.339.M.156.1934. XII (1934), pp. 14, 60).

43 League of Nations, International Institute for the Unification of Private Law, Appointment of the Members of the Governing Body, Doc. C.37.1933.V.

3.1 The Advisory Committee of Jurists (1920–1921)

In 1920, Loder became the chairperson of a preparatory conference of neutral powers and vice-president of the League of Nations's ACJ – both of which convened in The Hague. In the latter capacity, he participated in the drafting of the Statute of the PCIJ. The general agenda of the ACJ encompassed 11 sections: (1) preliminary questions regarding the outcome of the work of the Committee; (2) general principles; (3) competency of the Court; (4) seat of the Court; (5) composition of the Court; (6) organization of the Court; (7) material law to be applied by the Court; (8) res judicata; (9) enforcement of judgments; (10) procedure; and, (11) expenses. The sections below mirror these on the ACJ's general agenda, insofar as Loder made any contribution to the discussion. At the outset of the ACJ's work, there was an extensive discussion as to who should be its President – Loder was one of the names mentioned, but as he was not appointed in the end, this chapter does not elaborate on this.[44]

3.1.1 Election, composition, and seat of the court

Loder contributed to a number of topics in this regard: first, how to balance the need to elect high quality judges against the desire of some countries (particularly the Great Powers) to have a judge of their nationality on the bench; second, whether it ought to be possible to add ad hoc judges or disqualify sitting judges in a given case due to their nationality; and third, that The Hague ought to be the seat of the Court.

First and foremost, all members of the ACJ agreed that it was important to ensure the election of high quality judges regardless of their nationality. But simultaneously they realized that the judges would often belong to the Great Powers since in these countries, which represent the 'great civilisations' according to the prevailing views at the time, 'the intellectual minority is more numerous than in the smaller States'.[45] In any case, the judges must not consider themselves representatives of their countries: for this reason, Loder rejected the proposal by Ricci Busatti.[46] A discussion raged among ACJ members as to whether Great Powers ought to always have a judge of their nationality on the Court if only to make potential unfavourable judgments more palatable to a domestic audience. Perhaps rather unsurprisingly, opinions were largely divided between members

44 For an extensive overview of this discussion, see Ole Spiermann, '"Who Attempts Too Much, Does Nothing Well': The 1920 Advisory Committee of Jurists and the Statute of the Permanent Court of International Justice' (2002) BYIL 193–95.

45 Procès-Verbaux (n 31) 363; Spiermann (n 44) 202.

46 Procés-Verbaux (n 31) 363; Ricci Busatti proposed that each member of the League of Nations would nominate one person (chosen by its delegates at the Permanent Court of Arbitration), the persons chosen by the States represented permanently on the Council and those named by at least three members would be judges of the Court. The Assembly would then choose from the other persons a certain number not to exceed a third. Procés-Verbaux (n 31) 302.

who were nationals of Great Powers (and therefore 'sided' with their country) and members who were not.

Invoking the fundamental principle of equality of States, Loder 'thought that it would be possible to reconcile the different opinions by establishing guarantees to ensure that in a Court where the representatives of small States would form the majority, these representatives should not oppose the activity of the great States'.[47]

Disagreeing with the UK member (Phillimore) who was of the opinion that 'the equality of States did not exist in the Covenant', Loder maintained that 'Article 1 of the Covenant upheld equality between States' as '[e]ach State had but one vote and Great Britain was no exception'.[48] The main task at hand, in his view, was 'to find a system which would ensure good judges, possessing all the necessary qualifications of character and knowledge'.[49] He discussed various options to achieve this goal: first, allowing the Assembly of the League of Nations to choose judges, whereby only a third of the candidates presented by each State could be nationals of that States, while the others had to be 'the most eminent men of all the world'. A second option would be to let the members of the Permanent Court of Arbitration choose the judges – but this option met with quite some resistance.[50]

Originally, Loder supported the former option but withdrew this support when it became clear that it would not result in the appointment of 'the most distinguished' persons for political reasons.[51] He felt attracted by the option put forward by Descamps which was to draw upon the members of the existing Court of Arbitration,[52] because it allowed for a 'unification of the organisation of international law' and because it gave an active part in the election of judges to a body of jurists of 'great importance' and 'widely recognised authority'. However, together with Root and Phillimore, he was of the opinion that the final say should remain with the Assembly, with the proviso that 'the only difficulty consists in finding for this election a method which will defend the large States against the small, as well as the small against the large'.[53] For this purpose, there must be collaboration between the Assembly and the Council, even though this may open 'the door wide to political intrigues' and giving 'no assurance that the

47 Procés-Verbaux (n 31) 124.

48 ibid.

49 ibid.

50 ibid 125 *et seq*, Loder's position regarding the members of the Court was previously reflected in his speech as transcribed in the ILA Reports of Conferences of 1920, where he indicated that the judges 'belong to no country, represent no nation'. See also Loder (n 30) 146.

51 Procès-Verbaux (n 31) 160; Spiermann (N 44) 203–4.

52 Procés-Verbaux (n 31) 142–43.

53 ibid 161.

best candidates will be elected'.[54] Loder then proceeded to combine the two proposals: allowing the Court of Arbitration to draw up a closed list of candidates, upon which the Assembly and the Council subsequently voted.[55] This proposal met with the approval of Hagerup and Phillimore.

In Loder's opinion, the Court should be composed of a very limited number of 'eminent men' who 'should be able to work well together' – a number which he put at nine, as he predicted it would be hard to find a large number of persons 'sufficiently qualified and at the same time willing to accept the duties of judges'.[56] Furthermore, he thought the right of challenge should be excluded so as to distinguish the new Court from the Court of Arbitration.[57] Loder found himself in a minority on this regard (some ACJ members wanted 15 members while others thought five would already be sufficient) and relied on his personal experience to argue that a Court composed of a limited number of judges works better than a large tribunal because 'discussions are more to the point and the members have a greater sense of their responsibility'.[58] Moreover, he did not think it necessary that the Court should always sit *in pleno*: 'the essential thing was to decide on the quorum of the chambers'.[59] He repeatedly pointed out the fundamentally different functions of 'arbitration and justice': whereas the latter is 'to found a tribunal before which one party might call the opposing party; submission to the jurisdiction of the Court of Arbitration is purely optional.'[60] Moreover, he proposed that judge's terms should be limited to ten years, while other ACJ members advocated terms as short as six years (all members opposed lifetime appointments).[61]

Further, Loder was opposed to the idea that judges would have to be representative of the different legal systems in the world, arguing that '[o]ur Court is to apply International Law; in this particular case it consists of treaties, special conventions, and unwritten International Law'.[62] This idea of 'representation of different legal systems' returned on several occasions in the discussions of the ACJ but its meaning was never clearly explained. Loder admitted that he did not exactly know what was meant: in case a national law would have to be applied

54 ibid 162.

55 Loder proposed drafting amendments to the Statute proposed by Messrs. Root and Phillimore, in relation to the composition of the Court, in particular Loder referred to the number of judges (proposing that it be fixed at 9 and capped at 15), the election process, the conditions required of the judges, and rejecting that all judges must have different nationalities. Procés-Verbaux (n 31) PCIJ Series D, 379 *et seq*, 387, 396, 430.

56 Procés-Verbaux (n 31) PCIJ Series D, 169.

57 ibid 170.

58 ibid 173; Spiermann (n 44) 207; Antonio Sanchez and Elizabeth F Read de Bustamante (tr), *World Court* (American Foundation; MacMillan Co. 1925) 134.

59 Procès-Verbaux (n 31) 178.

60 ibid 180; Spiermann (n 44) 206.

61 Procés-Verbaux (n 31) 194.

62 ibid 164, 531.

'the international judge will do the same as judges do every day in all countries: he will make himself conversant with the subject before him'.[63]

Second, Loder's position on the election and composition of the Court (that the personal qualifications of the judges ought to be stressed, rather than their nationality) logically resulted in his opposition to the modification of the composition of the Court, either through the incorporation of ad hoc judges in a particular case, or the disqualification of judges in a particular case on grounds of nationality.[64] One option considered by the Committee was the incorporation of assessors of the nationality of the States in dispute. Loder was not highly in favour of incorporating assessors as he thought distinguished men should be able to 'disregard their nationality' and contesting parties should not have the power to appoint judges. If assessors were to be accepted, they should not be given deliberative but only advisory powers, in his view.[65] He considered the participation of national judges in the deliberations unnecessary. He rejected Root's proposal, that there always be a judge of the nationality of the parties in the dispute, on the basis that it was impractical. For example, where only one party would name an ad hoc judge, an even number of judges would result, making it impossible for the Court to proceed.[66] He insisted that the number of judges of the Court had to be fixed, otherwise the nature of the Court would be changed when ad hoc judges were appointed.[67] Later on, Loder returned to this issue when the PCIJ drafted the Rules of the Court in 1922: his solution then was to propose that where several States were acting jointly, the ad hoc judge ought to be chosen by the parties and not the Court,[68] as was later reflected in Article 4 of the Rules of the Court.

Advisory opinions were not regulated in the PCIJ Statute,[69] thus, in the 1926 amendments to the Rules of the Court, the PCIJ discussed whether the rules should reflect the appointment of ad hoc judges for advisory opinions.[70] Loder raised the issue of whether the Court had a right to make that change given that Article 25 of the Statute referred to the full court as consisting of 11 judges, and that Article 31 (referring to the incorporation of ad hoc judges) was an exception that ought to be strictly construed.[71] A committee was therefore elected, on which he participated along with John Bassett Moore and Deniso Anzilotti, concluding that there was no obstacle to incorporating this modification in the Rules

63 ibid 164, 178.

64 ibid 121, 169, see also Norman L Hill, National Judges in the Permanent Court of International Justice (1931) 25(4) American Journal of International Law 670, 672.

65 Procès-Verbaux (n 31) 199–200, 531; Spiermann (n 44) 231.

66 Proces-Verbaux (n 31) 534.

67 ibid 537.

68 Publications of the Permanent Court of International Justice, Series D, No. 2, "Preparation of the Rules of the Court", p. 97; Hill (n 64) 670, 675–76.

69 The Court considered itself to 'impliedly powered' by the Statute to give such opinions. Publications of the Permanent Court of International Justice, Series E, No. 4, p. 76.

70 Publications of the Permanent Court of International Justice, Series E, No. 4, p. 74.

71 ibid.

of the Court.[72] In relation to the discussion on challenges, Loder maintained that a challenge by a party should only be admitted where it was 'founded upon personal interest in the case'.[73]

Third, the choice of The Hague as seat of the PCIJ and later the ICJ seems to have been largely due to the efforts of Loder.[74] He did recognize the difficulty of finding judges prepared to establish their homes in The Hague.[75] For this reason, he proposed that 'the Court, although always accessible, should only sit during four separate periods in each year' so that the judges would not be obliged to live permanently in the Netherlands.[76] Depending on whether only States but also individuals might appeal to the Court (see next section), he thought the Court would simply not have sufficient work to warrant such a demand, and he doubted that enough qualified persons would be found who were 'prepared to give their whole time to their work as international judges'.[77] For this reason, judges would not be barred from taking up other work, with the exception of 'public duties' and 'duties of a nature entailing personal interests or a political objects'.[78] Even this (fairly limited) restriction to the ancillary activities of judges was met with strong opposition from the other ACJ members, such as Ricci Busatti who feared that 'a provision of this sort would result in limiting the choice for the duties of judge to those men for whom their countries had no use', so Loder accepted Phillimore's and Adatci's ideas of allowing PCIJ judges to take up adjudicatory and educational duties elsewhere.[79]

3.1.2 Standing, jurisdiction, and applicable law

Within the context of standing, jurisdiction, and applicable law, Loder took a number of strong stances which were, more often than not, not fully shared by the other members of the ACJ. He advocated in favour of private standing, compulsory jurisdiction, and a broad understanding of the applicable law before the PCIJ.

First, ACJ members spent a considerable amount of time discussing whether individuals should be able to appeal to the Court – eventually they decided against private standing, since States would be able to present claims of their subjects as their own.[80] Loder opposed this decision, however, because he saw 'no reason for limiting the competence of the Court by stipulating that private individuals must

72 ibid 77.
73 Proces-Verbaux (n 31) PCIJ Series D, 478. The importance of their financial compensation to guarantee their independence is also addressed in the ILA piece: See also Loder (n 30) 149–50.
74 Hoge Raad (n 9); Roelofsen (n 8); Procés-Verbaux (n 31) 204.
75 Procés-Verbaux (N 31) 186.
76 ibid 186.
77 ibid 188.
78 ibid 192.
79 ibid 192; Spiermann (n 44) 226; Sanchez (n 58).
80 Procés-Verbaux (n 31) 205; Spiermann (n 44) 208.

be represented by their Governments in order to have access to the Court'.[81] He argued that with the creation of the League of Nations, sovereignty should no longer be used to prevent private action against States, regardless of the number of cases that might result.[82] This desire to keep access to the Court open for as many as possible also informed Loder's position on non-contracting States, where he maintained that States other than League members should be admitted (with some special conditions regarding procedural costs).[83] He agreed with Hagerup that non-signatory States should be offered access to the Court at the invitation of the Council or as the result of an agreement between two disputing non-member States. In such cases, the Court would not only be competent but also compelled to hear the case.[84]

Second, Loder advocated for compulsory jurisdiction for all disputes,[85] for which no separate agreement between the parties was required.[86] He submitted a special memorandum dealing with the question of whether a unilateral summons was sufficient to have access to the PCIJ or whether a previous agreement between the parties was required.[87] Relying on his work distinguishing arbitration from justice, Loder noted that '[a]rbitration means a combat before the combat'. The intention of the Covenant was the creation of a Court of Justice where 'the plaintiff would no longer have to wait upon the good will of his opponent' which could only be created within the institution of the League of Nations.[88] He saw some issues with regard to the requirement that all diplomatic means must be exhausted before recourse to the Court could be exercised as this system was liable to cause difficulties.[89] Moreover, the Court should always have the competence to adjudge its own competence, in cases where States disagreed on whether a dispute related to the interpretation of a certain treaty, or whether it qualified as a 'legal dispute'.[90]

Third, in relation to the competence of the Court in terms of applicable law, this issue overlaps slightly with the discussion on jurisdiction as there was some concern among the members of the ACJ that an overly broad description of the applicable law (also described as rules or sources) would have the effect that States would not accept compulsory jurisdiction of the Court. Loder, Root, and Phillimore were part of an interesting discussion,[91] on the basis of Descamps'

81 Procés-Verbaux (n 31) 206; Loder also received a letter from W. Elink Schuurman, a Dutch public servant, to this effect; see also Loder (n 30) 152.
82 Procés-Verbaux (n 31) 206.
83 ibid 220–21.
84 ibid 291.
85 ibid 224; Spiermann (n 44) 210; Sanchez (n 58) 100–1.
86 Procés-Verbaux (n 31) 229 and 234.
87 ibid 249–51; Spiermann (n 44) 244–45; 250–51.
88 Procès-Verbaux (n 31) 251, as opposed to the attempts of 1907 which could not create a Court of Justice, without such bond between the States.
89 ibid 259–60.
90 ibid 261–62.
91 ibid 293–96.

proposal regarding the rules to be applied by the PCIJ.[92] Root considered that States would be induced to accept the establishment of compulsory jurisdiction as long as that jurisdiction were clearly defined.[93] He thought that such jurisdiction should be limited to 'the interpretation of treaties and questions of international law generally', as the only questions that the Covenant's authors had agreed would be within the Court's competence.[94] To 'make laws for it', as the Committee intended in the draft, would exceed their mandate.[95] If the Committee nevertheless did decide to undertake this task, he was not certain that 50 States would agree on the issue of custom, but his greatest concern was in relation to the third and fourth clauses of the proposal: 'rules of international law as recognised by the legal conscience of civilised nations' and international jurisprudence. These were 'an enlargement of the jurisdiction of the Court which threatened to destroy it'.[96] Root clarified that he 'thought the world was prepared to accept the compulsory jurisdiction of a Court which applied the universally recognized rules of international law. But he did not think that it was disposed to accept the compulsory jurisdiction of a Court which would apply principles.'[97] When asked by Loder what he meant by these limits to competence, Root explained that the Committee 'must limit itself to rules contained in Conventions and positive international law; but there were no statutes in international law'. In response, Loder argued that he did not think there was 'any great difference between statutes and custom in international law'.[98] In his eyes, the world had changed with the acceptance of the Covenant of the League of Nations. It was the duty of the Committee to point out to the Court how it should carry out its task, the application of international law. With regard to the disputed third and fourth clauses, he did not agree that they were overly vague. They referred to:

> Rules recognised and respected by the whole world had been mentioned, rules which were, however, not yet of the nature of positive law, but it was precisely the Court's duty to develop law, to "ripen" customs and principles

92 Descamps proposed the following text for what would eventually become article 38 of the Statute of the PCIJ, 'The following rules are to be applied by the judge in the solution of international disputes; they will be Considered by him in the undermentioned order: 1. conventional international law, whether general or special, being rules expressly adopted by the States; 2. International custom, being practice between nations accepted by them as law; 3. the rules of international law as recognised by the legal conscience of civilised nations; 4. international jurisprudence as a means for the application and development of law.' Procés-Verbaux (n 31) 306.

93 Procés-Verbaux (N 31) 293.

94 ibid 293.

95 ibid.

96 ibid 294.

97 ibid 308. Root in particular stressed that he had defended such broader wording in the context of the US-France Treaty of 1907 but had been unable to convince the US to ratify, ibid 309.

98 ibid 294.

> universally recognised, and to crystallise them into positive rules; in a word, to establish and international jurisprudence.[99]

Phillimore on the other hand, agreed with Root, noting that legislation in matters of international law could only be carried out by the universal agreement of States. If there were sufficiently general rules as described in the third clause, they should be considered custom under the second, so the Court need not go beyond the limits of that clause.[100] Hagerup then raised the question of what the Court ought to do if it found that there were no actual rules of international law with regard to a dispute brought before it.[101] Loder seconded this question, rejecting Root's suggestion that where there were no rules of international law only a recommendation ought to be made, and adding that it should be inadmissible, as a denial of justice, for the Court to declare itself incompetent by reason of the law being silent on the matter.[102] This understanding of the evolution of international law, which was later reflected in Loder's dissent in the *Lotus* case, could be considered one of his key contributions to the development of international law. It is noteworthy, however, in consonance with the theme of this book, that current scholars have not frequently referred to Loder's positions, perhaps mindful of some of his more controversial positions, as developed above.

3.1.3 International criminal law

At one of the ACJ meetings, Descamps proposed that the Committee discuss the establishment of a High Court of International Justice for the purpose of trying crimes against the universal law of nations.[103] Loder's intervention in this regard had significant foresight. Though he held that the proposed topic exceeded the Committee's mandate, he still thought that the discussion should take place. In his view, the President's idea was 'good', but relying on the adage *nulla poena sine praevia lege poenali* (no punishment without a pre-existing penal law), the time was not ripe for its realization as the substantive law that such a court would apply had not yet been defined. He emphatically rejected the creation of what he coined a 'political Court', that would apply 'undefined penalties to undefined crimes'.[104] Loder's intervention in this regard is foretelling of the criticisms that were later aimed at international criminal tribunals after the Second World War.

99 ibid 294; Spiermann (n 44) 214–15; Ole Spiermann, 'The History of Article 38 of the Statute of the International Court of Justice: "A Purely Platonic Discussion"?' in Samantha Besson and Jean d'Aspremont (eds), *The Oxford Handbook of the Sources of International Law* (OUP 2017) 170.

100 Procés-Verbaux (n 31) 295.

101 ibid 307.

102 ibid 311.

103 ibid 498.

104 ibid 504.

3.2 The Permanent Court of International Justice (1922–1930)

Loder was the first President of the PCIJ from 1922 to 1924, he then continued to be a member of the Court until his retirement in 1930. His main goal in this period was to build State confidence in the PCIJ generally, but the best account of his personal views on international law can be found in his dissent in the *Lotus* case.

3.2.1 Strengthening state confidence in the PCIJ

As the PCIJ's first President, Loder's focus was on strengthening State confidence in the PCIJ to resolve their disputes. He regarded the establishment of the Court as 'the arrival of a new era in the civilisation of the world'.[105] When describing the task of the PCIJ judges, Loder stressed the Court's role in establishing principles of law, reflecting one of the more controversial discussions in which he participated during his time as a member of the ACJ:

> The Court of International Justice will likewise possess a collection of Treaties and Conventions which it will have to apply, but it will equally have to take into consideration international custom, as proof of generally accepted practice and as representing law. It will have to establish those principles of law which are recognised by civilised nations, and finally, as a further means of assistance, it will be guided by legal decisions and by the opinions of the most eminent Jurists.[106]

Throughout his time on the bench, Loder continued emphasizing the importance of the Court's jurisdiction, differentiating it from arbitration.[107] Significantly, he described the process of acceptance of the PCIJ Statute, including the need for compulsory jurisdiction to be recognized unanimously: 'the establishment of a world institution, such as the Court was intended to be, can only be successful if it is supported by general sympathy; especially a Court whose judgments cannot be executed any other way'.[108] The first years of the Court were key: '[i]t will do the Court no harm if, in the first years of its existence, it knows it has to make a reputation'.[109] In his view, it was crucial that the Court be seen as a judicial organ, and not a political body. This was recognised: '[w]hatever one may think of the Court, and whatever opinion one may have regarding its work, it is certain that politics play no part therein', Anziolotti considered that this was the result of Loder's work at the helm: '[t]hat I think is as high praise as can be paid

105 League of Nations, BCJ Loder, 'The Permanent Court of International Justice' (1922) 3(4) Official Journal 312, 314.
106 ibid 312, 315.
107 BCJ Loder, 'The Permanent Court of International Justice and Compulsory Jurisdiction' (1921–1922) 2 BYIL 6, 8 *et seq.*
108 ibid 6, 23.
109 ibid 6, 26.

to our institution, and it is only right to remember how much its first President has done to deserve it'.[110] Nevertheless, in 1927, Loder described the Court (of which he was still a member at the time) as a 'work in progress', even though it had been functioning for five years: 'there is room for further development and improvement of its statute. The principle of its compulsory jurisdiction has not yet been definitively established, but progress has been made and in any case, the Court is in operation.'[111] This remains as true today as it was in 1927.

3.2.2 The Lotus case dissent

Perhaps as a result of the custom at the Dutch Supreme Court not to issue dissenting opinions, Loder only ever wrote one dissenting opinion during his time on the PCIJ bench – in the *Lotus* case.[112] As a result, it is difficult to gauge his position within the Court, though his *Lotus* dissent sheds some light on his thought processes. In the *Lotus* case, the Court had to issue a decision in relation to a collision between a French ship (*Lotus*) and a Turkish ship (*Boz-Kourt*), in which the Turkish ship sank and eight Turkish passengers and sailors lost their lives. The Turkish authorities brought criminal proceedings before a domestic court against the officer of the watch on board the French ship. The dispute before the Court was whether such proceedings were in breach of Article 15 of the Convention of Lausanne of 24 July 1923.

In his dissent, Loder focused on the 'spirit of international law', and in particular its unwritten character, which reflected his earlier work at the CMI, the IDI, as well as the ACJ. As described above, he had previously expressed the opinion that, while treaties were useful instruments for the unification of international law, to find unity in more volatile aspects it would be necessary to rely on the legislation of States. His discussion with Root in the ACJ focused on the importance of general principles of international law and jurisprudence as sources of international law. Also in his speech as President of the IDI, he requested that the members collaborate with the League of Nations in its Committee of Experts to study the codification and progressive development of international law.

110 Publications of the Permanent Court of International Justice, Series E, No. 4, 'Fourth Annual Yearbook of the Permanent Court of International Justice' p. 20.

111 BCJ Loder, 'La Cinquième Conférence de Droit International Privé' [1927] Grotius Annuaire International 1, 2. Authors' own translation of '"Il y a de la matière pour la développer et pour améliorer son statut. Le principe de sa jurisdiction obligatoire n'est pas encore définitivement établi, mais il fait des progrès, et en tout cas, la Cour opère."'.

112 In fact, when they were discussing the Rules of the Court Loder, along with Weiss and Nyholm, were the minority opposing the use of dissenting opinions Permanent Court of International Justice Publications, Series D, Acts and Documents, Addendum to No. 2, pp. 194–98; see also Forest L Grieves, 'Notes and Comments: Reform of the Method of Rendering Decisions in the International Court of Justice' (1970) 64(1) AJIL 144, 148–49; Edvard Hambro, 'Dissenting and Individual Opinions in the International Court of Justice' (1958) 17 Zeitschrift für ausländisches öffentliches Recht und Völkerrecht 229, 237.

Looking at the evolution of international law, Loder seems to have been concerned that international law could not solely evolve through the adoption of 'positive law' (a term coined at the time for customary international law as well as treaties). International law had to rely on general principles, as reflected in the common legislation of States (one might discuss whether this is indeed a form of State practice that could be reminiscent of custom) as well as the jurisprudence of an international court. In his *Lotus* dissent, he opined that 'the contention that, under international law, every door is open unless it is closed by treaty or by established custom' is 'at variance with the spirit of international law'. In particular, international law

> is for the most part unwritten and lacks sanctions; it rests on a general consensus of opinion; on the acceptance by civilized States, members of the great community of nations, of rules, customs and existing conditions which they are bound to respect in their mutual relations, although neither committed to writing nor confirmed by conventions.[113]

The main message was that international law is not complete, in that the number of explicit rules would be limited.[114] Without referring explicitly to Loder's dissent, Lauterpacht wrote that:

> [i]n international law this reliance upon freedom and independence as a substantive source of law is the more dangerous as, because of reasons particular to international law, the number of explicit rules restricting freedom of action is limited and their ascertainment is difficult. A combination therefore of a rigid theory of completeness of international law (which renders it difficult to define restrictions freedom of action through the normal exercise of judicial activity) with an emphasis upon the sovereignty of States as a law-creating principle may easily produce results inimical to the purposes of law.[115]

This allows for the rules to be 'gradually modified, altered or extended, in accordance with the views of a considerable majority of these States'.[116] However, 'the municipal law of a minority of States' is not sufficient to 'abrogate or change

113 The Case of the S.S. "Lotus" (France v. Turkey) (1927), Judgment, PCIJ Series A, No. 10, Dissenting Opinion by Loder, 34.

114 The importance of Loder's dissent is addressed in Henri de Waele, 'A New League of Extraordinary Gentlemen? The Professionalization of International Law Scholarship in the Netherlands, 1919–1940' (2020) 31(3) EJIL 1005, 1020; as well as Antonio Augusto Cançado Trindade. 'The Illegality under Contemporary International Law of All Weapons of Mass Destruction' (2006) 6(6) Revista do Instituto Brasileiro de Direitos Humanos 11, 22.

115 H Lauterpacht, *The Function of Law in the International Community* (Clarendon Press 1933) 96.

116 The Case of the S.S. "Lotus" (France v. Turkey) (n 113).

them'.[117] The *application* of municipal law, in this case the exercise of jurisdiction and acquiescence by other States, would be evidence of usage, not necessarily solely the existence of such provisions.[118] This description of the evolution of international law is key in the study of rules of international law,[119] however, Loder's dissent is not frequently referred to in the study of this issue, it seems to be a forgotten precedent. Further, Loder referred to the issue of sovereignty and independence of States, noting that 'the fundamental consequence of their independence and sovereignty is that no municipal law, in the particular case under consideration no criminal law, can apply or have binding effect outside the national territory'.[120] Criminal law, he added, '*cannot* extend to offences committed by a foreigner in foreign territory, without infringing the sovereign rights of the foreign State concerned, since in that State the State enacting the law has no jurisdiction'.[121] The rule, he concluded,

> has gradually undergone an important modification in the legislation of a somewhat large majority of civilized States . . . [it] tends to except from the strict rule governing the jurisdiction over offences committed by foreigners abroad . . . in so far as they are directed against the State itself or against its security or credit.[122]

3.3 The Committee of Experts for the Progressive Codification of International Law

In 1924, the Assembly of the League of Nations requested that the Council convene a committee of experts, which was to reflect the representation of the main forms of civilization and principal legal systems of the world, to determine which subjects of international law were ripe ('desirable and realisable') for codification and inform the Council of the procedure which could be followed to prepare conferences to that effect.[123] The Council approved the appointment of Loder on the Committee on 12 December 1924.[124] Loder himself was rather sceptical about the chances of success of the Committee noting, in 1927, that '[t]he

117 ibid.

118 ibid; see also WE Beckett, 'Decisions of the Permanent Court of International Justice on Points of Law and Procedure of General Application' (1930) 11 BYIL 1, 3.

119 Anthea Roberts, 'Traditional and Modern Approaches to Customary International Law' (2001) 95 AJIL 757, 784; Martti Koskenniemi, 'Hierarchy in International Law: A Sketch' (1997) 8 Eur J Intl L 566, 573. This is not to suggest that treaties might not also evolve, through subsequent practice, modification, agreement, or evolutive interpretation: see e.g., Eirik Bjørge, *The Evolutionary Interpretation of Treaties* (OUP 2014).

120 The Case of the S.S. "Lotus" (France v. Turkey) (n 113) 35.

121 ibid.

122 ibid 35–36.

123 League of Nations, Official Journal, Special Supplement, No. 21, p. 10 (1924).

124 League of Nations, Official Journal, No. 6, pp. 149, 274 (1924).

Council has nominated a committee of experts, whose task is perhaps a little too restricted and not overly well defined'.[125]

While serving on the Committee, Loder took a strong position in relation to two issues of international law: the law of treaties and the immunity of States. In relation to the law of treaties, one of the questions of the Council of the League was the admissibility of reservations to general conventions. Though Loder was not the rapporteur (Henri Fromageot was), he concluded from the report[126] that a signature to a general convention with reservations was null and void, and would not bind the State or other States with respect to that State.[127] In order to satisfy Loder, Fromageot proposed that a sentence be added clarifying that, if a reservation is not accepted by all contracting parties, both the signature and the reservation would be null and void.[128] In relation to the possibility of establishing, by way of a convention, international rules concerning the competence of the courts in regard to foreign States, Loder was again not the rapporteur (Michikazu Matsuda was). However, this was an issue close to Loder's heart, on which he had already commented previously, so he drew parallels with the immunity of jurisdiction of States when they acted in the same position as private companies, for example as shipowners or guarantors. True to form, he maintained that such State immunity was intolerable for any operations carried out by the State as a trader.[129]

4. Conclusion: Loder's legacy

At the time of his passing, Loder was recognized for his role as the first President of the PCIJ, where he set solid and durable precedents for decisions that were fair, positive, and practical, thereby contributing to the development of international law. He was said to have made the Court a living force in the international sphere, a position he held with incontestable authority and extraordinary energy.[130] Perhaps the success of his role as President of the Court is best reflected in the very limited individual opinions he left behind, in all likelihood a consequence of attempting to find stronger majorities in the decisions issued by the newly minted international court, that was aimed at strengthening the confidence of States in its ability to resolve their disputes. Though almost a century has passed since his *Lotus* dissent was issued, its key issues remain relevant today as a reflection of Loder's professional convictions. These issues include his thoughts regarding the

125 BCJ Loder, 'La Cinquième Conférence de Droit International Privé' [1927] Grotius Annuaire International 1, 3. Authors' own translation of "Le Conseil a nommé un Comité d'experts, dont la tâche est peut-être un peu trop restriente et pas trop bien définie"

126 The final version was published in League of Nations, Official Journal, No. 8 (1927), p. 880.

127 League of Nations, Committee of Experts for the Progressive Codification of International Law, Minutes of the Third Session, 22 March to 2 April 1927, C.576.1927.V, p. 26.

128 ibid.

129 ibid 52, 54.

130 J Klosters, 'B.C.J. Loder' [1936] 8 Grotius Annuaire International 8.

relationship between international law and domestic (criminal) law, the evolution of international law, customary international law, and criminal law.

Loder was an ardent believer in the internationalization of dispute settlement and the ability of 'eminent judges' to transcend their own nationality. He even denied the need to ensure that representatives of the different legal systems of the world were elected to the PCIJ bench, insisting that judges were meant to decide on the basis of international law, whereby their national laws were irrelevant.[131] Even though he was not an eminent publicist in the modern sense (being a practicing lawyer and judge, not a scholar or prolific writer), he nevertheless contributed to laying the foundations of the PCIJ's practice, taking a number of controversial stances in the process. For example, he was in favour of compulsory jurisdiction for the Court, allowing individuals to bring cases against States and an expansive definition of applicable law, so as to include not only treaties but also customary law and general principles.

To the modern reader, his thoughts on applicable law may seem somewhat confusing as they conflated our understanding of customary international law ('recognised and respected') and soft law ('not yet of the nature of positive law'). Moreover, Loder's reference to the Court's duty to develop the law extends beyond our concept of judicial decisions as subsidiary sources of law – not merely 'finding' customs and principles but actively creating them.[132] Although the ACJ minutes do not provide any evidence either way, it is doubtful whether he felt as confident that the 'writings of eminent publicists' should be given a similarly prominent place in the hierarchy of norms. On the contrary, the disagreement between Loder and the Dutch government upon his retirement from the PCIJ might serve as a strong indication of his limited regard for publicists. In 1930, he publicly disapproved of the Dutch government's decision not to nominate Loder's preferred successor (the Dutch law professor and member of the Supreme Court, Jan Kosters), in favour of the professor of public international law and *rector magnificus* of Leiden University, Willem van Eysinga, whom Loder considered 'unsuitable for the exercise of a judicial function'.[133] His own reputation was not so much built on his merits as a legal scholar, but rather on his integrity as a judge, as for example also demonstrated by his 1921 appointment to the British-Hungarian mixed arbitration committee. Even as a PCIJ judge, Loder never shied away from conflict: in 1925, he participated in the creation of the contentious Indological Faculty at Utrecht (to promote Dutch colonial rule and train colonial administrators), serving as its president-curator until his death in 1935.[134] This faculty was intended to function as a counterpart to Leiden University which was considered overly progressive – a sentiment towards which the

131 Procès-Verbaux (n 31) 164.

132 See also, Spiermann (n 44) 221.

133 Roelofsen (n 8); De Waele (n 114) 1020.

134 In the Netherlands, the term 'Indologie' was used to designate the study of Indian history and culture in preparation for colonial service in the Dutch East Indies. Upon the independence of Indonesia, the Faculty was abolished in 1950.

conservative Loder felt presumably sympathetic.[135] The controversy surrounding the new, fervently pro-colonialist Faculty did not deter Loder, whose combativeness frequently led to him making strong and uncompromising statements.

It could be considered telling of his recognition as an eminent international lawyer at the time that his role at the League did not end after his time at the PCIJ, but rather continued in different positions until his age did not permit him to continue. In 1929, four Dutch law professors (Costers, De Louter, Verzijl and Suijling), together with Tobias Asser's eldest son Carel Daniel, even nominated Loder for the Nobel Peace Prize.[136] Loder did not win, however – the 1929 Nobel Peace Prize went to Frank Billings Kellogg 'for the Kellogg-Briand Pact, whose signatories agreed to settle all conflicts by peaceful means and renounced war as an instrument of national policy'.[137] Both Rotterdam and Amsterdam have named a street after Bernard Loder to publicly honour his achievements – not so in The Hague, even though that is the city where he spent most of his professional life and where he died on 4 November 1935.

135 Roelofsen (n 8).
136 <www.asser.nl/media/1554/eyff_asser-100_book_lr.pdf>
137 <www.nobelprize.org>

10 The Italian jurist and diplomat at the Advisory Committee of Jurists

Arturo Ricci Busatti (1868–1923)

Elisabetta Fiocchi Malaspina

1. A life entirely dedicated to diplomacy

Arturo Ricci Busatti was one of countless figures of jurists and diplomats who, despite having played a decisive role in the field of international law and having participated in numerous diplomatic conferences, have been relatively little studied in depth. An overall study of Ricci Busatti is lacking, bringing together and reconstructing his intense activity and his thinking. Yet Ricci Busatti was, in 1906, among the founders, together with Dionisio Anzilotti, of the journal *Rivista di diritto internazionale*, he took part in the Second International Peace Conference held in The Hague in 1907, and in 1920 he was on the Advisory Committee of Jurists in charge of drafting the statute for the Permanent Court of International Justice.[1]

His scientific output and his diplomatic commitment, evident in archival documents that will be analysed in this article, are the demonstration of a life lived intensely, cut short when Busatti was only 55 years old. He was born in Siena on 25 January 1868 to Federigo Ricci and Ada Busatti, from two important Tuscan families, originally from the Sorano area in the province of Grosseto, who gave their double surname to Arturo and his brother Alberto.

On 29 June 1887 he graduated in Law at the Royal University of Siena having studied under Vittorio Scialoja, at the time professor of Roman law. Ricci Busatti was to remain in contact with Scialoja throughout his life, especially between 1919 and 1920 when he directed, for some time, the Litigation and Legislation Office of the Ministry of Foreign Affairs and Vittorio Scialoja was Foreign Minister.[2]

1 For a complete reconstruction of international law in Italy and its history, see the very recent volume Giulio Bartolini (ed), *A History of International Law in Italy* (The History and Theory of International Law, 1st edn, OUP 2020); as regards international law and jurists in the early part of the twentieth century during the First World War, see Giulio Bartolini, 'World War I and the Italian International Law Scholars' [2020] Journal of the History of International Law 1.

2 For the life of Ricci Busatti, see: Direzione Rivista di diritto internazionale, 'Necrologio di Arturo Ricci Busatti' (1923) 15 Rivista di diritto internazionale 3. For a comprehensive profile of Vittorio Scialoja, his activity as a lawyer and politician, see: Giovanni Chiodi, 'Scialoja

DOI: 10.4324/9781003020882-11

Barely 20 years of age, in 1888 he began his diplomatic career, obtaining the position of volunteer for first category jobs at the Ministry of Foreign Affairs[3] and the following year he obtained in Rome the qualification to practice as a lawyer. From 1890 his diplomatic career at the Italian Ministry of Foreign Affairs continued to grow and he was appointed second vice-secretary, then first secretary in 1891.[4] In 1895 he was awarded the honour of Knight of the Crown of Italy and he participated in the work of the commission responsible for drafting consular law, whose aim was to reform regulation of the diplomatic service, in particular governing the powers of individual consular officers, the powers of consuls relating to civil status deeds, notarial authority and civil and commercial jurisdiction.[5]

In 1902 he was a first secretary, holding very important positions both internationally and diplomatically. As mentioned, he was among delegates to the Second Peace Conference held in The Hague in 1907 in which the nations, on the invitation of Tsar Nicholas II, endeavoured to translate into law and practice their commitment to containing conflicts, limiting armaments and regulating warfare on both land and sea.[6]

Busatti's opinion on the conference was crystallized in some important letters written to famous Italian statesman and economist Luigi Bodio,[7] and these merit perusal for an understanding of the personal aspect of the Tuscan jurist's character. On 19 September 1907, Busatti informed Bodio that he was happy to

---

Vittorio' in Italo Birocchi, Ennio Cortese, Antonello Mattone, and Marco Nicola Miletti (eds), *Dizionario Biografico degli Italiani* (Il Mulino 2012) vol 2, 1833–37.

3 Direzione Rivista di diritto internazionale (n 2) 4.

4 ibid 5.

5 ibid 5. For a view of Italian diplomacy from Unification to the early twentieth century, see: Fabio Grassi, *La formazione della Diplomazia Nazionale (1861–1915) repertorio bio-bibliografico dei funzionari del Ministero degli affari esteri* (Istituto Poligrafico e Zecca dello Stato 1986).

6 On the Hague Peace Conferences see Claire Vergerio, 'The Berlin and Hague Conferences' in Mlada Bukovansky, Edward Keene, Maja Spanu, and Christopher Reus-Smit (eds), *Oxford Handbook of History and International Relations* (OUP forthcoming). See also: Shabtai Rosenne (ed), *The Hague Peace Conferences of 1899 and 1907 and International Arbitration: Reports and Documents* (T.M.C. Asser 2001). See: Maartje M Abbenhuis, Christopher E Barber, and Annalize R Higgins, *War, Peace and International Order?: The Legacies of the Hague Conferences of 1899 and 1907*, vol 23 (Routledge Studies in Modern History, Routledge 2017). And also Laura Passero, 'Dalle Convenzioni di Ginevra alla 'bancarotta' del diritto internazionale. Il rapporto tra il 'nuovo' *jus in bello* Otto-Novecentesco e la catastrofe della prima guerra civile europea' (2009) 39(2) *Quaderni Fiorentini per la storia del pensiero giuridico moderno. I diritti dei nemici* 1479–504.

7 Luigi Bodio (1840–1920) in 1878 assumed the position of general manager of statistics, a subject in which he excelled, making a significant contribution to the discipline in Italy. In 1901 he headed the newly established General Commissariat for Emigration. In 1885 he became secretary of the International Institute of Statistics (later president in 1909). In 1900 he was also appointed senator of the Kingdom of Italy. See: Franco Bonelli, 'Bodio Luigi' *Dizionario Biografico degli Italiani* (1969) 11 <www.treccani.it/enciclopedia/luigi-bodio_%28Dizionario-Biografico%29/> accessed 31 December 2020; also Marco Soresina, *Conoscere per amministrare. Luigi Bodio: statistica, economia e pubblica amministrazione* (FrancoAngeli 2001).

have been able to attend the meeting 'on politics and law' and specified that he had been able to acquire a 'varied experience', for the 'fine and interesting things' he had been able to see.[8] Busatti, however, did not conceal his true thoughts on the effects of the conference, stating that 'the result of these three very long months . . . will make very little change to the fates of peace and war and the conduct of events'.[9]

In 1912 Busatti sent Bodio the text of the conventions and declarations of the First Peace Conference in The Hague in 1899 'which we ratified and which still bind us'.[10] Busatti recalled the importance of the 1899 Hague Convention with which the Permanent Court of Arbitration was established and wrote that '*all States* signed and adhered to it later, except for Honduras which only joined the 2nd and 3rd conventions, still in force; the American states have never adhered: all the others without exception'.[11] He added that it concerned the '*moral commitment*' that should have led to ratification of the 1907 agreements, a ratification that Italy was slow to carry out.[12]

Between 4 December 1908 and 26 February 1909 Ricci Busatti attended the London Naval Conference as *attaché*, with Guido Fusinato and Count Giovanni Locatelli;[13] the objective of the conference was a sort of continuation of the discussions that had taken place at The Hague Conference of 1907 for establishing the International Prize Court.[14] The result was the signing of the London Declaration on the law of maritime warfare, which was never ratified. Among various topics, Article 1 covered naval blockades that 'must not extend beyond the ports and coasts belonging to or occupied by the enemy', their effects, application and duration. Detailed rules were also laid down on smuggling, hostile assistance, destruction of neutral prey, change of flag, the enemy or neutral character of

8 Letters conserved at the Braidense National Library in Milan: letter from Arturo Ricci Busatti to Bodio, Bodio papers 1976, letter no. 1.

9 'il risultato di questi tre lunghissimi mesi . . . modificherà assai poco sensibilmente le sorti della pace e della guerra e la condotta degli eventi' (author's translation) Bodio, Bodio papers 1976, letter no. 1. Ricci Busatti himself wrote that the result of the conference, as far as Italy was concerned, was the signing of all the conventions; however he 'abstained' from signing the 'declaration' relating to launching projectiles from airships: Arturo Ricci Busatti, 'Ratifica delle convenzioni dell'Aja, 17 ottobre 1907' (1909) 4 Rivista di diritto internazionale 403–18.

10 'che noi ratificammo e che tuttora ci vincolano' (author's translation). Letter conserved at the Braidense National Library in Milan: letter from Arturo Ricci Busatti to Bodio, Bodio papers 1976, letter no. 2.

11 'tutti gli Stati firmano e vi aderiscono in seguito, salvo l'Honduras che aderì soltanto alle 2° e 3°, tuttora vigenti, non hanno mai aderito gli Stati americani: tutti gli altri senza eccezione' ibid.

12 ibid.

13 Carlos I Fuentes, *Normative Plurality in International Law: A Theory of the Determination of Applicable Rules*, vol 57 (Ius Gentium, Springer 2016) 82. See also Direzione Rivista di diritto internazionale (n 2) 8.

14 On the Conference see Dieter Fleck, 'London Naval Conference (1908–1909)' in Frauke Lachenmann (ed), *The Law of Armed Conflict and the Use of Force*, vol 2 (The Max Planck Encyclopedia of Public International Law. Thematic Series, OUP 2017) 669 ff.

a ship and its cargo, resistance to exercise of the right to visit, and compensation for unjust sinking of ships.[15] Busatti gave an account of participation in the Conference, publishing the 'chronicle' in the *Rivista di diritto internazionale*, underlining that the provisions relating to 'enemy character' (chapter VI, art. 57–60)[16] were 'the proof of the lack of consensus on the most challenging questions' which were addressed but not particularly successfully.[17]

For Busatti, this last issue represented, together with the transformation of commercial ships into warships, 'one of the two points in which the Conference did not achieve its aim'.[18] It should be noted that the American jurist James Brown Scott was also critical about the outcome of the conference, underlining how discussion had been focused much more on theory than on practice.[19]

From 1908 to 1919 Ricci Busatti headed the Litigation and Legislation Office of the Ministry of Foreign Affairs, established in 1908 and strongly desired by that ministry,[20] which offered him

> the singularly propitious opportunity to demonstrate what was perhaps the most characteristic disposition of his spirit, to unite and equally reconcile in himself two different tendencies, the habit of the man of science who seeks

15 Declaration of London of February 26, 1909 <https://ihl-databases.icrc.org/applic/ihl/ihl.nsf/Article.xsp?action=openDocument&documentId=78B780093633B347C12563CD005177B6> accessed 31 December 2020.

16 Article 57 established that 'Subject to the provisions respecting transfer to another flag, the neutral or enemy character of a vessel is determined by the flag which she is entitled to fly.

The case where a neutral vessel is engaged in a trade which is closed in time of peace, remains outside the scope of, and is in no wise affected by, this rule': The declaration of London of February 26, 1909 <https://ihl-databases.icrc.org/applic/ihl/ihl.nsf/Article.xsp?action=openDocument&documentId=9400EFEB4F19598BC12563CD00517AC7> accessed 31 December 2020.

17 Arturo Ricci Busatti, 'La Conferenza Navale di Londra' [1909] 4 Rivista di diritto internazionale 52.

18 'uno dei due punti in cui la Conferenza non ha raggiunto il suo scopo' (author's translation) Ricci Busatti (n 17) 61–62.

19 'As in the blockade, so in contraband, the Declaration seems to be rather a reconciliation of divergent theories than a compromise of divergent practices, if substance be considered rather than form': James Brown Scott, 'The Declaration of London of February 26, 1909' (1914) 8(2) The American Journal of International Law 274–29, here 329. See also: Elihu Root, 'The Real Significance of the Declaration of London' (1912) 6(3) The American Journal of International Law 583. And also Enrico Catellani, *La Dichiarazione di Londra relativa al Diritto della Guerra Marittima* (Fratelli Drucker 1912).

20 The documents relating to the diplomatic activity of Ricci Busatti are conserved in the archive of the Ministry of Foreign Affairs, see: Laura Pilotti (ed), *Il fondo archivistico Serie Z-contenzioso*, Ministero degli Affari esteri, Direzione generale dell'emigrazione e degli affari sociali, Archivio storico diplomatico (Istituto poligrafico e Zecca dello Stato 1987). On the Ufficio del contenzioso e della legislazione see: Matteo Camboni, '"I sacri diritti di nazionalità". La giurisprudenza del Consiglio del contenzioso diplomatico del Regno d'Italia sui reclami degli Italiani all'estero' (PhD thesis, tutor Claudia Storti, University of Milan, cycle XXVIII, 2016/2017) 101; also: Enrico Serra, *La diplomazia in Italia* (FrancoAngeli 1988) 37.

principles rather than facts, and that of the diplomat, who is naturally more drawn to giving facts the greater attention and importance.[21]

In 1910 during the signing of the Arbitration Convention between Italy and the Netherlands he distinguished himself for his efforts regarding the enforceability of arbitration sentences pronounced in absentia.[22] In 1911 he held the prestigious position of Minister Plenipotentiary.

As an expert in international law he took an active part in numerous international issues in the first two decades of the twentieth century. Between 1912 and 1913 he appears as Agent at the Permanent Court of Arbitration in two crucial international disputes between Italy and France regarding the seizure of the mail steamers 'Carthage' and 'Manouba', in which Dionisio Anzilotti also took part, as counsel for the Italian government.[23] The 'Carthage' and the 'Manouba' had been seized by the Italian government on suspicion of smuggling during the Italo-Turkish war in Libya (1911–1912).[24] France and Italy, on the verge of a diplomatic crisis and a possible conflict, agreed on 26 January 1912 to resolve the dispute at the Permanent Court of Arbitration, which on 6 May 1913, found that Italy was within her rights.[25]

Ricci Busatti's most decisive contribution was made after the First World War. In the Paris negotiations, between 1919 and 1920, the global and legal order created as a result of the conflict was drawn up, and Ricci Busatti was a member of the *Comité de rédaction*, established to draft peace treaties and to provide legal and diplomatic counsel on specific issues of international law.

In 1920 he was a member of the commission in charge of drafting the statute for the Permanent Court of International Justice, whose role will be analysed in the following pages, and was an *attaché* at the First Assembly of the League of Nations, which met in Geneva on 15 November 1920.

In 1921 he was elected President of the Legal Commission at the Conference in Rome of the newly established states following the dissolution of the

21 'gli offrì l'occasione singolarmente propizia per spiegare quella che fu forse la disposizione più caratteristica dello spirito suo, di congiungere e di contemperare egualmente in sé due tendenze diverse, l'abito dell'uomo di scienza diretto a ricercare i principî più che i fatti, e quello del diplomatico, che è naturalmente condotto a dare più ai fatti la maggiore attenzione ed importanza' (author's translation). Direzione Rivista di diritto internazionale (n 1) 7.

22 Direzione Rivista di diritto internazionale (n 2) 7.

23 Dionisio Anzilotti, 'Le questioni di diritto sollevate dagli incidenti del "Carthage" e del "Manouba"' (1913) 7 Rivista di diritto internazionale 200–36 and 398–413. See also Giovanni Di Stefano and Robert Kolb, 'Some Contributions and Influence of the Italian Doctrine of International Law' in Giulio Bartolini (ed), *A History of International Law in Italy* (OUP 2020) 463. See also: Giorgio Bosco and Dionisio Anzilotti, *L'attività diplomatica e giurisdizionale* (Edizioni Nagard 2006).

24 For a reconstruction of both cases, see: Constantine Antonopoulos, *Counterclaims before the International Court of Justice* (T.M.C. Asser Press 2011) 14–15.

25 For the decision of the Permanent Court of Arbitration see, concerning the Manouba <https://pca-cpa.org/fr/cases/68/>, concerning the Carthage <https://legal.un.org/riaa/cases/vol_XI/449-461.pdf> (accessed 31 December 2020).

Austro-Hungarian Empire.[26] Here, too, Ricci Busatti did not fail to distinguish himself on a delicate legal problem. The Italian Under-secretary for Foreign Affairs, Marco Aurelio di Saluzzo, had written to the representatives of the participating States, informing them that some delegates to the Rome Conference had not been provided with powers broad enough to guarantee regular, timely conduct of the work, and that therefore integration was needed. In 1922 Ricci Busatti was among those in charge of verifying the conferral of powers on the diplomatic representatives, in order to complete the work of the conference.[27]

He was the Italian delegate to the Geneva Conference whose work began in October 1921 on the non-fortification and neutralization of the Åland Islands.[28] At the time the Åland Islands were under Finnish sovereignty, but their inhabitants wanted to be annexed to Sweden, appealing to the principle of self-determination of peoples. The Council of the League of Nations resolved on 24 June 1921 that the States concerned should meet in conference to discuss the matter, on the one hand, establishing certain guarantees in favour of the islands' population and, on the other, ensuring neutralization of the archipelago.[29] The Geneva Conference established Finland's sovereignty over the islands; the principle of demilitarization of the islands was restored and it was also accepted that the Ålands would constitute neutral territory in time of war.[30]

Also in 1921, in recognition of his scientific and also practical merits, Busatti was elected 'associé' of the *Institut de Droit International*.[31] He took an active part in reorganizing the duties, within the Ministry of Foreign Affairs, of the Litigation and Legislation Office and of the Treaties and League of Nations Office, the latter established after the signature of the Treaty of Versailles in 1919.[32]

26 Direzione Rivista di diritto internazionale (n 2) 9.

27 For the role of Ricci Busatti at the Rome Conference, interesting documentation has been collected by the Istituto di Studi Giuridici Internazionali of the Consiglio Nazionale delle Ricerche available on <www.prassi.cnr.it/prassi/content.html?id=1048> accessed 31 December 2020.

28 Direzione Rivista di diritto internazionale (n 2) 9.

29 Deborah Paci, *L'arcipelago della pace. Le isole Åland e il Baltico (XIX–XXI secolo)* (Unicopli 2016). Also Roberto de Cardona, 'Autonomia delle Isole Aland' (1960) 27(4) Rivista di studi politici internazionali 534.

30 See Norman J Padelford and KGA Andersson, 'The Aaland Islands Question' (1939) 33(3) The American Journal of International Law 465; Rowan Nicholson, *Statehood and the State-like in International Law* (Oxford Monographs in International Law, 1st edn, OUP 2019) 132–33.

31 *Annuaire de l'Institut de Droit International* (1921) vol 28, XXIV. At the time the president was André Weiss, and honorary members included Tomaso Tittoni, while among the effective members were Anzilotti, Enrico Catellani and Adriano Diena.

32 Ricci Busatti argued that it was better to keep the League of Nations Office separate from the Treaties Office, to which all matters relating to peace treaties and related conventions should be devolved. Following Ricci Busatti's thinking, the two offices were separated under an 'Internal Disposition' of 28 September 1921. The first would deal with the collection and publication of international conventions and the preparation of the international conferences and congresses of a legal-administrative nature. The second, with questions concerning the League of Nations. Studies on legal or legislative issues were addressed to the Secretariat of

After Busatti's death on 11 February 1923, the management of the *Rivista di diritto internazionale*, composed of Anzilotti, Arrigo Cavaglieri and Tomaso Perassi, described the intense activity of Ricci Busatti as follows: 'Few men, for innate disposition of spirit, for natural versatility of resourcefulness, for vast and brilliant culture, for amiability of manners, were similarly prepared to meet the various demands made of him during a ceaselessly industrious life'.[33]

2. Ricci Busatti's writing on international law and the founding of the *Rivista di diritto internazionale*

His first works dealt with issues of citizenship, a theme that he returned to on several occasions throughout his life. In 1891 he came to fame for the publication of his 'Principle of the family unit in the acquisition and loss of citizenship'.[34] Ricci Busatti examined the question under every aspect. He considered the articles of the Italian Civil Code regarding the acquisition of citizenship by the wife and minor children, the loss of citizenship and the possibility of its re-acquisition (Articles 4–15 of the Civil Code). He reconstructed the major doctrinal positions and legislative decisions, comparing the system in which wife and children were expected to 'follow in citizenship' the *pater familias* with the other system modelled on a very individual requirement of citizenship. Ricci Busatti, who believed in the importance of a strong, united family in terms of citizenship too, embraced the former system. It should be noted that this question chosen by Ricci Busatti seems to herald what was to be the leitmotiv of his entire existence: relations between family and State, especially in international contexts, with particular attention to Italians abroad.[35]

The problem of the legal status of Italians abroad was central in an era in which Italy saw massive emigration to various European and non-European countries.[36] In 1901 Italy repealed part of Article 11 of the Civil Code, which had deprived of citizenship anyone who, without the Italian government's authorization, had accepted or had entered foreign military service. Law no. 217 followed on

---

the Diplomatic Litigation Council, as discussed in Luigi Vittorio Ferraris, *L'amministrazione centrale del Ministero degli esteri italiano nel suo sviluppo storico (1848–1954)* (Biblioteca della Rivista di studi politici internazionali 1955) 60. See: Laura Pilotti (ed), *Il fondo archivistico Serie Z-contenzioso*, Ministero degli Affari esteri, Direzione generale dell'emigrazione e degli affari sociali, *Archivio storico diplomatico* (Istituto poligrafico e Zecca dello Stato 1987) 42–45. Also: Camboni (n 20) 102–3.

33 'Pochi uomini furono, per innata disposizione dello spirito, per naturale versatilità dell'ingegno, per vasta e geniale cultura, per gentilezza di maniere, al par di lui preparati a disimpegnare le svariate funzioni a cui lo chiamarono le vicende di una vita costantemente operosa' (author's translation). Direzione Rivista di diritto internazionale (n 2) 3.

34 Arturo Ricci Busatti, 'Principio dell'unità di famiglia nell'acquisto e nella perdita della cittadinanza' (1891) 12(1) Rivista italiana per le scienze giuridiche 25–53.

35 ibid 25 ff.

36 See: Gabriele Scotti, 'Dimensioni dell'emigrazione italiana tra il 1880 e il 1930' (2017) 3(17) Italian Review of Legal History 1–24.

17 May 1906, facilitating the acquisition of citizenship.[37] Three years later in 1909 Parliament discussed the possibility of regulating in a more streamlined manner the re-acquisition of citizenship by emigrants. Scialoja presented to the Senate the bill on citizenship, which was then approved as Law no. 555 of 13 June 1912, containing important measures on the maintenance of Italian citizenship for Italian children born abroad.[38] Before its promulgation this law had also been discussed in June 1911 during the second congress of Italians abroad, in which Ricci Busatti had taken part. Together with the Hon. Vittorio Polacco, he had discussed Scialoja's bill, assisting its passage through Parliament.[39]

Along with Dionisio Anzilotti, at the time professor of international law at the University of Bologna, and Leone Astolfo Senigallia, lawyer at the Court of Cassation, as well as member of *Comité Maritime International*, Ricci Busatti was among the founders in 1906 of the *Rivista di diritto internazionale*,[40] which has been described by Laura Passero as 'the rallying point for all scholars called to represent a doctrine that was ready for consideration in Europe'.[41] The *Rivista* can in fact be considered as the first attempt to create an Italian and international platform at both doctrinal and practical level. Significant are the words of Anzilotti, in a letter to Ricci Busatti dated 28 January 1905, expressing his enthusiasm to be part of the creation of 'an effective tool for the studies of international law' in Italy.[42]

As Passero notes, the mind behind the *Rivista* was that of Ricci Busatti.[43] He strongly desired a professional journal devoted entirely to international law. The

37 See Dolores Freda, 'La regolamentazione dell'emigrazione in Italia tra Otto e Novecento: una ricerca in corso' (2014) 6(9) Historia et ius 1–20, <www.historiaetius.eu>. Also Dolores Freda, *Governare i migranti: La legge sull'emigrazione del 1901 e la giurisprudenza del Tribunale di Napoli* (G. Giappichelli Editore 2018).

38 See Federico Sciarra, 'La cittadinanza nell'Italia liberale' in Paolo Bonini, Ettore William di Mauro, Gaetano Iovino, Martina Menghi and Federico Sciarra (eds), *Immigrazione e cittadinanza* (Sapienza University Press 2019) 27–35.

39 Vittorio Polacco and Arturo Ricci Busatti, 'Il problema della cittadinanza specialmente nei rapporti degli italiani all'estero' in *Atti del Secondo Congresso degli Italiani all'Estero (11–20 giugno 1911)*, vol I (Tipografia editrice nazionale 1911) 51–84. Sabina Donati, *A Political History of National Citizenship and Identity in Italy, 1861–1950* (OUP 2013) 303.

40 On Anzilotti, for a profile of his life and works, see Francesco Salerno, 'Anzilotti Dionisio' in Italo Birocchi, Ennio Cortese, Antonello Mattone and Marco Nicola Miletti (eds), *Dizionario Biografico degli Italiani* (Il Mulino 2012) vol 1, 84–87; Antonio Tanca, 'Dionisio Anzilotti (1867–1950) Biographical Note with Bibliography' (1992) 3 European Journal of International Law, 156. For a complete examination of the Italian school of international law in the first half of the twentieth century and in particular the role of Anzilotti: Giulio Bartolini, 'Italian Legal Scholarship of International Law in the Early Decades of the Twentieth Century' in Giulio Bartolini (ed), *A History of International Law in Italy* (The History and Theory of International Law, OUP 2020) 127–67.

41 'il polo di aggregazione per tutti gli studiosi chiamati a rappresentare una dottrina ormai pronta al colloquio europeo' (author's translation). Laura Passero, *Dionisio Anzilotti e la dottrina internazionalistica tra Otto e Novecento* (Giuffrè 2010) 10.

42 'un efficace strumento degli studi di diritto internazionale' (author's translation). Thus cited in Passero (n 41) 273.

43 Passero (n 41) 266–67.

management of the *Rivista* themselves said: 'We do not believe we are lacking in due modesty, if we say that the main claim to merit of Arturo Ricci Busatti towards the science of international law is represented by this journal.'[44] Ricci Busatti also supported the publication financially.[45]

Together with Anzilotti, Ricci Busatti also organized the journal's structure and the questions that the *Rivista* would deal with, paying close attention to balancing them to ensure, for example, that references to published sentences did not prevail but that, on the contrary, sentences were selected and were 'often accompanied by notes summarizing the state of the jurisprudence on that given point'.[46] Anzilotti and Ricci Busatti succeeded in their intent to launch the *Rivista* in an international, professional perspective, while also contributing on the methodological side to growing the discipline of international law in Italy.

The sincere friendship that bound Ricci Busatti to Anzilotti was strong and based on mutual esteem, and this is evidenced in the many letters that the two exchanged, which have been extensively studied by Passero, to whom we refer for a more detailed profile of Ricci Busatti as a member of the Advisory Committee of Jurists.[47]

Ricci Busatti invested heavily in the *Rivista* and published several articles, both doctrinal and practical in nature. For example, in 1909 in the section 'Practical cases of international law' he examined a thorny question: was it up to the Ottoman authority or the Italian consular authority to try an Italian accused of complicity with an indigenous subject, in a crime committed against a compatriot, in a country where Capitulations applied?'[48] The case concerned Father Giustino Pacini, an Italian subject, assigned to the French mission in Tripoli, who was 'Turkishly' killed in Derna on 22 March 1908.[49] The local authority accused Brother Felice (Aurelio di Leonardo) and a native employed at the royal vice consulate of Derna. The trial was held by the royal consular authority in Benghazi,

44 'Non crediamo di mancare alla nostra doverosa modestia, se diciamo che il principale titolo di benemerenza di Arturo Ricci Busatti verso la scienza del diritto internazionale è rappresentato da questa rivista' (author's translation). Direzione Rivista di diritto internazionale (n 2) 6.

45 Passero (n 41) 277. On the *Rivista di diritto internazionale*, its foundation and methodology, see Ivan Ingravallo, 'The Formation of International Law Journals in Italy. Their Role in the Discipline' in Giulio Bartolini (ed), *A History of International Law in Italy* (The History and Theory of International Law, OUP 2020) 196 ff.

46 'accompagnate spesso di note che riassumano lo stato della giurisprudenza su quel dato punto' (author's translation). Passero (n 41) 280, note 44.

47 See Passero (n 41).

48 'all'autorità ottomana o all'autorità consolare italiana processare un italiano accusato di complicità con un suddito indigeno, nel delitto commesso in danno di un connazionale, in paese di capitolazioni?' (author's translation). Arturo Ricci Busatti, 'Spetta all'autorità ottomana o all'autorità consolare italiana processare un italiano accusato di complicità con un suddito indigeno, nel delitto commesso in danno di un connazionale, in paese di capitolazioni?' (1909) 4 Rivista di diritto internazionale 412.

49 'Turkishly killed' reads the engraving on the marble inscription in the convent of San Francesco di Borgo a Mozzano (Lucca) with reference to Father Giustino Pacini.

with the assistance of the consular *attaché* of Constantinople, Sir Menzinger di Preussenthal. The native was acquitted and Brother Felice, freed from custody, was transferred to the naval vessel *Varese* flying the Italian flag. Meanwhile, Tal Mohamed Teraboulsi confessed to the murder and accused Brother Felice of complicity in the crime. A long diplomatic procedure began, as the Ottoman authorities intended to take a series of actions against Brother Felice, in the meantime being protected by the consul, who declared there was no case to answer against him, by virtue of the extraterritoriality of the ship *Varese*. In commenting on the international case, Ricci Busatti proved that he knew how to deal not only with issues of international law and diplomatic law, but also with both Italian and Ottoman criminal law. Ricci Busatti affirmed that if the consul had handed Brother Felice over to the Ottoman authorities he would have committed a very serious violation 'since the offender was on board an Italian warship, that is, in a place that the universally accepted principles of the law of nations equate, in every respect, to national territory'.[50]

Penal questions again appeared in the 1909 issue of the *Rivista di diritto internazionale*, in the 'Jurisprudence' section, where Ricci Busatti addressed various matters relating to extradition, commenting on the admissibility of appeal to the Supreme Court in such cases, after publication of a ruling that had rejected this possibility as not being contemplated in law.[51] After reconstructing legislation regarding extradition, Ricci Busatti, who supported its admissibility to the Supreme Court, examined the matter in more detail from the viewpoint of both domestic and international law, expressing a wish for radical change in decisions and in a specific provision to regulate its content.[52]

On another occasion he analysed the civil jurisdiction of consuls on a doctrinal and practical level as regards maritime disputes, reconstructing the legal situation before and after Italian unification.[53] The problem lay in determining the powers and limits of the local judge and the consul with respect to certain legal relationships, of a private nature, between the members of a ship's crew. Ricci Busatti demonstrated how the recognition, within certain limits, of the consul's exclusive jurisdiction over merchant ships, derived from an actual ruling of international law, and from a 'general principle that the collective will of the States, through long custom, has imposed on the conduct of each one'.[54]

During the First World War he published an interesting article concerning a proposal of the Russian government regarding Italian prisoners of war. In October 1914, when Italy was still neutral, the Tsar of Russia, 'wanting to give proof

50 'dal momento che il reo si trovava a bordo di una nave da guerra italiana, cioè in luogo che i principî universalmente accolti dal diritto delle genti equiparano, sotto ogni riguardo, al territorio nazionale' (author's translation). Ricci Busatti (n 48) 418.

51 ibid 418.

52 Arturo Ricci Busatti, 'Dell'ammissibilità del ricorso in cassazione in materia di estradizione' (1909) 4 Rivista di diritto internazionale 80.

53 Arturo Ricci Busatti, 'La giurisdizione civile del console nelle controversie marittime' (1909) 4 Rivista di diritto internazionale 261–88.

54 Ricci Busatti (n 53) 276.

of his great regard for Italy',[55] had informed the Italian government of his intention to free prisoners of war who were Austrian and Hungarian subjects but Italian nationals, and who had been taken prisoner in (Austrian) Galicia, provided that the Italian government undertook to take care of them, 'guarding' them, in order to prevent them rejoining the Austro-Hungarian armies.[56] The proposal had a sensational impact on public opinion, and articles were published in the newspapers by leading experts in international law.[57] Ricci Busatti was commissioned by the Hon. Antonio Salandra, at the time President of the Council of Ministers and Minister of the Interior, to study and evaluate the Russian proposal from a legal point of view. Ricci Busatti carried out a detailed analysis, illustrating the reasons why it was not possible to accept such a proposal; this was accepted by Salandra and communicated to Russia. For Ricci Busatti, the Russian request implied a question of changing the condition of soldiers of Italian nationality from that of prisoners of war to enemies interned in the territory of a neutral country; 'a better condition without doubt, but still different from liberty'.[58] The 'liberation' of the prisoners was effectively subordinate to 'custody', preventing them from returning to enlist. Ricci Busatti referred to the fifth Hague Convention of 1907, concerning the rights and duties of powers and neutral persons in the event of land warfare, where in Article 11 it was decreed that

> a neutral Power which receives on its territory troops belonging to the belligerent armies shall intern them, as far as possible, at a distance from the theatre of war. It may keep them in camps and even confine them in fortresses or in places set apart for this purpose. It shall decide whether officers can be left at liberty on giving their parole not to leave the neutral territory without permission.[59]

Ricci Busatti analysed Article 11, specifying that this Convention formally conferred an obligation and specific faculties in two cases: in the case of belligerent troops who, to escape the enemy, take refuge within the borders of a third State, keeping them away 'from the theatre of war'; and in the case of sick or

55 'volendo dare un attestato della sua alta simpatia all'Italia' (author's translation).'Comunicato ufficiale' *Corriere della Sera* (Milano, 25 October 1914).

56 Arturo Ricci Busatti, 'La proposta del Governo russo circa i prigionieri di nazionalità italiana' (1915) 4 Rivista di diritto internazionale 3.

57 For example, Giulio Cesare Buzzati with the article published in the *Corriere della Sera* of 25 October 1914, 'Il Nodo della questione. Caso impreveduto', stated: 'Russia intends to give proof of great regard for Italy: that is fine: but Italy cannot become the keeper of prisoners under a condition in itself unfair, and especially unfair to those our guests, who share our lineage and which together would cause difficulties and responsibilities of the neutral State towards its neighbouring Empire' (author's translation).

58 Ricci Busatti (n 56) 3–4.

59 Convention (V) respecting the Rights and Duties of Neutral Powers and Persons in Case of War on Land. The Hague, 18 October 1907, consulted in <https://ihl-databases.icrc.org/applic/ihl/ihl.nsf/385ec082b509e76c41256739003e636d/85e344e491c102e5c125641e003934b7> accessed 31 December 2020.

wounded, introduced by the opposing army into the territory of a neutral power, or entrusted to the latter by the same army to which they belong, in accordance with Article 14 of the Convention.[60] Article 13 made it clear that when a neutral Power received escaped prisoners of war, it was obliged to give them their liberty even when they were brought by troops fleeing to the territory of the neutral power.[61] Ricci Busatti showed that, given the tenor of these articles, the rules of international law would be seriously violated by accepting the Russian proposal: the internment requested by the Russian government and not contemplated in the fifth Hague Convention 'would constitute . . . an interference and a concurrence in the operations of the war, contrary to that strict duty of abstention, which is the fundamental character of neutrality. . . . Acceptance of the proposal would have constituted . . . an act of authentic hostile assistance'.[62]

At the end of the First World War, Ricci Busatti took part in the international debate that arose around Wilhelm II of Germany.[63] The crux of the matter concerned the possibility of bringing the German sovereign to trial for war crimes.[64] Cristiano La Lumia highlights that already in 1917 Alexandre Mérignhac, in an article published in the *Revue général de droit international public*, had spoken out for the need that a common solution be found at international level for the punishment of all the atrocities committed in Belgium by the Kaiser, as Head of State.[65] The 'four protagonists' of the Paris Conference did not remain indifferent.[66] David Lloyd George asked the opinion of a commission of jurists, who through Sir Frederick Edwin Smith declared themselves in favour, invoking the

60 'A neutral Power may authorize the passage over its territory of the sick and wounded belonging to the belligerent armies, on condition that the trains bringing them shall carry neither personnel nor war material. In such a case, the neutral Power is bound to take whatever measures of safety and control are necessary for the purpose. The sick or wounded brought under these conditions into neutral territory by one of the belligerents, and belonging to the hostile party, must be guarded by the neutral Power so as to ensure their not taking part again in the military operations. The same duty shall devolve on the neutral State with regard to wounded or sick of the other army who may be committed to its care': Convention (V) (n 59).

61 ibid.

62 'costituirebbe [. . .] una ingerenza e un concorso nelle operazioni della guerra, contrariamente a quel rigoroso dovere di astensione, che è il carattere fondamentale della neutralità. [. . .] L'accettazione della proposta avrebbe costituito [. . .] un atto di vera e propria assistenza ostile' (author's translation). Ricci Busatti (n 56) 9.

63 Cristiano La Lumia, 'Giustizia solenne o una "sciocchezza"? Dibattito sul processo al Kaiser Guglielmo (1918–1920)' (2019) 27 Annali, Museo Storico della Guerra 8–31. This article very clearly highlights how the Kaiser was seen in the media and in literature.

64 The reference was, for example, to the transatlantic Lusitania which was sunk by a German submarine on 7 May 1915, but also to the sovereign's conduct towards Belgium: La Lumia (n 63) 11.

65 La Lumia (n 63) 11; Alexandre Mérignhac, 'De la sanction des infractions au droit des gens' (1917) 24(1) Revue Générale de Droit international Public 52.

66 La Lumia (n 63) 11.

support of illustrious authorities of the past such as Hugo Grotius.[67] Georges Clemenceau turned to Ferdinand Larnaude and Albert de Lapradelle:[68] both jurists had been attentive campaigners for a serious international effort that was truly capable of punishing those who violated The Hague Conventions of 1899 and 1907.[69] In 1919, at the Paris Conference, Clemenceau and Lloyd George pressed for the emperor's trial, while Woodrow Wilson opposed it, also supported by Vittorio Emanuele Orlando. Among the American jurists, Robert Lansing and James Brown Scott were against it, without however denying the responsibilities of Wilhelm: according to Scott the Kaiser had already had his 'punishment' with dethronement and exile.[70]

Already during the war Italian opinion was hesitant regarding the possible trial of the sovereign. Ricci Busatti in the *Rivista di diritto internazionale* first addressed Mérignhac, arguing very critically that French jurist had been incapable of understanding or adequately evaluating the distinction and the relationships between international law and domestic law. Ricci Busatti's terse comment was that 'some of his practical conclusions seem to be, quite frankly, very impractical'.[71]

His position was followed by that of Vittorio Emanuele Orlando, who during the preparatory meeting of the Paris Peace Conference argued that there was no need to treat the matter as a priority.[72] After the signing of the Treaty of Versailles, too, the Italian position remained immoveable: once again Arturo Ricci Busatti saw a dangerous confusion between the legal question and the political one. In fact, he wrote to the Foreign Minister Tomaso Tittoni on 12 July 1919 that 'the judgment to which the former emperor will have to be subjected and the request for extradition to the Dutch government are nonsense'.[73] Although Ricci Busatti acknowledged that Article 227 of the Treaty established the so-called

67 ibid 12. See David Lloyd George, *The Truth about the Peace Treaties* (Victor Gollancz 1938) vol 1, 103–4.

68 La Lumia (n 63) 12.

69 ibid 13. The outcome of their work, thanks also to the collaboration of criminal lawyers, was the publication of the *Examen de la responsabilité pénale de l'Empereur Guillaume II* (Imprimerie Nationale 1918), requesting the institution of a court to try the sovereign for crimes against the law of nations. See also Martti Koskenniemi, *The Gentle Civilizer of Nations: The Rise and Fall of International Law 1870–1960* (Hersch Lauterpacht Memorial Lectures, CUP 2001) and also Stefano Mannoni, *Da Vienna a Monaco, 1814–1938: Ordine europeo e diritto internazionale* (Giappichelli 2014). On Italy between the two world wars Giulio Bartolini, 'Italy between the Two World Wars' in Giulio Bartolini (ed), *A History of International Law in Italy* (The History and Theory of International Law, OUP 2020) 359–79.

70 James Brown Scott, 'The Trial of the Kaiser' in M House and C Seymour (eds), *What Really Happened at Paris* (C. Scribner's Sons 1921) 475.

71 'alcune delle sue conclusioni pratiche sembrano, a dir vero, poco pratiche' (author's translation). Arturo Ricci Busatti, 'Bibliografia' (1918) 3 Rivista di diritto internazionale 130.

72 La Lumia (n 63) 20.

73 'il giudizio a cui dovrà essere sottoposto l'ex imperatore, e la domanda di estradizione al Governo olandese sono un'assurdità' (author's translation). Cited in La Lumia (n 63) 21.

'sanctions',[74] he argued that the article was in essence of a legal but exclusively political nature.[75] As is well known, Wilhelm II was neither extradited nor tried, but Ricci Busatti's position is interesting in considering the tensions between national criminal law and international law and between politics and law. In order to understand Ricci Busatti in his capacity as a jurist and diplomat, it is worth noting that he did not take a 'conservative' position but analysed the problem of the Kaiser's possible trial from a legal, not a political point of view.

Ricci Busatti's ability to manage to combine practice with theory and above all to know how to legally address important diplomatic issues, without being influenced by political decisions, was undoubtedly a characteristic that facilitated his appointment to the Committee of Jurists specially set up to draft the statute of the Permanent Court of International Justice.

3. Advisory Committee of Jurists set up to draft the statute of the Permanent Court of International Justice: the role of Ricci Busatti

Article 14 of the Covenant of the League of Nations provided that

> The Council shall formulate and submit to the Members of the League for adoption plans for the establishment of a Permanent Court of International Justice. The Court shall be competent to hear and determine any dispute of an international character which the parties thereto submit to it. The Court may also give an advisory opinion upon any dispute or question referred to it by the Council or by the Assembly.[76]

The Council thus proceeded in February 1920 to establish a Committee of Jurists charged with drawing up the draft statute of the Permanent Court. In the committee, besides Adatci from Japan, Altamira from Spain, Descamps from Belgium, Hagerup from Norway, de Lapradelle from France, Loder from Holland,

74 Art. 227 established: 'The Allied and Associated Powers publicly arraign William II of Hohenzollern, formerly German Emperor, for a supreme offence against international morality and the sanctity of treaties. A special tribunal will be constituted to try the accused, thereby assuring him the guarantees essential to the right of defence. It will be composed of five judges, one appointed by each of the following Powers: namely, the United States of America, Great Britain, France, Italy and Japan. In its decision the tribunal will be guided by the highest motives of international policy, with a view to vindicating the solemn obligations of international undertakings and the validity of international morality. It will be its duty to fix the punishment which it considers should be imposed. The Allied and Associated Powers will address a request to the Government of the Netherlands for the surrender to them of the ex-Emperor in order that he may be put on trial.' The treaty was consulted at: <www.nationalarchives.gov.uk/pathways/firstworldwar/aftermath/p_versailles.htm> accessed 31 December 2020.

75 La Lumia (n 63) 21.

76 The Covenant was consulted at: <www.ungeneva.org/en/covenant-lon > accessed 31 December 2020.

Lord Phillimore from Great Britain, and Root from the United States, there was also Arturo Ricci Busatti. Descamps was elected President and Dionisio Anzilotti, general secretary. Between 16 June and 24 July 1920, a draft scheme was prepared by the Advisory Committee, which worked relentlessly and tenaciously, and was subsequently submitted to the Council of the League of Nations.[77]

The work was complex and difficult because it involved drafting the statute of the International Court of Justice, under three distinct profiles: organization, competence, and procedure. The Committee itself stated that in addressing these profiles there were considerable difficulties, which were also reflected in all the minutes of their sessions. The sources used by the Committee for pursuit of its objective were the workings of the two Hague Conferences of 1899 and 1907, as well as the plan of the five neutral powers (Denmark, Norway, the Netherlands, Sweden, and Switzerland), which met at The Hague in February 1920.[78] The Committee was 'called upon to pay homage, in a special resolution, to the labours of its predecessors, whether Governments, international scientific bodies, or jurisconsults of all nations'.[79] It was also specified that this onerous task be carried out 'with the conviction that, thanks to their aid, it could undertake the solution of the three great problems before it, in spite of their real difficulty, with complete confidence'.[80]

Léon Bourgeois asked that they worked toward a 'true Permanent Court', which would become the 'symbol' of international law: a proper court with judges 'always present, to whom can always be brought the appeal of the weak and to whom protests against the violation of right can be addressed'.[81] The setting up of a Permanent Court of Justice and the establishment of its legal bases necessarily meant that the starting point of the discussions would be the Permanent Court of Arbitration, especially as regards its organization. In fact for Ricci Busatti, as he stated during the session of 18 June 1920, the Court of Justice would gradually emerge from the Court of Arbitration. It was essential that all matters relating to the Permanent Court of Justice be addressed by separating law from politics: on the one hand there were 'arbitration decisions' and on the other 'judicial decisions'.[82] Ricci Busatti was firmly convinced and would

77 Advisory Committee of Jurists, *Procès-Verbaux of the Proceedings of the Committee, 16 June–24 July 1920, with Annexes* (Van Langenhuysen, The Hague, 1920). For the establishment of the Permanent Court see: Marija Dordeska, *General Principles of Law Recognized by Civilized Nations (1922–2018): The Evolution of the third Source of International law Through the Jurisprudence of the Permanent Court of International Justice and the International Court of Justice*, vol 39 (Queen Mary Studies in International Law, Koninklijke Brill NV 2020). And also Malgosia Fitzmaurice and Christian J Tams (eds), *Legacies of the Permanent Court of International Justice*, vol 13 (Queen Mary Studies in International Law, Nijhoff 2013).

78 See Antoine Vauchez, 'Transnationale Expertenfelder als schwache Felder. Der Entwurf des ersten Weltgerichtshofs und die Entstehung eines internationalen Expertentums' (2014) 24(2) Berlin Journal für Soziologie 201.

79 Procès-Verbaux (n 77) 697.

80 ibid 697.

81 ibid 7.

82 ibid 107.

continue to argue in all Committee meetings that it would be necessary 'to link the Court of Justice with the Court of Arbitration and to guarantee its independence by excluding all political influence'.[83]

But there must be dialogue between the two institutions and he was in agreement with Descamps' proposal[84] that the appointment of judges, to avoid political prevarication by some States, be entrusted to the Permanent Court of Arbitration and not to the Assembly of the League of Nations.[85] Underlying all Ricci Busatti's interventions in the Advisory Committee was his belief that 'the essential point was to maintain a basic unity in international jurisdiction'[86] and that there should be a 'fundamental association' between the jurisdiction of the Court of Arbitration and that of the Permanent Court of Justice.[87] Thus, in the session of 23 June 1920, Ricci Busatti proposed the following articles: the Court of Justice should be connected 'as intimately as possible' to the Court of Arbitration, and 'the functions of which it merely develops'; the Permanent Court of Justice would have a number of members 'possessing the necessary qualification' for appointment to the Permanent Court of Arbitration;[88] all the States of the League of Nations would have the right to appoint a member 'who shall be elected by a college of its delegates to the Court of Arbitration'.[89]

Furthermore, in the session of 25 June 1920, President Descamps questioned his colleagues as to whether the Court of Justice was to be established for jurisdiction between States or whether its competence also extended to private individuals. Adatci, Altamira, and Hagerup were keen advocates of its jurisdiction covering exclusively disputes between States. Loder, on the other hand, referenced the plan of the five neutral States, which had accepted the hypothesis that individuals, too, could use the Court.[90]

Ricci Busatti was resolute in arguing that individuals and States could not be put on an equal footing, and to avoid the term 'international disputes' being interpreted broadly, he specified that individuals were not subject to international law and therefore should be excluded from the jurisdiction of the court.[91] He was also convinced, agreeing with Root, that access to the Court should be granted to all States, in compliance with Article 17 of the Covenant of the League of

83 ibid 388.

84 ibid Annex no 2 Organization 114.

85 ibid 107, the discussion continues on 128 ff.

86 ibid 153. Ricci Busatti insisted on the need to provide a list of judges, who were always' ready to sit 'and chosen from among the best qualified and stated: 'it must not be forgotten that the new Court would be called upon to try cases submitted from all parts of the world and dealing with all kinds of questions': Procès-Verbaux (n 77) 154.

87 Thus in the session of 29 June 1920, Procès-Verbaux (n 77) 246.

88 Procès-Verbaux (n 77) 183.

89 ibid.

90 ibid 184.

91 Ricci Busatti argued: 'To bring a dispute between a State and a private citizen of another State within the domain of International Court, the State of the private individual must consider itself injured through the rights and interests of its subject; thus it "internationalises" the conflict': Procès-Verbaux (n 77) 208.

Nations. He recalled Lapradelle's arguments, but with a 'reservation' regarding the composition of the Court, which

> affects rather the interests of justice than those of the contesting parties; if it were considered necessary or advisable that the contesting parties should be represented in some way on the Court in cases concerning Member States of the League, the same rights should be granted to States which are not Members.[92]

In the session of 30 June 1920, Ricci Busatti proposed specific changes to Articles 1, 2 and 3. With regard to Article 1 he suggested alignment with the contents of Article 13 of the Covenant and with the five neutral powers' plan, therefore to 'strike out the words disputes concerning cases of a legal nature, that is to say, those dealing with and to add after the word "disputes" the words "between states"'. Furthermore, he meticulously requested the substitution of the last paragraph of Article 1 with the following: 'It will also be competent to decide on all disputes, no matter of what description, which the parties have agreed to submit to a judicial decision'.[93] The text was accordingly modified by the President and proposed to the Committee, having also received the changes of Lord Phillimore.[94] The Article was further discussed in the session of 1 July. Ricci Busatti asked that paragraph b of Article 1 be replaced the words 'the application of general rule of international law' with 'any point of international law'.[95] Ricci Busatti's changes to Article 1 were not approved while those presented for Articles 2 and 3 were partially accepted in the final draft.[96] Similarly, in Article 2, he proposed replacing the words 'when the legal nature of a case is disputed' with 'if a question arises whether a certain dispute is or not included in the categories enumerated in the preceding article'.[97] This was 'reformulated' by Phillimore who recommended: 'in cases of a dispute on the question whether a given case does or does not fall within the classification of the preceding article, the Permanent Court will render an interlocutory decision'.[98] In that same session Ricci Busatti submitted to the Committee his draft for the articles concerning the organization of the Court.[99]

One article much discussed by the Committee was what would later become Article 38, concerning the type of sources on which the Court of Justice could base its judgments, recalling its content. During the thirteenth session, the Committee chairman, Belgian jurist Descamps, argued that the Court should

92 Procès-Verbaux (n 77) 223.
93 ibid 274.
94 ibid 275.
95 ibid 284.
96 ibid.
97 ibid 274.
98 ibid 277.
99 ibid 302–5.

judge according to conventional international law, international custom, but also according to the 'rules of international law as recognised by the legal conscience of the civilised nations'.[100] Descamps appeared to refer to the Statute of the *Institut de Droit International* founded in Ghent on 8 September 1873 by his compatriot Gustave Rolin-Jaequemyns. Article 2 of this Statute stated that the purpose of the *Institut* was to promote the progress of international law: 'by striving to formulate the general principles of the subject, in such a way as to correspond to the legal conscience of the civilized world'.[101] The reasoning behind Descamps' idea was to allow the Court, in the event that no treaty or customary laws existed, to reference all those rules, arising from natural law, crystallized in the law of nations in the treatises of authors such as Hugo Grotius or Emer de Vattel, and consolidated in the international community in the 'legal consciousness of civilised peoples'.[102] This would have avoided the Court being obliged to refrain from giving justice.

The question was a thorny one. If on the one hand most of the Committee's members agreed with the proposal of Descamps, on the other hand, some of the members opposed it. In particular Root, Lord Phillimore, and Ricci Busatti proposed variations. Root argued that the nations effectively submitted to positive law arising from the conventions but not to the principles that had not been agreed by the States:[103] 'it is inconceivable that a Government would agree to allow itself to be arraigned before a Court which bases its sentence on its subjective conceptions of the principles of justice' and ended by saying succinctly: 'the Court must not have the power to legislate'.[104] For Lapradelle it was not acceptable for the International Court to declare *non-liquet*, but it was necessary to 'find out in which cases no universally rules really existed'.[105] Arturo Ricci Busatti intervened, beginning his speech by referring to Root's statement: if the Court cannot act as a legislator, then it is crucial that the competences not be confused. Legislation on international law arose exclusively from the States. But

100 Procès-Verbaux, Proposition du Baron Descamps, Annexe No. 3 (n 77) 306. See Anne Peters and Jonathan Huston, *Beyond Human Rights: The Legal Status of the Individual in International Law* (Cambridge Studies in International and Comparative Law, Revised and updated by the author, CUP 2018) 428. And also Ole Spiermann, 'Historical Introduction' in Andreas Zimmermann and others (eds), *The Statute of the International Court of Justice: A Commentary* (Oxford Public International Law, 3rd edn, OUP 2019) 60.

101 Procès-Verbaux (n 77) 306.

102 Descamps ended his speech with the dramatic statement: 'On the threshold of the Palace of Peace where we meet daily there is a mosaic bearing the inscription: Sol Justitiae Illustra Nos. Let us draw inspiration and encouragement from this and let us recognise that the conception of justice and injustice as indelibly written on the hearts of civilised peoples, and with the two additional guarantees that I would give it, is not only the element par excellence making for progress of international law, but an indispensable complement to the application of law, and as such essential to the judge in the performance of the great task entrusted to him': Procès-Verbaux (n 77) 324–25.

103 Procès-Verbaux (n 77) 309 ff.

104 ibid 309.

105 ibid 313.

'that fact does not prevent the administration of justice'. Ricci Busatti's legal position was crystal clear: in declaring the absence of a positive ruling of international law, 'nevertheless a legal situation is established. That which is not forbidden is allowed; that is one of the general principles of law which the Court shall have to apply.'[106] According to Ricci Busatti, if a dispute was submitted to the Court and if after careful analysis the absence of specific regulations emerged, the Court should declare the absence of rights that one party might have asserted over the other and therefore that the conduct of the accused State was not contrary to any accepted regulation. Ricci Busatti was also of the idea that 'there are other principles of the same character (that which forbids the abuse of right or that of *res judicata*), and certain general rules of equity and justice which come into play in each case'. Therefore it was not a question of creating rules but of applying general rules to resolve any issue.[107] Lapradelle declared against Ricci Busatti's opinion, while for Lord Phillimore the Committee's task was to establish an International Court of Justice and not to create laws. In fact Phillimore agreed with Ricci Busatti, who in his opinion 'did not wish to give international judges wider powers than municipal judges; he did not wish in any case, to give international judges legislative powers'.[108] For Descamps, in the event that there was no law or custom, the judge should apply general principles of law. In fact, the judge should pronounce his decision 'in keeping with the dictates of the legal conscience of the civilised peoples and for this same purpose make use of the doctrines of publicists carrying authority'.[109]

As is known, the draft article accepted was that of Root, in which the Court adopted 'the general principles of law recognised by civilised nations'. Ricci Busatti entered into the discussion on this draft, too, observing that this draft laid out not so much 'rules', but rather 'sources of law' and suggested that 'principles of equity' also be added.[110]

Ricci Busatti and Phillimore embarked on an intense debate, in which the English jurist pointed out what 'equity' meant in England and consequently in the 'common law' system.[111] The addition of a reference to equity would have generated confusion and several problems of interpretation and it was decided not to accept Ricci Busatti's proposal.

Ricci Busatti believed it was necessary to take 'jurisprudence and doctrine into account, but . . . it was inadmissible to put them on the same level as positive rules of law'[112] and proposed a series of amendments to Phillimore's idea. A separate paragraph therefore read: 'The court shall take into consideration the judicial

106 ibid 314.
107 ibid 315.
108 ibid 316.
109 ibid 318–19. On Article 38 also: Alain Pellet, 'Article 38' in Andreas Zimmermann and others (eds), *The Statute of the International Court of Justice: A commentary* (Oxford Public International Law, 3rd edn, OUP 2019) 677, particularly 923.
110 Procès-Verbaux (n 77) 334.
111 ibid.
112 ibid.

decisions rendered by it in analogous cases, and the opinions of the best qualified writers of the various countries, as means for the application and development of law'.[113]

In the session of 6 July, Ricci Busatti again presented his draft with some changes regarding the organization and composition of the Court, referencing, as he himself said, the system of the 'Roman Rota', which comprised 'a college of judges who sit in turn according to certain rules of procedure'. Ricci Busatti proposed to establish a separate section that 'could be composed in such a way as to be especially competent to deal with certain classes of cases'. He argued that 'no judge can be equally competent to deal with all cases'. The solution to the problem was for the Presidency of the Court to decide on the designation and attribution to the competent section.[114] He reiterated the need, when appointing judges, in order to ensure impartiality: 'to entrust nomination to the national groups of three or four persons who are members of the Court of Arbitration',[115] in agreement with the proposal of Phillimore and Root. Ricci Busatti submitted to the Committee a further Amendment,[116] which was discussed in subsequent sessions,[117] and further rewritten before being embodied in the final draft.

The work carried out by all the jurists charged with writing the draft statute of the Court was extremely technical and precise. The pace was relentless in every meeting, and all the jurists, even where there was disagreement, brought 'to the table' their experience and knowledge. They were committed to achieving the ideal of international justice, through creating the statute of the Permanent Court. Ricci Busatti shared his experience as a diplomat and his technical expertise as a lawyer and jurist, in the hope that international law would play the central role it deserved, in order to maintain peace between States for as long as possible. All the jurists were well aware of the arduous task entrusted to them: clarity and certainty in formulating the statutory provisions would allow the 'machinery' of the Permanent Court to function without hitches of 'interpretation'.

4. Conclusions: Ricci Busatti and the Resolutions of the Committee

The conclusion of the Committee's work was reached on 24 July 1920 when three Resolutions (*Voeux*) were discussed, accepted, and then presented to the Council some days later, on 3 August, together with the draft statute for the Permanent Court of International Justice. These Resolutions envisaged that in future a High Court of International Justice could be established 'for the purpose of trying crimes against international public order, and against the universal law

113 ibid 351.
114 Procès-Verbaux (n 77) 392, see also 402.
115 ibid 418.
116 ibid 443.
117 ibid 448 ff. On 9 July he proposed a further modification, Procès-Verbaux (n 77) 462.

of nations';[118] that the Academy of International Law founded in The Hague in 1913 could collaborate with the Permanent Court of Arbitration, the Permanent Court of Justice at the Peace Palace; and finally that a conference should be organized as soon as possible to discuss the advancement of international law, through its codification. The proposal to establish a High Court of International Justice had already been the subject of extensive discussion by the Committee at the 23rd meeting held on 13 July.[119]

Lapradelle had stated that the League of Nations 'was born of suffering of the nations and its object was to prevent repetition of the calamities which gave rise to its creation'. To achieve this 'a stable judicial organisation was required which could take action against those guilty of crimes against international justice, no matter what nation they belonged to'.[120] Ricci Busatti said he was sceptical because 'he did not quite know what was to be understood by "a crime against the universal law of nations"'.[121] Here too, from a purely legal point of view, Ricci Busatti dissected the problem: he argued that in international affairs it was not possible to distinguish between civil law and criminal law 'as was done in national law in accordance with certain principles, the application of which could be not applied to international law'.[122] Ricci Busatti asked his colleagues on the Committee 'whether the criminals in question would be States or private individuals' and if they were individuals, which criminal laws would be applied. The problem needed careful attention and for Ricci Busatti this attention was not the specific objective of the Committee, which instead must keep exclusively to drafting the Statute of the Permanent Court of Justice. Ricci Busatti's positions were also supported by Loder because, in the absence of a specific discipline regarding crimes, the Court could be considered as a political court.[123] The Spanish delegate Fernandez managed to obtain universal agreement, suggesting they proceed gradually and progressively 'to the effect that steps should be taken to define the crimes and assess the penalties in order to make the operation of the High Court possible'.[124]

In another Resolution the Committee recommended holding an 'interstate conference' with the aim of continuing the work carried out in the two Hague Conferences in order to (i) re-establish the existing rules of the law of nations, in particular those overridden by the events of the First World War; (ii) formulate and approve all necessary changes that had arisen from the conflict; (iii) reconcile the different opinions regarding the application and interpretation of the rules; and finally (iv) to work for a general agreement that would constitute a sort of international codification.[125]

118 Procès-Verbaux (n 77) 747.
119 ibid 497 ff.
120 ibid 500.
121 ibid 501.
122 ibid 503.
123 ibid 504.
124 ibid 505.
125 ibid 747.

The committee suggested entrusting the preparatory work to specialist institutions, such as the *Institut de Droit International*, the *American Institute of International Law*, the *Union Juridique Internationale*, the *International Law Association*, and the *Iberian Institute of Comparative Law*.[126] It was also decided that the conference would be called the *Conference for the Advancement of International Law*.[127]

A few months later, on 16 December 1920, at the meeting of the Third Commission of the First Assembly of the League of Nations, this latter Resolution was discussed, examining in particular the role that the various institutes and associations would play in the process of studying the advancement of international law.

The issue was addressed from multiple angles: the work of codifying international law could not start before the Permanent Court was functioning, but at the same time the Court 'ought not to be allowed to fix the law it would have to apply'.[128] Ricci Busatti, member of this Third Commission, declared that 'the task of codifying international law should be left entirely to governments' but that in any case the issue of codification was extremely complex. He pointed out that by its very nature international law could not be codified and that it could only be 'a collection of conventions' referring to the content of the Resolution. It should be interpreted not so much for creating a new organization, but as authentic cooperation among associations, scientific institutes that would plan tasks according to a sort of codification in international law, thus confirming the contents of the Resolution.[129]

Once the work was completed, the Third Commission proposed that the Assembly of the League of Nations adopt the Resolution, which incorporated Ricci Busatti's suggestions. The Resolution underlined the importance of solid cooperation between institutions of international law, 'which have long possessed undisputed authority in international law'. It envisaged that institutions and associations would be sent a formal 'request to consider what would be the best methods of co-operative work to adopt for the more precise definition and more complete co-ordination of the rules of international law which are to be applied in the mutual relations of States'.[130]

The Statute, together with the Resolutions, was adopted by the Assembly of the League of Nations on 16 December 1920.

Ricci Busatti's dedication to the Statute of the Permanent Court of Justice had its roots in his activities as diplomat and director of the Litigation and Legislation Office of the Ministry of Foreign Affairs and in his commitment to founding the *Rivista di diritto internazionale*. There were always dual concepts at play deep

126 ibid.

127 ibid.

128 Court Permanente de Justice Internationale, *Documents au sujet de Mesures prises par le Conseil de la Société des Nations aux termes de l'Article 14 du Pacte et de l'Adoption par l'Assemblée du Statut de la Cour Permanente* (League of Nations, without date) 274.

129 ibid 274.

130 ibid 278. For further information on the work of the Third Commission, see also <www.prassi.cnr.it/prassi/content.html?id=999#note1> accessed 31 December 2020.

within him that he carefully considered in solving every difficulty he encountered, including during his work as member of the Advisory Committee. On the one hand lay the practice and theory of international law, which Ricci Busatti always held in mutual dialogue, never forgetting his combined experience as diplomat and jurist. On the other hand there was the association of politics and law: Ricci Busatti was well aware of the role exercised by law and often throughout his life fought constantly so that all decisions might be independent of political rationale, which was too often dictated by a desire for prevarication among States, and instead be based firmly upon the law.

Index

Page numbers followed by 'n' indicate notes.

Abellán, José Luis 9n4, 13n26
abolition of slavery 53, 53n91
Abranches, Sérgio 51n80
Academy of International Law, The Hague 238
active neutrality 18, 18n57
Act of Berlin, 1885 160
Adachi, Mineichiro 1, 22, 74–75, 76n1, 81n11, 90n46; ACJ 74, 84, 86; birth 75; civilizational pluralism and inegalitarianism 81–88, 81n12, 83; compulsory jurisdiction 88; early life 74–77; education 75–77; experience in foreign service 77; failure in persuading the Japanese government for compulsory jurisdiction 84–85; on importance of international law 76; international law, attitude toward 79; Japan's inegalitarianism in revising unequal treaties 79–81; Japan's refusal of compulsory jurisdiction 82–83; in Mexico 77; Paris, moved to 77; Peace Conference at Portsmouth 77; professional experience 77–78; realism and idealism 88–90; Rome, posted in 77; scholarly opinions as subsidiary source of law 85–88; Visscher, Charles De, worked with 87
Advisory Committee of Jurists (ACJ) 1, 2n2, 6, 10n9, 39, 91n1, 139, 171n102, 185n23, 203, 232n77; Adachi, Mineichiro 74, 84, 86; Altamira y Crevea, Rafael 8, 10, 21; candidate selection 27; Descamps, Edouard 171–178; election, composition, and seat of the court 203–207; Fernandes, Raul 43, 62–66; first meeting, 1920 27, 39; general agenda of 203; Hagerup, George Francis 100–110; International criminal law 210; Lapradelle, Albert G. De in 139, 141–143; Loder, Bernard C. J. 195, 203; Phillimore, Walter George Frank 187–193; Ricci Busatti, Arturo 218, 231–237; standing, jurisdiction, and applicable law 207–210
Aguinaldo, Emilio 113
Aín Vergara, Rafael 8n3
Alberola, Armando 8n3
Altamira y Crevea, Rafael 1, 8, 8n1, 8n3, 74; ACJ 8, 10, 21; active neutrality 18; arbitrator at the Court of Mining Litigation in Paris 20–21; bourgeois elitism 17; Centre for Studies in Seville 15n43; chair in History of Law, University of Oviedo 9, 13; chair in *History of Political and Civil Institutions in America* 15–16, 16n45; 'civilized' Spain 13; cosmopolitan scholar 20–23; in defense of international law 20; education 11, 11n17; education, technical thought on 25; elected associate of the *Institute de Droit International* (IDI) 37n161; Fernando Ortiz, controversy with 14; *La guerra actual y la opinión pública Española* 17; historiographic work 16; honours, received with 14; ideology 17; ILE 11, 37; international career 21; international judge 26–29;

international jurist, role as 35; judge in the Chamber for Social Affairs 17; judge of PCIJ 16n50; judicial justice 23–25; jurisdiction of PCIJ 23; justice, sum of virtues and values 37; legal education 11–17; legal questions 23–25; liberal education 9; modern intellectual archetype 8–9; moralism in idea of justice 23–29; at *Museo Pedagógico Nacional* 11; naturalism 9; pacifist in face of war 17–20; positivism 9; post-university training 9; pragmatism and scientific technique 29–37; rationalism 9; re-configuration of 'post-classical' international legal system 16; regenerationism 12, 16; Senator with Liberal party 16; sociological idealism 13; Spanish civilization 26; spiritual guide 9; teachings 11–17; teaching staff at Diplomatic and Consular Institute 16; travelling 11–17; writings of publicists 10
Alvarez, Alejandro 137, 143, 145, 155, 171
Álvarez Junco, José 13n27
Ambos, Kai 42n20
American Law Institute (ALI) 132
American Society of International Law in 1923 128, 139
Anaís Passos 72n225
anarcho-syndicalist ideologies 61
Andersson, KGA 223n30
Andrade, Daniel 72n230
Anghie, Antony 71n220, 148, 148n52, 149, 153, 153n76
Anglo-American flair 152n72
Anglo-Japanese Treaty of Amity and Commerce, 1858 79
Anglo-Saxon system 34
anti-formalism 137n12
anti-slavery mission 159n19
Anzilotti, Dionisio 3, 218, 222n23, 225
Arendt, Guillaume (Wilhelm) 163, 163n47–48
Arendt, Léon 159n19, 166
Article 14 of the League's Covenant 121
Article 76 of Dutch Constitution 196n7
Asín Vergara, Rafael 25n96
Asser, Tobias 188, 199
Association of American Law Schools 132
Aurelio di Saluzzo, Marco 223
Azcárate, Gumersindo de 11, 11n19
Badin, Michelle 48n61
Bajer, Fredrik 158n14
Bances, R Prieto 8n3
Banning, Emile 159n19
Barbosa, Rui 39, 41, 41n17, 67
Basdevant, Jules 32n129
Becker, T 148n55
Beernaert, August 156, 161
Belgium 163; Belgian neutrality 162; Belgian permanent neutrality 163n53; conventional neutrality 165; conventional permanent neutrality 163–164; declarations of permanent neutrality 164–168; declassification 171; Hymans, Affairs Paul 163; international constitution 163–164; and Paris Peace Conference 162
Bercovici, Gilberto 72n229
Berman, Harold 173n120
Bernheim, Ernst 13n31
Besson, Samantha 5n22, 9n6
Bevilaqua, Clovis 22, 39–40, 42–43, 62
Bjørnson, Bjørnstjerne 96
Blandhol, Sverre 101n38
Bliss, Tasker H. 120
Bodington, Oliver E 184n22
Bodio, Luigi 219–220, 219n7
Boissonade, Gustave 75
Bolhander, M 9n8
Borah, William E. 130
Bourdieu, Pierre 42n24, 46–48n44–60
Bourgeois, Léon 3, 21, 100, 100n30, 232
Boyle, Alan 9n6
Branco, Barão do Rio 39, 70
Brazil: capitalist centre-periphery dynamic 53–54; capitalist economic premises 54; colonial legacy 53; Constitution of 1891 55; Constitution of 1934 56; Constitution of 1946 56; Constitution of 1967 57; Constitution of 1988 51n80; constitutions 50–51; Euro-American political centrality 54; ex-slaves 55–56; industrial aristocracy 52; monarchy 52, 55; national development 67; non-official social prestige 72; official state discourse and a public opinion 72; oligarchy 54–55; political dispute between oligarchies 52–53; political regime changes 53; trust in Catholic Church 72; trust on armed forces 72

Brazilian Democratic Republic's aristocracy 52
Brazilian Empire's aristocracy 52
Brazilian legalist tradition 70
Briand, Aristide 177
Briand-Kellogg Pact 171, 176
Brooks v Inland Revenue 185
Buckle, Henry Thomas 13n30
Bunmeiron no Gairyaku (Fukuzawa) 80
Busatti, Ada 218
Butler, Judith 49n66
Buzzati, Giulio Cesare 228n57

Cardim, Carlos 39n1
Carnegie, Andrew 118
Carnegie Endowment for International Peace 119
Carnegie Foundation 139, 141
Carr, Raymond 21n75
Carthage 222
Carvalho, Antônio 41n15
Casdagli v Casdagli 186, 186n30
Casella, Paulo 39n1, 40n8
Castro, Douglas 48n63
Central American Court of Justice 115
Central Organization for a Durable Peace 200n28
Centre for Studies in Seville 15n43
Cervo, Amado 53n91
Charlersworth, Hilary 49n71
Chauí, Marilena 72n227
Chinkin, Christine 9n6, 49n71
civilizational inegalitarianism 80
civilizational pluralism 3, 83
civilization egalitarianism 83
civilized nations 62
Clark, Ch Martin 18n58
Clayton Antitrust Act of 1914 118
Clemenceau, Georges 230
Clerc, Louis 136
Climate of the Centenary 14
Cohn, Gabrel 52n85–87
Comité Maritime International (CMI) 198
communal property 11n18
Conde y Luque, Rafael 33
Conference of Associations for the League of Nations 27n102
Congo Free State 159, 159n20, 160
Congress of Vienna 166
conservatism 13, 13n27
contingency of international law 136n7
conventional permanent neutrality 163
Coolidge, Calvin 129
Corrêa, Luís 45n36
Cossío, Manuel B. 11–12
Costa, Joaquín 11, 11n21, 12n23
Council of the League of Nations 1, 4, 4n17
Court of Arbitration 204
Court of Mining Litigation 21n75
Court packing plan 134
Covenant of League of Nations 91
Craeybeckx, Jan 156n2
cultural legacy of Spain 14

d'Aspremont, Jean 5n22, 9n6
Dauchy, Serge 92n6
Declaration of London of February 26, 1909 221n15, 221n19
declarations of permanent neutrality 164
Decock, Wim 173n116
dédoublement fonctionnel 49
De Lapradelle, Albert Geouffre 109–110, 176
Delcour, Charles 156
Descamps, Edouard 1, 6, 22, 31–32, 62–64, 74, 95–96, 108n94, 110, 156–162, 159n24, 176n143, 188–189, 209n92, 235n102; 1889 anti-slavery conference 159n19; absorption of neutrality 158; adviser to King Leopold II 167; Advisory Committee of Jurist 171–178; associate member in the *Institut* 's Geneva meeting 158n16; Bar of Leuven 156n3; Belgian permanent neutrality 160; Belgian Royal Academy 158; Belgian Senate 157; classical neutrality 158, 178; on colonial endeavours 178; colonization of Africa 159n19; combination of LoN covenant and Briand-Kellogg Pact 171; *Conseil Supérieur* 159; counsel to the United States of America 162n41; degrees of doctor of law 156; degrees of permanent neutrality 169–170; against the deniers of neutrality 165–169; doctor in political and administrative sciences 156; education 156; extended neutralisation 169–170; general principles of international law 171–176; honorific memberships 158n17; inaugural address at Meeting of the ACJ, 1920 171n103; Institute-members Feodor von Martens 159;

international constitution of Belgium 163; interventions in the Belgian Senate 161; *L'Afrique Nouvelle* 159; legal expert to the Belgian delegation 162; member of the Institut de France 158; member of the Permanent Court of Arbitration 158; Minister for the Arts and Sciences 160; national synthesis 162–164; naturalism 157; negative neutrality 157; new international law 176–178; *pacta sunt servanda* 173; Paris Peace Conference of 1919 171; permanent neutrality 157, 163–165, 169; positive concept of neutrality 162–170; president of School for Political and Social Sciences 157; proposal to compel states 161n39; quintessence of the Belgian Catholic elite 178; radical neutralisation 170; secretary-general of the Institute of international law 158; *Société juridique* in Leuven 156n3; Vice-President of the Senate 161
Dhondt, Frederik 156n3, 160n27
Diggelmann, Oliver 140n21
Doe, Norman 181n3, 182n10
Dohlnikoff, Miriam 51n78
Draft for an International Juridical Organisation 101
Drago, Luis 42n22, 67
Droit international et législation consulaire 157
Drummon, Eric 21
Drumont, Eric 9n7
Duguit, Léon 25
Durkheim, Émile 13n28

East Greenland 94
Egido León, María Ángeles 10n15
equality of states 4
Eslava, Luís 49n69
Espadas Burgos, Manuel 21n79
Eurocentrism 155
extended neutralisation 169–170
Eyffinger, Arthur 198n17

Faria, José 72n228
Fausto, Boris 52n88
Favereau, Paul de 161
Faviani, V Salavert 12n22
Federal Trade Commission 118
Fernandes, Raul 1, 39–40, 74; academic and non-academic career 57–59; academic texts on international responsibility 44; ACJ debates, contributions to 43, 62–66; agency 42, 70; agency in ACJ meetings 65; arguments 44; birth and early life 50, 57; birthplace 57; Brazilian approaches to international law 70–73; Brazilian delegation to the Peace Conference 59; Brazilian Democratic Republic's aristocracy 52; Brazilian Empire's aristocracy 52; Brazilian legalism 46; champion of PCIJ 41; contributions to ACJ debates 62–66; death 50; development of international law 50; *doctor honoris causa* degree 59, 66; documents authored by 43–44; domestic material and immaterial political disputes 46; Fernandes Formula 41; at General Assembly of the United Nations, 59; Governor of Rio de Janeiro 58; industrial aristocracy 52; institutional design of PCIJ 41; institutional responsiveness 46; Inter-American Conference for the Maintenance of Continental Peace and Security 59; international law institutions, development of 46; jurist responsible for writing the Constitution of 1934 59; lawyer in Rio de Janeiro 58; legal and political changes during life 51; literature reviews 45; lived during institutional changes 51; Minister of Foreign Affairs 60, 66, 69; nominated to position of General Consultant of Brazilian Republic 58–59; non-academic activities 59; *Pax Americana* 67; *Pax Britanica* 67; during political disputes 52; President of IAJC 60; quadruple role at international level 60–69; representative of Rio de Janeiro state 58; role at ACJ 71; speeches on the LoN and on the PCIJ 43–44; structural political tensions 45–50; studying law 58; substitute of Clovis Bevilaqua 43; supported the candidacy of Getulio Vargas 58; União Democrática Nacional (UDN), founder member 59; voting rights 40; writing of publicists 43; writings on international law 66–69
Field 46
Fillon, Catherine 139n18

First Peace Conference, The Hague *see* The Hague Convention of 1899
First World War 2, 9; limits of international law 19; Spanish neutrality in 19
Fitmaurice, Malgosia 10n11
Fitzmaurice, Malgosia 2n6, 5n22, 29n110, 171n106
Fleck, Dieter 220n14
Fontaine, Henri La 161, 163n53
Foraker Act of 1900 114
Foster, Joseph 180n2
Fourth Hague Convention on the Laws and Customs of War on Land 173
Franco-British intervention 166
Fraser, Nancy 49n67
Freda, Dolores 225n37
Free Institution of Education (ILE) 11
free-law movement 93
French ship *(Lotus)* 212
Fröbel, Friedrich 12
Fromageot, Fadda 221
Fuentes, Carlos I 220n13
Fukuzawa, Yukichi 80
Fuller, Melville 117
Fur, Louis Le 145
Furtado, Celso 52n84, 53n94

Gagnér, Sten 92n4
Gamarra, Yolanda 10n14
García Arias, Luis 25n95
Gaurier, Dominique 145n38
Geikie-Cobb, WF 182n8
General Act for the Pacific Settlement of International Disputes 2, 174n146, 177
General Assembly's General Act 177
General Treaty for the Renunciation of War 171n101
Geneva Protocol for the Pacific Settlement of Disputes 201n40
Genin, Vincent 162n42, 163n53, 171
George, David Lloyd 120, 120n18, 229–230
Geouffre, Albert 154
German unification 166
Giannattasio, Arthur 43n25
Gibbons, George 4n12
Giner de los Ríos, Francisco 11
González, J Becker 18n61
González Posada, Adolfo 15n44
Goulé, Paul 146
Governing Body of the International Institute for the Unification of Private Law (UNIDROIT) 202
Gram, Gregers W. W. 21
grande bourgeoisie 12n22
Grotius, Hugo 9n5, 36, 230
Guani, Albert 41n16
Guerilla warfare 113
La guerra actual y la opinión pública Española (Altamira) 17
Guimarães, Feliciano 46n41

Hagerup, George Francis 1, 22, 31, 74, 91n2, 176, 192; ACJ 100–110; article on international arbitration 95; birth 91; on court's competence 107; death 91; *Draft for an International Juridical Organisation* 101; on election mechanisms 105; foreign languages 92; free-law movement 93; general penal law, book on 92; The Hague Conference of 1907 98; international arbitration 95; international committee of lawyers in Hague 91; internationalization in science of private law 92; international law 1890–1919 94–98; on international organization 97; involvement with International Court 110; as law professor 95; leader of the Norwegian governmental committee 91; legal adjudication 93; legal education 91–92; as legal scientist and politician 91–94; member of *Stortinget* (The Parliament) 93; Minister of Justice 93; Nobel Peace Prize Committee 96; obligatory jurisdiction 111; *Om Kvindesagen* 93n7; in PCIJ 91; penal law and criminal procedure 92; Permanent Neutralitet 96n14; politicization of international law 96; Prime Minster of Norway 92–93; Prize Court Convention 97; Professor in Law 92; role in meetings in 1920 101n38; Scandinavian states 91; *Tidsskrift for retsvitenskab* 92; vision of international law and First World War, 1915 98–100
Harrison, Brian Howard 181n3
Hay, John 115
Hobart, Garrett 114
Hoover, Herbert 130–131
House, Edward M. 120

Hudson, Manley Ottmer 27, 27n101, 129
Hughes, Charles Evans 129
Hymans, Affairs Paul 163

Immunity of sovereign States vs. compulsory jurisdiction of an international court 200–202
Indologie 216n134
inegalitarianism 83
Inoue, Kowashi 81
Institut de Droit International (IDI) 198
Inter-American Human Rights Court 42
Inter-American Juridical Committee (IAJC) 60
International Bureau of Peace 161
international constitution of Belgium 163
International Court of Justice (ICJ) 1–2, 9, 40, 212n112, 232, 236; Americans and 109; Article 38 of the PCIJ 127, 210n99; Statute of 2n1, 2n3, 29n110, 30n116, 40n4
International Criminal Court (ICC) 42
international criminal procedure 9
International Criminals Tribunals 9
international custom 5n22
International Human Rights Courts 9
international investor-state dispute settlement, 150
internationalization 25; of dispute settlement 216; of private-public agreements 152n75
international judicial mechanism 40
international jurisdiction 5n22
International Labour Organization (ILO) 60–61
International Law Association (ILA) 184, 198
international law in Nordic countries 94, 107
international legal order of 1920 3
International Maritime Committee 199n20, 200n32
International Prize Court (IPC) 5, 5n20, 29, 173
international public authority 40
international security 4
international social solidarity 25
Inter Parliamentary Union 158n11
Inter Ruinas Publicas Scriptum 156n3
'irreconcilable' senators 121
Italian Wars of Independence 166
Italo-Turkish war in Libya 222
Italy: Arbitration Convention between Italy and the Netherlands 222; Article 11 of the Civil Code 224; discipline of international law in 226; ratification of the 1907 agreements 220; reconstruction of international law 218n1

Jadot, JM 156n3, 157n9
Janis, Mark Weston 5n22, 128n61
Japan: Japanese immigration 116; Japanese Society of International Law 80; refusal of compulsory jurisdiction 82–83
Jessup, Philip C 113n1, 151, 151n68
Jiménez, JC 15n46
Jiménez-Landi Martínez, Antonio 11n20
Jones, Shepard 100n32
José de Américo Pinheiro Peregrino 57
Jouannet, Emmanuelle 46n40
judicial-churchman for peace *see* Phillimore, Walter George Frank
judicial justice 8
Juliá, Santos 18n59
justice, sum of virtues and values 37

Karlstad Treaties 1905 97n16
Karlstad treaties of 1905 97
Kellogg, Frank B. 130
Kellogg-Briand Pact 20, 85
Kelsen, Hans 39n2
Kent, James 172
Kévonian, Dzovinar 141n23
Kitagawa, Tadaaki 78
Kleen, Richard 167, 167n72
Kogoro, Takahira 116
Koskenniemi, Martti 5n21, 9n6, 32n130, 73n232, 137n9, 145–146, 159n18
Krausism 12, 12n24
Krauso-positivism 12–13, 12n26, 16

Lafer, Celso 52n83
Lambermont, Auguste 159n19
Langlois, Charles-Victor 13n29
Lansing, Robert 120
Lapradelle, Albert G. De 1, 21–22, 31, 62, 64, 74, 101, 135–136, 135n1, 141n23, 151n70, 174–175, 230; in ACJ 139, 141–143; Aerial Warfare and International Law 139n19; Comtean posivitism 140; *concours*

d'agrégation, passed 138; early years of league 141–143; French allegiance 138n14; French international lawyer 136; French international legal scholarship 137; international investor-state dispute settlement 150; internationalist 140; international law, progress of 138; lawyer 136–141; lectures of Louis Renault 138; *Lena Goldfields* 150; liberal internationalist 135; lost legacy 143–153; *Nationalité d'origine* 136n6; Politis and Alvarez 145; Proctor's project on ignorance 145; professor of international law in Paris 140; rights of Hungarians in Romania 152n74; Second World War 140; *Société Rialet* 150; on traditional international law 152; unity and universality 142; visiting professor in Columbia University in New York 139
Lapradelle, M. de 190
Larnaude, Ferdinand 139n17, 141, 230
Lasala Llanas, Manuel 19, 20n68
Lauterpacht, Hersch 3n9, 213
Law School of the Ministry of Justice, Japan 75
League of Nations (LoN) 1–2, 20, 39, 109n110, 120, 202n42, 208; Argentina 22; Article 14 of the Covenant 231; Belgium 22; Brazil 22; conciliation commission 177; courts 154; covenant of 4n11, 4n13, 91; England 22; founding members 4n10; France 22; Italy 22; Japan 22; the Netherlands 22; Norway 22, 97; peace and 'international security' 4; Spain 21–22; USA 22
League of Nations Pact 10, 20
Legacies of the Permanent Court of International Justice (Tams, Fitzmaurice, and Merkouris) 5n22
legal adjudication 93
legal equality of states 41
legalistic internationalism 139
legal positivism 6
Lejeune, Jérôme 156n3, 157n9
Lena Goldfields 150
Leopold, Richard W. 113n2, 133
Leopold II 159
léopoldiste convaincu 159
Leo XIII, Pope 157
liberal conservatives 6
Loder, Bernard C. J. 1, 22, 31, 74, 174, 190, 195, 200n29–31; ACJ 195, 203; background 195–198; birth 196; Board of Assistance of the Directorate of Economic Affairs within the Ministry 197; with CMI 198; committee of experts for progressive codification of international law 214–215; development of private international law 195n2; dissent is addressed in Henri de Waele 213n114; Dutch practicing lawyer 195–198; early life and education 195–197; election, composition, and seat of the court 203–207; forefront of Dutch foreign policy 197–198; *Immunity of sovereign States vs. compulsory jurisdiction of an international court* 200–202; international criminal law 210; internationalization of dispute settlement 216; international rules of responsibility for maritime accidents 199–200; legacy 215–217; at LoN 202–210; *Lotus case* dissent 212–214; maritime lawyer and Supreme Court judge 196–197; Permanent Court of International Justice 195, 211–214; professional associations focusing on international law 198–202; Progressive Codification of International Law 214–215; Royal Dutch Petroleum Society 197; spirit of international law 212; standing, jurisdiction, and applicable law 207–210; strengthening state confidence in PCIJ 211–212
Lodge, Henry Cabot 120–121
London Declaration of 1909 30
Lorca, Arnulf 39n1
Lumia, Cristiano La 229

Macalister-Smith, Peter 159n21
MacKonchie litigations 193
MacKonochie v Lord Penzance 187
Malksoo, Lauri 5n22
Malagón Barceló, Javier 8n3
Manouba 222
Maquiavel, Nicolau 73n231
Martens Clause 173
Martin, L 18n60
Martínez Cachero, José María 8n3
Massoneto, Luís 72n229
Mathisen, Trygve 97n22

Matthew, Henry Collin Gray 181n3
McKinley, William 113–114
Mérignhac, Alexandre 95
Merkouris, Panos 2n6, 5n22, 10n11
Metzger, Ernest 3n7
Meyer v. Nebraska 119n15
Meynen, Alain 156n2
Michalsen, Dag 92n5, 101n38
Monod, Jacques 13n29
Moore, John Bassett 30n113, 129
moralism in idea of justice: international judge 25–29; judicial justice 23–25; legal questions 23–25
Moreira, Adilson 49n68
Moreli, Alexandre 39n1
moyenne bourgeosic phenomenon 12n22
Müller, D 29n112, 30n114
Museo Pedagógico Nacional (National Museum of Education) 11

Nagaoka, Harukazu 83n17
Nagy-Böszömenyi, Emil 184, 184n21
natural law 10
Navarro Ordoño, Andreu 19n62
neo-Thomism 157
neutrality 169
neutrality-independence-guarantee 168
Nicholas II, Czar 115, 119
Niño, Antonio 17n53
Nobel, Alfred 95–96
Nobel Institute in Oslo 96
Nobel Peace Prize 96
Norway: on constitutional law and international law 95; East Greenland 94; in First World War 98–99; international arbitration 95; Inter-Parliamentarian Peace Movement 95; Inter-Parliamentarian union 94; modern states 100; Nobel Institute in Oslo 96; peace and international arbitration 94; Sweden, relationship with 94
Norwegian Foreign Service 97
Nussbaum, Arthur 150n63
Nys, Ernest 156, 163n53

Obregón, Liliana 171n107
Oliveira, Adna 60n143
Oppenheim, Lassa 33, 33n136
Organization of American States (OAS) 60
Orlando, Vittorio Emanuele 230
Ortiz, Fernando 14, 14n40, 15n42
Otto, Diane 49n70
Oxford Handbook of the Sources of International Law, The (Besson and d'Aspremont) 5n22

Paci, Deborah 223n29
pacigérat désarmé 169
Pact of Paris 178
Padelford, Norman J 223n30
Panhispanism 15
Papa Leão XIII 60n149
Paris Peace Conference of 1919 2, 4, 74, 98, 163, 171–172, 230
Paris Peace Treaty of 1919 163n53, 166n66
Paternostro, Alessandro 76n3, 79
Payk, Marcus M 97n19
peace and 'international security' 4
peaceful settlement of disputes 4
Peace Palace Library, The Hague 43
Pellet, A 29n112, 30n114
Pereira, Juan Carlos 19n65
Périn, Charles 156–157
Permanent Court of Arbitration (PCA) 4–5, 5n19, 24, 115, 162, 232, 238
Permanent Court of International Justice (PCIJ) 1, 2n2, 3, 20, 177, 191, 211; Article 2 of Statute of 28; Article 4 of Statute of 26n99; Article 5 of Statute of 26n99; Article 9 of Statute of 26; Article 25 of Statute of 206; Article 31 of Statute of 5n22; Article 34 of Statute of 189; Article 35 of Statute of 34n140, 189; Article 36 of Statute of 189; Article 38(4) of Statute of 34; Article 38 of Statute of 1, 3, 3n8, 30, 33–34, 37, 127; Chamber of Summary Procedure 201; committee of experts for progressive codification of international law 214–216; function of 33; General principles of international law 174; history of 8; Lotus case dissent 212–214; Spanish legal culture 9; Statute 8, 8n2, 9–10; strengthening state confidence 211–212; writings of publicists 33–34
Permanent International Court of Justice 153
permanent neutrality 96, 165n63, 167–168
Pestalozzi, Johann Heinrich 12

petite phenomenon 12n22
Phillimore, John George 181
Phillimore, Joseph 181, 181n5
Phillimore, Robert Joseph 180, 182
Phillimore, Walter George Frank 1, 6, 6n25, 22, 28, 34–35, 62, 64, 74, 102, 106, 108, 124, 180–184, 181n4, 182n11, 183n13–20, 210; ACJ 187–193; birth 180–181; *Brazil and League* 183; death 184; disagreement with Bernard Loder 190–191; 'domicile' of the English Hugh Court 186; at the *fin-de-siècle* 182; formation of legal authority in the house of lords 184–187; intellectual life 182–183; international law 183; judge at the House of Lords 182, 185; judgments 185; judicial-churchman 184, 193–194; jurisdiction proposed 191–192; legal writings 182–183; literary legal demonstration 187; *Procès-Verbaux* 189; role during the formation of LoN 182; role in ACJ 182
Pijnappel, Menso Johannes 199
pleonasm 32
plural voting 160
Polacco, Vittorio 225n39
political arbitrariness 68
Politis, Nicolas 137, 137n12, 139n15, 143, 145, 155
Ponce Marrero, Francisco Javier 19n64
Portsmouth Peace Conference, 1905 86
positive laws 11n18
Poullet, Prosper 157n7
Paris Peace Conference of 1919 230
Prado, Gustavo 14n37
pragmatism and scientific technique: general principles of law 29–32; writings of publicists 33–37
Preussenthal, Menzinger di 227
Prida, Joaquín Fernández 19
Prize Court of 1907 5, 5n20
Procès-Verbaux 2, 174n122
Proctor, Robert N 144n35
Proctor's project on ignorance 145
Progressive Codification of International Law 202

Raad, Van Haven tot Hoge 197n9
radical neutralisation 169–170
Ramos, Vicente 8n3
Rappard, William 27, 27n103
Rasulov, Abkar 5n22
regenerationism 12
Renaissance 9n5
Renan, Ernest 13n29
Renault, Louis 138, 145
renunciation of interwar project 146n47
Research Council of Norway 195n1
restatements 132
Ricci, Federigo 218
Ricci Busatti, Arturo 1, 22, 32–35, 74, 203, 218n2; ACJ 218, 231–237; and acquisition of citizenship by the wife and minor children 224; Arbitration Convention 222; Artical 11 of Hague Convention (V) 228–229; Artical 13 of Hague Convention (V) 229; birth 218; and Civil Code 224; *Comité de rédaction*, member of 222; Committee of Jurists 231; death 224; diplomacy 218–224, 221n20; education 218; first secretary 219; International Prize Court 220; Italian Civil Code 224; Italian delegate to Geneva Conference 223; on judges competence 237; Knight of the Crown of Italy 219; lawyer 219; League of Nations Office separate from the Treaties Office 223n32; Litigation and Legislation Office 221; London Declaration on the law of maritime warfare 220; London Naval Conference 220; member of the commission in charge of drafting the statute of PCIJ 222, 231; at Ministry of Foreign Affairs 219; President of the Legal Commission 222; professor of international law 225; resolutions of committee 237–240; *Rivista di diritto internazionale* 224–231; Second International Peace Conference 218–219; writing on international law 224–231
Rio de Janeiro State 50n77
Ripley, Charles 113n3
Rivier, Alphonse 159
Roberts, Anthea 10n16, 214n119
Roelofsen, CG 196n8
Rolin, Socialist Henri 177
Rolin-Jaequemyns, Gustave 159, 235
Romano-Germanic systems 34
Romero Salvado, Francisco J. 19n64
Roosevelt, Franklin D. 131

Roosevelt, Theodore 114, 117
Root, Elihu 1, 4n12, 22, 26, 28, 30–31, 62–63, 74, 86, 101, 103, 112, 123; American proponent of PCIJ 112; anti-corruption measures 113; Army War College 114; authoritarian Republican machine 113; birth 112; Central American Court of Justice 115; centralized military commands 114; chair of the Republican National Convention 118; colonial policies of McKinley Administration 113; and disputes to arbitrators of the PCA 116; early life 112; education 112; Federal Reserve Act 118; goodwill mission to Russia 119; Japan, improving relations with 116; and League of Nations (LoN) 120; marriage 112; opposed women's suffrage 118; at PCIJ 173; president of Association of the Bar 114; president of the Carnegie Endowment for International Peace 118; Republican presidential nomination 119; resigned as Secretary of War 114; Secretary of State 115; Secretary of War 113; Senate, 1909 117; Seventeenth Amendment, opposed 117; speeches 112; temporary chair of the Republican National Convention 114–115
Root, Nancy Whitney Buttrick 112
Root, Oren 112
Rosenberg, Barbara 45n39
Rosenne, Shabtai 2n2
Ross, Alf 151, 151n69
Ross, William G 120n17
Rousseau, Charles 135, 135n2
Royal Dutch Society of International Law (KNVIR) 198
Rubio Cremades, Enrique 8n3
rules of international law 5n22
Russell, Lord 166
Russo-Japanese War of 1904–1905 116, 117
Ruze, R 21n75
Rygiel, Philippe 141n23

Sáez, F Moreno 8n3
Salandra, Antonio 228
Salmerón, Nicolás 11
Salmon, Patrick 97n20
Sanchez, Michelle 45n39
São Sebastião do Rio de Janeiro Province 50n77
Scelle, Georges 25, 25n94, 49n72, 140n21, 143, 144n38, 147, 151, 152n72
Schabas, William 108n95, 146n50, 147
Schachter, Oscar 49n73
Schjatvet, Cecilie 95n11, 97n15
Sciarra, Federico 225n38
Scott, James Brown 26, 28, 28n108, 30n113, 101n35, 137n8, 139, 171n104, 230n70
Seaman's Act of 1915 118
Second Peace Conference, The Hague *see* The Hague Convention of 1907
Seignobos, Charles 13n29
Sela Sampil, Luis 8n3
Serbian Loans decision 148
Shaffer, Gregory 45n39
Skouteris, Thomas 10n12, 137n11
Smith, Charlotte 182n9
Smith, Frederick Edwin 229
socialization 25
Société Rialet 150
sociological idealism 13
sociological theory (Durkheim) 13n28
Solé, G 22n80
solidarity 10
Sources of International Law, The (Thirlway) 5n22
sovereignty 10
Soviet Revolution of 1917 61
Spain: cultural legacy of 14; cultural renewal 13; First World War and 18; neutrality 21n79; peace and 20; Spanish regenerationism 14
Spanish-American War 9, 17
Spanish-American War of 1898 113
Spanish Krausism 12n25
Spanish legal culture 9, 26
Spanish liberalism 12
Spanish neutrality in First World War 19
Spanish powerlessness 19
Spanish regenerationism 9, 14–15
Spiermann, Ole 2n4, 6, 6n26, 30n116
spiritual Re-Conquest of America 14
Stachurska-Kounta, Marta 100n31
Steine, Bjørn Arne 96n13
structural rationality 50
Suárez Cortina, Manuel 12n22

Tallgren, Immi 155, 155n78
Tams, Christian 2n6, 5n22, 10n11
The Hague Academy of International Law 178

The Hague Convention of 1899 24, 115, 129, 161, 172, 190, 219–220, 219n6, 230
The Hague Convention of 1907 24, 30, 41–42, 67, 95, 97, 102, 122, 129, 138–139, 161, 171–172, 190, 219n6, 228, 230
theory of civilization 80
Third Commission of the First Assembly of the League of Nations 239
third The Hague Peace Conference 197
Thirlway, Hugh 5n22, 9n6
Togores, JE 15n46
Tokugawa Shogunate 79
Toyoda, Tetsuya 83n18
Transnational Law lecture 151
Treaties and Conventions 192
Treaties and League of Nations Office 223
Treaties of Versailles 191
Treaty of Integrity of 1907 97
Treaty of London, 1839 163n53, 166
Treaty of Rio de Janeiro 50
Treaty of Versailles 2, 42, 60–61
Treaty to Limit the Responsibility of Shipowners 199
Trindade, Antônio Augusto Cançado 135n3, 171n105
Turkish ship *(Boz-Kourt)* 212
Tweed, William M. 113

unequal treaties with Japan 80
União Democrática Nacional (UDN) 59
United States 112–115; global leadership 117; goodwill mission to Russia 119; Hague Conference participation in 115; Panama Canal 115; relationships with Latin American countries 115
universalism 10
University Extension Programme 13

Valero, E 15n41
Valero Juan, Eva María 8n3
Vanderlinden, J 151n67
Vattel, Emer de 135n3
Vauthier, Maurice 159
Veeder, VV 150n64
Vélez, Palmira 14n38
Vergerio, Claire 219n6
Versailles Treaty 4
Visscher, Charles De 157, 157n8, 163
Vitoria, Francisco de 9n5, 10

wage-based labour force 53
Wales, Clara Frances 112
Ward, Leslie Matthew 180n1
Warren G. Harding 128
Wertheim, Stephen 140n20
White, Henry 119
Wickersham, George W. 129
William II of Hohenzollern 231, 231n74
Wilson, Woodrow 21, 78, 89
Witte, Els 156n2
World Court 3
Wright, Shelley 49n71
writings of publicists 33, 43

Yakemtchouk, Roman 157, 157n4–6, 159n19, 159n23
Yanagihara, Masaharu 76n2

Zachmann, Urs Matthias 83n18
Zimmerman, Warren 133n93

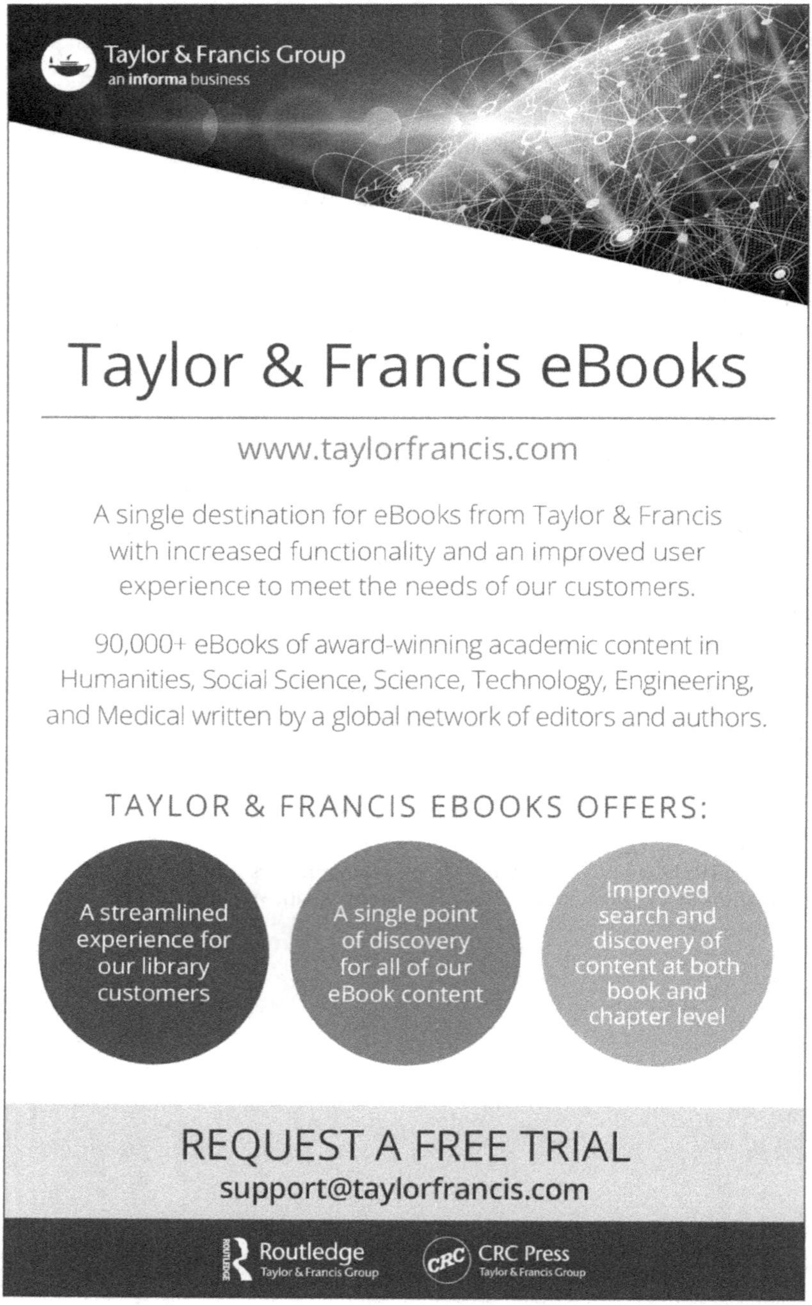
Taylor & Francis Group
an informa business
Taylor & Francis eBooks
www.taylorfrancis.com
A single destination for eBooks from Taylor & Francis with increased functionality and an improved user experience to meet the needs of our customers.
90,000+ eBooks of award-winning academic content in Humanities, Social Science, Science, Technology, Engineering, and Medical written by a global network of editors and authors.
TAYLOR & FRANCIS EBOOKS OFFERS:
A streamlined experience for our library customers
A single point of discovery for all of our eBook content
Improved search and discovery of content at both book and chapter level
REQUEST A FREE TRIAL
support@taylorfrancis.com
Routledge
Taylor & Francis Group
CRC Press
Taylor & Francis Group

For Product Safety Concerns and Information please contact our EU representative GPSR@taylorandfrancis.com
Taylor & Francis Verlag GmbH, Kaufingerstraße 24, 80331 München, Germany

www.ingramcontent.com/pod-product-compliance
Lightning Source LLC
LaVergne TN
LVHW011123300926
849160LV00008B/491

* 9 7 8 1 0 3 2 0 6 5 0 0 7 *